NORMANDY BEFORE 1066

Normandy before 1066

David Bates

Longman
London and New York

Longman Group Limited
Longman House
Burnt Mill, Harlow, Essex, UK

Published in the United States of America
by Longman Inc., New York

© David Bates 1982

All rights reserved. No part of this publication may be reproduced, stored in a retrieval system, or transmitted in any form or by any means, electronic, mechanical, photocopying, recording, or otherwise, without the prior permission of the Copyright owner.

First published 1982

British Library Cataloguing in Publication Data

Bates, David
　Normandy before 1066.
　1. Normandy – History
　I. Title
　944'.2021　　DC611.N856

　　ISBN 0-582-48492-8

Library of Congress Cataloging in Publication Data

Bates, David, 1945-
　Normandy before 1066.

　　Bibliography: p.
　　Includes index.
　　1. Normandy (France) – History. I. Title.
　DC611.N856B37　　944'2　　81-17154
　ISBN 0-582-48492-8　　AACR2

Set in 10/12 pt Linotron 202 Bembo
Printed in Singapore by
Singapore National Printers Pte Ltd

Contents

Preface	vi
Abbreviated references	viii
List of maps	x
Introduction	xi

PART ONE
The tenth century — 1

1 Origins and consolidation — 2

PART TWO
The eleventh century — 45

2 Normandy and its neighbours — 46
3 Economy and social structure — 94
4 Ducal government — 147
5 The Church — 189
6 Achievement — 236

Appendix A The dates of William II's campaigns against Geoffrey Martel, 1048–52 — 255
Appendix B Two supposed 'feudal' documents of William II's reign — 258
Appendix C A list of Norman archdeacons to *c.* 1080 — 260

Maps — 263–274
Index — 275

Preface

When first projected, this book was intended as an up-dating of early Norman history in the light of the scholarship of the last twenty years. It was only during research and writing that I became convinced that our whole approach to the duchy of Normandy's history needed reappraisal and that this book would have to be composed accordingly. It also became apparent that an exploration of the Norman archives was essential; unpublished material has provided fresh evidence on a number of subjects. All this said, the names of Marjorie Chibnall, Michel de Bouard, David Douglas, Charles Homer Haskins, Jean-Francois Lemarignier, John Le Patourel, Lucien Musset, and Jean Yver, must head any list of acknowledgements since it is on their devoted attention to the history of eleventh-century Normandy that this book tries to build. Where disagreement on general interpretation or on a point of detail has to be registered, it is done with a profound awareness that any history of the duchy which neglected or belittled their endeavours would be a miserable thing.

It is hoped that technical problems have been overcome in as convenient a way as possible. Place-names are given in their modern form and personal names in their modern English equivalent where it exists. Obscurity has been avoided where possible, and names such as William de 'Warenne' retained, even though to do so is not strictly accurate. For the same reason the eleventh-century Norman rulers are consistently referred to as dukes, despite this not becoming the sole title until the twelfth century. It has, however, been necessary to number these dukes according to succession. For this reason William the Conqueror appears as duke William II throughout.

The book was read in typescript by Mr David Crouch, Dr Elizabeth Hallam, and Professor Henry Loyn. All three made numerous

Preface

valuable comments and criticisms, and their suggestions have done much to clarify argument and to give direction and precision to parts of the text. Important help on particular points has been given by Mrs Kathleen Thompson. Research in Normandy would not have been possible without the aid of two grants from the British Academy. Numerous librarians have given assistance, notably those responsible for the Inter-Library Loan Section of the Library of University College, Cardiff, Mrs Shelagh Pollard and Miss Hilary Calwell. In France, the librarians and archivists at the various institutions were always courteous, kind, and helpful, contributing immensely to my enjoyment of research. Thanks are also due to my medievalist colleagues at Cardiff, Dr Peter Edbury and Dr Clive Knowles, for carrying increased teaching loads during the year 1979–80, so that I could press ahead with writing during a 'light year'. Mrs Christine Morgan typed the manuscript with exemplary patience and care. Miss Karen Fryer gave invaluable assistance with the maps.

The writer must also pay tribute to the good fortune which made him a pupil of Professor Frank Barlow at the University of Exeter. Such qualities as this book possesses draw deeply on the example given by his rigorous and exacting scholarship and try to provide some thanks for all his generous advice and encouragement. My wife Helen bore nobly the oppressions of an irritable and demanding author; she and my two children, Jonathan and Rachel, created the conditions under which a book could be written. Lastly, I must thank my father, to whose memory this book is dedicated. It was he who first awakened my interest in history. It is an inconsolable sadness that he should not have lived to see the result.

Abbreviated references

AAC	Les actes de Guillaume le Conquérant et de la reine Mathilde pour les abbayes caennaises, ed. L. Musset (Caen, 1967)
Acta Sanctorum	Acta Sanctorum, ed. J. Bollandus et al., (Antwerp and Brussels, 1734–)
A.D.	Archives départementales
AN	Annales de Normandie
Arch. méd.	Archéologie médiévale
BIHR	Bulletin of the Institute of Historical Research
BN	Bibliothèque nationale
BSAN	Bulletin de la société des antiquaires de Normandie
CCM	Cahiers de civilisation médiévale
CTR	Cartulaire de la Sainte-Trinité-du-Mont de Rouen, ed. A. Deville, in Cartulaire de St-Bertin, pp. 403–87, ed. B. E. C. Guérard (Paris, 1840)
EHR	English Historical Review
Etudes ... Yver	Droit privé et institutions régionales: Etudes historiques offertes à Jean Yver (Paris, 1976)
GC	Gallia Christiana (Paris, 1715–1865)
MGH	Monumenta Germaniae Historica
OV	The Ecclesiastical History of Orderic Vitalis, ed. and trans. Marjorie Chibnall, 6 vols. (Oxford, 1969–80)
PL	Patrologiae cursus completus: series latina, ed. J.-P. Migne (Paris, 1844–64)
Recueil	Recueil des actes des ducs de Normandie de 911 à 1066, ed. Marie Fauroux (Caen, 1961)
Regesta	Regesta Regum Anglo-Normannorum, vol. i, ed.

	H. W. C. Davis (Oxford, 1913); vol. ii, ed. C. Johnson and H. A. Cronne (Oxford, 1956)
RHDFE	*Revue historique de droit français et étranger*
RHF	*Recueil des historiens des Gaules et de la France*, ed. M. Bouquet *et al.*, new edition, ed. L. Delisle (Paris, 1869–1904)
SHN	*Société de l'histoire de Normandie*
TRHS	*Transactions of the Royal Historical Society*
WJ	*Guillaume de Jumièges, Gesta Normannorum Ducum*, ed. J. Marx (Rouen and Paris, 1914)
WP	*Guillaume de Poitiers: Histoire de Guillaume le Conquérant*, ed. Raymonde Foreville (Paris, 1952)

List of Maps

1	*Pagi* and dioceses	264
2	The probable stages of the Norman settlement	265
3	Scandinavian place-names in Upper Normandy	266
4	Scandinavian place-names in the Cotentin	267
5	Normandy and the surrounding regions	268
6	Central Normandy, showing Beaumont and Tosny possessions	269
7	The extension of aristocratic estates into Lower Normandy	270
8	Location of property granted to the Church by William II before 1066	271
9	The property of ducal vassals in pre-1066 charters	272
10	Rural churches granted in Richard II's reign to the three main Norman monasteries	273
11	Monasteries and colleges founded before *c* 1080	274

Introduction

This book sets out to describe and to analyse the first century and a half of the evolution of a Viking settlement made in the early tenth century around the upper reaches of the river Seine in northern France. By the fateful year of 1066 this settlement had expanded and developed into a well-organised territorial principality ruled by duke William II, known now by the nickname of 'the Conqueror'. There should not be any need to justify a study devoted specifically to the early history of the duchy of Normandy. The doings of the Normans have been a subject of fascination for historians at least since Dudo of St-Quentin wrote his 'On the Manners and Deeds of the First Dukes of Normandy' (*De Moribus et Actis Primorum Normanniae Ducum*) at a date between 1015 and 1026. The reason for this interest is obvious. Normandy was always to some extent special since its founders were the Vikings. In the eleventh century its inhabitants played a large part in two movements of military expansion, one, which from *c.* 1020 led to the establishment of a series of territorial principalities in southern Italy which were joined in the early twelfth century to form the kingdom of Sicily, and the other, which from 1066 brought about the conquest and colonisation of the English kingdom. There can be no doubt, therefore, that anyone who examines the development of the province is going to confront a society possessing remarkable qualities. The prime purpose of this book is to concentrate attention on Normandy itself and to examine its evolution in its northern French context, divorced from the subsequent history of the Normans' conquests. In this way it may be possible to discover something of the true origins of the Norman movements.

In the period between 911 and 1066 the original settlement was greatly expanded in size. By 1066 the name Normandy meant largely what it means now: that is, a maritime province stretching from the vicinity of Dieppe on its eastern boundary to Mont-St-Michel and the borders of Brittany in the west. Its northern boundary was always the English Channel: its southern was in some places a series of small rivers such as the Bresle, the Epte, the Eure, and Avre, and in others, the limits of Carolingian administrative districts known as *pagi*.

This eleventh-century province of Normandy was subdivided into units of ecclesiastical government, namely the dioceses, and of secular government, the *pagi*. By 1066 the duchy included in whole or in part seven dioceses: the archbishopric of Rouen and the six suffragan bishoprics of Evreux, Lisieux, Sées, Bayeux, Coutances, and Avranches. Of these, only Rouen and Sées were not entirely within the frontiers of the duchy: Rouen included the outside region of the French Vexin and Sées, that of Perche. Although there were often long intervals during the tenth century when some of these dioceses had no bishop, their boundaries in the eleventh century were still essentially those of the pre-Norman period. This same continuity applies to the *pagi*, of which there were twelve. Of these, the Vexin and the Méresais were alone in not being completely Norman. The others, from east to west, were the Pays de Talou, the Pays de Caux, the Roumois, the Lieuvin, the Evrecin, the Séois, the Hiésmois, the Bessin, the Cotentin, and the Avranchin. Geographically and economically the duchy's most prominent feature was the river Seine which bisected the north-eastern part of the duchy and passed through the populous and wealthy town of Rouen. The special importance of this single large river and the one large town tended for most of the tenth century and for the early decades of the eleventh century to have the effect of concentrating most of the political and religious life of the province in their vicinity. Two further points require emphasis. One is the near coincidence of the frontiers of the duchy with those of the ecclesiastical province of Rouen. The other is the fact that the territory of eleventh-century Normandy had no existence prior to the tenth century: its extent and its boundaries were entirely the result of events which took place during the tenth and eleventh centuries (see Map 1).

The study of the Norman tenth century is an arduous and delicate task. The one relevant early history, that by Dudo of St-Quentin, which was composed in the second and third decades of the eleventh century, is a thoroughly untrustworthy document, a bombastic and rhetorical text, embroidering a long and frequently tedious discourse around a very small number of facts. The eighteenth-century monks who started to compile that encyclopaedic collection of historical sources, the *Recueil des Historiens des Gaules et de la France*, rejected Dudo's composition as being beneath contempt. Modern scholars usually regard it as little more than a curiosity.[1] But without it, there is little else. As an eleventh-century source tells us, charters were not written in the time of the first two Norman rulers, Rollo (911– *c.* 925) and William Longsword (*c.* 925–42).[2] Only four charters, two of which are very suspect documents, and none of which survive in an original text, exist for the long reign of Richard I (942–96). For almost the first century of its existence, the government of the Norman rulers was illiterate. There is some compensation in non-Norman sources such as the excellent *Annales* of Flodoard of Rheims, completed in the 960s, but great reliance has inevitably to be placed on the testimony of non-literary evidence, notably place-names containing Scandinavian features and archaeological finds. The former, which can tell us a great deal about the nature of the Scandinavian settlements, are very numerous in many parts of the province. The latter, much more miscellaneous, provide information on a number of problems: particularly valuable is the large hoard of coins which was found at Fécamp in 1963, and which can tell us a lot about the government of the first Norman rulers and something about the region's economy.

The eleventh century is a very different proposition. Sources are still far from plentiful, but, in comparison with the tenth century, the historian faces an overwhelming flood. The pre-1066 ducal charters, of which there are some 230, are available in an excellent modern edition by Marie Fauroux. In addition, there are many non-ducal charters – some still accessible only in manuscript – and literary sources such as saints' lives or the local histories of monastic houses. There are also two important historical works which, like Dudo's before them, set out very consciously to describe the achievements of the dukes: the 'Deeds of the Norman Dukes' (*Gesta Normannorum Ducum*) by William, a monk of the Norman abbey of Jumièges, which was written in the early 1070s, and the 'Deeds of William, Duke of the Normans and King of the English' (*Gesta Guillelmi Ducis Normannorum et Regis Anglorum*), compiled in *c.* 1077 by William of Poitiers, an archdeacon of Lisieux cathedral. These two have to be used carefully, since both set out quite deliberately to present a selective version of events in order to praise the achievements of the Norman rulers. The same reservations have to be made about the marvellous 'Ecclesiastical History' of Ordericus Vitalis, a gold-mine of material for the eleventh-century history of the duchy, but a source composed in the first half of the twelfth century and, therefore, both distant from events and liable to impose its own preconceptions on them. If the tenth century can be perceived only through a glass darkly, the eleventh is apt to appear as if it is being viewed through a series of distorting mirrors.

An important consideration, which must be borne in mind by all who examine the province's development, is that the history of Normandy and of the Normans has never been entirely freed from anachronism. Dudo of St-Quentin was as ready as anyone to present the past in terms of the conditions which existed in his own day. His book's title contains two gross – and quite deliberate – inaccuracies. The first is the statement that the Norman rulers were dukes. In Dudo's opinion, the very first Norman leader, the Norwegian Viking Rollo, was the first duke of Normandy. This was just not true. The title most frequently attributed in contemporary texts to Rollo, to his son William Longsword, and to his grandson Richard I, was 'count of Rouen'. The earliest reference to the ducal title in a reliable document dates only from 1006. The first duke to use it was Richard II (996–1026), the Norman ruler at the time that Dudo was writing and the man whom he was seeking to flatter.[3] Dudo's second deception was to suggest that these early 'dukes' ruled over a place called Normandy. In fact Dudo himself was almost the first person to call their territory by that name, although by *c*. 1020, when he was writing, he did have good warrant for doing so (see p. 56). In making these two assertions, Dudo was simply guilty of trying to suggest that the political and territorial circumstances of his own time extended back to the foundation of the province. In reality, the territory of Normandy was forged by the aggressive wars of its tenth-century rulers. The assumption of the title of duke by their eleventh-century successors was a reflection of their successes and of their consolidation of their power.

The preconceptions of those who came after Dudo are more complex and not so easily penetrated. The most difficult anachronism of all is the idea of a specifically 'Norman' achievement, the view that the Normans were a people especially endowed with a talent for conquest and for the government of their acquisitions. This notion was expressed in most of the major historical writings of the later eleventh and twelfth centuries and has subsequently passed into some of the best and most influential treatments composed during the twentieth century, notably the books of Charles Homer Haskins and Professor David Douglas. Douglas, for example, could write of 'the quality of Norman rule, ... the Norman ability to respect the traditions, and to utilise the aptitudes of those they governed, ... the over-mastering energy of a dominant people'.[4] Although Douglas elsewhere denies that the Norman movements could be inspired by 'national sentiment',[5] the idea of specifically national characteristics, or at least of qualities belonging to a single people, is unmistakable in this and other passages.

Are a people by nature dominant? As Professor R. H. C. Davis has persuasively argued, the modern idea of the Normans as a sort of 'chosen people' of conquest goes back in large part to a single source, the 'Ecclesiastical History' of Ordericus Vitalis.[6] Ordericus, who wrote between *c.* 1114 and 1141 *after* the great Norman conquests had already taken place, could include, for instance, an excursus on the Norman character which he chose to place in the death-bed speech which he attributed to William the Conqueror:

If the Normans are disciplined under a just and firm rule they are men of great valour, who press invincibly to the fore in arduous undertakings and, proving their strength, fight resolutely to overcome all enemies. But without such rule they tear each other to pieces and destroy themselves, for they hanker after rebellion, cherish sedition, and are ready for any treachery.[7]

Passages such as this were part of a literary theme which became widely prevalent during the twelfth century, and which could find very flamboyant expression in, for example, a battle speech written by Ailred of Rievaulx in *c.* 1155–57 for his account of the battle of the Standard, fought against the Scots in 1138:

We have seen – we have seen with our own eyes – the king of France and his whole army turn their backs upon us, while all the best nobles of his kingdom were captured by us, some to be ransomed, others loaded with chains and others condemned to a dungeon. Who has conquered Apulia, Sicily and Calabria but your Norman? Have not both emperors on the same day and at about the same hour turned their backs on the Normans, though the one was fighting the father and the other his son?[8]

Around sentiments such as these was woven what Professor Davis has called 'the Norman Myth'.

If these ideas evolved as a result of the conquests, then we must ask how the Normans viewed themselves before success came their way. It is readily apparent that the eleventh-century Normans saw their collective character in much less simple terms than those which have sometimes been drawn from passages such as that above. Dudo's history contained a set of ideas which persisted throughout the century. Essentially these came down to the view that, as a result of intermarriage and colonisation, Normandy had become a land in-

xv

habited by a distinct race, a people who were by now well integrated into their Frankish environment. In identifying the Normans as a unique people, Dudo was certainly ready to praise their military skills, but he was also concerned to belittle the memory of the Scandinavian past, which seems to have remained very much alive in the eyes of some of his contemporaries: Richer of Rheims, a writer who lived within 100 miles of the province, could still stigmatise its inhabitants as 'pirates' in a work written in the very late tenth century.[9] Dudo, who was not himself a Norman, must have been very sensitive on this particular point. His purpose was to flaunt the independence of the Norman lands and the achievements of the 'Norman dukes'. This could include boasts about their military exploits, but it certainly did not comprise anything as extreme as endowing either the dukes or their subjects with a special mission to conquer others.

Dudo's themes, along with some of those aspects of Norman history which he had tried to deny, remained the chief ones current throughout most of the eleventh century. The idea that the province had existed intact since 911 was indeed taken further in the late eleventh century by a writer at the abbey of Fécamp, as well as by William of Apulia in southern Italy, with the opinion that Rollo and his followers called their new home 'Normandy' after the north wind which had blown them there.[10] In spite of Dudo's version of the Norman character, there are sporadic references throughout the eleventh century to the people's Scandinavian origins. These must indicate a continued awareness, both within and outside Normandy, of the unusual background of the rulers of the province. A charter written for the abbey of Marmoutier, which is near Tours on the river Loire, could describe a piece of land in Normandy as being made up of 'thirty acres, or as we would call them, arpents', a reference to a change in agrarian terminology which had taken place as a result of the Scandinavian settlements. The monks of the abbey of St-Florent of Saumur, also in the Loire valley, could still be cagey about acquiring property in Normandy as late as the 1050s, despairingly referring to the problems of identifying place-names which had changed, and so pestering duke William II that he was driven to an oath on the integrity of the Norman people.[11] The existence of a similar sentimental attachment to the Scandinavian past is epitomised by the famous boast of Roger II de Montgommery, one of the closest of William II's followers, that he was 'a Norman of Norman stock'.[12] The sum of this material is far from constituting evidence of a set of 'national' values driving the Normans on to conquest. They would seem to have retained a sense that they were a different and unusual people, a fact which was acknowledged by their non-Norman contemporaries.[13] Yet this distinctiveness did not place them in an inflexible category: it was the case, in both northern and southern Europe, that the terms 'Norman' and 'Frenchman' could be used apparently interchangeably, as if to show that the Normans were seen in the eleventh century as being part of a wider racial spectrum which was unquestionably Frankish.[14]

There is one possible hint of a more radical view of racial and national character in the work of the poet Garnier, a contemporary of Dudo's, who could brand the French as 'haughty'. This must, however, be treated as an isolated comment devoid of any special significance, and not as evidence of any sharp separation of Normans and French on Garnier's part: he also composed a eulogy of the contemporary French king, Robert the Pious (996–1031).[15] New ideas on the Norman character, very obviously the result of recent events, began to appear only in the wave of literary sources which celebrated the conquest of England. William of Jumièges, in the early 1070s, commented that ill-feeling between French and Normans was long-standing, the former's envy as good as a fact of life. William of Poitiers, in c. 1077, seems to have been the first to allude to the range of Norman victories in northern and southern Europe; he was soon followed in this in the 1080s by Amatus, a monk of the renowned abbey of Monte Cassino in southern Italy.[16] This was the beginning of our 'dominant people' syndrome. It is significant, however, that Dudo's comments about the multiracial character of Norman society could still be repeated in a source written in the last decade of the eleventh century.[17] The novel idea of the Normans as a conquering people was far from widespread at this stage, and did not become so until the next century. It would be foolish on the basis of this evidence to think that the Normans had by 1066 developed any ferocious racial or national drive towards a career of conquest.

The moral is that a study of pre-1066 Normandy must set aside such sentiments as 'the over-mastering energy of a dominant people' and concentrate instead on drawing conclusions from an analysis of social and political conditions in the duchy. The history of the province should be written as the history of a Scandinavian settlement which evolved into a northern French territorial principality. Any such study must examine the specific impact of the Scandinavian settlers on the tenth-century history of the province and must discuss how far these changes contributed to the duchy's remarkable evolution in the eleventh century. Close attention must be given to the very points which Dudo sought to overlook: the territorial and political instability of the early settlement and the survival of Scandinavian features. This requires an examination of the place-name, legal, and archaeological evidence from the duchy, matters on which several excellent modern publications make conclusions feasible. On this subject, the Norman material can be illuminated by reference to the numerous studies on Scandinavian settlements in the British Isles; a comparative approach, undertaken carefully, can be most helpful. If, as Dudo proclaimed, and as modern commentators have generally suggested, the Scandinavian influence on most aspects of the province's life was largely dissipated by the end of the tenth century, then eleventh-century Normandy must be analysed entirely in its French context. By this stage its people all spoke French and its social and governmental structure was almost exclusively Frankish. Here, too, in addition to the many excellent studies of aspects of the province's history, there is good comparative material available. The many publications of recent years on the early medieval histories of France's regions provide an admirable focus for such discussion. As instruments of comparison, these monographs are not always very easily used, since all are inevitably influenced by the specific character of their region's history and by the great variation in the quality of available sources: Robert Fossier's study of Picardy is an analysis of the evolution of a rural society over a long period of time, whereas Olivier Guillot's book on Anjou concentrates on the fortunes of the redoubtable dynasty of eleventh-century counts and is therefore essentially a study of political power.[18] Where these works are especially useful, however, is in their common philosophy that a more profound and precise understanding of social and political change can be obtained through an analysis of structure. Although Normandy, because of its unique beginnings, does present special problems, considerable progress can be made by applying the techniques which others have applied to different regions and different problems.

The shape of this book is governed by the quantity of available material. The formative period of the tenth century has perforce to be treated in a single chapter. The eleventh century can be given a more expansive discussion, so the next four chapters deal in turn with the province's relations with its neighbours, social structure, ducal government, and the Church. The final section will seek to draw together conclusions on the nature of the Norman achievement within Normandy, its strengths, as well as its deficiencies. The purpose throughout is to reject simplified explanations of this achievement, to rely as far as is possible on the testimony of strictly contemporary and reliable sources and to place Normandy and its history as far as is possible in their contemporary context. But for all this, it should never be forgotten that the Scandinavian settlements did take place and that, for this reason if for no other, Normandy occupied a unique place in the history of the Medieval West.

NOTES

1. The most recent edition is Dudo of St-Quentin, *De moribus et actis primorum Normanniae Ducum*, ed. J. Lair (Caen, 1865). The most comprehensive demolition is that by H. Prentout, *Etude critique sur Dudon de St-Quentin* (Paris, 1916).
2. *Recueil*, no. 53.
3. For the ducal title, see K. F. Werner, 'Quelques observations au sujet des débuts du "duché" de Normandie', in *Etudes . . . Yver*, 691–709.
4. D. C. Douglas, *The Norman Achievement* (London, 1969), 215.
5. *Ibid.*, 11.
6. R. H. C. Davis, *The Normans and Their Myth* (London, 1976), especially, 7–17, 49–69. Important qualifications to Professor Davis's thesis are made by G. A. Loud, 'The *Gens Normannorum* – Myth or Reality?', to appear in *Proceedings of the Battle Conference*, iv, 1982. I am grateful to Dr Loud for providing me with a copy of his paper.
7. OV, iv, 82. The practice whereby 11th- and 12th-century writers put speeches into their subjects' mouths was very common, deriving from classical models.
8. Ailred of Rievaulx, *Relatio de Standardo* in *Chronicles of the Reigns of Stephen, Henry II and Richard I*, ed. R. Howlett (Rolls Series, 1886), iii, 186. The translation is taken from Davis, *The Normans and Their Myth*, 66–7. The events referred to are the battle of Mortemer (1054), and the campaigns of Robert Guiscard at Rome in 1084 and probably of Bohemond in Greece in 1082. I am grateful to Professor Davis for permission to use his translation.
9. For example, *Richer, Histoire de France (888–995)*, ed. R. Latouche (Paris, 1930), i, 156, 168, 172; ii, 328. This appreciation of Dudo is based on Davis, *The Normans and Their Myth*, 50–63; Loud, above note 6.
10. *Libellus de revelatione, aedificatione et auctoritate Fiscannensis monasterii*, PL, cli, col. 713; *Guillaume de Pouille: La geste de Robert Guiscard*, ed. Marguerite Mathieu (Palermo, 1961), 98.
11. *Recueil*, nos. 163*bis*, 199; *Chartes normandes de l'abbaye de St-Florent près Saumur*, ed. P. Marchegay (Caen, 1879), no. 2.
12. R. -N. Sauvage, *L'abbaye de St-Martin de Troarn* (Caen, 1911), preuves no. 3. See also, *Vita Herluini*, ed. J. Armitage Robinson, in *Gilbert Crispin, Abbot of Westminster* (Cambridge, 1911), 89.
13. See, for example, the letter, dating from 1050 to 1054, of abbot John of Fécamp to pope Leo IX, PL, cxliii, cols. 798–99, in which he refers to *gens illa Northmannorum bellica* and complains about being attacked in the suburbs of Rome because he was a Norman.
14. Davis, *The Normans and Their Myth*, 54.

15. L. Musset, 'Le satiriste Garnier de Rouen et son milieu (début du XIe siècle)', *Revue du moyen âge latin*, x (1954), 245, 266.
16. WJ, 129; WP, 228; *Storia de' Normanni di Amato di Montecassino*, ed. V. de Bartholomeis (Rome, 1935), 11. The reference in *The Carmen de Hastingae Proelio of Guy, Bishop of Amiens*, ed. Catherine Morton and Hope Muntz (Oxford, 1972), line 259, has been left on one side. A strong case has been made out to suggest that the *Carmen* is a literary exercise undertaken in the early twelfth century, R. H. C. Davis, 'The *Carmen de Hastingae Proelio*', *EHR*, xciii (1978), 241–61.
17. 'Inventio et Miracula Sancti Wulfranni', ed. Dom J. Laporte, *SHN, Mélanges*, xiv (1938), 27.
18. R. Fossier, *La terre et les hommes en Picardie* (Paris and Louvain, 1968); O. Guillot, *Le comte d'Anjou et son entourage au XIe siècle* (Paris, 1972).

In memory of my father

PART ONE
The tenth century

CHAPTER ONE
Origins and consolidation

During the autumn of the year 911 the Carolingian king Charles the Simple granted 'certain districts (*pagi*) bordering the sea-coast, along with the city of Rouen'[1] to a band of Viking raiders. This obscure event, usually referred to as 'the Treaty of St-Clair-sur-Epte', after the place in the Vexin at which the agreement between king Charles and Rollo was probably made, is customarily identified with the foundation of 'the duchy of Normandy'. The 'treaty' was not, however, in its contemporary context, an especially unusual event. 'St-Clair-sur-Epte' was just one instance of the ways in which the rulers of ninth- and tenth-century western Europe sought to dilute the Viking menace. The first stage towards an understanding of the origins and early history of 'Normandy' is to place its beginnings against the general background of the raids and the settlements which followed.

THE SCANDINAVIAN SETTLEMENTS

Although it is not quite their earliest recorded appearance, the start of the Viking raids on the West can be conveniently marked by the sack of the famous monastery on Holy Island off the Northumberland coast in 793. The event gains especial poignancy from the idea of the destruction of a secluded and unprotected church and because the reaction of Alcuin of York, an Englishman, but also the confidant of the emperor Charlemagne, has been preserved:

. . . it is nearly three-hundred-and-fifty years that we and our fathers have inhabited this most lovely land, and never before has such terror appeared in

Britain as we have now suffered from a pagan race, nor was it thought that such an inroad from the sea could be made.[2]

Many others were subsequently to feel the same sense of shock. The raids became a constant element in the life of the ninth-century West, with the inhabitants of the Seine valley first experiencing their effects in the 840s. Although recent studies have contributed to a much more subtle interpretation of the nature of the Viking migrations, notably with regard to the numbers involved and the aims of the raiders, and have made us aware of the peaceful and constructive sides to the pirates' endeavours, their fundamental menace is something which should never be forgotten. The Vikings were the representatives of a pagan culture. Their speed of movement usually gave them the advantage of surprise. That their target was movable wealth, usually in the form of precious metals, meant that they attacked the Church and the towns, which were among the more vulnerable elements in western society. Because they broke so many of the rules of accepted conduct, they constituted a threat of a specially dangerous kind.

The acquisition of land, as well as that of plunder, had always been a fairly consistent element of Viking activity: it explains the colonisation of the fringe lands of Greenland, Iceland, and the Scottish Islands. Such aims became an altogether different matter when they were directed against regions where there was already a measure of political organisation. An important landmark in a new and very dangerous phase was the landing in eastern England of 'the Great Army' in 865 with the deliberate purpose of conquest. The ancient kingdoms of Northumbria and Mercia went under very quickly. A Viking territory was set up in northern England which evolved into the kingdom of York. The whole of England might well have been overrun but for the heroic stand of Alfred the Great of Wessex (871–99). His victories mark another crucial moment in the history of the Vikings' relations with western Europe since, for the first time, a serious check had been imposed on their advance. The Vikings themselves would have become much more aware that there were limits to what could be achieved.

Alfred's success opened the way for a series of attempts to integrate the Vikings into western European life. The Treaty of Wedmore made with Guthrum in 878 sought a *modus vivendi* on the basis that he and his followers would, in return for their territory, keep the peace and convert to Christianity. The advantages of this sort of agreement for hard-pressed native rulers were significant ones. In theory the Vikings' appetite for land was met and kept within definite territorial bounds. The poacher was turned into the gamekeeper by being given responsibility for maintaining order. It was hoped to tame the Vikings by integrating them into the existing political and religious structures. But at the same time Alfred's defensive victories had the accidental result of diverting those Vikings who wished to continue raiding across the Channel, thereby intensifying the pressure on the lands under the theoretical control of the Frankish kings.

The initial response in the territory which we would now call France to the Viking onslaught was somewhat different from what happened in England. There was, for example, no widespread capitulation after the fashion of the English 860s and 870s. Nor, however, were the invaders faced by the co-ordinated resistance which developed under the auspices of the Wessex monarchy in the later years of the ninth century. Despite the energetic efforts of some of the Carolingian kings, effective defence came increasingly to mean local defence, organised independently of the monarchy. What this involved in terms of fortifications in the territory which was later to become Normandy is a subject on which archaeological investigation has only just begun.[3] The insistence of the raids and the progressive dissolution of the powers of the Frankish monarchy meant that both the kings and the local men who were in the process of succeeding to their authority began to offer compromises similar to Wedmore. In 897 Charles the Simple had been dissuaded from ceding territory on the grounds that it would be wrong to ally himself with pagans. By 911 practical necessities had evidently come to outweigh such sensibilities and the king made the treaty with Rollo. Charles' example was followed in 921 by his arch-rival, Robert, son of Robert the Strong, marquis of the Neustrian March, who granted a territory which was described as Brittany and the *pagus* of Nantes to a group of Vikings based on the river Loire. Like Wedmore, both these agreements envisaged conversion to Christianity (see pp. 11–12).[4]

The raids on northern France were an important factor in the social changes which ensured that the medieval histories of the English and French kingdoms would travel different paths. If the organisation of resistance under Alfred's unified command was a crucial phase in the evolution which led to the formation of an English kingdom ruled by the Wessex monarchy, the localisation of defence in France was equally crucial to a complex set of social changes which shifted effective political power to new levels. The most obvious manifestation was the disintegration of the power of the once magnificent Carolingian monarchy. The Empire founded by Charle-

Origins and consolidation

magne on Christmas Day 800 came to an end with the deposition of his undistinguished descendant, Charles the Fat, in 888. Thereafter there were separate monarchies for the west and east Franks. A bastard Carolingian named Arnulf ruled in the east over a territory approximating to what we would now call Germany. In the west, the Carolingians were temporarily set aside and replaced by Odo (888–98), a son of Robert the Strong, but were then recalled in the person of Charles the Simple. The steady dismemberment of royal power meant that the kings lost lands and subsequently control over their local officials. This contributed to the formation from the late ninth century of what are generally termed for convenience territorial principalities, new units of political authority which were to play a central part in the history of tenth-, eleventh-, and twelfth-century France. The county of Flanders, for example, was created by military expansion by count Baldwin II between 883 and 918 on the basis of a much smaller area given to his father, count Baldwin I, by king Charles the Bald. Further south, a similar process enabled Richard the Justiciar to build up what later became the duchy of Burgundy, again in the last years of the ninth century.

The particular origins of what later became Normandy have to be set against the background of the numerous and ultimately futile attempts to establish some sort of stability within the region of northern France which was known as the Breton or Neustrian March. In Charlemagne's time this had stretched from Calais to the borders of Brittany. Its purpose was to check the incursions of the Bretons who had never been incorporated into the Carolingian Empire. In 862 Charles the Bald had granted the March to Robert the Strong. The objective of restraining the Bretons seems to have failed, since in 867 they were granted possession of the Cotentin and the Avranchin. The agreement by which this transfer was effected, conferring as it did all royal rights except that of nominating bishops, strongly prefigures the grant made to Rollo in 911. The Bretons subsequently pushed further east into the region around Bayeux without being able to consolidate their grip. The instability became chronic in the second half of the ninth century, not simply because of Breton pressure, or because of the Vikings, but because of the additional complication of the feuds between the Carolingians, the Robertians, and other aspiring territorial rulers.[5] In one sense, the grant of a territory to Rollo and his followers was nothing more than the creation of another local power in a region which was already fragmenting into a number of increasingly independent units. Their introduction was not, therefore, a simple matter of the

5

peace-loving Franks trying to assimilate a group of uncivilised brigands. Despite receiving their lands 'for the safety of the kingdom',[6] Rollo and his men were in fact being welcomed into a region already shredded by violence and in the midst of far-reaching social changes.

Once they had been installed, the Scandinavians were in control of a territory whose tenth-century evolution must be seen against the background of the events and social changes which took place throughout northern France. The new settlers in the Seine valley were from the first embroiled in the incessant wars which were being fought among their neighbours. The best source for the history of the first half of the tenth century, the *Annales* of Flodoard of Rheims, presents a plain, factual record of the seemingly continuous warfare in which the chief participants were Charles the Simple himself, Robert the son of Robert the Strong, Arnulf I of Flanders (918–65), and count Herbert II of Vermandois (900/07–43). The effect of these struggles was finally to frustrate the formation of a stable principality covering the entire Neustrian March. Instead authority continued to fragment. The Carolingians grew weaker and weaker. Charles the Simple was imprisoned and superseded by his rival Robert (922–23), who was killed in battle against Viking raiders, and then by Robert's son-in-law, Ralph (923–36). Ralph, however, was followed by Louis IV (936–54) and a succession of Carolingians up until 987, when the dynasty failed in the direct male line. During this period when Carolingian power was sliding downhill, the territorial strength of the Robertians was also dissolving, to the extent that when Robert the Strong's great-grandson, Hugh Capet, became king in succession to the Carolingians, his own lands were largely confined to the district around Paris. This general fragmentation of all large areas of authority had by the 950s and 960s brought about the establishment of a new and still more local stratum of effective power, at the level by this stage often of no more than a single county, such as Anjou, Blois, or Maine.

Amidst such unstable conditions, the Scandinavian settlers showed a notable unwillingness to abandon previous habits and connections. The experiment of granting lands to the Vikings did not lead to an immediate alleviation of the danger which they presented. The conversion to Christianity tended to be superficial and the agreement to reside within a defined territory was often kept only with reluctance. In many respects, western rulers discovered that bringing the wolf to dinner merely invited him to consume more. The new Viking settlements became bases from which to launch fresh raids and an attraction to newcomers who often tried to extend the acquisitions. There seems to have been a strong feeling of community among the various fledgling settlements. Rollo himself was closely related to the Norwegian rulers of the Orkneys.[7] 'Normandy' received settlers who had dwelt in other territories: the existence of place-names containing an Anglo-Saxon element in the Pays de Caux suggests the immigration of Scandinavians who had lived for a considerable period of time in England, while Celtic toponyms in the north of the Cotentin indicate Irish–Scandinavian colonisation there, a pattern of movement which parallels that from Ireland to northern England.[8] On the bloodier side of things, there was the expedition of *c.* 935 which was fitted out at Rouen and which pillaged in the vicinity of Thérouanne. The approach of king Ralph's army caused the raiders to strangle their prisoners and to try to make a quick getaway.[9] These contacts across the Scandinavian North proved very long-lasting. Duke Richard II of Normandy (996–1026) made an agreement with Sven Forkbeard, king of Denmark, to divide the loot taken in the latter's invasion of the England of the luckless Aethelred the Unready.[10] At about the same time, men from Normandy appear alongside Scandinavians at the battle of Clontarf (1014) in Ireland, and an Irishman, sold into slavery at Corbridge in Northumberland, after a long journey located his wife at Le Vaudreuil in Normandy.[11] Still later the Scandinavians in England are supposed to have formed a 'fifth column' which welcomed king Harold Hardrada of Norway in 1066.

These enduring links were in many ways a cause of profound instability for all the Viking principalities which had come into existence in the late ninth and early tenth centuries. The continuation of the raids must have been a great stimulus to attempts at reconquest by the rulers who had made the original grants, while the constant immigration must have been extremely unsettling for those who lived in the Scandinavian colonies. At York, the inability to maintain steady political control and the surliness of the people, both English and Scandinavian, led almost inexorably to voluntary, temporary, submissions to the Wessex monarchy in 919 and 944, a period of dramatic military expansion into the Midlands under Olaf Guthricsson in 939–41, and, finally, to the expulsion of the last king of York, a Norwegian immigrant named Eric Bloodaxe, in 954. The Norse kingdom of Dublin was beset by similar problems. Its survival seemed often to depend more on the dissensions of the native Irish than on its own strengths. The settlement on the river Loire soon collapsed. With the single exception of 'Normandy', the continuation of the very same piratical and adventurous instincts which had brought the Viking principalities into existence also made a large contribution to their speedy elimination.

The grant of lands to Rollo and his followers must therefore be seen as a typical response of the harassed western European ruling classes to the Viking menace. The 'Treaty of St-Clair-sur-Epte' was made between a Frankish king whose successors might easily seek to overthrow it and a Viking chief who could not guarantee to control the new settlers. What was to become the duchy of Normandy came into existence within a society which was itself highly unstable and in the midst of profound social change. Contrary to the story put around by Dudo of St-Quentin in the early eleventh century, there was nothing very certain about the first years of the province's existence.

THE FIRST YEARS

The known facts about the 'Treaty of St-Clair-sur-Epte' are very small in number. Dudo of St-Quentin's account, written over 100 years after the event, told of the grant to Rollo not only of the territory which was by Dudo's time known as Normandy, but of Brittany as well. The land was given in full ownership (*in alodo et in fundo*) and, in order to emphasise that from the very beginning the Norman rulers were remarkably independent of the French kings, Dudo included a story about Rollo's refusal to bend his knee before king Charles. Instead, one of his soldiers was delegated to take part in the ceremony and his attempt to kiss the king's foot without bending down sent the unfortunate Carolingian tumbling backwards. Dudo does, however, admit that Rollo did homage. He also records that he agreed to convert to Christianity and that he was given Charles' daughter Gisla in marriage.[12]

Some of this story is demonstrably false; some of it at best fabulous. The territorial provisions, for example, are an invention. Rollo and his followers received no more than the *pagi* of Talou, Caux, Roumois, and parts of the Vexin and the Evrecin (see Map 2). The marriage is known in no other source. If the Norman ruler did enjoy a privileged status within the kingdom of France, no tenth-century writer noticed it: Flodoard, for example, carefully records William Longsword's homages to king Charles, king Ralph, and king Louis IV, in 927, 933, and 940 respectively, in the same language which he used for other such acts by other princes.[13] But with Dudo largely

Origins and consolidation

discarded, the remaining information on 'St-Clair-sur-Epte' is very meagre. The earliest documentary reference appears in a diploma of king Charles dated 14 March 918 for the abbey of St-Germain-des-Prés, which mentions 'the portion which we have granted to Rollo and his companions for the safety of the kingdom'. Otherwise, there is only Flodoard, who, in his annal for 923, referred to the lands beyond the river Epte given so that the Normans should convert to Christianity and keep the peace, and who, in his 'History of the church of Rheims' mentioned the grant of the maritime *pagi* and the city of Rouen.[14]

The two features which stand out in this sparse collection are the conversion to Christianity and the conferment on Rollo of a formally constituted authority within the territory. Neither of these would appear to have been any deterrent to the Normans expanding the area under their control during the reigns of Rollo (911–c. 928) and his son William Longsword (c. 928–42). The chronology of the conquests is clearly set out by Flodoard. In 924 king Ralph agreed to the concession of Bayeux and Maine (*Cinomannis et Baiocae pacto pacis eis concessae*), a region which is generally equated with central Normandy. The grant probably did not in the end include the county of Maine, of which there is no other record of Norman possession. In 933 William Longsword received 'the land of the Bretons situated on the sea-coast' (*terra Brittonum in ora maritima sitam*), which must be the Avranchin and Cotentin, the region previously granted to the Bretons by Charles the Bald in 867.[15] The three 'grants' of 911, 924, and 933, if Flodoard's reference to Maine is rejected, brought the territory under Norman control to approximately the same limits which existed in 1066.

The acquisitions of territory which resulted from Rollo's and William Longsword's campaigns seem to have been largely accidental, since alongside the agreements of 924 and 933, the sources also record a succession of apparently indiscriminate wars, which in turn suggest the same tendency to lash out in all directions which was typical of all the Viking settlements. In 923 Normans from Rouen were in the district around Beauvais fighting alongside the army of Charles the Simple. In 925 they launched a very violent raid, sacking Amiens and Arras, and penetrating eastwards as far as Noyon.[16] William Longsword maintained an interest in this same region, but also embarked on a significant push westwards. The tantalising find at Mont-St-Michel of a single coin bearing the legend + VVILEIM DUX BRI is likely to be that of a money of William Longsword issued as duke of Brittany.[17] This fortuitous discovery may make a

9

little less fantastic Dudo's assertion that the original grant to the Normans included Brittany, just as the vagaries of the campaigning may make Flodoard's strange reference to the grant of Maine a little more plausible. It looks very much as if during the first decades of the tenth century the Norman rulers simply extended their control to those regions which they could subdue by force.

The corollary is that the Normans were kept within the restraints which their neighbours could impose on them. To the east, they both benefited and suffered from the rivalries of contending princes. Their excursion into the Beauvaisis in 923 in support of Charles the Simple makes the grant of Bayeux and Maine in 924 by Charles' enemy, king Ralph, look suspiciously like an attempt to buy them off. The prospects in this easterly direction did, however, receive a serious set-back in 925 when Rollo suffered a military defeat at Eu, a place right on what was to become the Norman frontier. His conquerors were king Ralph's allies, counts Arnulf I of Flanders and Herbert II of Vermandois. This was an important set-back against the chief powers contending for dominance in the political vacuum of what we would now call Picardy. In the west, the removal of the Avranchin and the Cotentin from Breton control constituted a significant gain. But the recorded details of the military engagements of the 930s suggest that further encroachments westwards went no further beyond what was eventually to become the frontier on the river Couesnon than the region of St-Malo and Dol. During the whole of this period William Longsword's dealings may have been somewhat devious, since, while his father had favoured the Carolingians, William for a long time supported the Robertians. But in 940 he again changed over to the side of Charles the Simple's son, Louis IV. In any event, however, all Norman expansion, both to east and west, was brutally halted on 17 December 942 when William was assassinated on the island of Picquigny in the river Somme near Amiens on the orders of count Arnulf of Flanders.

It is generally accepted that the terms of 'St-Clair-sur-Epte' included the provision that Rollo become count of Rouen, that he take over the royal lands, and represent royal authority in his territory.[18] We know almost nothing about the way in which he set about the task of government. Dudo provides a fanciful picture of legislation against robbery and violence which may be worthy of some credence (see p. 22). But it is also to Dudo that we owe the notorious story of Rollo taking over a region reduced to a desert and subsequently reapportioning it among his followers. A series of studies by Professors Lucien Musset and Jean Yver, published over the last forty years and culminating in the latter's magisterial survey of the province's institutions, have consigned Dudo's opinions to an oblivion from which they will surely never return.[19] In 911 the Scandinavians took over a going concern, albeit a somewhat dented one: a Carolingian-appointed count was still in office at Rouen in 905, so was a bishop at Coutances, while the archbishop of Rouen remained at his post over 911 to co-operate actively with his colleague at Rheims in the conversion of the newcomers. The long-term perspective more than justifies the general conclusion that the first settlers must have taken over many existing institutions, since, by the eleventh century, when documents become available, it is clear that rural estates had preserved essentially Carolingian features and that ducal government operated largely through mechanisms which were inspired by Carolingian notions of authority. This indicates that, from the very beginning, Rollo and his followers must have made a serious attempt to sustain organised government within their territory. Interpreted literally, Flodoard's annal for 925, which noted laconically that the Normans of Rouen had broken the peace which they had formerly agreed, might even be taken to mean that they abided by the terms of 'St-Clair-sur-Epte' for some fourteen years.[20]

The records of the tenth-century Norman Church underline rather more forcefully the positive side to the efforts at organisation made in Rollo's time. What was achieved must be set against a background of a region in which the structure of ecclesiastical authority had been as good as completely wrecked. The continuous occupation of the archbishopric of Rouen contrasts markedly with most other dioceses, which were abandoned in the later ninth century: there is no record of any bishop at Avranches from 862, Bayeux from 876, and Sées from 910. Similarly, a once vigorous monasticism almost entirely disappeared during this same period as the monks of once prosperous abbeys such as St-Wandrille, Jumièges, and St-Ouen of Rouen took to the roads with their precious ornaments and relics. Despite being a comprehensive exodus, it was also one which was fairly well organised.[21] And despite the carnage, the reception of the pagan newcomers at Rouen was carefully prepared by the ecclesiastical authorities, who, at least at first, seem to have looked upon the new arrivals in a liberal frame of mind. Pope John X in c. 914 counselled patience to archbishop Hervey of Rheims. Hervey himself sent to Guy, the archbishop of Rouen and, therefore, the prelate unfortunate enough to find himself in the middle of the new settlement, a sort of handbook for converting the heathen. This consisted of twenty-three texts ranging through the conversions of St Paul, the emperor Constantine, and the Frankish king, Clovis, to advice given by popes Gregory the Great and Leo I, St Augustine, and St Ambrose.[22] Guy's efforts to apply this guidance are not documented. Rollo at least would seem to have responded positively, welcoming the return of the relics of St Ouen to Rouen and endowing the monastery named after that saint with a substantial patrimony largely made up of its former estates.[23] A non-Norman monastery, the abbey of St-Denis near Paris, was able to resume possession of a vill near Dieppe. According to an early twelfth-century source, Rouen even became a town of refuge for relics from Coutances cathedral, a place which was at this stage not within the Norman lands.[24] Churches outside the land assigned to the new settlers appear to have been ready to resume contact and even to attempt a recolonisation. Rollo himself was not indifferent to Christianity.

A much more general accommodation to Frankish practices became obvious in William Longsword's reign. William's marriage to a Christian wife, Leutgarde, the daughter of count Herbert II of Vermandois, was accompanied by the provision of a dowry organised along Frankish lines.[25] The Rouen mint was revived, a direct recreation of an institution of Carolingian government. It produced money in a typically Carolingian style, but at the same time displayed a remarkable spirit of independence by suppressing all reference on the coins to the Frankish kings, and including instead William's own name.[26] A mixture of literary and archaeological evidence suggests that William may have begun the construction of a palace at Fécamp according to the pattern which was normal among his fellow northern French princes.[27] William Longsword also showed a more than conventional commitment to Christianity and made a large contribution to the restoration of religious organisation in a territory which had grown to approximately the full extent of the later duchy. The willingness of the surviving inmates of the monasteries of the pre-invasion period to return to their old sites was exploited as two monks were allowed to come back to Jumièges, along with further monks and a new abbot obtained from the abbey of St-Cyprien of Poitiers, a house which had come under the novel reforming influence of the abbey of Cluny (founded 909).[28] Rouen cathedral, St-Ouen of Rouen, Jumièges, and Mont-St-Michel, which at this date housed a community of canons, all received substantial grants of land.[29]

The process by which the Norman rulers tended to organise their authority along the same lines as other territorial princes is already in evidence under Rollo and William Longsword. To judge by the large scale of the restorations made to the Church, and by the immense landed resources available to the early-eleventh-century dukes, the first counts of Rouen succeeded in taking over a remarkable proportion of the lands within their new territory; mostly the old Carolingian fisc, that is, the royal and comital estates, and much ecclesiastical property as well. Quite how they were able to do this is entirely obscure; nothing can be known of the extent to which former Frankish holders of estates were dispossessed, and to whose benefit. In the long run, this accumulation of landed wealth provided the foundations on which the later Norman rulers established their power-base, from which they were able to sustain their control over the province. In the early tenth century, however, the territory under their control lived a very turbulent life. The region continued to receive considerable numbers of new settlers. Tensions between the Frankish natives and their new masters, and among the Scandinavians themselves, disturbed the precarious peace. The people of Bayeux, officially placed under Scandinavian rule in 924, revolted in 925. Dudo's unconfirmed account mentions the rising of 933–34, led by a Scandinavian named Rioul, which was put down by William Longsword. The same literary evidence which describes the building of the Fécamp palace, also mentions the employment of large gangs of slaves in typically Scandinavian style.[30] Another eleventh-century source, the Aquitanian chronicler, Adhemar of Chabannes, retailed the story of how Rollo on his death-bed had taken out the double insurance of benefactions to Christian churches and some human sacrifices to the old gods.[31] The already highly volatile existence of the new territory was thrown into chaos when William Longsword was murdered in 942, to be succeeded by his young son Richard I (942–96), the product of a union with a Breton mistress.

During the period between 942 and 946, the lands assembled by Rollo and William Longsword were subjected to all the strains and stresses which destroyed other Viking principalities. Scandinavian war-bands intervened in force. Soon after 942 a group of warriors arrived under the command of a chief who has been cautiously identified as Sihtric Sihtricsson, an exile from York, and the brother of king Olaf Sihtricsson.[32] Another chief named Harold seems to have set himself up in an independent power-base at Bayeux, while there was a pagan reaction within the province led by a certain Turmod. In addition, a Frankish quisling named Ralph *Torta*, at least according to Dudo, encouraged the armed intervention of king Louis IV.[33] All this went on against the background of a serious attempt at reconquest. In 944, a two-pronged campaign, in which Louis IV

13

moved against Rouen and Hugh the Great, duke of the Franks and chief of the Robertians, attacked Bayeux, the main town in Lower Normandy, was launched. After some early successes the threat to the Norman province's existence evaporated with the collapse of the fragile alliance between the two men, ostensibly as a result of Louis' refusal to allow Hugh to take possession of Bayeux. Thereafter, at least from a Carolingian point of view, all was a shambles. In 945 Louis was captured by Harold, the Viking in command at Bayeux, subsequently to be ransomed into a second captivity in the hands of duke Hugh. Through all this the young Richard I had been a helpless bystander whose life may at times have been endangered. But by 946 the threat to the continued existence of the Norman principality had passed.

It would be difficult to over-state the seriousness of this crisis. Quite simply, 'Normandy' had survived the symptoms which overwhelmed the other Viking principalities. What would appear to have saved it from annihilation was the perennial jealousies among the Franks which prevented the impoverished Carolingians from acquiring the lands needed to equalise resources with their stronger rivals. In comparison with the singleness of purpose displayed towards the Scandinavians at York by the kings of Wessex from Edward the Elder onwards, the Frankish monarchy offered only a pallid and inconsistent threat. After 946 the assistance of duke Hugh the Great allowed Richard I to re-establish himself in 'Normandy'. There are signs of a close alliance: Richard married Hugh's daughter Emma and Hugh appears to have provided auxiliaries to support Richard's wars. In particular, Hugh's campaign in 954 against a certain Harold looks very like an attack on that same Harold who had held Bayeux in 944–45, and therefore like deliberate aid in re-establishing Richard's power in Lower Normandy.[34] The youthful Richard I seems to have been capable of the aggressive attitudes of his predecessors, launching a violent raid against Theobald, count of Blois-Chartres, in the late 950s. The scheme seems to have backfired since Richard soon faced a strong coalition comprising Theobald, the Carolingian king Lothaire (954–86), and the counts of Anjou and Flanders. Their riposte was parried only by a military victory in the suburbs of Rouen and by a summons for the assistance of unruly Scandinavian auxiliaries.[35] This last manoeuvre was too much for Dudo of St-Quentin, who had known Richard I personally, and wished to present him in a favourable light. He therefore added that Richard personally preached to the pagans unceasingly for sixteen days in order to convert them to Christianity. The peace settlement of 965, which ended this particular war, may be a significant turning-point, since thereafter Richard seems to have abandoned the sallies into *Francia* typical of his predecessors. The first two decades of his reign had witnessed a perilous few years when the province's very existence had been called into question, followed by the steady re-establishment of power over the regions controlled by William Longsword. The last thirty years of his rule from 965 onwards were devoted to the consolidation of this authority. The substance of Dudo's Norman Utopia started to assume definite form.

THE SCANDINAVIAN IMPACT

The result of the grant made to Rollo in 911 and of subsequent events was the creation of a new political unit in northern France. Seminal to any understanding of this region's history in the tenth and eleventh centuries is an estimate of the effects which the Scandinavian settlements had on the society of the province. A beguiling image of a vigorous Viking society which sustained a continuity of aggression over a century and a half is readily available to anyone who wishes to put forward easy explanations for the expansion of the Normans from *c.* 1020 onwards. Social and political change is, however, far more complicated than this. The 150-odd years between 911 and 1066 turn out to be a complex period in which the Scandinavian settlers shed most of the characteristics associated with the Vikings and changed into the inhabitants of a well-organised territorial principality.

Both contemporary evidence and the conclusions of modern scholarship enable us to dismiss out of hand any simplistic view of the Scandinavian impact. The Norman historians who wrote in the eleventh century offer no cause to think that their subjects regarded themselves as a specially warlike people or one whose life-style had remained obdurately Viking. When we turn to the results of modern research, we find complete agreement that the Scandinavian language had as good as ceased to be spoken in the province by the end of the tenth century and that the 'thing', the regional assembly characteristic of the political organisation of Scandinavia, never took root on Norman soil.[36] Most modern studies have, in short, belittled the Scandinavian contribution to the province's institutions and have instead stressed the immense depth of continuity, both in the organisation of government and of rural society, from the Carolingian period through to the eleventh century.[37] Continuity of this kind is, however, a delicate animal. We find much of the Carolingian legacy assumed in 911 preserved within later Norman society, yet at the same time we also know that connections with Scandinavia were maintained right up until the early eleventh century. A simple statement that the Scandinavian impact was small just will not do. Tenth-century 'Normandy' presents that paradox which troubles the historians of many medieval conquests: heavy institutional continuity combined with a drastic rupture in the personnel of the ruling classes. The general conclusion which is therefore emerging in several recent studies is that of a very pronounced initial Scandinavian impact, which was steadily absorbed into a Frankish matrix which had survived over the invasion period and which eventually came to dominate the character of Norman government and society.[38] It is also important to set this 'continuity' against the pattern of evolution elsewhere. If attention were focused solely on 'Normandy', then the nature of this 'continuity' might easily be misunderstood; especially since a similar continuity turns out not to have existed in neighbouring regions. It is best to begin with the specific evidence for the density and nature of the Scandinavian settlement.

The density of the settlement has always been a controversial subject. Place-names containing a Scandinavian element are scattered liberally throughout many areas of the province. Their form in general is either one where a Scandinavian personal name has been appended to a Frankish suffix – 'Toki's' -*ville* (Tocqueville) or 'Osbern's' -*ville* (Auberville) – or where a Scandinavian element, usually a suffix, has been included to describe a natural feature – 'tot' (toft) in Yvetot or Hautot and 'lundr' in Etalondes. Exhaustive studies of Norman toponomy, principally those of the late M. Jean Adigard des Gautries, have produced a composite list of all place-names which show a definite or possible Scandinavian influence.[39] Their distribution has been plotted on the map to show that the heaviest concentrations are in the north of the Cotentin peninsula and in the maritime regions of Upper Normandy, from the mouth of the river Dives along the coast to the Seine estuary and then eastwards into the Pays de Caux where their incidence is especially intense (see Maps 3 and 4). There is also a considerable number in all other coastal areas, namely, in the Bessin which is between the two regions of heaviest concentration mentioned above, and in the Pays de Talou to the east of the Pays de Caux. This general location is probably a predictable one: an originally sea-faring people would inevitably settle near the coast, while the two regions where the names appear in the largest quantities were, in the case of the Seine estuary, the area of initial entry, and in that of the Cotentin, the one place where serious institutional disruption can be proved. That the names do not extend throughout what was later to be the duchy of Normandy indicates that its creation derived from a mixture of settlement, of whatever density, and political conquest. It is also true that whereas the number of Scandinavian place-names in some regions is very high – there are, for example, almost 80 names containing a Scandinavian personal name in the Cotentin peninsula alone, many more than this in the Pays de Caux, and about 100 examples of '-tot' in the entire province – these names do not anywhere form a local majority over pre-existing Frankish names. Nor did the newcomers feel impelled to change the name of any large centre of population: Rouen and the six bishoprics, for example, kept their old names.

The interpretation of this material is an extremely delicate task. Like all place-name evidence, that from Normandy is slippery and at times mendacious. As a means of measuring density of settlement, it poses very great difficulties because there is no very definite means of knowing what number of name-changes are required to prove a large influx of new population, nor is it certain what name-forms automatically represent a change which took place very soon after the Scandinavians' arrival. To take one possible snag. Toponyms containing Scandinavian elements were probably still being formed in the eleventh century: Toutainville (Eure, cant. Pont-Audemer) may well have been named after Thurstan Goz who held land there and who was alive in 1020. Since Scandinavian Christian names continued to be popular in eleventh-century Normandy, it is very likely that other place-names which reflect conditions of lordship at a comparatively late date could be found. It is also probable that suffixes such as '-tot' or '-tuit' survived in Norman dialect on into the thirteenth century and might have contributed to new place-name forms well after the original settlements.[40] It is also the case, however, that some Scandinavian names might be in the process of disappearing by the eleventh century: a document in a late-eleventh-century collection refers to the island of *Torhulmus*, otherwise called Oissel, in the river Seine.[41] All this said, it none the less remains true that as a general rule the formation of place-names will reflect current linguistic usage. For this reason, the comparatively rapid demise of the Scandinavian language in the province must mean that those toponyms which contain a Scandinavian element are more than likely early formations, especially since the vast bulk of the Norman place-names conforms to types which English scholars now regard as early forms. It is also true that the great majority of place-names which do include a Scandinavian personal name are probably early since their large number would most logically derive from violent upheavals of lordship rather than from a slow evolution. The massive concentration in coastal regions supports this view. In brief, a very high proportion of the Norman place-names which contain a Scandinavian element are likely to be indicative of early settlement. This proportion might well be higher than in the English Danelaw, where Scandinavian and English languages co-existed over several centuries and the case for a more gradual increase in Scandinavian forms is stronger.

The type of the Scandinavian place-names in Normandy points to a relatively heavy early colonisation, followed by a very noticeable slowing-down. The most common forms are the combination of a Scandinavian personal name with an indigenous element, which an English specialist would call a 'Grimston hybrid'. In Normandy these are usually compounds with the suffix *-ville*: *Osbernivilla* (Auberville), *Bollivilla* (Boulleville), or *Ketelvilla* (Quetteville). The most recent interpretations of the toponomy of northern and eastern England suggest that such forms usually represent existing habitations taken over at an early stage of settlement and renamed before the newcomers had become accustomed to using the native names.[42] Some, a smaller number, may be fresh habitation sites named in imitation of local practice; others, resembling Toutainville, may be much later changes. There is no reason why precisely the same conclusions should not be drawn for Normandy, especially since, as will be argued in the next paragraph, the province does not have what are now regarded as indicators of name-changes which happened after the first settlement. Another argument in favour of a heavy, early, colonisation which was far more than a take-over by a military élite is the considerable incidence of place-names where Scandinavian was used to indicate a natural feature (Bacquetuit or Blanchelonde). It is hard to believe that these do not derive from a sizeable peasant influx, strong enough to influence the way in which men who tilled the soil referred to the surrounding landscape. Even if some of these are a consequence of dialect survivals into the eleventh and twelfth centuries, this is still an argument for peasant settlement, since fairish numbers would have been required to affect an essentially unsympathetic French linguistic environment. The likelihood of relatively intense colonisation is also suggested by the appearance of elements which describe an extension of the cultivated area: 'thorp' which indicates a secondary settlement is rare[43] – there are only sixteen examples from the whole province – but 'tuit', a clearing, is much commoner. Local studies, which will ultimately prove or disprove this argument, exist for the region around Bayeux, which on the basis of the place-name evidence was not one of the more heavily settled areas; they suggest a colonisation on the margins of cultivated land.[44]

In one very significant respect, the place-names of Normandy differ radically from English types. The province just does not possess the large number of '-bys' which are so familiar on the English scene. Their scarcity in the province may not, however, be a serious argument against a relatively large early colonisation. '-by' is now being abandoned as an indicator of primary settlement. Rather it is seen as marking the transfer, usually at a later date, of estates into new hands. Professor Peter Sawyer further suggests that '-by' came into use in England as a result of the persistence of Scandinavian speech, and that it came to be employed in predominantly Scandinavian-speaking regions as a substitute for the native '-tun'.[45] Therefore '-by' probably did not come into regular use in Normandy because of the relatively rapid extinction of the Scandinavian language and because '-by' was uncommon in Denmark, the land of origin of most of the settlers in the province. There is no reason why there should be a great number of 'by' forms in the toponomy of Normandy. The scarcity of 'thorp' names there may be explained in a similar way, since their very concentrated development in one area of England, the eastern Danelaw, suggests a localised and later evolution.

On balance, the Norman place-name evidence seems to be indicative of a heavy settlement during the first decades of the province's history. This would conform with the steady extension by Rollo and William Longsword of the territory under their control, a development which encouraged continuing immigration, some of it from England and Ireland, and with the instability prevalent during these early years. The settlement was in some respects merely that of a new, highly militarised, ruling group, but in many regions there was also a large settlement of farmers.

This conclusion is not undermined by the other evidence for the Scandinavian presence. Archaeological remains which relate to the settlement are scarce. Early settlers appear to have made use of the pre-Christian rampart known as the Hague-Dike, an earthwork some two miles in length, which was probably elaborated to protect a landing-stage on the narrow peninsula leading to the Cap de la Hogue. The existence of what, despite the endeavours of bounty-hunters and amateur archaeologists, appear to be burial sites in the vicinity also suggests that the fortification was utilised during the earliest and most precarious phase of settlement.[46] There was once a Viking grave at Pîtres in the Norman Vexin, from which two brooches were deposited in the Musée des Antiquités at Rouen during the nineteenth century, and there is a possible burial site on the beach at Réville on the north-east of the Cotentin peninsula which has yielded only mediocre results.[47] In addition, a number of swords and axes have been found at various places in the province. These do at least show the presence of weapons of purely Scandinavian design, despite the well-recorded practice by which the raiders utilised the armour of their victims. The weapons also strengthen the case for immigration from England, since three of the swords are of a style which is demonstrably Anglo-Saxon, while an axe from an unknown find within the duchy, now preserved at Rouen, is of a late-tenth-century Scandinavian type, suggesting the long duration of contacts with the North.[48] This overall picture is not very dissimilar from the results obtained for the English Danelaw. There, finds, although more plentiful than in Normandy, are as a whole very small in quantity. It may be important that no major excavation has ever been undertaken at Rouen itself; results along the lines of the substantial discoveries which have recently been made at York might be expected. The one obviously distinctive feature of English conditions, the numerous sculptures in the northern counties, for which there is no Norman parallel, may well be the results of a unique and late artistic evolution stimulated by the interaction of Scandinavian tastes and native English techniques. Fortifications are scarce on both sides of the Channel. The general arguments which are applied to England seem appropriate to Normandy. If an extensive colonisation can be argued for England despite the absence of significant archaeological finds, then the same conclusion seems feasible for Normandy. The evidence of the weapons, in particular, points to long-standing contacts between Normandy and the North.

Spoken Scandinavian disappeared rapidly in Normandy: the language survived much longer in England than it did in northern France. Superficially, therefore, the speed with which Scandinavian was abandoned might suggest sparse settlement. This may, however, be a reflection more of the very different linguistic environment in which the two settlements were made than of their densities. An axiom among scholars who study English conditions is that natives and settlers would usually have been intelligible to one another; there were sufficient points in common to make regular communication possible without significant linguistic changes. As a result the English language developed as a fusion of the two tongues. Such interaction was quite out of the question in northern France because French and all forms of Scandinavian were entirely incompatible; one or the other was certain to have to give way. The large numbers of place-names, along with the current opinion that Scandinavian had a large phonetic influence and an enduring effect on vocabulary, especially on nautical, marine, and agricultural terms, must show that the language was once strong and that it was widely spoken.[49] A well-known passage in Dudo's 'history' described how William Longsword was forced to send his son to Bayeux to learn the Scandinavian language because it was no longer spoken in the districts around Rouen. This must be an exaggeration in support of Dudo's campaign to diminish the province's debt to its northern heritage, since some of the earliest settlers would still have been alive in c. 940. But in any case, providing that Richard I was a good boy who learnt his lessons, the comment also carries the implication that a Norman ruler who was alive in the very late tenth century still possessed a smattering of the tongue of his ancestors.[50] The language may indeed have endured much longer than Dudo cared to acknowledge, since a poet from the court of Olaf Haraldsson, king of Norway, was still welcome at Rouen in c. 1025 in the later years of Richard II's reign.[51]

The fate of the Scandinavian language in tenth-century Normandy was most likely bound up with the history of an ethnic minority confronting a different and, in the context of northern France as a whole, dominant culture. Given the pre-eminently masculine composition of the Scandinavian settlers and the observed fact that families tend to speak the language of the mother, marriage and cohabitation with Frankish women would have speedily eroded the imported Scandinavian tongue. The first generation, and perhaps the second, used the language widely. Thereafter there was decline, hastened as the rate of immigration fell away in the second half of the tenth century. Adhemar of Chabannes, viewing the matter from Aquitaine in the 1020s, could write as if the abandonment of Scandinavian was part of the natural order of things.[52] We should, however, beware killing the language off too quickly.

The Scandinavian impact on the customs of Normandy suggests a solid and substantial contribution. By the late eleventh century the province's customs were unquestionably French and the basis of government was firmly rooted in a predominantly Carolingian tradition. These characteristics are even more apparent in the first compendiums of customary law, the earliest of which dates from the very late twelfth century. None the less, it would probably be correct to think in terms of an initially strong Scandinavian impact which gradually faded.[53] Despite the numerous relics of the Carolingian regime which were passed on to Rollo, he and his successors could only rule effectively if they did so in a manner which their subjects could understand and respect. The effect of this principle is very apparent in the peace-keeping powers of the eleventh-century dukes, which retained a right to exile (*ullac*) which drew on Scandinavian precedent, and which included protection for agricultural implements left lying in the fields and an exclusive power over the crimes of murder in secret (*murdrum*) and assault inside a house (*hamfara* in Normandy and *hamsocne* in England). The special interests of the newcomers were also reflected in a Scandinavian influence on maritime and family organisation: the laws relating to shipwreck (*varech*) and several other maritime customs, as well as the equal rights of all male heirs to an inheritance, were assuredly not the product of a Carolingian legacy. These were merely the features which survived to be recorded in the legal texts. Norman society during the obscure settlement period must have sustained a considerable initial impact. The multiple influences in play as the newcomers sought to organise the province for which they had assumed responsibility are brought together in Professor Yver's apparently preposterous suggestion that there may be truth in Dudo's statement that Rollo legislated against robbery and violence.[54] The idea may be credible: these same crimes were the subject of the last Carolingian legislation which related to the region. But, according to Dudo, Rollo exacted the death penalty, whereas Carolingian law normally prescribed a fine. The death penalty, however, does have parallels in the English laws of king Aethelstan (924–39). Which, if either, was Rollo's source? In the end, his responsibility and that of his successors was to find a means to maintain order in a society which had recently acquired a new ruling class and which had assimilated a significant peasant migration.

   The effect of the Scandinavian settlers on rural lordship was not apparently very great. Not only did their arrival scarcely affect the boundaries of the *pagi* and the dioceses, it also appears to have caused little change to the organisation and size of rural estates.[55] With the exception of the very north of the Cotentin peninsula, where there were changes, it has been possible to trace a good number of cases of continuity from the Carolingian period through to the eleventh century. This even applies in places where the density of Scandinavian place-names suggests that settlement was exceptionally heavy: in the Pays de Caux there is even good evidence for the continuity of the siting of seigneurial residences.[56] The same indications of continuity also appear in the evidence for social structure, since although the Normans did bring their own brand of personal slavery, the peasantry who appear on eleventh-century estates were described by a terminology which indicated that their organisation closely resembled that of the Carolingian period. English evidence suggests that neither of these continuities is a strong argument against a substantial Scandinavian settlement. Even in the northern Danelaw, continuity of estate organisation has been found except in regions where colonisation was overwhelmingly heavy. The whole problem has much in common with 'the free peasantry of the Danelaw', another instance where pre-existing tenurial forms appear to have been fixed by the Scandinavian immigration: as in Normandy, the terminology is one which stresses the remarkably free status of the peasants.[57] It may even be the case that, as in East Anglia, the settlements had the effect of ossifying existing tenurial forms: Normandy was later than most other parts of northern France in abandoning the subtle gradations of Carolingian nomenclature in favour of a brutal classification which divided lay society into the two categories of those who fought and those who worked.

The final rupture between 'Normandy' and the Scandinavian North came in the first decades of the eleventh century. The evidence of coin hoards puts the break in *c.* 1020 (see p. 36). The last recorded occasion on which Scandinavian troops set foot on Norman soil by invitation was in 1013–14 when they assisted Richard II in a campaign against the count of Blois-Chartres. The last reference to the Rouen slave-market comes from the late tenth century.[58] All this appertains to contacts of a somewhat rarefied type: high-level connections between the Norman dukes and the Scandinavian kingdoms, or to an economic role in the trade of the northern seas. For 'ordinary men', despite specialised dialect survivals and some influences on rural society, it is likely that the evolution had passed the point of no return at a significantly earlier date. It remains undeniable that Rollo, in assuming the title of count of Rouen, was identifying himself and the province that he ruled with Frankish forms. Conversion to Christianity could only accentuate this. But the placename and institutional evidence in particular suggests large-scale early settlement; there is also nothing in the archaeological or linguistic evidence to sustain the opposite view. Integration was therefore gradual. Tenth-century Norman society for a very long time retained a double face.

There remains an entirely conjectural, yet absolutely crucial, dimension: namely, the unrevealed, indirect, consequences of the settlements. The two apparently incompatible conclusions of heavy settlement and great institutional continuity are really the inseparable elements at the very base of the 'Norman Achievement'. The next part of this chapter and the later sections devoted to the eleventh century will stress, somewhat tentatively, the stability of ecclesiastical estates throughout the tenth century and, much more forcefully, the strongly authoritarian and Carolingian structure of Norman government and society. These features, as will be seen, set the province some way apart from neighbouring regions. It must be the case that the Scandinavian settlements, and more particularly the obscure deeds of the first counts of Rouen and their followers, provided 'Normandy' with a firmness of government and a stability which was not so completely maintained elsewhere. That the counts of Rouen were able to achieve this must be a consequence of the political and social structures which formed in the first half of the tenth century. The darkness of this period largely conceals the origins of such crucial features of eleventh-century Normandy as the immense resources in land held by the counts/dukes and the installation of a new aristocracy. The Scandinavian settlements, combined with the necessity to revitalise institutions which elsewhere merely evolved, must be regarded as the basis of the cohesion which is apparent in eleventh-century Norman society. The vital phase of consolidation was the second part of Richard I's long reign.

CONSOLIDATION

The period covered by the fifty-four or so years of Richard I's reign divides into two very distinct phases. The first, already discussed, comprises the 940s and 950s, a serious crisis which almost destroyed the new settlement. The second, which extended from then to the end of the reign, and whose basic character continued into the reign of Richard's son, Richard II (996–1026), was a time of stability and of consolidation. Our knowledge of this second phase is as usual hampered by the paucity of the sources: the information which can be gleaned from the existence of a small number of charters is a gain which is as good as cancelled out by the termination of the detailed *Annales* of Flodoard of Rheims in the 960s. We therefore have to rely on essentially the same eleventh-century histories as before, supplemented by some isolated scraps of contemporary documentary evidence, and by the remarkable collection of 8,584 coins which were buried at Fécamp at a date between 980 and 985. The result is that our knowledge of this very important formative period is extremely uneven: coinage and the recovery of the Church are tolerably well served, whereas the condition of all social groups is distressingly obscure.

A narrative of this second part of Richard I's reign is quite impossible. Richard in fact made very little impression in such chronicle sources as do exist; relatively speaking, the warfare of the Norman 930s and 940s is a more fertile terrain for descriptive history than the later tenth century. This suggests that the main thrust of Richard's endeavours was directed towards maintaining internal stability, since, after the ill-starred campaigns of the early 960s, he appears to have taken little part in the seemingly perennial conflicts of tenth-century *Francia*. In the late-tenth-century history of Richer of Rheims, the rather mediocre account which replaces Flodoard as the main source for events in northern France, all Richard's military interventions were in a subsidiary role, and would appear to have been somewhat inconsistently motivated: in *c*. 991 he helped Hugh Capet to take Melun from count Odo I of Blois-Chartres, but he then subsequently supported Odo against the king's protégé, count Fulk III 'Nerra' of Anjou (987–1040).[59] If there were invasions of the Norman territory by other rulers, we know nothing of them. Likewise, there is no report of any outward pressure from Normandy against its neighbours. This staidness is not what Dudo of St-Quentin would have wished us to believe about Richard: he portrayed him as a great peacemaker and the prime mover in Hugh Capet's accession to kingship in 987. Sources closer to this last event tell a rather different story, attributing Hugh's acquisition of the royal power to the agency of the archbishop of Rheims, supported by a coalition of princes, of whom Richard was merely one. Dudo's account, founded as always on a minimum number of facts, greatly exaggerates Richard's significance as an active participant in the political life of northern France. But it none the less presents an image which may not be that far removed from the truth; that of a territorial prince who ruled his lands firmly and who did try to keep the peace.

What undoubtedly did happen during Richard I's reign, and about which the sources are entirely silent, was a recovery of control over the territory which his father had ruled from the year 933: that is, a land approximating to that which started to be called 'Normandy' in the eleventh century. The refoundation under Richard's auspices of a monastery on Mont-St-Michel in 966 is a definite indication of the extension of authority into the far West by that date. Two specific points can be made about this reconstitution of the Norman territory. The first is that it may not have been complete. Or rather that, the frontiers established may not always have been stable; there was, for example, a clear failure to regain the earlier line of the boundary of the *pagus* of the Evrecin between the rivers Eure and Avre.[60] The second is that, in the 950s at least, if the assistance received from Hugh the Great is anything to go by, the recovery was accomplished only with the aid of Frankish reinforcements (see p. 14). The conclusion must be that, despite continuing relations with the Scandinavian North and the known disembarkation of Viking warriors there in the early 960s, the Norman province had already achieved a sufficient measure of acceptance and integration into *Francia* as to cause native rulers to exert themselves in its support. With outside help, by methods which are otherwise utterly obscure, and perhaps because a considerable degree of security was derived from the province's location on the fringes of the French kingdom, Richard I effected a consolidation which must be seen as laying the foundations for the achievements of the eleventh-century Norman dukes.

Other information demonstrates 'Normandy's' steady assimilation into the general economic and political trends current in northern France during this period. The numismatic evidence is crucial to the argument for economic integration. The presence in the Fécamp hoard of coins from a very large number of mints, including, among many types, money struck at Cologne, Arles, and Pavia, suggests strong and extensive contact, at least for the region of Upper Normandy where the count of Rouen's power was concentrated. The danger of arguing this conclusion from a single hoard is obviated by the earlier discovery of a similar, if much smaller, numismatic miscellany at Le Puy (Haute-Loire), over 500 miles from the Norman lands. This hoard, interred between 998 and 1002, also demonstrates a wide circulation of coin into which the Norman regions were very well incorporated. This evidence can only signify that later tenth-century 'Normandy' had developed very definite economic links with the Frankish hinterland.

Political integration is indicated by two very noticeable changes, both of which surface during the 960s, and both of which show that Richard I was acutely conscious of his status as the ruler of a French territorial principality. The first is Richard's new title. From 966 he began to refer to himself as a marquis (*marchisus* or *marchio*), inferring, within the contemporary meaning of the term, that he was someone who ruled over counts. The earliest known use of the new title, in the charter which recorded the refoundation of the abbey of Mont-St-Michel in 966, may well be symbolic of the reunification of the lands which William Longsword had controlled. Its appearance in a solemn diploma of the Carolingian king Lothaire suggests that it thereby received official recognition.[61] The second piece of evidence is Richard's first appearance in 968 as the vassal of Hugh Capet, documentary confirmation of a relationship which may well have been of several years' standing, since the alliance between Richard I and Hugh the Great and Hugh Capet, father and son, had existed from the 940s.[62]

Both these developments are a part of wider changes associated with the death-throes of the Carolingian monarchy, and with the disintegration of the Capetian/Robertian principality, which had been established for Robert the Strong in the second half of the ninth century, and which at that date had covered much of northern France. The quest for a more elevated title was a symptom of the growing autonomy of the local territorial rulers. The Robertians had raised themselves to the status of 'duke' in 936; the counts of Poitou assumed the additional title of 'duke of Aquitaine' in *c.* 965. Both were reacting against the trend whereby the local strong men who were consolidating their power started to call themselves 'count', a title first claimed by the *vicomtes* of Angers in 929, and which was recognised officially by the Robertians in 942, or in 957 by the erstwhile *vicomtes* of Blois.[63] More prestigious rulers such as the counts of Flanders, who had become established in the late ninth century, began to describe themselves as 'marquis' in the second half of the tenth century.[64] Richard I's acknowledgement of Hugh Capet's lordship was again something which can be observed in the case of other territorial rulers: the apparent contradiction between this relationship and the recognition given to royal authority in the Mont-St-Michel charter is a phenomenon which is closely paralleled in the history of the contemporary counts of Anjou.[65] The duality of allegiance demonstrates a weakening of the significance attached to any form of superior authority.

This pattern of change, the quest for more exalted titles and the dissolution of ties of allegiance, says a great deal about northern French political society in the second half of the tenth century. The rising territorial princes, remorselessly effective, yet deeply conservative, sought authentication for their increasing local power within the very conventions which they were in the process of modifying through their own actions. Effective power, which more and

Normandy before 1066

more meant local power, was reproduced in the same mould as the authority which it was steadily taking over. The counts of Rouen were as sensitive as anyone else to their own place within this shifting political spectrum. This of itself is another important indication of the extent to which the Norman lands were taking on the guise of a Frankish territorial principality. But, at the same time, this preoccupation with titles and status also draws attention to an oddity which might easily be overlooked; namely that, in the midst of the prevalent fragmentation and realignment of authority, Richard I's 'Normandy' represented a territorial unit of some antiquity. It is important to appreciate that Richard's grandfather had received a direct grant of authority from a Carolingian king well before the local autonomy of the likes of the counts of Anjou had become obvious. Despite the *parvenu* character of the ruling class of the Norman lands, this territory, along with the county of Flanders, represented the oldest, the most resilient, and after *c*. 960 the stablest, of the northern French territorial groupings.

The most accessible feature of Richard I's government is his coinage. The Fécamp hoard, containing 6,044 silver pennies from the Rouen mint, is indeed the only direct testimony we possess to illuminate the way in which Richard ruled 'Normandy'. The mere fact that these coins were produced demonstrates integration into the Frankish environment: the right to control the minting of money, once the monopoly of earlier Carolingian emperors and kings, was in the process of passing to the territorial princes and to others lower on the social scale during the tenth century. This was just one more incidence of the fragmentation of regalian authority. That the counts of Rouen should assume the right to mint money was only to be expected. But the way in which they did this is a testimony to exceptional power, consistently and effectively exercised. On the basis of the Fécamp hoard, for example, it appears that the counts of Rouen maintained a monopoly of minting within their lands: although a large number of pennies survive which were made for archbishop Hugh of Rouen (*c*. 942–*c*. 989), the concession does not seem to have passed to his successor and, in any case, the coins appear to have been made by the craftsmen of the Rouen mint. The same workshop produced the small number of coins known to have been minted in the name of a mysterious 'Hugh the Dane'. To the demonstration of power can be added that of efficiency: the numismatic evidence shows that minting was resumed in William Longsword's time; it also indicates the episodic operation of the former Carolingian mint at Bayeux, and, above all, the production of money of consistently good standard under Richard I.

These comments on efficiency are reinforced by the generally high silver content of the coins. Although the weight declined as the century advanced, this was a common pattern in tenth-century *Francia*. The dies were changed from time to time and, on the basis of the evidence of the one very large hoard, it would appear that a fair degree of success was achieved in recalling the coins of the previous issue in order to re-mint them. The achievement palls only before that of the English kings in the period after Edgar's reform of 973, which established a regular rhythm of re-coinages. The English monarchs, like the counts of Blois-Chartres, were also able to do something which the Norman rulers apparently could not; namely, increase the weight of their money. The self-assertiveness and independence of the Norman rulers is also clearly demonstrated. Richard's coinage broke quite deliberately from the traditional and widely observed rules codified in Charles the Bald's Edict of Pîtres of 864, the basis for most subsequent royal and princely coinages. The later tenth-century Norman money included the legend 'Richard' on all issues along with a design with a temple on the obverse, which had previously been used on the coins of the emperor Louis the Pious (814–40). In a Frankish context, the Norman rulers were among the first to display independence of this kind: other early departures from the Carolingian tradition appear on coins made for count William II of the Auvergne (918–26), with several mints in Burgundy not very far behind. The counts of Rouen were not, however, the patrons of especially imaginative designs: Mlle Dumas-Dubourg awards that particular prize to the counts of Blois-Chartres, whose coinage of the second half of the tenth century carried a representation of a human face. But the Normans' abandonment of the Pîtres regulations was consistent and, from Richard I's time, final. Other rulers were less single-minded: the mints of the pretentious count Herbert II of Vermandois (900/07–43), for example, made coins in both the count's name and the king's; likewise, duke Hugh the Great's mints produced money in his name, but the pre-987 coins of his son Hugh Capet reverted to the Carolingian royal style. In short, the evidence from the Fécamp hoard reveals the operation from almost the earliest period of a prerogative which was clearly ascribed to the duke of Normandy in the earliest statement of Norman custom, the *Consuetudines et Iusticie* of 1091. It also reveals a purpose, consistency, and stability which might reasonably be expected from other aspects of Richard I's government, if anything could be known about them.[66]

The history of the Church in the Norman territory during the tenth century offers an illuminating commentary both on the province's stability, which was in some respects remarkable, as well as on its deficiencies. The true significance of the Church's development during this period can be properly appreciated only if the destructive effects of the late-ninth-century invasions are kept in mind. In order to do this, it should be remembered that for England the prevailing orthodoxy is that the Church recovered slowly in the territories granted to Scandinavian pagans, despite their promise to convert to Christianity and the apparent rapidity with which they abandoned their old religion. In the eastern Danelaw, for example, episcopal authority was exercised from London until the see of Elmham was revived in 956, while in the North, the bishoprics of the pre-invasion period disappeared for good and monasticism had not recovered by 1066.[67] The position in Normandy was rather similar: diocesan organisation outside Rouen appears to have been moribund throughout most of the tenth century. Similarly, monasticism was slow to revive, with St-Ouen of Rouen being refounded in Rollo's time, Jumièges under William Longsword, and Mont-St-Michel and, much less solidly, St-Wandrille and Fécamp, under Richard I. But those few houses which were re-established suggest in some aspects of their existence a notable stability and prosperity. As a result, Richard I's reign exhibits two seemingly contradictory faces: little, if any, enthusiasm for a reconstruction of the full paraphernalia of ecclesiastical organisation in the province, combined with a solicitous protection of such sections of the Church as had revived.

The great turning-point in our knowledge of the bishoprics of tenth-century 'Normandy' occurs in 990, with the appearance in a charter of a newly appointed archbishop of Rouen named Robert and all six of his suffragans. Before that date very little can be known: for some dioceses, this charter in fact provides the first evidence that a bishop was in office since before 911. Continuity of occupation over the tenth century can only be established for Rouen, with lengthy vacancies the norm elsewhere. No tenth-century bishop of Avranches can be discovered before 990, while the bishop of Coutances only gained the confidence to return to his westerly cathedral city from the safety of the church of St-Lô of Rouen, where his predecessors had resided for approximately 100 years, in the early years of the eleventh century.[68] The only prelate about whom anything serious can be known is the former monk of St-Denis named Hugh,

Origins and consolidation

who held the archbishopric of Rouen from the last years of William Longsword's reign right up until the 980s. The brief late-eleventh-century tract on the history of the archbishops simply noted that Hugh fathered children and that he distributed ecclesiastical estates to his relatives, of whom the best known was his brother, Ralph I de Tosny. This was behaviour which a later age thought reprehensible. At the time, such patrimonial treatment of a bishopric was entirely normal.[69] Hugh may well have played a crucial role in the reorganisation of the Church in his diocese, although less markedly perhaps in the province as a whole. He negotiated with the extra-Norman abbey of St-Médard of Soissons for the text of a Life of St Romain, part of the reconstitution of the liturgical and historical resources of his cathedral.[70] The only clear evidence before 990 for the whole ecclesiastical province of Rouen for the existence of archdeacons or for regular episcopal administration of synods and visitations comes from the non-Norman part of Hugh's diocese, the French Vexin.[71] The appearance of the new archbishop in the 990 charter may well represent a tightening of Richard I's grip on matters ecclesiastical in the later years of his reign. Not only did Robert apparently forfeit his predecessor's right to mint coin, he was also – and this is very important – Richard's son. The Norman ruler appears to have become aware of the benefits to be reaped from a more positive co-operation with the Church.

The revival of monasticism in the Norman province presents a very similar picture of slow advance and, by the very last years of the century, good health in one or two places only. By 942 the abbeys of Jumièges and St-Ouen of Rouen had been revived, Mont-St-Michel housed a community of canons, and St-Evroult, if we believe Ordericus Vitalis' twelfth-century account, was about to be destroyed by the forces of Hugh the Great. By 996 there had been some development. Monks had been installed at Mont-St-Michel and Fécamp, and an attempt made to refound St-Wandrille. But the list of communities which had existed before the Scandinavian settlements, and which had not been re-established, including St-Pair, Deux-Jumeaux, and many others, is the most eloquent commentary there is on tenth-century conditions. In the year 1000 organised religious life remained confined within the very narrow geographical limits of the Seine valley, along with the exceptional foundation 'in peril of the sea' on Mont-St-Michel.

The explanation for this slow pace of reorganisation seems to lie more in an absence of active interest on the part of the laity, than in churchmen's lack of initiative. William of Jumièges's account of the refoundation of his abbey in the 930s describes the return of two of the former monks, named Baldwin and Gonduin, from their refuge at Haspres near Cambrai.[72] A similar interest in a return to the ancient site is exhibited in the attempts in c. 944 and c. 960 to recolonise the abbey of St-Wandrille from St-Pierre du Mont-Blandin of Ghent, the ultimate repository of the patron saint's relics. Along with the bones, the monks possessed some early charters to enable them to resume their church's former patrimony. According to a later St-Wandrille tradition, monastic property was the major stumbling-block. In c. 944, so we are told, the prospective restorer, St Gerard of Brogne, was well received by Richard I, but the count's followers refused to hand over lands acquired in war and with great effort.[73] The idea that land could be given over in perpetuity to the Church must have been a difficult one to comprehend. It was, none the less, the case that conditions had existed since Rollo's time in which churches outside 'Normandy' could confidently expect to regain and to hold property within the province. The restoration was continued into Richard I's time, with a confirmation of St-Denis's holdings and with gifts in favour of the abbeys of Corbie and St-Bénigne of Dijon.[74] Even more significantly, the property holdings of the small number of Norman monasteries seem to have been remarkably stable throughout the whole of the tenth century. The records of the benefactions of the early counts of Rouen, which appear in charters of duke Richard II's time (996–1026), still describe the properties granted as *villae*, extensive landed estates prevalent in Carolingian times, which centred on a lord's domain and were worked by a peasantry of free *coloni* and unfree slaves, and even make references to the restitution of encroachments.[75] This may be extremely significant for our appreciation of the province's tenth-century history. The trend elsewhere was towards the fragmentation in the later tenth century of *villae* in monasteries' possession, a movement characterised by lay appropriation of ecclesiastical property and an accompaniment to the breakdown of royal and princely authority.[76] In 'Normandy', despite the slow recovery of the Church in general, it does appear as if such monasteries as did exist did so in conditions of quite exceptional stability.

The internal life of these few monasteries seems to have flourished. Jumièges in the later tenth century possessed a useful library, built around manuscripts which had survived through the invasion period. Mont-St-Michel, to judge from a list of monks which was appended to a manuscript kept at the famous abbey of Fleury-sur-Loire in the early eleventh century, was a thriving house with some fifty inmates. Like Jumièges, it had collected the standard texts such as Cassian's Collations which the Rule of St Benedict made prescribed reading during meals in the refectory, or St Gregory's *Moralia in Job*, as well as a *corpus* of writings on the history of the abbey. In the late tenth century Mont-St-Michel's prestige was such as to attract a benefaction from St Mayeul, abbot of Cluny.[77] These small developments were part of a process which in time came to possess a wider significance. The survival of early charters, notably from Jumièges and Mont-St-Michel, illustrates the start of the process whereby the Norman rulers were conditioned to think in terms of a written record to preserve a permanent testimony of their benefactions and their protection. The request for such confirmation, the provision thereof, and the consequent document, would all feed the notion that the count of Rouen's authority was paramount within the province. Of little importance in themselves, Richard I's participation in the translation of the relics of St Ouen, or his judgement that the relics of St Sever should stay in Rouen, anticipate greater things in the eleventh century.[78] But tenth-century Norman monasticism remained a very small voice in a very large desert. In many respects the abbeys remained remote from the life of the province, retaining parts of their Carolingian properties in France and attracting most of their benefactions from outside the Norman lands. St-Ouen of Rouen went so far as to seek aid from Edgar, king of the English (959–75), and all the recorded grants received by Mont-St-Michel during the last years of the tenth and the early years of the eleventh century came from Brittany and the county of Maine.[79] The impetus from outside Norman territory towards a full recovery cannot have been that strong, with bishoprics in the control of territorial princes and aristocratic families, and monastic reform very dependent on lay sponsorship. As with bishoprics, significant advance for Norman monasticism came only in the later years of Richard I's reign, with the establishment of the new abbey at Fécamp, and the request for monks – which in the event was turned down – from St Mayeul, abbot of Cluny.

The most desperate problem of all is that of the aristocracy. Since almost every major political initiative during this period derived from the state of relations between the king or prince and his most powerful and warlike subjects, our almost total ignorance of the structure and the powers of the tenth-century Norman aristocracy is a disastrous *lacuna*. Almost the only information is that available from Dudo, who provides eight names, which are devoid of any context of land or family.[80] Most of those identified appear to have been *familiares*, or, as they would later be called, household officials. Anslech, Bernard, and Botho are described as *secretarii*, and Botho and Osmund appear as the tutors of William Longsword and Richard I respectively. Others seem to have been wealthy and independent landowners, like Rioul who led a rebellion against William Longsword, Ralph *Torta* who was a Frank who only left the province in the 940s, and the Harold, whom Dudo mistakenly transformed into a king of Denmark, but who was in all probability an important landowner in Lower Normandy.[81] To these can be added the long list of largely unidentifiable Christian names who attest Richard I's charter for the abbey of Fécamp of 15 June 990.[82] This mysterious group are on occasions described by Dudo as the *fideles* of the count, an entirely Carolingian description current in tenth-and early-eleventh-century *Francia*, implying a vague, personal, subordination.

The almost impenetrable fog which the absence of documentation draws over this subject has led to the view that a 'new aristocracy' emerged in the 1030s and 1040s (see p. 134).[83] This is not really acceptable. The probability is that some of these names conceal the ancestors of the families who came to prominence in the eleventh century. This was certainly the view held in the early twelfth century by Ordericus Vitalis, who opined that the powers and pedigrees of the Norman aristocracy went back to Rollo's day.[84] This was, however, a part of 'the Norman Myth', an assertion which Ordericus' own genealogical knowledge shows him to have been utterly incapable of proving. The results of modern research do, none the less, stress the continuity of aristocratic houses in many regions through the tenth century. It can be asserted that the impossibility of tracing any Norman genealogy back much before *c.* 1000, and the fact that the same exercise usually defeated twelfth-century historians, are no argument against the families' existence before that date. Exact genealogical research only became possible once the aristocratic houses had formed themselves into lineages, identifying their power with a specific residence and practising – to put the matter excessively simply – primogeniture. These structural changes only occurred in Normandy in the first decades of the eleventh century. Before that date, the aristocracy can be expected to have consisted of extended, ill-defined, kin-groups, holding often large estates as family concerns (see p. 135). Such a view would be entirely in conformity with charter attestations which recorded only a single Christian name and with the very loose subjection implied by the term *fidelis*.

Origins and consolidation

The supposed 'new aristocracy' of eleventh-century Normandy emerged out of well-established families.

This hypothesis is based on conclusions which have been reached for regions where documentation is more plentiful. Logically, its application to tenth-century 'Normandy' would suggest that the progenitors of the great families installed themselves in the period before *c.* 950 and that they consolidated their power after that date. There is a certain amount of evidence, most of it negative, to support this suggestion. The existence of Scandinavian names in the earliest recorded generations of the eleventh-century families probably indicates that they were neither newcomers nor men who had recently pushed themselves upwards. There are, not surprisingly, signs of instability in the pre-950 period with the departure of Ralph *Torta* and the decision by the family of Anno, abbot of Jumièges, to abandon an attempt to settle in 'Normandy' and revert instead to the Orléannais and the Touraine.[85] Conversely, in the second half of the tenth century, there are indications of stability, in addition to those provided by the Church. Excavation at Le Plessis-Grimoult (Calvados) has demonstrated continuity of occupation of a seigneurial residence from precisely this period up until the mid-eleventh century.[86] The reception in 'Normandy' before 989 of Ralph I de Tosny, a brother of archbishop Hugh of Rouen, has every appearance of being a planned exercise, since estates were passed to him out of the ducal demesne and the patrimonies of the two churches over which archbishop Hugh might be expected to have influence, namely, Rouen cathedral and the abbey of St-Ouen. There is no sign that violence was done to the property interests of any other family by Ralph's arrival.[87] This general absence of disorder in later tenth-century 'Normandy' is another argument in favour of the proposed thesis. Despite the feeble documentation, it is unlikely that Dudo or his adaptation at the hands of William of Jumièges would have failed to mention any such troubles: the latter did after all dwell on the famous peasants' revolt of *c.* 996, for which he is the unique source.[88] Finally, the well-known tendency for the eleventh-century families to splinter into collateral branches whose origins are often unknown is a further indication of their earlier amorphous form (see p. 135). Relations between Richard I and his territory's aristocracy probably resembled the conditions which existed in his son Richard II's reign, but which were fading by *c.* 1020. Government was staffed by what contemporary English charters would have described as *ministri*, a group set above the mass of Norman society. The social structure was very much one based on Carolingian notions of fidelity and on extensive and often wealthy kin-groups.

The ending of connections with the Scandinavian North can be charted with some accuracy, the prime evidence being the location of hoards containing Norman money.[89] Although the number of coins involved is fairly small, the regularity of the pattern which emerges justifies firm conclusions. Coins minted in Normandy have been found on Norwegian routes off the west coast of Scotland, in southern England, in Denmark, and further east in Poland and Russia. They seem to have been the currency of trade, since, like the Fécamp collection, the hoards involved contain money from a large number of mints – plunder would probably have produced a greater concentration of coins from a few mints – and because their burial can be fixed to the later tenth century, when relations between Scandinavia and the Norman province were apparently peaceful. The dominance in the hoards, numerically, of Norman coins over other Frankish types emphasises both the efficient organisation of the Norman coinage and the importance of the Norman province in the overall process of exchange. But after the first years of the eleventh century, Norman coins cease to appear in the northern hoards. Instead, they begin to occur in some numbers on very different routes, most especially in France itself and in Italy. This suggests a fairly abrupt rupture in relations between 'Normandy' and the Scandinavian North, a break which is inexplicable in terms of known movements of trade, since English coins continue to appear in Scandinavia right up until 1066. There must have been, over a period of time, a conscious redirection of Norman activity.

This general picture is supported by the literary evidence. The last traces of large-scale communication with the North are the well-attested visit of a Viking army to northern France in 1013–14 and the presence of Normans in Ireland in 1014 at the battle of Clontarf. Contemporaries could continue at this stage to regard the rulers of 'Normandy' with suspicion. Richer of Rheims, who wrote in the late tenth century, made a habit of referring to the inhabitants of the province as 'pirates', while during the first decade of the eleventh century, William of Volpiano expressed reluctance to undertake the reform of the Norman Church because of the barbarity of the people. The combination of numismatic and literary evidence suggests that the final break came during the period from 1005 to 1025. The very last vestiges are the presence at Rouen in c. 1025 of the poet from the court of Olaf, king of Norway, and a failed marriage project between a daughter of Cnut, king of England and Denmark, and the Norman ruler, duke Robert I (1027–35). In *c.* 1018 there appear the very first indications of a Norman presence in southern Italy, along with the record of Roger de Tosny's notorious campaign against the Moslems in Spain. The cord had finally been cut.

The breach had been in the making long before the early eleventh century, as the province steadily assumed the characteristics of a northern French territorial principality. By the end of the tenth century, the connections with the North had become very tenuous. The contacts with the Frankish hinterland, which are attested by the Fécamp hoard, contrast very obviously with Rouen's increasingly peripheral role in the economy of the Northern Seas: the number of Rouen coins in the northern hoards is very small, in proportion to their total content, while no money from even the busiest Scandinavian routes has been found in Normandy. Rouen's function as a mart at which booty was exchanged seems to have brought an exceptional prosperity to the region. But by *c.* 1000 'Normandy' had little to lose from severing its final links with a Scandinavia which was itself no longer despatching the old-style warrior bands to the West. There remained, therefore, only the political relations between the Norman and the Scandinavian rulers. The decisive event in this sphere is likely to have been the conquest of England, begun by Sven Forkbeard and concluded by his son Cnut in 1016. In spite of a non-alignment pact sponsored by pope John XV in 991, by which Richard I and Aethelred, king of the English, swore not to aid their respective enemies, both Richard I and Richard II gave the Danish armies the use of Norman harbours. Richard II even made a treaty with Sven Forkbeard in *c.* 1003 to divide the loot.[90] But Richard's other contacts may eventually have turned him against Sven, Cnut, and their Danish forces. His Scandinavian friends seem mostly to have been Norwegians, notably Olaf Haraldsson (St Olaf), converted to Christianity by archbishop Robert of Rouen and later canonised. In addition, his sister Emma had married the unfortunate king Aethelred (978–1016), the victim of the Danish attacks. From 1013 Richard gave shelter to the couple and, with fateful consequences, to some of their children, including the future king Edward the Confessor (1042–66). Richard is likely to have played a positive part in arranging Olaf's crossing to England in 1014 to support Aethelred's declining cause.[91] In the end, the Norman ruler turned against the organised phase of Viking activity which made Cnut and two of his sons into kings of England.

The longevity of these contacts between 'Normandy' and Scandinavia deserves emphasis. That they were eventually reduced solely to commerce, and political relations between rulers does not very much weaken the force of this point.*It was precisely these groups – and notably of course the landed aristocracy – who made by far and away the greatest contribution to the Norman movements of the eleventh century. Their attitude was crucial to any reorientation of political and military activity. Such enduring links were an important element in the two phases of the history of tenth-century 'Normandy', the instability of the first half of the century and the consolidation of the second. But the essentially Carolingian and Frankish context in which the settlement was made needs equally forceful emphasis. From the very beginning the counts of Rouen made very definite efforts to rule in a Carolingian tradition. The discoveries of archaeologists are helping to demonstrate just how strong this continuity was; it is certain, for example, that the residence of the counts at Fécamp was built on the site of the former abbey.[92] There are paradoxes in the history of tenth-century 'Normandy': violent invasion, yet in the longer term a settlement which preserved many essentially Carolingian features and which maintained an exceptionally stable social structure. In the end, we must think in terms of a fusion of cultures; not of a massive, dominating, Scandinavian presence – no one would now argue this case any way – nor of a small group of settlers easily assimilated. The effects of the settlements were felt throughout the social structure of the province: the Carolingian core remained, but changes were made to rural society and the counts of Rouen gave authority a new strength.

To emerge into the Norman eleventh century is to leave darkness for bright sunlight. The sources suddenly become almost numerous, a fact which itself illuminates changed social conditions. The territory which scrambled across the millennium was a rather backward child, dominated by able and wealthy rulers, but with a Church largely untouched by the movements of reform which were influential in other regions, and an aristocracy as yet unaffected by structural changes which were taking place elsewhere. It arrived in an eleventh century in which the dominant powers were the territorial rulers whose local independence had evolved throughout the later tenth century, into a harshly competitive and exceptionally brutal world in which a further phase in the progressive decomposition of authority whipped up violence and uncertainty.

NOTES

1. Flodoard, *Historia Remensis Ecclesiae*, in *MGH, Scriptores*, xiii (1881), 577.
2. For convenient translations, *English Historical Documents*, i, ed. D. Whitelock (London, 1953), 776; H. R. Loyn and J. Percival, *The Reign of Charlemagne* (London, 1975), 108.
3. J. Le Maho, 'Châteaux d'époque franque en Normandie', *Arch. méd.*, x (1980), 153–66.
4. *Les annales de Flodoard*, ed. P. Lauer (Paris, 1906), *s.a.* 921.
5. For this section, J. Boussard, 'Les destinées de la Neustrie du IXe au XIe siècle', *CCM*, xi (1968), 20–7. Indispensable for this early period is J. Dhondt, *Etudes sur la naissance des principautés territoriales en France (IXe–Xe siècle)* (Bruges, 1948).
6. *Recueil des actes de Charles III le Simple, roi de France*, ed. P. Lauer (Paris, 1949), i, no. 92.
7. D. C. Douglas, 'Rollo of Normandy', *EHR*, lvii (1942), 418–23.
8. On these settlements, for a summary of evidence and full bibliography, see L. Musset, 'Pour l'étude comparative de deux fondations politiques des Vikings: le royaume d'York et le duché de Rouen', *Northern History*, x, *Essays in Honour of John Le Patourel* (Leeds, 1975), 47–52.
9. *Cartulaire de l'abbaye de St-Bertin*, ed. B. E. C. Guérard (Paris, 1840), 138.
10. WJ, 80.
11. L. Musset, 'Le satiriste Garnier de Rouen et son milieu (début du XIe siècle)' *Revue du moyen âge latin* x (1954), 250–3.
12. Dudo of St-Quentin, *De moribus et actis primorum Normanniae Ducum*, ed. J. Lair (Caen, 1865), 168–9. Discussions of the grant and of the early history of 'Normandy' can be found in Douglas, 'Rollo of Normandy', 425–32; J. -F. Lemarignier, *Recherches sur l'hommage en marche et sur les frontières féodales* (Lille, 1945), 74–85; D. C. Douglas, 'The rise of Normandy', *Proceedings of the British Academy*, xxxiii (1947), 103–7; L. Musset, 'Naissance de la Normandie (Ve–XIe siècles)', in *Histoire de la Normandie*, ed. M. de Bouard (Toulouse, 1970), 96–129; idem, in *Documents de l'histoire de la Normandie* (Toulouse, 1972), 73–82; K.F. Werner, 'Quelques observations au sujet des débuts du "duché" de Normandie', in *Etudes . . . Yver*, 695–6. For an excellent survey, J. Le Patourel, *The Norman Empire* (Oxford, 1976), 3–15.
13. *ibique se filius Rollonis Karolo committit; eidem regi se committit; et se illi commisit. At ille dedit ei terram quam pater ejus Karolus Nordmannis concesserat*, *Les annales de Flodoard*, 39, 55, 75.
14. *Ibid.*, 16; above, notes 1 and 6.
15. *Les annales de Flodoard*, 24, 55.
16. *Ibid.*, 16, 30.
17. M. Dolley and J. Yvon, 'A group of tenth-century coins found at Mont-Saint-Michel', *British Numismatic Journal*, xl (1971), 7–11. Also, *ibid.*, 14–16, for a most useful chronology of events.
18. A point recently emphasised by Musset, in *Documents de l'histoire de la Normandie*, 76; and Werner, *Etudes . . . Yver*, 695–7.
19. See J. Yver, 'Les premières institutions du duché de Normandie', *Setti-*

20. *Nordmanni de Rodomo foedus quod olim pepigerant irrumpentes, pagum Belvacensem et Ambiacensem depopulantur, Les annales de Flodoard*, 29–30.
21. See, for example, *Recueil des actes de Charles le Simple*, no. 53; L. Musset, 'L'exode des reliques du diocèse de Sées au temps des invasions normandes', *Bulletin de la société archéologique et historique de l'Orne*, lxxxiii (1970), 8–9, 16–17.
22. These comments depend entirely on O. Guillot, 'Les conditions religieuses de l'installation des Normands autour de l'année 911', *RHDFE*, 4e série, lii (1974), 545–7. The dossier is printed in *Sacrosancta Concilia ad regiam editionem exacta quae nunc quarta parte prodit auctior*, ed. P. Labbe and G. Cossart (Paris, 1671), xi, cols. 483–94.
23. *Recueil*, p. 20, no. 53.
24. *Ibid.*, no. 3; *GC*, xi, instr. col. 217.
25. L. Musset, 'Actes inédits du XIe siècle. III. Les plus anciennes chartes normandes de l'abbaye de Bourgueil', *BSAN*, liv (1959, for 1957–58), 29–30.
26. Françoise Dumas-Dubourg, *Le trésor de Fécamp et le monnayage en Francie occidentale pendant la seconde moitié du Xe siècle* (Paris, 1971), 48–51.
27. Annie Renoux, 'Recherches historiques et archéologiques sur le château de Fécamp, ancien palais des ducs de Normandie', *Château Gaillard*, vii (1975), 188–9, 199–200.
28. WJ, 38–9.
29. *Recueil*, nos. 36, 49, 53, 66, 67. Also, Cartulaire de la cathédrale de Rouen, Rouen, Bibliothèque municipale, MS. 1193 (Y. 44), fo. 31r.
30. *Libellus de revelatione, aedificatione et auctoritate Fiscannensis monasterii*, *PL*, cli, col. 713.
31. *Adhémar de Chabannes, Chronique*, ed. J. Chavanon (Paris, 1897), 148. Rollo was buried in Rouen cathedral.
32. Dolley and Yvon, 'A Group of tenth-century coins', 11; J. Adigard des Gautries, *Les noms de personnes scandinaves en Normandie de 911 à 1066* (Lund, 1954), 68–9. These authors' opinion that the Harold who intervened was identical with Harold Bluetooth, later king of Denmark, should probably be rejected in favour of the earlier dismissal of this idea by H. Prentout, *Etude critique sur Dudon de St-Quentin* (Paris, 1916), 360–1, especially in the light of a Harold's presence in Lower Normandy in 954, see note 34 below.
33. The main source for the events of these years is Flodoard, sometimes substantiated by Dudo. The existence of Ralph *Torta* may be independently confirmed, *Recueil*, no. 53.
34. 'Annales Nivernenses', in *MGH, Scriptores*, xiii, 88.
35. On this war, F. Lot, *Les derniers Carolingiens* (Paris, 1891), 346–57, although needing correction on some points, remains the basic account.
36. L. Musset, 'Gouvernés et gouvernants dans le monde scandinave et dans le monde normand (XIe–XIIe siècles)', *Gouvernés et Gouvernants. Recueils de la société Jean Bodin*, xvii (1968), 456–7.
37. For the basic studies, see note 19 above.

38. M. de Bouard, 'De la Neustrie carolingienne à la Normandie féodale: continuité ou discontinuité?', *BIHR*, xxviii (1955), 1–14; L. Musset, 'Les apports scandinaves dans le plus ancien droit normand', *Etudes... Yver*, 559–75; L. W. Breese, 'The persistence of Scandinavian connections in Normandy in the tenth and early eleventh centuries', *Viator*, viii (1977), 47–61.
39. Adigard des Gautries, *Noms de personnes scandinaves, passim*; and his series of articles, 'Les noms de lieux de la Normandie entre 911 et 1066', *AN*, i–ix (1951–59). For an excellent map, *Histoire de la Normandie*, 104.
40. L. Musset, 'L'aristocratie normande au XIe siècle', in *La noblesse au moyen âge, XIe–XVe siècles. Essais à la mémoire de Robert Boutruche*, ed. P. Contamine (Paris, 1976), 73–4; J. Adigard des Gautries, 'Etudes de toponymie normannique. I. Les noms en *-Torp*', *Etudes germaniques*, vi (1951), 6.
41. ...*insulam super alveum Sequanae quam dicunt nomine Turhulmum, alio quidem vocabulo Oscellum, Recueil*, no. 61.
42. See, in general, Gillian Fellows Jensen, 'Place names and settlement in the North Riding of Yorkshire', *Northern History*, xiv (1978), 39–42; K. Cameron, 'Scandinavian settlement in the territory of the five boroughs: the place-name evidence, Part III: the Grimston hybrids', in *Place-Name Evidence for the Anglo-Saxon Invasion and Scandinavian Settlements*, ed. K. Cameron (English Place-Name Society, 1975), 170–1. For a general account of the settlements in Britain, H. R. Loyn, *The Vikings in Britain* (London, 1977).
43. It is now doubted whether most of the Norman *-torp* names were Scandinavian at all, L. Guinet, 'Les toponymes normands "Torp(s)", "Torpt", "Tourp(s)", "Tour(s)"', *AN*, xxx (1980), 193–7.
44. Musset, *Northern History*, x, 46.
45. P. H. Sawyer, *From Roman Britain to Norman England* (London, 1978), 163–4.
46. M. de Bouard, 'Le Hague-Dike', *Cahiers archéologiques*, viii (1956), 117–45, especially, 138–45; *idem*, 'A propos de la datation du Hague-Dike', *AN*, xxiv (1964), 270–1.
47. Birgitta Elmqvist, 'Les fibules de Pîtres', *Meddelanden fran Lunds Universitets historiska Museum* (1966–68), 203; M. de Bouard, 'Sépultures énigmatiques à Réville', *AN*, xiv (1964), 263.
48. H. Arbman and N. -O. Nilsson, 'Armes scandinaves de l'époque viking en France', *Meddelanden fran Lunds Universitets historiska Museum* (1966–68), 163–6, 171–5, 194–202.
49. This is the argument of R. P. de Gorog, *The Scandinavian Element in French and Norman* (New York, 1958).
50. Dudo, 221.
51. Adigard des Gautries, *Noms de personnes scandinaves*, 70.
52. *Adhémar de Chabannes, Chronique*, 148.
53. For the whole problem, Musset, *Etudes... Yver*, 559–75. On the Carolingian basis of Norman law, Yver, 'Les premières institutions', 316–23. For an addition to the Scandinavian *corpus*, E. Hall and J. R. Sweeney, 'The "Licentia de Nam" of the Abbess of Montivilliers and the origins of the port of Harfleur', *BIHR*, lii (1979), 2–3.

54. Yver, 'Les premières institutions', 317–19.
55. Musset, 'Les domaines', 42–78.
56. J. Le Maho, 'L'apparition des seigneuries châtelaines dans le Grand-Caux à l'époque ducale', *Arch. méd.*, vi (1976), 94–101.
57. Musset, 'Les domaines', 68–78. For England, in general, Loyn, *The Vikings in Britain*, 130–3; Sawyer, *From Roman Britain to Norman England*, 161–4. For specific aspects, R. H. C. Davis, 'East Anglia and the Danelaw', *TRHS*, 5th series, v (1955), 33–6; C. D. Morris, 'Northumbria and the Viking settlement: the evidence for land-holding', *Archaeologia Aeliana*, 5th series, v (1977), 96–101; Fellows Jensen, *Northern History*, xiv, 37–40.
58. WJ, 85–7; L. Musset, 'La Seine normande et le commerce maritime du IIIe au XIe siècle', *Revue de la société savante de la Haute-Normandie*, no. 53 (1969), 9–11.
59. *Richer, Histoire de France* (888–995), ed. R. Latouche (Paris, 1930), ii, 272, 292.
60. Musset, 'Les plus anciennes chartes... de Bourgueil', 36–47.
61. The argument in this paragraph relating to the title is that of Werner, *Etudes... Yver*, 697–700. The charter is printed in *Recueil des actes de Lothaire et de Louis V, rois de France, (954–987)*, ed. L. Halphen and F. Lot (Paris, 1908), no. 24.
62. *Recueil*, no. 3.
63. For Anjou, Guillot, *Le comte d'Anjou et son entourage au XIe siècle* (Paris, 1972), i, 133; citing, K. F. Werner, 'Untersuchungen zur Frühzeit des französischen Fürstentums', *Die Welt als Geschichte*, xviii (1958), 265–7, 269, 283–4. Also, J. Boussard, 'L'origine des familles seigneuriales dans la région de la Loire moyenne', *CCM*, v (1962), 308–10.
64. F. L. Ganshof, 'La Flandre', in *Histoire des institutions françaises au Moyen Âge*, ed. F. Lot and R. Fawtier (Paris, 1957–62), i, *Institutions seigneuriales*, 356.
65. Guillot, *Le comte d'Anjou*, i, 4–5. Numerous local studies chart the decline of royal authority. See, in general, Dhondt, *Etudes sur la naissance des principautés territoriales*, 139–42; J. -F. Lemarignier, 'Les fidèles du roi de France (936–987)', in *Recueil de travaux offert à M. Clovis Brunel* (Paris, 1955), ii, 138–62.
66. This section relies on Francoise Dumas-Dubourg, *Le trésor de Fécamp*, passim.
67. See Dorothy Whitelock, 'The conversion of the Eastern Danelaw', *Saga Book of the Viking Society*, xii (1941), 159–76; D. M. Wilson, 'The Vikings' relationship with Christianity in northern England', *Journal of the British Archaeological Association*, 3rd series, xxx (1967), 37–46.
68. For continuity at Rouen, as opposed to other dioceses, J. Dubois, 'Les listes épiscopales témoins de l'organisation ecclésiastique et de la transmission des traditions', *Revue de l'histoire de l'église de France*, lxii (1976), 12–13. For Coutances, J. Le Patourel, 'Geoffrey of Montbray, bishop of Coutances, 1049–1093', *EHR*, lix (1944), 134–5.
69. *Acta Archiepiscopum Rotomagensium, PL,* cxlvii, col. 277.
70. BN, MS. latin 1805, fo. 41v.
71. *Recueil des chartes de l'abbaye de St-Germain-des-Prés*, ed. R. Poupardin (Paris, 1909), no. 44.
72. WJ, 38–9.

73. 'Inventio et Miracula Sancti Wulfranni', ed. Dom J. Laporte, *SHN, Mélanges*, xiv (1938), 29–30. On this episode, Dom J. Laporte, 'Gerard de Brogne à St-Wandrille et à St-Riquier', *Revue bénédictine*, lxx (1960), 156–7.
74. *Recueil*, no. 3; pp. 22–3.
75. *Ibid.*, nos. 36, 49, 53, 66, 67.
76. Marie de la Motte-Collas, 'Les possessions territoriales de l'abbaye de Saint-Germain-des-Prés, du début du IXe au début du XIIe siècle', *Revue de l'histoire de l'église de France*, xliii (1957), 65–80; J. -F. Lemarignier, *Le gouvernement royal aux premiers temps capétiens* (Paris, 1965), 90–1.
77. For the libraries, Geneviève Nortier, 'Les bibliothèques médiévales des abbayes bénédictines de Normandie', *Revue Mabillon*, xlvii (1957), 137–8; xlviii (1958), 100–1. For Mont-St-Michel, J. J. G. Alexander, *Norman Illumination at Mont-St-Michel, 966–1100* (Oxford, 1970), 8, 35–6, 38–40; Dom J. Laporte. L'abbaye du Mont-St-Michel aux Xe et XIe siècles', in *Millénaire monastique du Mont-Saint-Michel*, i (1967), 64–70. For Mayeul's gift, Cartulaire du Mont-St-Michel, Avranches, Bibliothèque municipale, MS. 210, fo. 55rv.
78. *Translatio S. Dadonis vel Audoeni episcopi*, in *Acta Sanctorum*, August, iv, 823–4; *Recueil*, p. 23, note 19.
79. For St-Ouen, *Memorials of Saint Dunstan*, ed. W. Stubbs (Rolls Series, 1874), 363–4. For Mont-St-Michel: *Cartulaire de St-Victeur au Mans*, ed. A. Bertrand de Broussillon (Paris, 1895), nos. 1–4; 'Cartulaire de l'abbayette (997–1421)', ed. *idem, Bulletin de la commission historique et archéologique de la Mayenne*, 2e série, ix (1894), supplément, nos. 1–2; Alexander, *Norman Illumination at Mont-St-Michel*, 7–8.
80. Rioul, Bernard, Ralph *Torta*, Anslech, Botho, Osmund, Tetger. Harold should be added, see note 33 above. Of the names, only Osmund and Ralph *Torta* receive any independent confirmation, *Recueil*, nos. 3, 53.
81. See note 33 above.
82. *Recueil*, no. 4.
83. The idea was fully developed by Professor David Douglas.
84. OV, iv, 122.
85. Musset, 'L'aristocratie normande au XIe siècle', 75.
86. Elisabeth Zadora-Rio, 'L'enceinte fortifiée du Plessis-Grimoult, résidence seigneuriale du XIe siècle', *Château Gaillard*, v (1970), 237–9.
87. L. Musset, 'Aux origines d'une classe dirigeante: les Tosny, grands barons normands du Xe au XIIIe siècle', *Francia*, v (1978, for 1977), 50, 70–3.
88. WJ, 73–4.
89. For this section, L. Musset, 'Les relations extérieures de la Normandie du IXe au XIe siècle, d'après quelques trouvailles monétaires récentes', *AN*, iv (1954), 31–8; Francoise Dumas-Dubourg, *Le trésor de Fécamp*, 55–60.
90. *Recueil*, p. 22, note 15; WJ, 80.
91. S. Keynes, *The Diplomas of King Aethelred 'The Unready', 978–1016* (Cambridge, 1980), 227.
92. Annie Renoux, 'Le château des ducs de Normandie à Fécamp (Xe–XIIe s.). Quelques données archéologiques et topographiques', *Arch. méd.*, ix (1979), 12–15.

PART TWO
The eleventh century

CHAPTER TWO
Normandy and its neighbours

NORTHERN FRANCE IN THE ELEVENTH CENTURY

The history of the Norman lands in the eleventh century after the final severance of regular contact with the Scandinavian fatherland can be analysed in basically the same terms as the history of any other northern French territorial principality. Such a discussion involves consideration of a wide range of subjects, such as the effects of the prevailing economic growth, or of the spread of the ideas of the Church reformers. It is best, however, to begin by setting out the main lines of social and political change in early-eleventh-century northern France, with the aim of providing a context in which Normandy's development can eventually be placed. This will be followed by a discussion of Normandy's constitutional position within the French kingdom and of its territorial identity. Finally in this chapter, the course of relations between Normandy and the other territorial principalities of northern France will be charted.

The predominant trend in early-eleventh-century French society was a progressive localisation of effective power. The monarchy grew steadily weaker as the disintegration of the large Robertian/Capetian principality during the tenth century left the field to a number of local powers. The descendants of Robert the Strong, by the late tenth century described as the Capetians, finally ousted the Carolingians from the kingship of the west Franks in 987. A succession of Capetian kings ruled during the eleventh century: Hugh Capet (987–96) was followed by his son, Robert II the Pious (996–1031), and he in turn by his son Henry I (1031–60) and his grandson Philip I (1060–1108). The modern view is that the achievements of these kings should not be belittled. All had some degree of ability; all wrestled with crushing difficulties against opponents who were often much stronger than they were. It must be said, however, that the change of dynasty in 987 was in many respects a serious blow to the prestige and power of the monarchy, since the Capetians could not aspire to the dignity of the descendants of Charlemagne. All pretension to power south of the river Loire disappeared at a stroke from 987. Despite the maintenance of theoretical claims and a general awareness that royal power should possess special qualities, the area under Capetian control contracted to a small region around Paris and Orléans. Their authority over their once large principality dwindled and by the eleventh century had almost entirely passed to a number of local powers. The Capetian monarchy in the eleventh century is therefore best considered as just another territorial principality, albeit one whose ruler bore the title of king.[1]

The counts of Blois-Chartres and the counts of Anjou were the most obvious beneficiaries of this process of dissolution. Both lines were represented by some formidable personalities during the first half of the century. Blois-Chartres under count Odo II (996–1037) achieved a considerable expansion of territory, annexing the county of Champagne in 1019, and as a result threatening to suffocate the Capetian principality. In 1044 Odo's successor was defeated at the battle of Nouy by count Geoffrey II Martel (the Hammer) of Anjou (1040–60). The consequences of this battle, which made Anjou the dominant power in northern France, must be seen as a culmination of a mixture of steady consolidation and brilliant military successes under counts Fulk Nerra (987–1040) and Geoffrey Martel. In similar manner to Blois-Chartres, Anjou had pushed outwards during the first half of the eleventh century, gaining control over the county of Maine to the north and parts of the duchy of Aquitaine to the south. The victory at Nouy cemented and extended these gains. After 1060, however, Normandy, which was, along with Flanders, one of the two relatively older and more stable principalities, emerged as 'top dog' within northern France. This was during the reign of duke William II and after the disintegration of the enlarged Angevin principality. Flanders was consistently influential – count Baldwin V (1035–67), for example, acted as guardian to the young Capetian king, Philip I – but the ambitions of its rulers tended to be directed eastwards towards the lands of the German emperors. Alongside these five should also be placed the counts of Rennes, usually the dominant power in Brittany, a region with a long tradition of independence,

Normandy before 1066

but one which lacked political cohesion. In the eleventh century the Breton counts and their lands tended to be more the focus for the ambitions of other rulers than a positive influence on events.

There existed a great deal of land in northern France which never came entirely under the control of the major territorial rulers. The intervening spaces between the principalities were dominated by lesser territorial rulers, men over whom their stronger neighbours fought to extend their power, but who would prey on their prospective masters when opportunity arose. The land between the county of Champagne, which was ruled from 1019 by the family of the counts of Blois-Chartres, and the Norman, Flemish, and Capetian principalities was segmented into small territories ruled by individual counts. In the middle of the eleventh century, one of these, Ralph IV, count of Amiens, Valois, and the Vexin (1038–74), battered his way to a precarious hegemony over some of the others. The 'principality' so assiduously constructed fell to pieces in 1077 when his son and heir left the world to become a monk. To the south of Normandy, two families, the counts of Maine and the lords of Bellême, stand out in the midst of a similar fragmentation of power. They fought each other, with the bishopric of Le Mans a frequent bone of contention, but tended also to come into the orbit of their strongest neighbours, the counts of Anjou and the dukes of Normandy. The Bellêmes, about whom a great deal can be known because of an unusually extensive documentation, in many respects typify the violence and insecurity of an extremely unstable time. Ordericus Vitalis, looking back from the comparative security of the early twelfth century, was deeply prejudiced against them: vassals of several lords, ensconced in what was in northern French terms a relatively secure afforested region, they pillaged the lands of those around them. Yet on one scale of values they were merely small men surrounded by inherently stronger powers, a family which lost many of its members through violent deaths. Throughout the eleventh century, they clung resolutely to their power-base, subjugated for a time by Geoffrey Martel and then by William of Normandy, but in 1100 almost independent again under the infamous Robert de Bellême (see Map 5).

The ambitions of the strongest territorial rulers within this northern French cockpit tended to be circumscribed by a crude 'balance of power'. The rise of one to pre-eminence usually led to the others forming an alliance against him. Thus, Odo II of Blois-Chartres was opposed in the early 1020s by a coalition composed of Robert the Pious, Fulk Nerra, and Richard II of Normandy. Similarly, in the late 1040s, Geoffrey Martel had to fight against king Henry I, William II of Normandy, and Theobald of Blois-Chartres. From the 1050s, this mechanism turned everyone to face the expansionist ambitions of duke William II. The greater princes could also aspire to aggrandisement into lands on the periphery. The counts of Flanders pushed eastwards into Germany during much of the eleventh century, while the counts of Blois-Chartres were infiltrating Berry from the late tenth century and also held on to hopes of gain in both the duchy and the kingdom of Burgundy. Likewise, the counts of Anjou were able to push south-west, and, after the battle of Moncontour (1033) in which the young Geoffrey Martel defeated the duke of Aquitaine, William VI the Fat, Geoffrey was able to lay the foundations of a precarious domination over parts of the duchy. For the Norman dukes, as also for lesser men like the counts of Boulogne, one logical direction for expansion lay across the Channel against the large, wealthy, but very vulnerable, English kingdom.

The background to these struggles was a process of social change which affected all regions, although at different times, and with varying degrees of intensity. Numerous studies, published during the last three decades, and now thankfully at last beginning to be made available to English readers, have done much to clarify our understanding of the processes involved. What is thought to have happened in the midst of the struggles between the territorial rulers is a transformation in the structure and organisation of family groupings, which began to take effect in the later tenth century. Around the year 1000, the strongest families among the aristocracy, most of them securely established since the ninth century at the very latest,[2] evolved from extended kin-groups, in which each son had a theoretically equal share in the inheritance, into lineages which placed a heavy emphasis on the integrity of family property and on the right of one son, usually the first-born, to inherit. The claims of other sons were reduced, even eliminated. Psychologically this can be interpreted as an evolution away from families, which were essentially groups of blood relations with no consciousness of past or future, into lineages, which were tenacious of lands, rights, and even status, over successive generations. Associated, and often as near as not coincidental in time with these changes, was the proliferation of what were both status symbols and new bastions of power: castles – usually simple wooden structures at first – and endowed monasteries or colleges of canons. This combination, fortified residence and religious foundation, became the typical possession of most powerful families.[3]

Normandy before 1066

These developments had a profound political significance. Essentially they represented an extension to a lower social stratum of the phenomena which in the tenth century had dissolved the authority of the Carolingian kings, and subsequently that of the Robertians/Capetians, and which had brought about the emergence of the new power groupings such as Anjou and the Capetian demesne. These territories now in their turn started to suffer the symptoms of disintegration. The effect of the changes at the higher social level had been to cause kings and territorial princes to lose control over their local officials, the counts, who had as a consequence obtained exclusive power over their area of jurisdiction, the *pagus*. During the eleventh century, the count's powers over his *pagus* tended to be broken down and taken over by the castle-holding families. The kin-group, which had arguably always been the basic unit of political society, in its new lineal form evolved towards a much stronger sense of possession, which became a great threat to organised authority. All manner of rights and powers tended to be converted into hereditary family possessions. The result was that authority over the mass of the people became the subject of territorial redefinition, with, at different times in different regions, the castellanry replacing the *pagus* as the basic unit. A further consequence was that what had once been royal rights passed to these families and were progressively devalued, so that from the early eleventh century, the writers of charters began to lump them together simply as 'customs' (*consuetudines*).[4] In some regions, of which the Mâconnais in Burgundy, the subject of a brilliant study by Professor Georges Duby, is a prime example, there is a straightforward chronological coincidence around the year 1000 between the appearance of the new family structures and the final disintegration of the *pagus* and of all forms of the Carolingian institutions designed to administer public authority. The castellanry became the highest level of political power; the dominant group in society was a military élite, unchecked by any superior notions of public peace or by any judicial authority greater than that which could be maintained by force.[5]

The intrinsic nature of these changes is difficult to grasp. It is at least clear that they were part and parcel of chronic social instability. Even in Flanders, a consistently well-organised and relatively peaceful principality, it can be said that 'after the year 1000, and perhaps even earlier, the clash of arms accompanied every appearance of the nobility'.[6] A case can be made out for a progressive militarisation of society in some regions: the armies with which rulers such as the counts of Anjou and Blois-Chartres fought their battles from the later tenth century onwards appear to have been much larger than those of their tenth-century predecessors.[7] This in turn seems to have been associated with the spread of ties of dependence and the granting of benefices to military followers. The dissolution of the *pagus* and the evolution of the new family structures were a crucial stage in the creation of a 'new feudalism' by which previously free families were brought into ties of lordship and by which the castle-holding families strengthened their local territorial power. A period of extreme violence and disorder laid the foundations for what was to become a new framework of power.

The older tradition, brought together in the vital work of synthesis, Marc Bloch's *La société féodale*, first published in 1940, explained these changes as being the result of a rising class of knights enveloping and transforming the aristocracy, thereby leading to a drastic reorganisation of the social, political, and institutional structure of French society. This view drew its strength from a widespread trend whereby the aristocracies in some regions came to be described in the documents as *milites* ('knights'); apparently identifying themselves increasingly with the social ethos of the warriors. Knighthood, so it seemed, absorbed the nobility. Carolingian terminology, which had distinguished between a group of superior families (*nobiles, proceres, optimates,* and similar terms) and the inferior fighting-men (*milites*), vanished from the charters during the eleventh century. It was replaced by the single status of knighthood. In the Mâconnais, for example, all levels of the aristocracy, including the families strong enough to own castles and to wield judicial powers, were described as *milites* by the late eleventh century. In the Capetian demesne in the Ile de France, the word *miles* was being regularly applied to the holders of castles by 1060, although not apparently to the most powerful ones.[8] A similar eleventh-century evolution has been discerned further south in Berry and Provence.[9]

The modern emphasis on the continuity of noble families through from the Carolingian period to the eleventh century has produced a significant revision of Bloch's general conclusions. The demonstration of continuity means that the survival of economic and political distinctions between the long-established more powerful families and the lower group of warriors is now widely accepted. The change in descriptive terminology, devised as it was by the clerics who wrote the charters, is seen, not as evidence of the rise of a 'new aristocracy', but as a recognition by the stronger families of the essential *raison d'être* of the aristocracy, the profession of arms. The acceptance of the novel designation as *milites* is regarded as a sign that the Carolingian institutions associated with the *pagus* had collapsed, to be replaced by territorial castellanries, thereby removing the need for those who were predominant in the count's or territorial prince's court to stress their distinctive position through terms such as *proceres* or *nobiles*. The whole process was accompanied by a spread of ties of vassalic dependence, and, while it was taking place, by a serious weakening in the significance attached to the tie of fidelity between lord and vassal. From *c*. 975 the practice, already widespread since the later ninth century, by which men became vassals of more than one lord, seems to have proliferated much more rapidly. The overall result was that in some regions the theoretical treatises, which described the natural order of society, had effected a significant redefinition by *c*. 1030. Laymen, divided in Carolingian times into those who were free and those who were unfree, with the former category including significant numbers of the peasantry, tended to be viewed instead in terms of those whose way of life was to fight and those who worked the land. This development reflected the extinction of a regime; the dissolution of a Carolingian world which gave pre-eminence to those who exercised public authority. It was replaced by the spread of the term *miles* and an accent on the military role of the aristocracy.[10]

The general picture of a society in considerable disarray is summed up by the famous letter of *c*. 1021 in which Fulbert, bishop of Chartres, an acknowledged fount of wisdom in his day, replied to count William V of Aquitaine's enquiry about the respective duties of lord and vassal. The fact that the question could even be asked, along with the bishop's somewhat platitudinous and theoretical replies – he had had to undertake research in order to answer – point to a grave enfeeblement of all conceptions of authority.[11] The maintenance of power and status became as a result dependent on something resembling almost a daily flexing of muscle, requiring constant vigilance and the consistent exercise of those prerogatives which a ruler claimed as his own. The Mâconnais is the archetypal example of a region in which the break-up of the *pagus* and the spread of ties of multiple dependence destroyed the count's authority and tended to paralyse the actions of the more powerful families. In Aquitaine, bishop Fulbert's correspondent, count William V (995–1030), may well have lacked the determination of his predecessor, count William IV 'Iron-Arm' (963–95), and as a result territorial dismemberment took place. The powers which had been upheld as customs by count Geoffrey Martel of Anjou faded away during the succession dispute between his two nephews, count Geoffrey the Bearded (1060–68) and count Fulk Rechin (1068–1109), which followed his death. At the same time the conquests which count Geoffrey Martel had made disintegrated.[12] In Normandy itself William the Conqueror's sons were obliged to hold an inquest within four years of his death in 1087 in order to define the customary powers which he had exercised while duke. The power of all territorial princes was vulnerable.

The clearest overt reaction to this state of affairs came from the sections of society most at its mercy, the Church and the non-military classes. Monasteries sought to escape the oppression of the castellans by securing immunity from all secular jurisdiction. They tried, too, to gain exemption from episcopal authority, since in many regions the bishoprics were dominated by the same families who controlled lay society. The most dramatic development was the popular peace movement known as the Peace of God, which appeared in the very disturbed regions of southern and central France from the last years of the tenth century.[13] The bishops appear to have been the chief propagators of a movement whose chief aims were the protection of the weak and of ecclesiastical property. Direct appeals to the people in large assemblies at which the relics of saints were displayed could sometimes produce amazing results: in the 1030s Haimo, archbishop of Bourges, recruited a popular army which was launched against the men of war with tragic and entirely predictable consequences.[14] Thereafter the Peace tended to abandon 'direct action' and to concentrate on prohibiting fighting on set days of the week. It was introduced into northern France at the time of the council of Compiègne of 1023.

The reaction of lay aristocratic society can also be interpreted as being in some senses motivated by a search for stability, rather than by a simple enjoyment of violence for its own sake. Castle-building, the new emphasis on the rights of succession of one son, and the accumulation of the powers to command, to judge, and to tax were all up to a point defensive measures on the part of powerful families who were seeking to protect themselves against the fragmentation of their property through the excessive alienation of benefices and to thwart neighbours who were competing with them for the loyalty of the *milites*. The pressure on the landed resources of the aristocracy also frequently tempted them to extend their estates at the expense of the Church: in the Ile de France, for example, the failure of the institutions of the *pagus* in the late tenth century coincided with the dilapidation of the patrimonies of the monasteries which had survived the Viking invasions (see p. 32). Change was therefore a complex amalgam of aggressive and defensive reactions. In regions to the south and east of Normandy, the result was the breakdown of the *pagi* and the emergence of the power of near-independent lineages such as the Bellêmes. But the fact that so many families should have succeeded in preserving the basis of their power through this turbulent period also reflects a somewhat surprising phenomenon which has been the theme of several recent studies: namely, the resilience of the government of many of the territorial princes. The Capetian monarchy, for example, was feeble in 1000 and still feeble in 1100, but it had in the meantime considerably refashioned its power preparatory to the advances made in Louis VI's reign (1108–37). Anjou, very impressive under Fulk Nerra and Geoffrey Martel, could bounce back under Fulk Rechin in the later eleventh century and become a formidable military power in the first half of the twelfth century.[15] The changes in the structure of aristocratic power, despite the threat which they offered to organised authority, were in varying degrees absorbed within the principalities. The two pillars of princely survival were an intelligent use of those powers which remained available, coupled with the adaptation of developments such as the Peace of God, and a diet of consistent external aggression.

Most principalities provide examples of novel and effective administrative devices, designed to exploit new sources of wealth. A new official, the *prepositus* (provost), appears in many of the principalities – in the very early eleventh century in both Anjou and Blois-Chartres – with the general task of supervising other officials. Formal households made up of stewards, marshals, and the like, can be discerned at various times. Most princes developed the rudiments of an organised writing-office during the second half of the century. In its very last years, several of these evolved a new kind of document which enabled them to direct orders to local officials: the *mandatum* of the Capetian and Angevin principalities, and the writ, which was transferred from England to Normandy during William Rufus' tenancy (1096–1100). The phraseology of the princes' charters emphasised that they were the successors to the authority of kings and all made strenuous efforts to uphold the powers which they had acquired. They tried, for example, to maintain the Carolingian prerogative which prohibited the construction of unlicensed fortifications. A careful attention to chronology can show that the appearance of aristocratic castles was usually a gradual process, as also was the fragmentation of princely control over them.[16] Castles tended to be built conditional on a ruler's consent and to form the basis of castellanries only when his power was weakened. In the principalities where a territorial ruler did maintain authority, the chief families were obliged to moderate their ambitions accordingly. Some would be likely to co-operate with the prince, others might not. The result was that in regions where older notions of public authority remained strong, the fusion of nobility and knighthood did not take place during the eleventh century. Thus, in the county of Ponthieu, which was adjacent to Normandy's eastern frontier, and where the *pagus* resisted disintegration, the two remained distinct until the middle of the twelfth century. In the counties of Champagne and Flanders, fusion was delayed until the later twelfth century, while in the Empire, they could still be distinguished in the thirteenth century.[17] The aristocracy in these regions might assume some of the symbols of knighthood, but the more powerful continued in the charters to fall within the general descriptions of Carolingian terminology, *proceres*, *optimates*, etc. The prince therefore maintained a dominant role within the military aristocracy, a conclusion even applicable to some areas where fragmentation was very severe. The Capetian kings, for example, as Professor Lemarignier has shown, were able to found their power on a social stratum lower than that of the castellans.

External aggression is a feature of the eleventh-century history of all the principalities. This was directed not only into warfare with neighbouring rulers but also found expression in a series of fabulous schemes. Odo II of Blois-Chartres, for example, contested the kingdom of Burgundy with the emperor Conrad II during the 1030s. Earlier, along with counts William V of Aquitaine and Odo-William of Mâcon, he had taken an interest in the succession to the kingdom of Italy.[18] Geoffrey Martel, in addition to his career of conquest within France, clearly regarded himself as a man of European stature, marrying a daughter to the German king Henry III and attending his son-in-law's coronation as emperor in Rome in 1046. The purpose of all this aggression has generally been seen as being the diversion of potentially disruptive violence against other principalities. A more extreme formulation identifies the more extravagant ambitions as the expression of a society teetering on the brink of anarchy – because everything was so uncertain, all schemes seemed to be possible.[19]

Any appreciation of eleventh-century society must take full account of the essentially military ethos of the life-style of the ruling classes. Aggressive war was a vital ingredient of effective government in a world in which notions of authority and of the obligations demanded by ties of fidelity between man and man had been gravely weakened. The society of eleventh-century northern France was changing rapidly and conclusively. The pace was one which posed a serious threat to all who sought to maintain themselves as territorial rulers. Yet, in the end, although many among them might have trembled inwardly during such private moments as they enjoyed, most had no cause to despair.

THE IDENTITY OF NORMANDY

The name 'Normandy' was first used in the early eleventh century. Its earliest forms, 'the land of the Normans' (*terra Normannorum*) or, more simply, 'Normandy' (*Normannia* or *Nortmannia*), occur at precisely the time that Dudo of St-Quentin was composing his history of the first Norman rulers.[20] This clear territorial identity was sustained for the rest of the eleventh century, attaining from the 1060s an even stricter definition through a steady stream of references in the charters which locate particular properties by their position relative to the Norman frontier: the earliest example is the grant in 1055 to the abbey of Marmoutier at Tours of property 'in Normandy, in the Vexin'. Two much more precise instances from 1067 describe St-James-de-Beuvron as 'on the boundary of Normandy and Brittany' and the river Epte at Gisors as 'flowing between France and Normandy', while, finally, a charter drawn up in the 1070s alludes to the river at Aumale as dividing Normandy from the district of Amiens.[21] It should be added that this remarkable clarity of the line between Normandy and the neighbouring lands was a subject for specific comment in a literary source written between 1074 and 1087.[22]

The way in which contemporary documents use 'Normandy' and 'the land of the Normans' as equivalents demonstrates that 'Normandy' was understood as being the land in which the descendants of the Scandinavian settlers lived. But, as we have seen, an adequate definition cannot be so simply arrived at: writers from Dudo's time onwards stated what is obvious from the place-name evidence; namely, that Normandy was not racially monolithic, it was a land peopled by several races. Normandy's identity may have derived from the Scandinavian settlements, but it had become a recognisable territorial entity because its rulers had been able to maintain power over it during a long period of time. This point is reflected in the eleventh-century documents by its frequent description as a 'principality' (*principatus* or even *regnum*),[23] by the practice by which its rulers sometimes described themselves as 'counts' or 'dukes' of 'Normandy' as opposed to the more usual title of 'count/duke of the

Normans', by the inclusion of the word *Nortmannia* on the duke's coinage in the second half of the century, and by the idea of 'the custom of the land' co-terminous with the territory ruled by the dukes which appears as early as 1031/32–1035 in an original charter.[24] The name 'Normandy' therefore reflected the ethnic origins of its ruling class. But its well-defined frontiers were the result of the consistent exercise of political power by the tenth-century counts of Rouen and the eleventh-century dukes of Normandy.

Normandy's well-defined territorial identity and the strength of ducal authority within it were the subject of contemporary comment. An inspired observation by the scribe of a Marmoutier charter, written in *c.* 1055, sums the matter up very effectively: William II, he remarked, was 'ruler of his whole land, something which is scarcely found anywhere else'.[25] The duchy was a notably coherent political unit in comparison with other eleventh-century principalities. This state of affairs had not, however, been achieved without effort. The construction in frontier regions of castles which, during Richard II's reign at least, were usually entrusted to the duke's relatives, must have made a considerable contribution. Several close relations, bearing the title of count, were made responsible before 1020 for castles at Mortain, Ivry, Evreux, Eu, and briefly, Exmes. Castles were also established at intermediate places such as Tillières-sur-Avre. William II subsequently strengthened this barrier with fortifications at, among other places, St-James-de-Beuvron, Breteuil, and Neufmarché. But, as will be shown below, it was only after Richard II's death that there are clear signs of a deliberate policy of concentration on extending and clarifying these frontiers. Under Richard and, to a lesser extent, under Robert I, the dukes were involved in enterprises into remote regions such as Burgundy or Flanders in support of the Capetian kings. With William II, this dispersal of effort ceased. His wars were consistently aimed to defend or expand the Norman frontiers (see pp. 75–83).

A similar narrowing of endeavour as well as the same basic chronology can also be inferred from the dukes' monastic patronage. Richard II made grants to a large number of churches outside Normandy and enjoyed a wholly justified reputation for generosity which extended as far as the monastery on Mount Sinai. Robert I, however, did nothing beyond reorganise an earlier grant to the abbey of St-Bénigne of Dijon in Burgundy and, along with his brother Richard III, make a donation to St-Benoît-sur-Loire. William II, although he did give consistent support to the abbey of Marmoutier at Tours and did make a grant to St-Florent of Saumur, showed none of his grandfather's propensity for wide-ranging liberality with Norman land.[26] He enjoyed a European renown for his generosity to the Church, but this was founded on financial gifts: he was, for example, a contributor towards the restoration of Le Mans cathedral, and the donor of the wherewithal to construct a dormitory at Marmoutier and a tower, which fell down before it was finished, at St-Denis.[27]

The coincidence of a changed, more concentrated, and more distinctly Norman attitude in William II's time with the increased sharpness of the frontier in the second half of the century cannot be accidental. It represents a change of crucial importance in the approach of the Norman rulers to the task of government. Why it happened is a matter of pure speculation: it should most probably be related to the increasing pressure on the Norman frontiers from the 1020s onwards; to the great increase in financial resources at the duke's disposal, especially since many of William's most generous gifts were made after the conquest of England, which made it unnecessary to grant land; and to the development of the Norman Church itself which made it less essential to encourage outside interest. Whatever the explanation, it is clear that the changes as a whole were not just a reflection of new thinking on the part of the duke. The way in which the abbey of Jumièges, which, after its refoundation in c. 940, had acquired property in regions as distant as Poitou, began to jettison such remote possessions in the early eleventh century and at the same time to acquire properties in Lower Normandy – an example subsequently followed by the abbeys of St-Wandrille and St-Ouen of Rouen – suggests that the dukes' behaviour reflected the operation of deeper forces at work in Norman society.[28] There appears to be a pronounced turning-point in the period between 1025 and 1050 when the duchy turned in on itself, and out of which an even firmer definition of the frontiers and more intensely 'Norman' attitudes emerged.

Normandy's territorial unity was not unshakeable. Although the integration of Frankish natives and Norman settlers in the tenth century meant that racial tension was no threat, the territory's independence, and possibly also its unity, might be qualified by the fact that Rollo had received his land by a treaty with a Frankish king and that he and his successors had acknowledged the lordship of successive monarchs. This recognition of external authority had persisted throughout the tenth century, and despite the universal weakening of the significance attached to ties of fidelity, had survived into the eleventh century. It must be asked how far this continued acknowledgement of royal lordship affected the authority of the eleventh-century Norman rulers. In addition, the security of Normandy's frontiers might at any stage be corroded by the economic and property interests of Norman and non-Norman families and religious houses. A lineage, or indeed a church, might build up an estate which traversed the frontier in such a way as to attach Norman land to a centre of power outside the duchy. Such an occurrence could be part and parcel of the way in which families and churches extended their property interests. On occasions, however, it could lead to a serious fragmentation of ducal authority. In extreme circumstances, it caused war.

The question of Normandy's independence of outside authority must be seen against the wider background of the developments in northern France as a whole. The general problem – '*Fidèles ou vassaux?*' – of whether the territorial rulers were simply *fideles* who accorded no more than an honorary precedence to the kings, or whether they were truly vassals who were required to perform services along lines which all acknowledged, has been hotly debated among French historians for at least a century.[29] It can also be asked to what extent the kings retained powers which were regalian, applicable in such matters as keeping the peace and protecting subjects. On both counts, the modern view emphasises the destructive and disruptive effects of the prevailing localisation of power. Ties of fidelity had no binding force for either king or territorial prince; rulers such as the counts of Anjou, Blois-Chartres, or Flanders were the vassals of several lords, of whom the king was merely one. *Mutatis mutandis*, regalian powers had also broken down almost to nothing.

The evidence of terminology suggests that the tenth-century fidelity of the Norman rulers to the Capetian king was maintained into the eleventh century up until the reign of William II. Richard II is explicitly described as a *fidelis* of king Robert the Pious by the well-informed contemporary, bishop Fulbert of Chartres.[30] Richard III (1026–27) ruled for too short a time for there to be clear evidence: it may be significant, however, that he visited king Robert's court at Senlis in 1027.[31] For Robert I's status, there is the rather ambiguous statement by William of Jumièges that the duke was asked to assist in the restoration of king Henry I in 1033 on the basis of 'the duty of fidelity'.[32] A clear change appears only in William II's time, the crucial text being supplied by William of Poitiers, who wrote his history of William's reign in *c.* 1077. Poitiers acknowledged what appears to have been the truth – that previous Norman rulers had done homage. Duke William, however, he announced, was neither the friend nor the vassal of the Capetians.[33] Emanating as it does from a writer who was William's unashamed panegyrist, and who may not have been above tinkering with the truth when it suited his purpose, this statement that the duke was independent of Capetian lordship, is automatically suspect. Yet since the purpose was to please duke William, William of Poitiers is likely to have presented the version of a tricky problem which the duke wanted to hear. He therefore made no attempt, as Dudo had done, to suppress past acknowledgements of Capetian superiority. In general, Poitiers, on the evidence of his full treatment of the respective claims of William and Harold to the English kingdom in 1066, was a man who liked to give a well-researched, if partisan, legal opinion. At the least he was retailing a version of relations with the Capetians which duke William would have found acceptable.

William of Poitiers' thesis is supported by the negative evidence that there is no actual contemporary reference that William was a vassal of the Capetians. A statement in an almost contemporary source that in *c.* 1034 Henry I confirmed duke Robert's anticipatory designation of his young son as his successor may indicate that William had done homage to that king.[34] There is similar evidence for Philip I's reign. Although William of Poitiers' description of a treaty between William and the new king in *c.* 1060 is often interpreted as showing that homage was performed, its vague language and its incompatibility with Poitiers' other statements make this unlikely.[35] More serious is the evidence of the 1079 annal of the 'D' version of the *Anglo-Saxon Chronicle* that king Philip had given his consent to the designation of Robert Curthose as William's heir to the duchy, an event which must be dated to 1060–63.[36] This implies some form of homage, although it does not explicitly mention it. But, in any case, like all eleventh-century records which refer to contacts between the Norman rulers and the Capetians, the *Chronicle* does not refer to any clearly formulated rules which might have governed the relationship. It is unfortunate that there is no statement from the Capetian side: of the eleventh-century kings, only Robert the Pious attracted a biographer, the pedestrian Helgaud of Fleury. To the extent that there is nothing clear to go on, the contemporary evidence justifies William of Poitiers' opinion. We should think in terms of the maintenance of the formal links of fidelity through to Robert I's time, but of their denial, and possibly of their rejection, under William II. Conditions had changed to the extent that a claim to an independence of external authority not enjoyed by previous Norman rulers could be made on William's behalf.

A final assessment of the nature of the relationship between the Norman rulers and the Capetians has to take account of a wider range of evidence, and most especially of the statements of twelfth-century historians who sometimes described eleventh-century dealings between the two parties in terms of a lord–vassal relationship. Thus, for example, the assistance which duke William received in 1047 from king Henry I, and which enabled him to win the battle of Val-ès-Dunes, was described by the English historian William of Malmesbury, who wrote in the 1120s, as an official guardianship and, by implication, as a lord giving protection to a vassal.[37] This view of events was also recorded independently in a chronicle compiled at Tours in *c.* 1137.[38] A little later, the Englishman Henry of Huntingdon wrote as if Normandy had been taken into the Capetian demesne, a view influenced by contemporary notions of wardship, and a statement which was reproduced verbatim by the Norman chronicler Robert of Torigny. None of this appears in an early source: William of Jumièges, for example, simply noted that William asked for Henry's help (see pp. 74–75).[39] The same difficulty, namely that twelfth-century sources might describe in institutional terms something which would not have been so understood in the eleventh century, dogs discussions of the military assistance which the Normans gave to the Capetians. This might have been in response to an obligation to provide a definite service, of the kind recorded in the 1133 inquest into the fiefs held of Bayeux cathedral, an enquiry whose purpose was to discover what conditions had existed in the late eleventh century.[40] But, in the same way that Henry I's support for William in 1047 might have stemmed from a necessary reaction to the growth of Geoffrey Martel of Anjou's power, all four occasions on which Norman aid was given to the kings can be explained in terms of immediate considerations. Help in 1006 and 1033 can be seen as a consequence of a long-standing alliance, that of 1048–49 as a repayment of the debt incurred to Henry I in 1047, while the small Norman force which was sent to Flanders in 1071 could well have been intended to support duke William's beleaguered young nephew count Arnulf III or to advance the personal ambitions of William fitz Osbern who led the unsuccessful expedition.[41]

The essence of this particular problem is that the natural accumulation of precedent produced custom. The twelfth-century writers interpreted what had happened more than half a century before within the legal forms of their own day, and in terms of the stronger powers which lordship was coming to embody. The eleventh-century documents employ no precise vocabulary to describe the feudal relationship. It should therefore be concluded, in conformity with the broad conclusions reached for other principalities, that the fidelity of the Norman dukes to the monarchy imposed no definite obligations. As far as we can see, the last occasion on which a Capetian king overtly exercised authority in the duchy was in 1006 when Robert the Pious confirmed Richard II's far-reaching grant of privileges to the abbey of Fécamp.[42] The Norman rulers could still appreciate that the monarchs represented a theoretically superior level of authority; hence, the ratification of the succession arrangements in *c.* 1034 and 1060–63. But the history of relations in the first half of the eleventh century is essentially one of mutual assistance in times of need and of the occasional attendance of Norman dukes at such ceremonial occasions as coronations. At this stage indeed the Norman rulers appear to have displayed a quite exceptional single-mindedness: unlike other princes such the counts of Anjou or Flanders, they remained the vassals of the Capetians and of the Capetians alone. The evidence suggests that co-operation faded after Richard II's death in 1026. From 1052 William II and the Capetians were enemies. It was this rupture which led William of Poitiers to deny that duke William was a royal vassal. The declaration of independence was taken to its logical conclusion in 1108 when the Anglo-Norman Henry I stated bluntly that homage was not owed, a position which proved to be untenable. It was Louis VI's reassertion of lordship over the Norman rulers in 1113 which allowed twelfth-century writers to reinterpret eleventh-century conditions.

The physical threat to the Norman territory's stability was an ever-present one throughout the eleventh century. In the 1050s it took the form of organised invasions, but usually it existed in the more subtle form of encroachment or of the acquisition of property interests through marriage or inheritance. It must be said at the outset, however, that not all instances of cross-border estates constituted a danger which had to be combated. Immediately before 1066 we find a Richard fitz Herluin with lands in both the Norman and French Vexins, apparently in peaceful possession of his properties. His family's cross-border status seems to have been a long-standing one: his aunt Helvise had earlier married a Norman named Azor with lands in the Pays de Caux, before subsequently retiring to live as a recluse near the abbey of Coulombs in the Ile de France of which Richard's brother was abbot. Richard may also have held estates in central Normandy.[43] This capacity to combine Norman and non-Norman properties was shared with the monasteries of Upper Normandy, who were busy obtaining lands and exemptions from tolls on river

Normandy and its neighbours

traffic on the Seine towards Paris from the early eleventh century. Their interests both as religious communities and great landowners made these desirable, if not essential.[44] Later monastic foundations, such as Le Bec or St-Evroult, followed the same policy. So, too, in a different region did Mont-St-Michel, situated at the point where Normandy, Maine, and Brittany met, and the recipient of extensive property in all three. Mont-St-Michel does, however, differ in one respect from the other examples cited, since, at one period of its history at least, its position on the margin of the Norman lands tempted the monks to dabble in high politics (see p. 70).

The period from *c.* 1020 to *c.* 1050 was the time when the Norman frontier was most vulnerable. The southern sector suffered especially severely. The greatest threat came from the Bellême clan, who, with a secure power-base outside Normandy, were able definitively to extend their sway into the duchy during the 1020s. In spite of campaigns by duke Robert I and persistent harrying by the counts of Maine, the family seem to have got the best of the wars of the 1020s and 1030s, and, by *c.* 1035, the theoretically Norman bishopric of Sées had come into the hands of Ivo de Bellême, who had also inherited Bellême after the deaths of several elder brothers. There was, moreover, a strong current of turbulence at a lower social level which encouraged further the fragmentation of this section of the Norman frontier. The triumphs and tribulations of the family of Giroie, a story magnificently narrated by Ordericus Vitalis, a monk in the monastery which the family had founded at St-Evroult, demonstrate the extreme instability prevalent in the region. Between *c.* 1020 and *c.* 1060 they extended their lands by becoming the vassals of the Bellême, of a castellan named Geoffrey de Mayenne whose power-base was in Maine, and of the dukes of Normandy. The manipulation of their lords' rivalries, as well as the fortunes of marriage and inheritance, enabled them to effect a large extension of their lands. But it was also the cause of several tragedies: William fitz Giroie, for example, was savagely mutilated on the orders of William de Bellême, and Robert fitz Giroie died after holding the castle of St-Céneri-le-Gérei against duke William II in 1059–60.[45]

The first half of the eleventh century seems to have been the time when the majority of such encroachments took place. In a parallel case to those in the south, the counts of Ponthieu obtained a foothold over the north-eastern frontier in *c.* 1030 (see p. 74). At this stage the dukes do not seem to have deemed it necessary to resist most such developments. Robert I campaigned ineffectually against the Bellême family and more successfully against the aspiring alliance of the monks of Mont-St-Michel and the count of Brittany. But the arrival of the Giroie and of the counts of Ponthieu was confronted only by count Gilbert of Brionne, whose landed interests near Orbec and Eu respectively, were threatened. In both cases duke Robert intervened, not to repel an intruder, but to make peace.[46] This disturbed time left its scars on Norman institutional development. A charter, which dates from 1063–66, refers to a castellan at Moulins-la-Marche on the southern frontier exercising full-blown bannal lordship, the total domination over the people of the locality which was typical of regions where public authority was in the process of dissolution, but which was quite unknown anywhere else in Normandy.[47] The southern frontier, even in 1066, is in many respects best considered more as a zone than a line. It is doubtful whether the dukes' jurisdiction was ever fully exercised there, while the local coinage in the later eleventh century seems to have been money minted at Le Mans – ducal money certainly did not circulate there in the later twelfth century.[48]

The stabilisation of the Norman frontier was the work of William II. The counts of Ponthieu were ejected in 1053. A series of campaigns in the south brought William de Moulins-la-Marche, the Giroie, and even the Bellême to heel by 1060. How far William intended to suppress cross-border landed interests is uncertain. Enough of them survived, and several important new ones appeared, to suggest that there was no deliberate policy. But those who acquired undesirable connections had to tread carefully. Roger de Mortemer nearly lost his estates in 1054 for having assisted the flight of his non-Norman lord, Ralph, count of Amiens-Valois-Vexin, after the battle of Mortemer.[49] That the Norman frontier acquired a sharper definition from c. 1060 is therefore not a coincidence. The distinct existence of Normandy may have been the result of the endeavours of the tenth- and early-eleventh-century Norman rulers, but its final stabilisation was largely brought about by duke William II. The new concentration on Normandy and the more strident assertion of independence from the Capetian kings are further straws in the wind to suggest that the policies and even the basic political attitudes of the Norman rulers acquired a new direction from c. 1050. There is something of an old-fashioned quality about Richard II's rule; notably his devotion to the Capetians at a time when every other territorial prince was extending his lands by entering relationships of vassalage with numerous lords. His stable government contributed greatly towards Normandy's distinct identity. But it is also clear that Normandy's history entered a new phase in William II's time.

NORMANDY AND ITS NEIGHBOURS

Richard II's reign is invariably treated by eleventh-century writers as having been a great success. He is consistently praised for keeping the peace, for supporting the Church, and for winning his wars. William of Jumièges, for example, noted that the duke always defeated his enemies and that, while he ruled, the duchy resembled the church of God. Significantly, an independent writer, the Burgundian Ralph Glaber, echoed these sentiments, emphasising the firm peace which Normandy enjoyed during this period with dramatic metaphors of domestic harmony. As has been noted above, Richard also possessed a great reputation as a benefactor of churches, his generosity being acknowledged far beyond the confines of northern France.[50]

The main source for what can be conveniently termed 'external' relations during Richard's long reign is the fifth book of the *Gesta* of William of Jumièges, written about half a century after the events it describes. The subject-matter consists almost exclusively of the duke's campaigns and of events in early-eleventh-century England. A fuller picture can be assembled by the addition of references in other sources, but it must be assumed that Jumièges recounted what were later thought to be the most memorable and significant events of the reign.

The *Gesta* mentions one major war, against count Odo II of Blois-Chartres, which took place in 1013–14. The cause of the trouble was land on the river Avre and in the vicinity of the castle of Dreux, which had been given as a dowry with Richard's sister Mathilda when she married Odo. She had borne no children when she died and Richard proceeded to seek restitution of the property. In pursuit of this aim, he built a castle either within or very near the disputed region at Tillières-sur-Avre. Odo's unsuccessful assault on the new castle seems to have alarmed Richard sufficiently for him to call upon Scandinavian reinforcements. At this point king Robert the Pious intervened to mediate between the two sides: the resulting settlement, made at nearby Coudres, gave Dreux to count Odo and the land on the Avre to Richard.

From Richard's point of view, this was a victory. His father appears to have lost control over territory on the river Avre to the benefit of the counts of Dreux. In the last years of the tenth century, the land had passed via the Capetians to the counts of Blois-Chartres, and Richard's concession of it as part of Mathilda's dowry looks very like an admission that he had abandoned hope of recovering it. The war against count Odo therefore enabled him to regain long-lost Norman lands and to consolidate the frontier.[51] It may also have led to an extension of influence into the territory of the French Vexin, which borders Dreux, since two of the major castellans of that region, Dreux, count of the Vexin, a generous benefactor of Norman monasteries who became the husband of Edward the Confessor's sister Godgifu, and Waleran I, count of Meulan, attest ducal charters in the last years of Richard's reign. Waleran's appearance may be especially significant as an index of increasing Norman power: he had sided with count Odo in 1013–14.[52]

Other elements in William of Jumièges' account which relate to Richard's relations with other northern French princes are the assistance which the duke gave to Robert the Pious' campaigns to secure the duchy of Burgundy and the cordial relations between Richard and the dominant Breton ruler of the time, count Geoffrey of Rennes. On the former subject, Jumièges telescoped events considerably, making a single successful campaign out of fighting which lasted for fourteen years. Richard's actual contribution seems to have been to send troops to the siege of Auxerre in 1005–06. With regard to Brittany, Richard married Geoffrey's sister Judith at a date between 996 and 1008, while Geoffrey married another of Richard's sisters, named Havise. Richard subsequently acted as guardian to Geoffrey's young sons during their father's pilgrimage to Rome, a journey from which he did not return. Other sources suggest that the campaign in Burgundy was merely one aspect of Richard's consistent support for king Robert the Pious, a policy so steadily pursued that it must be seen as the dominant characteristic of Richard's endeavours. He is known to have supported a royal campaign in Flanders.[53] The basic aim motivating Richard's actions would appear to have been the maintenance of good order in northern France. From the celebrated letter, written in 1023–24 to complain about king Robert's conduct towards count Odo of Blois-Chartres, we know that Richard attempted to arbitrate in the long and bitter struggle between the two men: Richard had tried to set up what might best be described as an independent enquiry, but had abandoned the idea once it became clear that the king was bent on wrecking the project by trying to put Odo on trial for breach of fealty.[54] Concern for public order of a different sort is suggested by his part in reporting an outbreak of heresy at Chartres to king Robert. Finally, Richard's general indispensability in important matters and his concern for peace are conclusively shown by his attendance at Compiègne in May 1023 to discuss the introduction of the Peace of God into northern France and to meet the ambassadors of the emperor Henry II in preliminary talks before the summit conference between the kings of France and Germany which was held three months later at Ivois.[55] This alliance with king Robert and the efforts for peace are fully in accord with the conclusions of the earlier discussion which suggested that he was the loyal vassal of the king.

The final feature of Book V of the *Gesta Normannorum Ducum* is the extensive treatment which it gives to English affairs, including the massacre of St Brice's Day (1002), some aspects of the conquest of the English kingdom by the Danish armies of Sven Forkbeard and Cnut, and the flight into exile in Normandy of king Aethelred and his young sons Edward and Alfred. The purpose of this section, as Jumièges explained, was to instruct the uninformed about the early life of king Edward the Confessor. The author, writing after 1066, composed his history with the deliberate intention of supplying the background for the events of the conquest of England.

From this material, the source of duke Richard's contemporary reputation as an upholder of peace and good order is easily appreciated. It is no surprise, too, that some of the traditions embodied in later *chansons de geste* emphasised the virtue of loyalty, and especially his devotion to the Capetians.[56] It must be said, however, that, with hindsight, Richard's endeavours appear almost eccentric in a period dominated by the almost incessant warfare between the counts of Anjou and Blois-Chartres, and subsequently by the beginning of hostilities between count Odo and the Capetians. Richard played no discernible part in the competition between Anjou and Blois-Chartres. His exertions for peace seem to have intensified once the Capetian monarchy was threatened. In military terms, it may be doubted whether Richard actually commanded the resources to take much part in warfare which included large pitched battles such as Pontlevoy (1016), which was eventually won by count Fulk Nerra of Anjou. It may be significant that the troops which he sent to assist Robert the Pious in Flanders were regarded by Ralph Glaber as being notably undisciplined, suggesting a lack of regular practice in the martial arts.[57] In terms of Normandy's external relations, Richard II's reign was most significant for the *volte-face* implied by the welcome given to king Aethelred's family, breaking previously maintained connections with the Scandinavian invaders, and instead creating an interest in the fortunes of the late Anglo-Saxon royal house. Against its northern French background, Richard II's Normandy has something of the character of a haven of peace in a very violent world, its ruler universally respected as someone who kept the peace at home and who was, in the broader context of northern French political life, a dedicated supporter of order and ecclesiastical reform.

For Robert I's reign (1027–35), it is again necessary to rely heavily on information supplied by William of Jumièges. As before, the bulk of his account is devoted to a description of the duke's wars. The greater volume of charter evidence does, however, allow a sharper critique of Jumièges' story than was possible for Richard II's reign. Five campaigns are recorded: against William de Bellême, in support of count Baldwin IV of Flanders (989–1036), in support of king Henry I, against count Alan III of Brittany (1008–40), and, abortively, in support of the claims of Edward and Alfred, two of the sons of king Aethelred, to the English kingdom.

Some of these wars represent a continuation of the policies of Richard II's reign. The sustenance given to Robert the Pious' son Henry I who had been expelled from the royal principality by a coalition headed by his mother queen Constance and Odo II of Blois-Chartres, is the most obvious example of this theme. Although Jumièges exaggerated Robert's contribution to Henry's recovery, there can be no doubt that the asylum which was given at Fécamp in 1033 provided essential relief in very desperate circumstances.[58] This same notion of duke Robert as the upholder of legitimate authority lurks behind the assistance given to his brother-in-law, count Baldwin IV of Flanders, who had been driven out by his son, later to be count Baldwin V, and also behind the encouragement given to his cousins Edward and Alfred. So proper indeed did Jumièges think Robert's support for the two young men that he was obliged to make divine intervention the reason for the rather unlikely diversion of a fleet, which was supposed to carry forces to England, from Fécamp to Mont-St-Michel. No doubt coincidentally, it proved to be useful there in a war which Robert happened to be fighting against count Alan of Brittany. Needless to say, Jumièges is the only source for this projected English expedition and the story may well be fictitious. But its basis, Robert's continuation of his father's aid to Aethelred's descendants, is testified to by other sources.[59] This support was not, however, entirely unequivocal: there was a lively exchange of illuminated manuscripts between that eleventh-century queen Gertrude, Emma, and her brother archbishop Robert of Rouen, while Emma's second husband, king Cnut, and subsequently their son, king Harthacnut (1040–42), were at least willing to implement a grant which king Aethelred had planned to make to the abbey of Fécamp, the burial-place of dukes Richard I and II.[60]

William of Jumièges' references to wars against William de Bellême and count Alan suggest that duke Robert was obliged, as his father had been, to exert himself against erosion of the Norman frontier. William de Bellême, almost all of whose lands lay outside Normandy, is quite improperly treated by Jumièges as a rebel. The immediate source of contention, so we are told, was the castle of Alençon which William had apparently been given as a benefice by duke Richard II. Since William de Bellême died in *c*. 1028, this war must have been among Robert's first actions as duke. Two campaigns reduced William to submission, but he was then allowed to retain Alençon.

Duke Robert's relative success or failure must be interpreted against the wider background of the expansion of the Bellême territory, a process which had been going on since the later tenth century.[61] The family's earliest gains had been made within the county of Maine, but mounting difficulties there, manifested most notably in the quarrels between count Herbert 'Wake-Dog' (1014/15–1032/35) and Avesgaud de Bellême, bishop of Le Mans (*c*. 1000–*c*. 1035) and brother of William de Bellême, caused some members of the family to turn their attentions towards Normandy. The acquisition of Alençon in Richard II's reign was merely one aspect of this,[62] since shortly before 1025 William de Bellême sponsored the restoration of the bishopric of Sées, in theory a Norman diocese. William's installation of new canons, the reference to the evils which the cathedral had suffered at his hands, the typically Bellême name of the presiding bishop (Sigenfrid, *c* 1017–*c* 1025), and the charter's confirmation by king Robert the Pious, all suggest a waning of Norman ducal authority in lands some way north of Alençon.[63] The grant of the *pagus* of the Hiésmois, which bordered that of Sées, to the future duke Robert at the beginning of his brother Richard III's short reign, and a campaign so early in Robert's own reign indicate that a determined attempt was made to stop the rot.

That some revival of ducal authority was achieved is confirmed by the appointment to Sées of bishop Radbod (1025–*c*. 1032), a man from the sort of family commonly advanced to the episcopate in Richard II's time (see pp. 210–11). Success seems, however, to have been brief. The number of the attestations of ducal charters by bishops of Sées during the reigns of Richard II and Robert I suggests that the diocese was never very securely integrated into Normandy.[64] Although duke Robert's demonstration may have temporarily diverted the family's aspirations back into Maine – William de Bellême's heir, Robert, was imprisoned and then killed at Ballon in 1033 – the clan were on Norman territory with a vengeance by

1035. By that date, one of William de Bellême's two surviving sons, Ivo, had assumed both the lordship of Bellême and the bishopric of Sées; the other, William Talvas, was the holder of extensive possessions in the vicinity of Sées.

Robert's wars against count Alan of Brittany appear to have been motivated by similar anxieties, but his efforts at consolidation were somewhat more successful in this sector. Jumièges reports that count Alan III was the aggressor, that Robert conducted two victorious campaigns, which were interspersed by a raid by Alan on the Avranchin, and that peace was eventually made at Mont-St-Michel under the auspices of the two adversaries' uncle, archbishop Robert of Rouen. The wars must have taken place in the early 1030s. Jumièges suggests that Alan was striving to break an obligation to serve the Norman duke, tantamount perhaps to an oath of fidelity.[65] Whatever the truth of this remark, it is certain that the good relations which had existed between count Geoffrey of Rennes and duke Richard II, and which had continued during Richard's protectorate of the young Alan, turned sour in the later 1020s. In a wider context Alan's alliance with Odo of Blois-Chartres, the enemy of the Normans' friends, the Capetian kings, may have been a factor. But the immediate focus of disagreement appears to have been the famous abbey of Mont-St-Michel, right on the frontier between the two territories, and geographically very remote from the centres of Norman ducal power. In the early eleventh century the abbey had received its most generous benefactions from the regions of Maine and Brittany. Its special significance for the counts of Rennes is demonstrated by the burial there of two counts, Conan I (died 992) and Geoffrey I (died 1008), suggesting the aim of converting it into a family mausoleum after the fashion of St-Denis for the Capetians or Fécamp for the Norman dukes.[66] None the less, duke Richard II's confirmation of the election of abbot Hildebert I at Rouen in 1009 indicates where ultimate control resided at that date.[67]

From the late 1020s, however, Breton designs seem to have been receiving encouragement from within the abbey. Abbot Almod (1027/28–33), a native of Maine, probably visited count Alan in 1030, and certainly did so in 1032: on both occasions his abbey received liberal grants. The abbey's records reveal signs of other involvements in Breton affairs at this time: it was, for example, offering military supplies and refuge in wartime to one family.[68] Its motives may not have been so blatantly treacherous as they at first sight appear, since the Norman Church was severely plundered in Robert I's early years. Mere self-preservation may have instigated the

Normandy and its neighbours

appeals to count Alan. But Robert's campaigns put a stop to whatever schemes were afoot. Norman interests were secured by the construction of a new castle just across the river Couesnon at Cherrueix, abbot Almod was moved sideways and made abbot of the recently established monastery of St-Vigor of Cerisy, and a series of generous grants were made to Mont-St-Michel.[69] For the time being, the frontier held firm.

William of Jumièges did not include what would, if it were true, rank as the one substantial territorial acquisition made by Robert I: namely, lordship over the whole of the French Vexin, which, according to Ordericus Vitalis, was granted to him by king Henry I out of gratitude for his assistance in 1033. The credibility of this statement has been much discussed. It should be rejected.[70] Both the inexplicable silence of William of Jumièges and the circumstances under which Ordericus' assertion appears make the story suspect. Jumièges is unlikely to have omitted a story which reflected so well on his hero, while Ordericus mentions the supposed grant as a justification for William the Conqueror's invasion of the Vexin in 1087, an attack which followed the Capetians' own assertion of suzerainty over the region in 1077. The documents for Robert I's reign do show strong Norman connections with the French Vexin, contacts which maintained those made under Richard II. The close friendship with Dreux, count of the Vexin, continued: he and his relations gave generously to Norman monasteries, received two estates in Normandy, and Dreux himself travelled on duke Robert's pilgrimage of 1034–35 (see p. 66).[71] Likewise, Waleran I of Meulan also kept up his Norman contacts, although these may have been much more intimate with the 'Beaumont' family than with the ducal house. Waleran's son Hugh was a boyhood companion of Roger de Beaumont and his daughter Adeline subsequently became Roger's wife. In contrast, there is a record of fighting between count Waleran and duke Robert.[72] These details do not add up to a case for overlordship along the lines suggested by Ordericus. Waleran, for example, despite his Norman connections, was also a vassal of king Henry I, of count Dreux, and, from a recent date, of Odo of Blois-Chartres.[73] In the region as a whole, count Odo was busy mopping up vassals during the 1020s. In the circumstances, it is very doubtful whether the Capetian king possessed sufficient control over the French Vexin to make such a grant, or whether duke Robert had the strength to take advantage of the gift, even if it had been made. Ordericus very probably reported a story elaborated later in order to justify William the Conqueror's claims in 1087; at best he was guilty of simplifying a

71

very complicated political situation. All that can be said with certainty is that duke Robert did acquire some influence in a region where political and personal relationships had become extremely unstable. It is, however, very unlikely that any formal grant was ever made. At most Henry I may have provided a *carte blanche* to meddle.

Taken as a whole, the record of the external relations of the Norman dukes up until 1035 is an unspectacular one. There is a consistent pattern of loyalty to the Capetians. But most of their campaigns were undertaken to plug threatening gaps in the frontier. Normandy during this period appears to have been very vulnerable to penetration from the outside, either as a result of simple aggression, or more often of a marriage or an inheritance. It looks, too, as if the dukes countered only the most severe infractions of the frontier, and as if they were quite willing to acquiesce in many of the developments which were taking place. Although the activities of the Bellême family were eventually resisted, duke Richard II appears to have approved of the arrival of the Giroie and the counts of the Vexin. A similar case occurred in Upper Normandy, where, in Richard II's time, a certain Guerenfrid is known to have held a territory which straddled the Norman frontier in the vicinity of Aumale. His daughter's marriage to Enguerrand I, who, by the time of his death in 1045, had assumed the title of count of Ponthieu, meant that from *c*. 1030 this powerful outsider had landed interests in the duchy.[74] Despite resistance to both the Giroie and the count of Ponthieu from count Gilbert of Brionne, the new arrivals seem to have been left undisturbed (see p. 64). Under both Richard II and Robert I, the dukes appear to have aimed to police serious breaches of the peace and not actively to seek to expand the Norman territory.

The military achievements of the early-eleventh-century Norman dukes are restricted ones. Robert I's victory over count Alan of Brittany scarcely compares, for example, with the buccaneering exploits of his contemporary, the young Geoffrey Martel, who was displeasing his ageing father during the 1030s by his campaigns in support of his stepson's claims to the duchy of Aquitaine, or with the ultimately disastrous attempt by count Odo II of Blois-Chartres to acquire the kingdom of Burgundy. Under both Richard II and Robert I, Normandy was very obviously an influential territorial principality, but also one which stood aside from the mêlée which had engulfed most of northern France. Under Richard II this aloofness probably derived from the internal stability which the province enjoyed; under Robert I, the cause may well have been his preoccupation with the turmoil within the duchy. It must also have been reinforced by the alliance with the Capetians and the severe fragmentation of the territories immediately adjacent to the Norman frontier, which, although it encouraged the numerous petty encroachments into the duchy, also created a sort of *cordon sanitaire* against the ambitions of the most aggressive territorial rulers. It looks very much as if Richard II succeeded in most things he undertook. It is clear, however, from cases such as the Giroie or Guerenfrid at Aumale, that the Norman frontier was being crossed by men seeking to augment their property. Robert I faced the more serious ramifications of these developments, and was not altogether successful in controlling them. When the military achievements of these rulers are placed in a northern French context, it becomes clear that an excessive concentration on the exclusively Norman literary sources, William of Jumièges and William of Poitiers, can cast a false light on their deeds. These two authors, who wrote in the 1070s, presented a story of consistent victory in war. As with Dudo, who had the tenth-century consolidation to celebrate, they too could look back on several decades of success, the military achievements of one of the most outstanding of all territorial princes, duke William II. They therefore tended to project backwards his interest in England and his expansion of the Norman lands. In fact, Richard II was a ruler of decidedly pacific tendencies and a loyal supporter of the Capetian kings. Robert I struggled manfully against internal and external disorder.

When William II became duke in 1035, he was at most eight years old. Conditions within the duchy having been fragile during his father's reign, the cohesion of Norman society collapsed almost completely while his minority endured. Amidst the murderous feuds of the aristocracy, duke William's survival remained perilous up until 1047 when, with the crucial assistance of king Henry I, he defeated a coalition comprising his own cousin, count Guy of Brionne, and a group of nobles whose power was based in Lower Normandy. This victory, at Val-ès-Dunes to the south-east of Caen, was a vital turning-point in William's career.

External relations as such were largely in abeyance during this early part of William's reign. Apart from the war of 1013-14, eleventh-century Normandy had never been the target for the ambitions of the more aggressive territorial princes. It may be that Richard II's and Robert I's basic policy of non-alignment reaped dividends during the 1030s and 1040s. In any case, the 'great powers' had other matters on their hands during William II's minority. Anjou was engaged on a course of expansion southwards into Aquitaine and northwards into Maine. Blois-Chartres meanwhile went into a decline after count Odo II had been killed at the battle of Bar in 1037. In 1044 the balance in the long-standing rivalry between Blois-Chartres and Anjou tilted sharply when Geoffrey Martel decimated the forces of Odo's sons, counts Theobald III and Stephen I, at the battle of Nouy. This was followed by a steady Angevin conquest of the Touraine and by Geoffrey Martel's visit to Rome in 1046 for the imperial coronation of his son-in-law.

With so much happening, the only outside powers to pay any attention to Normandy were count Alan III of Brittany and king Henry I. Alan's role, according to Ordericus Vitalis, was to act as the guardian of the young duke William. Alan died, possibly by poison, during the siege of Montgommery in 1040.[75] Two expeditions by Henry I into Normandy, recorded by William of Jumièges, are very difficult to reconcile with the supposed protectorate assigned to Henry by later sources, and have never been satisfactorily explained: on the first raid he captured the castle of Tillières-sur-Avre; on the second, he advanced into the Hiésmois, burnt Argentan, and then rebuilt the castle at Tillières for his own use. Many of the problems about these campaigns disappear if the idea of Henry's guardianship of the young William is forgotten, and they are seen as unsolicited interventions connected with Henry's defeat of a serious rebellion in *c.* 1041 within the Ile de France. One of his most obdurate enemies, count Waleran I of Meulan, is known to have been expelled from his estates and, from charter attestations, to have taken refuge in Normandy, where he could undoubtedly rely on a haven with his friends, the Beaumonts.[76] William of Jumièges' comment that the Normans were divided in their response to Henry's intervention would be explicable if the king's purpose was to punish a rebel and those who had given him shelter. It may not be a coincidence that two of the ducal charters which Waleran attests were also witnessed by Robert de Beaumont, son of Humphrey de Vieilles, and that one of them is also witnessed by Gilbert Crispin, a very infrequent name on such documents but the very man identified by William of Jumièges as the defender of Tillières against Henry I.[77] This explanation does not cover Henry's sack of Argentan, nor the presence of Capetian troops at Falaise. It does, however, identify good reasons for what looks like a brief punitive expedition, during the course of which he took over the embarrassing frontier castle of Tillières. Later, the succession of Angevin victories and count Guy of Brionne's direct bid for control over the duchy may well have persuaded Henry to act against the impotence of a vital northern

French ruler and to throw his weight behind William II.

After the victory at Val-ès-Dunes, duke William began to take a much more positive part in northern French politics than either his father or his grandfather had done. The character of the period up until *c.* 1060 is one of defence mixed with patient accumulation. Conditions within Normandy remained unsettled for some time after 1047. It may have taken as long as three years to eject count Guy from his castle of Brionne,[78] while the revolt by William's uncles, count William of Arques and archbishop Malger of Rouen, was in preparation from 1052 and exploded in 1053. In addition, the duke was obliged to resist two well-organised invasions: in 1053–54 a coalition, which included king Henry I, Geoffrey Martel, counts Enguerrand II and Guy I of Ponthieu, and count Ralph IV of Amiens-Valois-Vexin, was repulsed after a series of engagements; while in 1057 a second assault by Henry I and Geoffrey Martel was beaten at Varaville near Caen.

The full-scale invasion of 1053–54 constituted an especially grave threat, since William was already battling against internal opposition from his uncle, count William of Arques, who was receiving help from his brother-in-law, count Enguerrand II of Ponthieu, and indirectly from Henry I. It was the defeat and death of Enguerrand in a skirmish at St-Aubin-sur-Scie and the associated capture of the nearby castle at Arques, which provoked Henry I to assemble a large invasion force. This advanced in two columns: one, under the king, moving through the Evrecin towards Rouen, and the other, under the command of Henry's brother Odo, advancing into eastern Normandy through the region of Neufchâtel-en-Bray. Duke William led a force which moved against the king's army. The decisive engagement took place at Mortemer in February 1054 when a group of Normans, prominent among whom were count Robert of Eu, Hugh de Gournay, Walter Giffard, and William de Warenne, defeated Odo's army. This reverse prompted king Henry to retreat without offering battle. His return in 1057 was even less glorious, since duke William's force was able to effect tactical surprise as the royal army crossed the river Dives at Varaville, defeat one half, and thereby persuade Henry to abandon the venture. The two victories of Mortemer and Varaville followed defensive campaigns. Although both were probably followed by sallies into opposition territory, the overwhelming impression from what we know of the campaigns is of relatively easy penetrations by William's enemies deep into Norman territory, of encouragement and assistance from within the duchy,

Normandy before 1066

and, from William's side, of victories which came only as a result of a careful appreciation of the tactical situation. In 1054, William himself avoided fighting a pitched battle; in 1057, he carefully waited until his opponents were at a disadvantage. The smaller size of the 1057 invasion force[79] does suggest that William was gradually prevailing. None the less, his enemies gave him a hard time during the 1050s. The full power of William II's Normandy emerged out of watchful, embattled, defence.

The roots of future expansion can, none the less, all be found in the obscure years immediately after Val-ès-Dunes, a quagmire of uncertain dates and poorly recorded events. After 1047 William was free to assist Henry I in campaigns against Geoffrey Martel, taking part in the large expedition which captured the castle of Mouliherne near Angers in late 1049. Up until this point William was simply contributing to Henry's efforts to curb Angevin expansion. William himself, however, seems to have set out on his own policy of opposition to Geoffrey Martel's designs on the county of Maine from about this time. In 1051 he provided a refuge for Gervase de Chateau-du-Loir, bishop of Le Mans (1035–55), a determined opponent of the Angevins. In 1048–49, or more probably in 1051–52, he organised an expedition to take the castle of Alençon, which Geoffrey Martel had seized, and also Domfront, which lay in Maine.[80] In another direction, William's marriage to Mathilda, the daughter of count Baldwin V of Flanders, mooted by 1049 and celebrated in 1050–51, cemented a connection with the ruler of one of the strongest of the territorial principalities and may even have led to friendship with the emperor Henry III.[81] In yet another direction, earlier links with England may well have culminated in Edward the Confessor's promise of the succession to the kingdom, which was probably made in 1051.

These activities of themselves must explain the extensive opposition which had built up by 1053. William's ambitions had already demonstrated a verve absent during the reigns of all his immediate predecessors. In addition to the offence given to Geoffrey Martel, the attack on the castles of Alençon and Domfront must have alienated the family who held them, namely that of Bellême. Their chief, bishop Ivo of Sées, disappears completely from the witness-lists of Norman ducal charters during the 1050s (see p. 79). More significant, as a testimony to the effect which William's scheming produced, was the remarkable *rapprochement* between Geoffrey Martel and king Henry I, which had taken place by 15 October 1052. This ended the century-old alliance of the Capetians and the Norman rulers, a momentous change which does seem to have worried William, since he appears to have visited Henry on 20 September 1052, without any tangible result. It can only be surmised that Henry's readiness to come to terms with the count of Anjou, whose ambitions he had resolutely combated for several years, was caused by a greater anxiety about the potential effect of William's plans. This new alliance of Capetians and Angevins dominated the invasion of 1053–54. The coalition also drew in others who might well have been alarmed by the new duke's brash behaviour. Count William of Arques, a man imbued in the traditions of ducal authority as exercised by his father Richard II, may simply have lost patience (see p. 176). His family connections were in any case with others who might have something to lose from William's activities: the counts of Ponthieu may have feared for their Norman property, while Eustace, count of Boulogne, with whom count William eventually sought refuge, had a strong interest in the English succession and had himself, somewhat ignominiously, visited the kingdom in 1051.[82]

One result of the battle of Mortemer was that, for the first time, duke William's influence extended outside the duchy. The counts of Ponthieu appear to have abandoned their lands within Normandy, since they passed from Enguerrand I's widow Adelaide to her daughter of the same name, who married Odo, exiled count of Champagne. Guy I of Ponthieu was captured at Mortemer, held as a prisoner, and, after his release, became William's vassal. The narrow scrape experienced by Roger de Mortemer, who nearly lost his estates for having assisted the flight of his non-Norman lord, Ralph, count of Amiens-Valois-Vexin, must have been a warning to others against such engagements with outside powers.[83] Yet William's success was in some respects a qualified one. Henry I and Geoffrey Martel had left Normandy without hazarding battle, and, although bereft of allies, were very much alive to fight another day. Also, at least one of the threats to Upper Normandy had not been subdued. Further military activity by count Ralph of Amiens-Valois-Vexin enabled him to defeat Hugh de Grandmesnil, whom duke William had entrusted with the frontier castle of Neufmarché (Seine-Maritime, cant. Gournay), at a date between 1061 and 1066. This success must be connected either directly or indirectly with count Ralph's receipt of a life-lease on Gisors in the Vexin from archbishop Maurilius of Rouen (1054–67). Although Gisors did not yet possess its later strategic significance, since the Capetians had not yet taken over the French part of the Vexin, this was a large alienation. It may have purchased count Ralph's friendship, since he was in the party which welcomed king William back to Normandy in 1067, but Gisors was not restored to the estates of Rouen cathedral until 1075 after Ralph's death.[84] The achievement of Mortemer was essentially to remove organised internal opposition, to thwart invasion, and to create elbow-room by subduing neighbours around the limited region of Upper Normandy. William was ambitious and was playing for very high stakes. But life remained far from comfortable for the rest of the 1050s.

The hardest struggles took place on the southern borders of the duchy. Maine stayed within the firm grasp of the Angevins right up until Geoffrey Martel's death in 1060. His alliance with the Capetians permitted the 'promotion' of bishop Gervase from Le Mans to the archbishopric of Rheims in 1055, allowing his replacement by Geoffrey's protégé, Wulgrin, abbot of St-Serge of Angers. Geoffrey also kept control over the young count of Maine, Herbert II, the son of count Hugh IV who had died in 1051. Despite what the Norman sources suggest, this guardianship continued at least until 1056, and may well have gone on until the end of Geoffrey Martel's life.[85] William did no more than dent Angevin supremacy. Shortly after Mortemer he was able to erect a castle in Maine at Ambrières, some seven miles beyond the recognised Norman frontier, and beat off Geoffrey Martel's attempt to recapture the place. This victory enabled William to establish a very tenuous lordship over the man on whose lands the castle of Ambrières had been built, namely, Geoffrey de Mayenne, whose power-base was some six miles further south. William of Poitiers presented the whole story in very theatrical terms: duke William announced to Geoffrey Martel the day on which he intended to build the castle; a trembling Geoffrey de Mayenne fled to Geoffrey Martel to seek his assistance, which the count of Anjou promised in language drawn from Caesar's *Gallic Wars*.[86] A glance at the map shows how little William actually achieved. Against William of Poitiers' tale of flamboyant Norman victories, Angevin tradition recorded that Geoffrey Martel inflicted much harm on duke William during these years.[87]

A second perspective on the Norman-Angevin rivalry is provided by the history of the Bellême family during this period. Conditions on the southern limit of Normandy where their power was concentrated were very disturbed in the later 1040s and early 1050s: Ivo de Bellême, who had become bishop of Sées in c. 1035, and whose promotion to the see consolidated the family's grip in southern Normandy, was censured at the papal council of Rheims (1049) because of disorders which had led to a fire which damaged his cathedral church, while his brother William Talvas became embroiled in a war against his own son. In 1051–52, duke William repeated his father's campaign against the castle of Alençon, and subsequently extended operations against Domfront as well, but with no apparent effect on the family's political alignment, since their leader, bishop Ivo, was completely absent from the charters of the Norman duke after the 1040s. In contrast, he frequently appears in the company of Geoffrey Martel and can with confidence be identified as his ally and his vassal.[88] There are good reasons for thinking that this relationship and count Geoffrey's solid grip on the county of Maine may have at one stage threatened to extend Angevin power as far north as Sées, since a grant to the abbey of St-Vincent of Le Mans provides a clear reference to the presence of vassals of the count of Anjou at Sées.[89] The alliance between Ivo and Geoffrey was still in existence on 14 January 1056, the earliest possible date for a charter for the abbey of St-Aubin of Angers which Ivo witnessed and Geoffrey Martel confirmed.[90] It is likely to have remained active at least until the time of the battle of Varaville (1057), because the invasion force led by count Geoffrey and king Henry I entered Normandy through the district of Sées. None the less, it is clear that the town of Sées and bishop Ivo's allegiance were steadily incorporated into duke William's sphere of authority in the late 1050s. The Norman attack on the Bellême defences was spearheaded, not by William himself, but by Roger II de Montgommery, who had married Ivo's niece, Mabel de Bellême, in *c.* 1050. There was a *rapprochement* between Ivo and these two some time before ducal authority intruded itself. Bishop Ivo does in fact seem to have taken a positive decision to change sides: the battle of Varaville stands out as the most likely turning-point.

Since the course of events on this southern frontier has never been entirely clarified, it is worth spending a little time examining the evidence. The keys to the chronology are a charter, of which the original is extant, for the abbey of St-Aubin of Angers,[91] and the four versions of the *pancarte* recording the earliest grants to the abbey of St-Martin of Sées.[92] The St-Aubin charter records the gift by bishop Ivo of the church of St-Ouen of Villiers (Sarthe, cant. La Fresnaye-sur-Chédouet, comm. Roullé), a few miles east of Alençon and midway between Sées and Bellême, to St-Aubin. On internal grounds the charter cannot be dated more closely than 1051–62, but the grant clearly took place at a time when Roger de Montgommery was making his influence felt around Sées and Alençon, and while the Anjou–Bellême alliance was still in existence; its guarantors and witnesses comprise Ivo's relatives, count Geoffrey Martel (his successor, Geoffrey the Bearded, is improbable), count Herbert II of Maine, and Roger and Mabel. The first version of the St-Martin *pancarte*, which must have been drawn up a little after the time when the abbey was founded by Roger and Mabel in collaboration with bishop Ivo (before August 1057), mentions the grant of the church of St-Ouen of Villiers to this monastery. The transfer of the church from one abbey to the other cannot be interpreted otherwise than as a slap in the face for the counts of Anjou, the chief protectors and patrons of St-Aubin. It indicates the moment at which Ivo broke with Geoffrey Martel, an event which must be located between January 1056 and the first years of St-Martin's existence. The obvious time would be after the battle of Varaville. It is likely that pressure on Ivo from Normandy was building up throughout the 1050s. Roger de Montgommery seems to have become influential in the region of Sées by the middle of the decade – we know that he had to fight to establish himself there, in all probability against the followers of the late William Talvas (died ?1053), Mabel's father.

The foundation of the abbey of St-Martin a little time before 1057 was a proclamation of Roger's arrival, as well as a declaration that he intended to stay; the gift of St-Ouen of Villiers to St-Aubin most likely dates from a period of co-operation between him and Ivo around the year 1055; its re-grant to St-Martin came a little later when Ivo became certain that the Normans were winning. The initial colonisation of St-Martin with monks from St-Evroult, an abbey only seven miles to the north of Sées, is consistent with a period when Sées was still in the balance between Normandy and Bellême-Anjou, since at least one member of St-Evroult's founding family, Robert fitz Giroie, fought for Geoffrey Martel in the late 1050s.[93] It is only from the later 1050s that there are signs that bishop Ivo had started to take a part in Norman affairs; he was involved in the investiture of a new abbot of St-Evroult in *c.* 1059 in co-operation with duke William and attended the consecration of the new cathedral at Rouen in 1063.[94] The second text of the St-Martin *pancarte*, recording events which took place before 1060, and probably written before 1066, unlike the first version, mentions duke William's confirmation (*annuente Willelmo Normannorum principe*), as well as including the St-Ouen gift. This demonstrates the growing strength of ducal authority in the region by 1060, something which intensified through the 1060s, with the weakness of Geoffrey Martel's successors and the Norman conquest of Maine in 1063.

This gradual, if remorseless, penetration of Sées requires the abandonment of the oft-stated opinion that Bellême immediately came into close contact with Normandy after Roger and Mabel's marriage. As far as Bellême itself, which is outside the duchy, was concerned, nothing was entirely certain until bishop Ivo's death in c. 1070. There is simply no evidence for the exercise of ducal authority in Bellême. At a date between 1050 and 1064, Hugh de Rocé, founding the priory of St-Martin-du-Vieux-Bellême, named as his lords, count Geoffrey of Anjou, Odo the brother of king Henry I, and bishop Ivo. Much later, in 1069–70, Hugh's confirmation charter received the assent firstly of bishop Ivo and afterwards of the then Capetian king Philip I.[95] It may even be that Mabel's succession to Bellême was far from clear-cut: of two brothers of hers, one only became a monk in the abbey of Le Bec in old age and the other, a monk at St-Martin of Sées; while two nephews of bishop Ivo were alive in 1067.[96] There must have been an arrangement to regulate the succession between Ivo and his niece and her husband; Roger is known to have been active in the region of Bellême before 1068.[97]

The Norman 1050s is therefore a tale of steady but laborious progress against powerful opposition. Despite William's persistence, his enemies could launch a major invasion in 1057. The victory at Varaville secured Norman power over the Séois. It was followed by a campaign against the Capetian king. In 1058 William recovered Tillières-sur-Avre, lost during his minority, and then moved on to capture the castle of Thimert, some ten miles to the south of Dreux. Progress was not, however, very spectacular since Henry I was still maintaining a close siege of Thimert at the time of his death in 1060.[98]

The fruits of toil only came into sight with the deaths, within a few months of each other, of Henry I and Geoffrey Martel. Henry was succeeded by his infant son Philip I and Geoffrey by his nephew, Geoffrey the Bearded. Peace was quickly made between William and the Capetian, whose guardian was William's father-in-law, count Baldwin V of Flanders. Significant military progress was then made against Anjou, distracted by attacks from the south, and subsequently by the struggle for the succession between Geoffrey the Bearded and his brother Fulk Rechin. As far as Angevin power in Maine was concerned, the death of count Herbert II of Maine on 9 March 1062 prompted a crisis. William of Poitiers' story is that Herbert had fled from the Angevin domination of Maine, had done homage to duke William, and had promised that, should he die without heirs, William would receive the succession to the county. This cannot be checked against any non-Norman source; it has a suspicious ring about it, since it resembles closely the justification made for the conquest of England. William conquered Maine in 1063, meeting stiff resistance from the locals who had called in Walter, count of Mantes in the French Vexin, who had married a sister of count Hugh IV (died 1051), but little hindrance from Anjou. William had at last made a large territorial acquisition, although one whose ease needs to be set against the wider process of the fragmentation of Geoffrey Martel's enlarged principality, the first blow at which had been struck by count Guy-Geoffrey of Aquitaine's reconquest of the Saintonge in 1062. This first Norman conquest was not, however, followed by any significant colonisation of Maine. William seems to have been content to allow his eldest son Robert, who had married Margaret, Herbert II's sister, to do homage to Geoffrey the Bearded for the county and to rely for control on a local clientele. Charter evidence does, however, demonstrate that William's power in the county was very real. Also, in 1065 when the bishopric of Le Mans became vacant, he was able to press a Norman who was a member of the Le Mans chapter into office against count Geoffrey's wishes.

One final aspect of William's activities in northern France was his steady extension of his power on the Breton frontier. There was a very effective consolidation on the Norman side of the line. A castle was built at St-James-de-Beuvron, some nine miles east of the Couesnon. In *c.* 1060 the frontier *comté* of Mortain was conferred on William's half-brother Robert, replacing count William Werlenc, and seemingly enjoying the sort of licence which had allowed Roger de Montgommery to advance southwards at the expense of non-Norman neighbours.[99] Tough treatment was also meted out on the monks of Mont-St-Michel, who, having received liberal gifts from duke Robert I, appear to have burnt their fingers again by becoming involved in the rebellion of 1047. A notice in the twelfth-century cartulary of the abbey records a list of properties which William removed from the estates of the abbey, many of them the grants which his father had made. The abbot, Suppo, packed his bags and went home to Frutturia near Turin. A long tradition of internal appointments to the abbacy was brought to an end, and the monks found themselves under the rule of Ralph 'de Beaumont', a man from a family renowned for its loyalty to duke William.[100] At the same time, a pattern developed whereby landholders in eastern Brittany acquired properties across the Norman frontier. It is generally impossible to know whether these had initially been encroachments of the kind which had taken place in other sectors of the Norman frontier, or whether they were a part of deliberate ducal policy. William was, however, strong enough to assert his lordship over any intruders: Maino de Fougères (Ille-et-Vilaine), who held in Normandy at Savigny-le-Vieux (Manche, cant. Le Tilleul), acknowledged that this was a benefice held of the duke at a date between *c*. 1050 and 1064.[101] Norman property was sometimes deliberately conferred in order to build up an interest group: count Alan the Red, nephew of count Alan III (died 1040), held a church in Rouen up until 1067, while, in a much more explicit case, duke William granted tithes on a property belonging to the abbey of St-Ouen of Rouen to Juthael, bishop of Dol (1039–76) and a certain Hugh.[102] The whole operation is a splendid example of the extension of influence through the attraction of men's loyalty. Many of William's protégés, who tended to come from eastern Brittany and from the family of count Eudo de Penthièvre, the brother of Alan III, subsequently received estates in England.

Duke William's web did not, however, ensnare the most important Breton, namely, count Conan II (1040–66 – effectively, 1057–66), Alan III's son and heir. William indeed failed before 1066 to renew the superiority over the Breton counts which had apparently existed up until 1040: William of Jumièges wrote as if Alan III had been a vassal of duke Robert I, and Geoffrey I may well have been one of Richard II.[103] This relationship lapsed after 1040, since Eudo de Penthièvre, who had been Conan II's guardian, was free from all lordship, and Conan himself is said by William of Poitiers to have denied Norman superiority in precisely the same way that duke William had denied that of the Capetians.[104] A war was fought against Conan in either 1064 or 1065, in response to a summons from one of William's Breton supporters, Rivallon de Dol. The campaign, involving the relief of Conan's siege of Dol and a subsequent attack on Dinan, was directed against the young count's mounting assault on the Norman preponderance in eastern Brittany. Up to a point it may have succeeded since Conan was diverted towards the easier pickings of Geoffrey the Bearded's Anjou. But it did not prevent Conan from avenging himself on Rivallon de Dol, nor did it force Conan to swear homage.[105]

It is the interest in English affairs which distinguishes the policies of the Norman dukes from those of most of their neighbours. The simple fact of geography which gave their territory a long coastline facing England meant that their ambitions could realistically assume a dimension which might attract other maritime powers, but which would not be available to a ruler such as the count of Anjou. Connections between Normandy and England had existed in the tenth century with the frequent movement of settlers from one area to the other. Dudo of St-Quentin, with his customary penchant for the most unreasonable of stories, even recorded a tradition that Rollo had been granted half of England.[106] Edward the Confessor, cherished by Richard II and Robert I and restored peacefully to the English kingship in 1042, is supposed to have promised the succession to duke William in 1051, and to have confirmed this through the embassy of Harold, earl of Wessex, in either 1064 or 1065. The historical controversy about the relative value of Harold's and William's claims is littered with almost as many corpses as was the field of Hastings. The sources are almost exclusively Norman and present problems which, because they are so one-sided, are never likely to be resolved. The most eloquent account, that of William of Poitiers, advances a case which included devices very similar to those employed to justify the conquest of Maine, and is, at a number of points, illogical. It invites distrust. The sharpest recent commentaries continue to find fresh clues in the sparse evidence: it is possible, for example, that the designers of the pro-Norman Bayeux Tapestry were not as certain as their Norman patrons would have wanted them to have been about the purpose of earl Harold's mission of 1064/65, and that sources close to Harold's family were obliged to conceal the fact that no clear death-bed bequest had been made in his favour.[107]

It is, however, almost unhistorical to seek definitive law in such a matter in an age when very many successions provoked disputes, and where what was customary was so uncertain. William's claim to the English kingdom was merely one specimen of a very common breed: among many, king Robert the Pious tried in 1002 to take the duchy of Burgundy as the nephew of the deceased duke Henry against the claims of Odo-William, count of Mâcon, Henry's adopted son and designated heir; while in the years after 1019 Odo of Blois-Chartres and king Robert contested the county of Troyes, to which both had a distant claim; and subsequently, count Odo turned his attention to the kingdom of Burgundy which he claimed as the nephew of king Ralph III against the emperor Conrad II, the husband of the dead king's niece and his nominated heir. Vague, indeed unformulated, rules of succession, coupled with the extreme instability of social structures in general, lay behind most of these adventures. With the aid of a tame apologist like William of Poitiers, many of these enterprises could undoubtedly have been written up as heroic campaigns in pursuit of justice. Instead, there was only the simple statement in the tract written by count Fulk Rechin of Anjou that his grandfather Fulk Nerra 'took Maine'.[108] None the less, Fulk

Rechin himself, in 1068, having usurped Anjou from his brother, was soon describing himself as Geoffrey Martel's designated successor and his heir 'by hereditary right'.[109] What mattered in 1066 was that William believed himself to have a claim worth pursuing.

CONCLUSIONS

The history of pre-1066 Normandy's external relations falls into four phases: the stability of Richard II's time which can also be defined as a continuation of the consolidation during the second part of Richard I's reign, the relative ineffectuality of Robert I in the face of a number of aggressive neighbours, the weakness of William II's minority, and the inexorable drive towards expansion characteristic of his maturity. Through the period as a whole the province evolved a distinct territorial identity, as all the dukes emphasised their status as territorial princes and ruled in an increasingly effective independence of external authority. In this process, William II's reign constitutes a second and much sharper phase: the definition of the frontier becomes much clearer, the assertion of autonomy more strident, and the concentration on exclusively Norman interests more blatant.

Normandy's originality is clarified by a brief glance at the history of other principalities. The weakening of the links between monarchy and the principalities was a development which applied to the whole of France: geographical proximity sustained some scraps of authority in the North which faded out elsewhere. The Norman rulers were relatively slow to defy the Capetians openly, but, by the same token, the complete exclusion of royal authority from the duchy after 1006 is an exceptional demonstration of princely autonomy. This suggests firstly that the Norman rulers were remarkably successful as state-builders, an achievement which is reflected in the province's very clear territorial identity; something rivalled only by Flanders, which was called 'Flanders' from a date earlier than 'Normandy' in the tenth century. Anjou, in contrast, only sustained a definite identity during Geoffrey Martel's rule, while it has been doubted whether Blois-Chartres possessed sufficient cohesion even to be regarded as a true territorial principality.[110] The second important general observation is that the drive towards military expansion came much later in the duchy than it had done in the territories of other rulers. Up until the 1050s, the Norman rulers were rarely more than an audience to the struggles of the military powers – just occasionally they aspired to the status of umpire. From *c.* 1050 duke William II made slow progress against determined opponents up until 1060, thereafter breaking through to major triumphs only after the deaths of his strongest competitors. These two features – sustained stability and delayed military organisation and expansion – are fundamental to the so-called 'Norman Achievement'. They can only be explored by an examination of the internal evolution of the province.

NOTES

1. See the survey by Elizabeth Hallam, 'The king and the princes in eleventh-century France', *BIHR*, liii (1980), 143–56. The fundamental study of eleventh-century Capetian government is J. -F. Lemarignier, *Le gouvernement royal aux premiers temps capétiens* (Paris, 1965). On all matters the new book on the Capetians by Elizabeth Hallam, *Capetian France, 987–1328* (London, 1980), provides essential background.
2. The continuity of families from the Carolingian period was first proposed by K. F. Werner, 'Untersuchungen zur Frühzeit des französischen-Fürstentums', *Die Welt als Geschichte*, xviii (1958), 256–89; xix (1959), 146–93; xx (1960), 87–119. It has been reiterated for Anjou by O. Guillot, *Le comte d'Anjou et son entourage au XIe siècle* (Paris, 1972), i, p. VIII; and established for Flanders by E. Warlop, *The Flemish Nobility before 1300* (Kortrijk, 1975–76), i, 21–52. See also, J. Boussard, 'L'origine des familles seigneuriales dans la région de la Loire moyenne', CCM, v, 303–22.
3. On this, G. Duby, 'Lineage, nobility and knighthood: the Mâconnais in the twelfth century – a revision', and 'The structure of kinship and nobility. Northern France in the eleventh and twelfth centuries', in *The Chivalrous Society*, trans. C. Postan (London, 1977), 64–75, 134–48. For some general remarks, T. Reuter (ed.), *The Medieval Nobility* (Amsterdam, New York, and Oxford, 1978), 6–7; L. Génicot, 'Recent research on the medieval nobility', *ibid.*, 27. For more controversial arguments, K. Schmid, 'The structure of the nobility in the earlier Middle Ages', *ibid.*, 37–59.
4. J. -F. Lemarignier, 'La dislocation du "pagus" et le problème des "consuetudines" (Xe–XIe siècles)', *Mélanges Louis Halphen* (Paris, 1951), 401–10.
5. G. Duby, *La société aux XIe et XIIe siècles dans la région mâconnaise* (Paris, 1953). For a brief *exposé* of the point under discussion, *idem*, 'Structures familiales aristocratiques en France du XIe siècle en rapport avec les structures de l'état', in *L'Europe aux IXe–XIe siècles*, ed. A. Giesztor and T. Manteuffel (Warsaw, 1968), 57–62.
6. Warlop, *The Flemish Nobility*, i, 90.
7. J. Boussard, 'Services féodaux, milices et mercenaires dans les armées, en France, aux Xe et XIe siècles', *Settimane di Centro Italiano*..., xv (1968), 148–51, 158–63.

8. There is a large literature on this subject. For a recent survey in English, Génicot, in *The Medieval Nobility*, ed. Reuter, 17–35, and especially, 25–8. Also essential are G. Duby, 'The origins of knighthood', in *The Chivalrous Society*, 158–70; idem, 'Lineage, nobility and knighthood. The Mâconnais in the twelfth century – a revision', *ibid.*, 75–9. See note 17 below.
9. G. Devailly, *Le Berry du Xe siècle au milieu du XIIIe siècle* (Paris, 1973), 187–90; J. -P. Poly, *La Provence et la société féodale, 879–1166* (Paris, 1976), 137–41.
10. G. Duby, 'The origins of a system of social classification', *The Chivalrous Society*, 88–93.
11. *The Letters and Poems of Fulbert of Chartres*, ed. F. Behrends (Oxford, 1976), no. 51.
12. B. S. Bachrach, 'Toward a reappraisal of William the Great, duke of Aquitaine', *Journal of Medieval History*, v (1979), 11–21; Guillot, *Le comte d'Anjou*, i, 428–9.
13. For a good survey, H. E. J. Cowdrey, 'The Peace and the Truce of God in the eleventh century', *Past and Present*, no. 46 (1970), 42–67.
14. The material is analysed by Devailly, *Le Berry*, 142–8.
15. These changes form the substance of Lemarignier, *Gouvernement royal*, *passim*. Guillot's study of Anjou propounds similar ideas in a different way. For a general treatment, K. F. Werner, 'Kingdom and principality in twelfth-century France', in *The Medieval Nobility*, ed. Reuter, especially 249–61. An early essay on the same theme within a limited region is, L. Génicot, 'Noblesse et principautés en Lotharingie du XIe au XIIIe siècle', in *Scrinium Lovaniense. Mélanges historiques Etienne van Cauwenbergh* (Louvain, 1961), 191–206.
16. A point forcefully argued by Guillot, *Le comte d'Anjou*, i, pp. VIII–XII, 299–352.
17. Duby, *The Chivalrous Society*, 161–5. Also, R. Fossier, 'Chevalerie et noblesse au Ponthieu aux XIe et XIIe siècles', in *Etudes de civilisation médiévale, IXe–XIIe siècles. Mélanges offerts à E. -R. Labande* (Poitiers, 1974), 297–306; M. Bur, *La formation du comté de Champagne, v. 950–v. 1150* (Nancy, 1977), 416–21; Warlop, *The Flemish Nobility*, i, 55–70, 90–101.
18. For Odo, L. Lex, 'Eudes, comte de Blois, de Tours, de Chartres, de Troyes, et de Meaux (995–1037) et Thibaud, son frère (995–1004)', *Mémoires de la société académique d'agriculture, des sciences, arts, et belles-lettres du département de l'Aube*, 3e série, xxviii (Troyes, 1891), 231–4; R. Poupardin, *Le royaume de Bourgogne (888–1038)* (Paris, 1907), 145–71. For William V, *The Letters and Poems of Fulbert of Chartres*, nos. 111, 113.
19. J. Dhondt, 'Une crise du pouvoir capétien, 1032–1034', in *Miscellanea Mediaevalia in memoriam J. F. Niermeyer* (Groningen, 1967), 147–8.
20. See, for example, *Recueil*, no. 15; *Adhémar de Chabannes, Chronique*, ed. J. Chavanon (Paris, 1897), 148.
21. *Recueil*, no. 137; *Recueil des chartes de l'abbaye de St-Benoît-sur-Loire*, ed. M. Prou and A. Vidier (Paris, 1908–12), i, no. 58; BN, MS. latin 12878, fo. 230r; T. Stapleton, 'Observations on the history of Adeliza, sister of William the Conqueror', *Archaeologia*, xxvi (1836), 358.

22. 'Inventio et Miracula sancti Wulfranni', ed. Dom J. Laporte, *SHN, Mélanges*, xiv (1938), 27.
23. K. F. Werner, 'Quelques observations au sujet des débuts du "duché de Normandie, *Etudes... Yver*, 708–9. For *regnum* applied to Normandy, *Recueil*, nos. 61, 67, 74, 92, 95, 122, 158; Durand of Troarn, 'Liber de corpore et sanguine Domini', *PL*, cxlix, col. 142.
24. For the title *dux/comes Normanniae*, *Recueil*, nos. 15, 18, 104, 159, 185, 218, of which all except no. 104, which was written in the late 11th century, are originals. On the coinage, see now Françoise Dumas, 'Les monnaies normandes du Xe–XIIe siècle', *Bulletin de la société française de numismatique* (1978), 390. Note, *juxta morem patriae nostrae*, *Recueil*, no. 85.
25. *Ibid.*, no. 137.
26. Richard II: *Recueil*, nos. 18, 20, 23, 29, 32, 86. For the many references to his generosity, *Documents de l'histoire de la Normandie*, ed. M. de Bouard (Toulouse, 1972), 82–5. For Robert I: *Recueil*, no. 86; *Recueil des chartes de l'abbaye de St–Benoît-sur-Loire*, i, no. 58. For William II: *Recueil*, nos. 141, 150, 151, 160, 161, 199, 228.
27. *Nécrologe-obituaire de la cathédrale du Mans*, ed. G. Busson and A. Ledru (Le Mans, 1906), 238; 'Chronicon abbatum Majoris Monasterii', in *Recueil des chroniques de Touraine*, ed. A. Salmon (Tours, 1854), 318; *Self and Society in Medieval France. The Memoirs of Abbot Guibert of Nogent (1064–c. 1125)*, trans. J. F. Benton (New York and Evanston, 1970), 228.
28. L. Musset, 'Les destins de la propriété monastique durant les invasions normandes (IXe–XIe s.). L'exemple de Jumièges', *Jumièges. Congrès scientifique du XIIIe centenaire* (Rouen, 1955), i, 53–4.
29. See, in general, Hallam, 'The king and the princes', 143–56.
30. *The Letters and Poems of Fulbert of Chartres*, 152. See also, *Cartulaire de l'abbaye de St-Père de Chartres*, ed. B. E. C. Guérard (Paris, 1840), i, 112; Lemarignier, *Gouvernement royal*, 50.
31. *Recueil*, no. 59.
32. ... *Rodbertum per debitum fidei petens sibi ab eo subveniri*, WJ, 105.
33. ... *comitem Guillelmum suum nec amicum nec militem, sed hostem esse; Normanniam quae sub regibus Francorum egit ex antiquo, prope in regnum evectam; superiorum ejus comitum, quamquam arduo valuerint, nullum in haec ausa illatum*, WP, 66.
34. Raoul Glaber, *Les cinq livres de ses histoires (990–1044)*, ed. M. Prou (Paris, 1886), 108.
35. ... *inter quem et principem nostrum firma pax composita est ac serena amicitia*, WP, 82–4. See the basic work on the whole subject, F. Lot, *Fidèles ou vassaux?* (Paris, 1904), 200.
36. *Anglo-Saxon Chronicle*, 'D', 1079, translated in *English Historical Documents*, ii, ed. D. C. Douglas and G. W. Greenaway (London, 1953), 159. On Robert's designation, see now R. H. C. Davis, 'William of Jumièges, Robert Curthose and the Norman succession', *EHR*, xcv (1980), 597–606.
37. *Willelmi Malmesbiriensis Monachi, De Gestis Regum Anglorum*, ed. W. Stubbs (Rolls Series, 1887–89), ii, 285–7.

38. 'Chronicon Petri filii Bechini', in *Recueil des chroniques de Touraine*, 55.
39. *Historia Anglorum: The History of the English by Henry, Archdeacon of Huntingdon*, ed. T. Arnold (Rolls Series, 1879), 189–90; *Chronique de Robert de Torigni, abbé du Mont-Saint-Michel*, ed. L. Delisle (Rouen, 1872–73), i, 40.
40. H. Navel, 'L'enquête de 1133 sur les fiefs de l'évêché de Bayeux', *BSAN*, xlii (1935), 14.
41. Both motives are suggested for William fitz Osbern's expedition by William of Malmesbury, *De Gestis Regum Anglorum*, ii, 314–15.
42. References to Robert's charter, *Recueil*, no. 9, p. 79.
43. The details of the family's property can be built up from *Recueil*, no. 202; *AAC*, nos. 8, 11; *Cartulaire de l'abbaye de Saint-Martin de Pontoise*, ed. J. Depoin (Pontoise, 1895), 343–4.
44. The documentation is extensive. The general point is well made by L. Musset, 'La vie économique de l'abbaye de Fécamp sous l'abbatiat de Jean de Ravenne (1028–1078)', in *L'abbaye bénédictine de Fécamp*, i (Fécamp, 1959), 69.
45. For the Bellêmes and Normandy, see pp. 68–70, 78–81. The story of the Giroie can be built up from OV, ii, 14, 22–30, 78–80.
46. OV, ii, 12, 24. Enguerrand's attestation of ducal charters points to the same conclusion, *Recueil*, nos. 80, 85.
47. *Ibid.*, no. 225.
48. L. Musset, 'Observations sur l'histoire et la signification de la frontière normande (Xe–XIIe siècles)', *RHDFE*, 4e série, xli (1963), 546. Although 11th-century documents refer only infrequently to the mint from which coin originated, the cartularies of Mont-St-Michel and St-Martin of Sées suggest that Le Mans money was common. See also, T. N. Bisson, *Conservation of Coinage: Monetary Exploitation and its Restraint in France, Catalonia, and Aragon (c. A.D. 1000–c. 1225)* (Oxford, 1979), 19–20.
49. OV, iv, 88.
50. WJ, 72–3; *Raoul Glaber*, 20. Also, *christianissimum comitem ... Richardum*, *ibid.*, 75.
51. On this war, L. Musset, 'Actes inédits du XIe siècle. III. Les plus anciennes chartes normandes de l'abbaye de Bourgueil', *BSAN*, liv (1959, for 1957–58), 43–5.
52. For Dreux, the first of whose grants to a Norman abbey dates from 1024, F. Lot, *Etudes critiques sur l'abbaye de St-Wandrille* (Paris, 1913), pièces justificatives, no. 7; A.D. Seine-Maritime, 14 H, 805; *Recueil*, no. 63. For Waleran, *ibid.*, no. 25.
53. *Raoul Glaber*, 42; *Gesta Episcoporum Cameracensium*, in *MGH, Scriptores*, vii, 414, 452.
54. *The Letters and Poems of Fulbert of Chartres*, no. 86.
55. J.-F. Lemarignier, 'Paix et réforme monastique en Flandre et en Normandie autour de l'année 1023', *Etudes ... Yver*, 444–6.
56. R. Louis, 'Les ducs de Normandie dans les chansons de geste', *Byzantion*, xxviii (1958), 411–18.
57. *Raoul Glaber*, 43.
58. On these events, Dhondt, *Miscellanea ... Niermeyer*, 137–48.

59. E.g. *Recueil*, nos. 69, 70, 73, 76, 85.
60. OV, ii, 42; C. H. Haskins, 'A charter of Canute for Fécamp', *EHR*, xxxiii (1918), 342–4.
61. The family has been studied frequently, but a definitive treatment is badly needed. See, for now, G. H. White, 'The first House of Bellême', *TRHS*, 4th series, xxii (1940), 67–99; J. Boussard, 'La seigneurie de Bellême aux Xe et XIe siècles', *Mélanges Louis Halphen*, 43–54. Indispensable is OV, ii, Appendix I.
62 WP, 42, relying, as he admits, on oral testimony, attributes the foundation of the castle to duke Richard II. Since Alençon is some way south of Sées, there is a strong possibility that Poitiers was making a ducal castle out of what was in fact an independent fortification. His inclusion of the castle of Domfront in the same sentence increases the possibility. See, Guillot, *Le comte d'Anjou*, i, 70, note 313.
63. *Recueil*, no. 33.
64. Bishops of Sées witness only five known charters of Richard II and Robert I, *Recueil*, nos. 17, 33, 35, 51, 64. The next most infrequent attestors among the bishops are Coutances and Evreux with twelve and thirteen respectively.
65. *a ducis Rodberti servitio se surripere pertinaciter est aggressus*, WJ, 105.
66. For the benefactions, see p. 33, the burials, GC, xi, col. 514.
67. *Recueil*, no. 12. Richard was of course exercising a protectorate over Brittany at this time.
68. Avranches, Bibliothèque municipale, MS. 210, fos. 40r–42r, 46r–47r, 47rv.
69. *Recueil*, no.73. The grant included half the island of Guernsey.
70. For the most recent critique, OV, iv, pp. xxxii, 76.
71. For the grants, *Chronique de Robert de Torigni*, i, 33, a late source which is confirmed by other evidence.
72. *Chartes de l'abbaye de Jumièges (v. 825 à 1204) conservées aux archives de la Seine-Inférieure*, ed. J. J. Vernier (Rouen and Paris, 1916), i, no. 16.
73. Lemarignier, *Gouvernement royal*, 62, note 93.
74. The course of events suggested here is based on information in the neglected text of the earliest version of the *pancarte* of the college of secular canons at Auchy-lès-Aumale. This is printed by Stapleton, 'Adeliza', *Archaeologia*, xxvi, 358–60, apparently from an original text which has since disappeared, and by E. Sémichon, *Histoire de la ville d'Aumale* (Paris and Rouen, 1862), i, 391–3. The sole surviving MS. now seems to be a seventeenth-century copy in A.D. Seine-Maritime, 1 H, l. The *pancarte* contains information on the benefactions of Enguerrand II and Adelaide which was omitted from the late-11th-century *pancarte*, printed by L. Musset, 'Recherches sur les communautés de clercs séculiers en Normandie au XIe siècle', *BSAN*, xlv (1961, for 1959–60), 32–5.
75. Ordericus, interpolating WJ, 194; OV, ii, 304; iii, 88; iv, 76; *Recueil*, no. 97. The basic account of Normandy's external relations under duke William is D. C. Douglas, *William the Conqueror* (London, 1964), 44–80, 173–5. See also, J. Dhondt, 'Les relations entre la France et la Normandie sous Henri Ier', *Normannia*, xii (1939), 465–86.

76. *Les miracles de St-Benoît,* ed. E. de Certain (Paris, 1858), 251; *Recueil,* nos. 104, 105, 107.
77. *Ibid.,* no. 105. No. 107 is also relevant, if as seems likely it is a charter in which two witness-lists have been conflated.
78. The figure of three years comes from OV, vi, 210, which refers to Guy's stand at Vernon and Brionne. To read this as indicating that the siege of Brionne lasted for three years may be excessively rigid. WJ, 124, says that Guy was starved out and mentions elaborate siege-works.
79. WP, 80.
80. On the dates of these campaigns, see Appendix A.
81. On the marriage, Douglas, *William the Conqueror,* 391–2; Guillot, *Le comte d'Anjou,* i, 78–9.
82. For Eustace's interest in the English succession, F. Barlow, *Edward the Confessor* (London, 1970), 307–8.
83. These results are described in OV, iv, 88. For the documents on which the descent of Adelaide's lands is based, above, note 74.
84. WP, 260; OV, ii, 130, 198. Ralph's lease on Gisors is described in a charter whose transmission presents problems. There is a French translation by Dom F. Pommeraye, *Histoire de l'église cathédrale de Rouen* (Rouen, 1686), 569–70. I have so far located only a nineteenth-century copy of the Latin text by Achille Deville, BN, MS. nouvelles acquisitions latines 1243, fo. 161r, no. CXIII ('Archives de la Seine-Inférieure. Copie d'après l'originale'). Form and language are entirely acceptable.
85. For a statement that the Angevin tutelage over Maine lasted for ten years, *Actus pontificum Cenomannis in urbe degentium,* ed. G. Busson and A. Ledru (Le Mans, 1902), 366. It is not clear whether this tutelage was exercised continuously over count Herbert. See, Guillot, i, 80–1, 85–7.
86. WP, 74–80.
87. 'Chronica de gestis consulum Andegavorum', in *Chroniques des comtes d'Anjou et des seigneurs d'Amboise,* ed. L. Halphen and R. Poupardin (Paris, 1913), 62.
88. The conclusions of Guillot, *Le comte d'Anjou,* i, 82–5, can be expressed even more strongly. The charter, *Recueil,* no. 131, from which he concludes that Ivo appears in the duke's entourage in 1053 is a very insecure text. It survives only in a mediocre 18th-century copy whose witness-list includes, among others, count Guy of Brionne, and is not compatible with the date of 1053.
89. *Cartulaire de l'abbaye de St-Vincent du Mans,* ed. R. Charles and M. le vicomte Menjot d'Elbenne (Le Mans, 1913), no. 545.
90. *Cartulaire de l'abbaye de St-Aubin d'Angers,* ed. A. Bertrand de Broussillon (Paris, 1903), i, no. 287; Guillot, ii, 145, no. C214.
91. *Cartulaire de l'abbaye de St-Aubin d'Angers,* ii, no. 941; Guillot, ii, 153–4, no. C230.
92. I am grateful to M. Jean Gourhand, archivist of the Département of Orne, for supplying a microfilm of this manuscript. The 13th–14th-century cartulary of the abbey of St-Martin of Sées is preserved in the Bibliothèque de l'évêché at Sées. For my comments on this manuscript and on this phase of the history of the Montgommery-Bellême family, I am deeply indebted to the work of my student Mrs Kathleen Thomp-

son. The first version of the *pancarte* (c. 1055–57?) appears on fo. 7rv, the second (*c.* 1055–pre-1066?) on fos. 8v–9r, the third (post-1066) on fos. 9v–10v, and the fourth (*c.* 1077–*c.* 1082) in sequence on fos. 7v, 13rv, 8r (the folios have at some stage been incorrectly bound). A detailed commentary will appear in Kathleen Thompson's University of Wales Dissertation to be submitted for the degree of M.A.
93. OV, ii, 46–8, 66–8.
94. OV, ii, 74; *Acta Archiepiscopum Rotomagensium*, *PL*, cxlvii, col. 278.
95. *Cartulaire de Marmoutier pour le Perche*, ed. l'abbé Barret (Mortagne, 1894), no. 5; *Recueil des actes de Philippe Ier, roi de France, (1059–1108)*, ed. M. Prou (Paris, 1908), no. 50. For the received view, Douglas, *William the Conqueror*, 60–1. Marjorie Chibnall is rightly much more cautious, OV, ii, 362–5.
96. OV, ii, 363–4; Cartulaire de St-Martin de Sées, fo. 99v; *Recueil des actes de Philippe Ier*, no. 50.
97. *Cartulaire de l'abbaye de St-Vincent du Mans*, no. 769.
98. Douglas, *William the Conqueror*, 74.
99. For the date, I. N. Soulsby, 'The fiefs in England of the Counts of Mortain, 1066–1106' (University of Wales M.A. Thesis, 1974), 5–9. For the territorial gains, J. Boussard, 'Le comté de Mortain au XIe siècle', *Le Moyen Age*, lviii (1952), 274.
100. *Recueil*, no. 111; Avranches, Bibliothèque municipale, MS. 210, fos. 106v–107r. See, in general, J. J. G. Alexander, *Norman Illumination at Mont-Saint-Michel* (Oxford, 1970), 8–15; Dom J. Laporte, 'L'abbaye du Mont-St–Michel aux Xe et XIe siècles', *Millénaire monastique de Mont-St-Michel*, i (1967), 72–6.
101. *Recueil*, no. 162. See, in general, L. Musset, 'Aux origines de la féodalité normande: l'installation par les ducs de leurs vassaux normands et bretons dans le comté d'Avranches (XIe siècle)', *RHDFE*, 4er série, xxix (1951), 150.
102. Cartulaire de Saint-Ouen pour la Forêt-Verte, A.D. Seine-Maritime, 14 H, 18, p. 230; Dom F. Pommeraye, *Histoire de l'abbaye de St-Ouen de Rouen* (Rouen, 1662), 420–1.
103. WJ, 105–6, 110.
104. OV, iii, 88. The language employed by William of Poitiers is important: *Paternae dehinc rebellionis renovator, Normanniae hostis, non miles, esse voluit*, WP, 104.
105. OV, ii, 350–2, for an admission of William's failure. WP, 106–12, is the main source for the campaign. It is obvious that Conan deliberately avoided a battle, which might have been decisive. See, A. Le Moyne de la Borderie, *Histoire de la Bretagne*, iii (Rennes and Paris, 1899), 16–21.
106. Dudo of St-Quentin, *De moribus et actis primorum Normanniae Ducum*, ed. J. Lair (Caen, 1865), 147–8, 158–60.
107. The most impressive new ideas are those presented by N. P. Brooks and the late H. E. Walker, 'The authority and interpretation of the Bayeux Tapestry', in *Proceedings of the Battle Conference on Anglo-Norman Studies, i (1978)*, ed. R. Allen Brown (Ipswich, 1979), 10–13. The most recent general treatments, which reach very different conclusions, are, Barlow, *Edward the Confessor*, 220–9, 249–53; E. John, 'Edward the Confessor and the Norman succession', *EHR*, xciv (1979), 258–67.

108. *Ipse* (Fulk) *enim adquisivit Cenomannicum pagum et adjunxit eum Andegavino consulatui*, 'Fragmentum historiae Andegavensis', in *Chroniques des comtes d'Anjou*, 233–4.
109. Guillot, *Le comte d'Anjou*, i, 103, note 460. An original charter for the abbey of Jumièges says that duke Richard III *jure hereditario fratri suo Rodberto . . . reliquit*, *Recueil*, no. 74. Robert was accused of poisoning his brother, who left an illegitimate son, Nicholas. If there was scandal, it was pushed under the carpet.
110. Ganshof, in *Histoire des institutions françaises au Moyen Age*, i, 346, 365–6; Guillot, *Le comte d'Anjou*, i, 356–66.

CHAPTER THREE
Economy and social structure

Normandy's internal history before 1066 can be divided into three phases: one of peace and stability up until Richard II's death in 1026, one of disorder during Robert I's reign and the minority of William II, and a third period dominated by the reimposition of order in the years after William's victory at Val-ès-Dunes in 1047. It is inevitable that any study of the structural changes behind these phases will concentrate on the aristocracy, the chief participants in events and the cutting-edge of the Norman exploits in both southern Italy and England. It is important, however, to grasp something of the nature of Norman society as a whole; not so much the physical conditions under which the peasantry lived – these are irretrievably buried in the mists of time – as the characteristics of their tenures and of the powers which the lords wielded over them.

Social change within the duchy ought to follow the same basic patterns as elsewhere in northern France: the terminology employed in the documents is essentially the same as that used in neighbouring regions; those estates which it has been possible to trace through the period of invasion and settlement had usually retained their Carolingian boundaries. It is therefore no surprise to discover that the fortunes of the peasantry of Normandy conform in general terms to what has been demonstrated elsewhere. Slavery of the kind known in the Carolingian period had largely disappeared in the duchy by the eleventh century, a pattern of change shared with most of northern and western France. This shift away from a domestic labour force towards an economy based on the interdependence of seigneurial demesne and small peasant holdings is usually associated with the effects of the expanding economy which was prevalent everywhere in eleventh-century France.[1] The Norman peasantry was, however, unusual in that it continued to be described until the very late eleventh century in an archaic terminology which drew distinctions between wealthy and less burdened peasants such as *alodarii* or *liberi homines* and their social inferiors who were known by terms like *rustici, villani*, or *bordarii*.[2] This conservatism suggests that the peasantry's subjection to a stricter manorial regime of demesne and peasant holdings came at a date which was late relative to the rest of northern France; there are analogies here with the peasantry of eastern England who likewise resided within an exceptionally 'free' and fluid social structure. The persistence in Normandy of this varied terminology suggests that the extension of powers of lordship over the class of small 'free' landed proprietors was somewhat retarded within the duchy in comparison to what happened in neighbouring regions. This in turn points to a late evolution of the type of social structure which is frequently referred to as 'feudal'; that is, one associated with the spread of well-formed institutions of lordship and vassalage within a dominant military élite. The problem as a whole is, of course, one which has constantly preoccupied historians of early medieval Europe. Normandy, in general terms, would seem to possess close analogies with more conservative lands such as the Empire.

The study of Norman society raises difficult and sometimes insuperable problems. Above all the historian is hampered by the appalling lack of tenth-century information, a barrenness unparalleled elsewhere even in this dark documentary age. Social change over the entire period from 911 to 1066 is therefore exceptionally difficult to chart. What is particularly perplexing is that the decades when documentation becomes available in usable quantities – that is, from the 1020s onwards – are the same ones during which violent changes were taking place within Norman society. Attempts to breach this 'documentary barrier' and thereby ascertain the relationship between Norman society in the tenth century and in the eleventh have produced two received generalisations: the basic continuity of rural society over the whole period and the emergence of a 'new aristocracy' during the second quarter of the eleventh century. These are sufficiently contradictory to cause concern and to call for a fresh examination of the evidence.

ECONOMIC CONDITIONS

An English student of the Norman economy must immediately la-ment that there is no Norman equivalent of 'Domesday Book'. This said, however, the available charters and chronicles do at least provide the sort of vignette which suggests a thriving and varied economic life. A collection of miracles compiled at the abbey of St-Wandrille mentions a ship travelling with a cargo of grain from the estuary of the river Orne in Lower Normandy to Rouen,[3] perhaps evidence of a coastal trade supplying corn for the city of Rouen from the flat cereal-growing lands of the plain of Caen. The general buoyancy of exchange is in any event very clearly demonstrated by the frequency with which markets and fairs appear, often in places which were of little obvious significance, yet handling a trade which was much more than local.[4] Initiative could take many, sometimes slightly eccentric, forms. Roger II de Montgommery is known to have diverted the line of a Roman road, while dredging operations on the bed of the river Odon were undertaken on behalf of the monks of St-Etienne of Caen.[5] The predictable features of an active economy can usually be traced: industrial enterprise in the towns, whale-fishing around the coasts, and widespread viticulture, although the violent dislike for the ubiquitous Norman cider expressed by a monk of St-Benoît-sur-Loire who visited Bayeux in the early twelfth century, might suggest that the scale of vine-growing was limited.[6]

The duchy possessed what was for the eleventh century a highly developed money economy. The charters provide numerous instances of the disbursement of sums of money which would have involved the transfer of a quantity of silver pennies considerably greater than the 8,000 or so found in the late-tenth-century Fécamp hoard. A great landowner such as Goscelin, who was *vicomte* of Arques in the 1020s and 1030s, could pay £60 to buy a vineyard.[7] Recorded payments were invariably made in cash; transactions in kind were rare, although there are occasional instances where a sum of money was described in terms of an equivalent such as a horse.[8] From *c.* 1012, and much more regularly from the later 1020s, there are references to what appear to be payments by weight, rather than quantity, of coin. This may reflect the serious deterioration in the standard of Norman money from *c.* 1020: it also indicates a very definite attention to the value of money. Assaying (the melting-down of coin to produce silver weight), may also have taken place.[9]

The wide circulation of money affected the lives of aristocracy, townsmen, and peasantry alike. In one or two cases, the last-named were described specifically as rendering their dues in cash.[10] Financial transactions could assume quite sophisticated forms, with mortgages and payments by instalments widely recorded. The natural corollaries of this sort of arrangement are also evident: as early as Richard II's time, a certain Atto the Mad had fallen irredeemably behind on a payment of £100, while later a chaplain of William II's named Rainald complained bitterly about another chaplain named Samson who, it was claimed, had not paid all the instalments towards the purchase of a house in Bayeux.[11] This widespread use of money, combined with the prevailing economic growth, appears to have had the effect of diversifying the resources which could be drawn from the possession of land and power. Thus, the general character of the resources which the Norman rulers gave to the Church changes from land, often whole manors, during the tenth century, to a mixture of land along with the revenues and rights deriving from the possession of land in Richard II's time, towards purchases and revenues under William II.[12] It may be that the dukes over time became much more conscious of the need to preserve land as the ultimate basis of power, but it is more likely that the change represents a development in the nature of aristocratic wealth, associated with the plentiful circulation of coin. This same point is brought out, too, by the proliferation of seigneurial tolls on the sale and movement of goods, a trend apparent from the mid-eleventh century. In this case, a one-time ducal monopoly splintered under economic pressures and came to be shared with others in a position to draw revenue from the spread of exchange.[13]

The life of both town and countryside suggests prosperity. The foundation of new towns, and the expansion of old ones, is very evident throughout the province in the eleventh century. There are also many references to the extension of the cultivated area, a clear sign of rising population in an age where increased demand could not be met by technological improvement.[14] Great lords sponsored the establishment of rural *bourgs*, new settlements usually in the vicinity of a castle or a monastery, which, although not especially adventurous as colonising movements, would generally require the recruitment of a population. These *bourgs* proliferate widely from the middle of the eleventh century onwards.[15] Indeed, the picture as a whole, taking account of rural and urban enterprise – and especially of the exceptional growth of new towns and the evolution of the money economy – must place eleventh-century Normandy among the wealthiest regions of contemporary western Europe. The one available statistic of growth, supplied in a tract of *c*. 1100 from among the records of Coutances cathedral, shows that the annual revenue from the tolls taken by the bishops of Coutances at St-Lô (Manche) had risen from £15 to £220 following the construction of a *bourg* by bishop Geoffrey (1048–93).[16] Those with money to invest in pre-1066 Normandy must have done so confidently.

The sources of this exceptional prosperity are not entirely clear. The high population density recorded for the one Norman vill described in a Carolingian survey may suggest that great economic potential existed long before the Scandinavian settlements.[17] But a recent survey of Rouen's commercial development has shown that the city's trading prosperity was mediocre right up until the tenth-century boom, which derived from its role as a mart at which Viking booty was liquidated.[18] As in the parallel case of York, or to a lesser extent, Bristol, a commercial position between the Scandinavian North and the European hinterland could bring very great rewards. The eleventh-century evidence shows how the wealth drawn from such an intermediary role spilt over into other areas of activity. The most dramatic manifestation of all is the grand campaign of church-building, involving the reconstruction of all seven cathedrals of the province, new basilicas for all monasteries which had been refounded in the tenth century, and a church and conventual buildings for every new monastic and canonical foundation. At times outlay outran ready resources: both the cathedrals of Coutances and Sées, as well as the abbey of St-Evroult, required fund-raising in southern Italy. The effort by count Robert of Mortain, from *c.* 1060 onwards, to envelop poor and remote Mortain with an array of monastery, college of canons, *bourgs*, markets, and castle, provides an example of extravagant optimism on the part of a layman.

It must finally be emphasised that there is a broad coincidence between the periods of fullest economic expansion and the periods of internal peace.[19] The early-eleventh century supplies the earliest instances of growth – the first *bourgs*, an initial campaign of church-building, and the legendary wealth of duke Richard II. The disorders of the 1030s and 1040s constitute a phase of relative stagnation, which was followed by a second and very extensive period of growth from the 1050s onwards. By this stage the various elements of the Norman economy were working on one another in a wealth-creating cycle: increased cultivation of land, growth of towns, circulation of coin, the exchange of goods and property – all operated within the peace maintained by duke William II. None of these factors was likely to detract from the optimism and self-esteem of those with the power to harvest the rewards.

THE ARISTOCRACY

The aristocracy and their lands

It is fruitless to look for great changes in land tenure during Richard II's reign, which is notable as a period of peace and stability. The presumption must be that the pattern of land-holding remained largely that of the second half of the tenth century, of which we know almost nothing (see pp. 33–6).[20] Most of the Norman aristocracy of the time is hidden since the character of the witness-lists of Richard II's charters is such as to prevent us obtaining much knowledge of the families who were the duchy's greatest landholders during that period; the documents generally mention only a limited social group, the 'official' classes, the duke's relations, the bishops, his familiars, and his *fideles* (see pp. 158–9). There are, however, two significant types of change observable during the reign, both of which involved the establishment of new land-owning families. One was the creation of the *comtés*, special privileged territories dominated by men bearing the title of count, which were situated around a castle, and responsible for the defence of a sensitive region, often on the frontier. The *comtés* were the monopoly of the duke's closest relatives: Richard's uncle Rodulf received Ivry, while his brother, archbishop Robert of Rouen, was made responsible for Evreux; another brother, also called Robert, was given Mortain; two other brothers, Godfrey and William, of whom the former subsequently came to be associated with Brionne, appear to have held Eu in turn.[21] The second development, certainly not so carefully planned, was the reception of new families. The trail blazed by the Tosnys in the late tenth century was followed by, among others, the Taisson, who came from Anjou, or the Giroie, mentioned by Ordericus, who came from Brittany via Bellême, or by Baldric, the father of Baldric de Bocquencé, who came from Germany. In the case of the *comtés*, and of the estates of the Tosny and Taisson families, the source of their acquisitions was a mixture of ducal and ecclesiastical lands. It looks very much as if the tenth-century regime by which the dukes had based their power on their great landed wealth was in the process of modification. Instead they were beginning to exploit the potential of land as a means to sustain chosen followers.

Robert I's reign was characterised by the extension of the estates of numerous powerful families. It was as if everyone now assumed for themselves what Richard II had confined to a select few. The early years of Robert's reign were especially disturbed. There were rumours that he had disposed of his brother, duke Richard III, by poison; these stories were current in very early sources.[22] Robert had to fight at the start of his reign against his uncle, archbishop Robert, and against bishop Hugh of Bayeux, the two most prominent members of Richard II's entourage and the holders respectively of the *comtés* of Evreux and Ivry.[23] The reign was notable for the despoliation of church property, a movement which gave the duke a bad reputation which even so devoted a sycophant of the ducal house as William of Jumièges could not overlook.[24] Robert also has a remarkable renown for encouraging immigration into the province, an activity which later legends exaggerated to giant proportions. The famous story is that of the smith of Beauvais, interpolated into the *Gesta* of William of Jumièges in the late eleventh century to demonstrate Robert's liberality through the smith's amazement that someone from his humble station in the world should be so magnificently rewarded.[25] Another late-eleventh-century writer, the Burgundian Hugh of Flavigny, preserved a harsher verdict on Robert I's Normandy: according to him, the duchy during these years was 'debauched with anarchy'.[26]

The feast on church property, which is especially well documented, brings into prominence, as far as the historian is concerned often for the first time, many of the families who were to dominate Norman history in the second half of the century. Humphrey de Vieilles, for example, first appears in the sources during the last years of Richard II's reign, and can be shown to have pushed his property interests north-eastwards from his elementary possessions in the region of Pont-Audemer (Eure) into the forest of Brotonne and southwards where Beaumont, Beaumontel, and Vieilles were removed from the estates of the recently founded abbey of Bernay. Similarly rapacious was Roger I de Montgommery, who, in addition to plundering Bernay's lands, also pressed westwards and southwards to seize Troarn and Almenèches from the abbey of Fécamp.[27] A list of all similar actions would produce a lengthy catalogue. It would show that the movement involved well-established, as well as superficially 'new', families, and that the Church from one end of the duchy to the other suffered spoliation. Archbishop Robert of Rouen plucked a couple of properties from the abbeys of Jumièges and La Trinité-du-Mont of Rouen.[28] In Upper Normandy, Fécamp's estates were ravaged by Goscelin, *vicomte* of the Talou, a persecutor also of Rouen cathedral.[29] In Lower Normandy, the cathedrals of Bayeux and Coutances sustained losses, and the abbey of Mont-St-Michel granted properties to a mixture of predators who included a

Economy and social structure

ducal moneyer named Rannulf and Hugh, bishop of Avranches.[30]

Duke Robert's death on pilgrimage in 1035, and his replacement as duke by a young boy, meant the extension of estates at the expense of the Church and the duke's demesne turned into a struggle between rival families. There are in fact irrefutable signs that the fighting began in Robert's reign. His cousin, count Gilbert of Brionne, became involved in a succession of wars, attacking Giroie when the latter gained land which threatened Gilbert's power near Orbec, pursuing a hereditary claim to the *comté* of Eu which his father had held, and subsequently launching a wild and unsuccessful raid against Enguerrand I of Ponthieu.[31] Feuds of this kind proliferated during William II's minority, and, with the removal of the duke as an effective referee, deaths started to occur in numbers. The bloodiest among several recorded wars was that between Beaumont and Tosny, a series of battles which very pointedly illustrate how the expansion of estates after 1027 contributed to the 'anarchy' of William's minority. The two families had effectively set themselves on a collision course during the 1030s. Humphrey de Vieilles, having extended his lands southwards along what is now the route of the main Paris–Caen–Cherbourg railway, must have presented a considerable threat to the consolidation of Tosny estates around Conches, where Roger I de Tosny had recently founded a monastery and a *bourg*. The principal source for this war, Ordericus Vitalis, makes Roger de Tosny the aggressor. This must be an over-simplification.[32] Roger's assault on Humphrey's lands was countered by the latter's son Roger (de Beaumont), who killed Roger de Tosny. In retaliation, Roger de Clères, a Tosny follower, slaughtered Robert, another of Humphrey's sons. Among members of other families, Robert I de Grandmesnil died fighting for the Tosny cause (see Map 6).

William II's victories at Val-ès-Dunes and in 1053–54 restored the peace-keeping role of ducal government and social stability. The result was that from *c.* 1050 the opportunity to make territorial acquisitions was closely controlled. Within the duchy, extensive gain usually occurred only after a forfeiture. The flight of count William of Arques in 1053–54, for example, allowed his property to be used to reward, among others, Roger de Beaumont, William de Warenne, and Walter Giffard. After 1050 Normandy also seems to have ceased to be a land which gave opportunity for immigrants to make their fortunes. In consequence, the aristocracy appear to have turned some of their energies into consolidation. Seigneurial *bourgs* proliferated from *c.* 1050. The number of monastic foundations also multiplied, as several families followed the example set in the 1030s which had produced St-Pierre and St-Léger of Préaux, founded by Humphrey de Vieilles, and Conches and La Trinité-du-Mont of Rouen established by Roger de Tosny and Goscelin the *vicomte* respectively. There are also clear signs from after 1050 of the aristocracy profiting from the prevailing economic growth through the establishment of tolls and water-mills. In doing these things, the aristocracy displayed exactly the same administrative inventiveness which distinguished ducal government. There are numerous references to seigneurial *prepositi* and household officers. It is also worth emphasising that the aristocracy's response to the complexities of organising cross-Channel estates after 1066 seems to have paralleled that of the duke: the particularly rich records of the Montgommery-Bellême family supply an example of a land plea delegated to a subordinate, as well as what looks like a primitive writ *de ultra mare* addressed by Roger II de Montgommery to his son Robert de Bellême.[33]

A closer examination of the pre-1066 changes in land-holding suggests that we are dealing with a process which, although essentially an extension of powerful men's estates, was also one which contained much deeper implications for the structure of Norman society. There was a sense in which the expansion of estates meant the spread of the domination of stronger families over weaker ones. This is sometimes made explicit, as in the case of Lilletot (Eure, cant. Pont-Audemer, comm. Fourmetot), at which place the monks of Jumièges transferred a certain Adhemar to the lordship of Hugh de Montfort, at a date between 1037 and 1045, so that Adhemar should do service to Hugh, who would in return protect the abbey's estates in the neighbourhood.[34] A similar extension of lordship can be suggested from the history of the large domain of Montivilliers which passed out of ecclesiastical control into that of Walter I Giffard between 1025 and 1035, and on which he can be shown to have installed his own tenants as well as acquiring domination over men who were also vassals of the Malet family. This last group were probably erstwhile freemen who became subject to Giffard and Malet lordship.[35] The conclusion reached for Montivilliers, the result of meticulous research which takes full account of both genealogical and topographical considerations, is one which is likely to be obtained by a careful scrutiny of other extensions of aristocratic estates. It is also probable that the second quarter of the century witnessed the subjugation of less powerful branches of one family to a single lineage. The records of the two monasteries at Préaux show how the property of a younger brother of Humphrey de Vieilles named Turchetil reverted to Humphrey's son Roger and how the estates held by Roger's brother Robert were reunited after his death under Roger's control. There are also references to relatives (*consanguinei*) of the main branch and implications that other families of the neighbourhood, such as the Harcourts or the Efflancs, had descended from the same stock as the Beaumonts.[36] The conclusion that the events of the Norman 1030s and 1040s involved not just an extension of estates, but also one of power, although a subject requiring further investigations, seems inescapable.

The changes of this period also have something of the character of an Upper Norman colonisation of Lower Normandy. The steady, albeit unspectacular, acquisition by many families of property interests in the West was a process which seems to have been continuous throughout the period up until 1066. A clear early example is the Tosny acquisition of St-Christophe-du-Foc (Manche, cant. Les Pieux), which had formerly been ducal demesne and then a part of the dowry of Richard II's first wife, in 1017–18.[37] A similar case from Richard II's time must be the grant of property near Valognes (Manche) to archbishop Robert of Rouen.[38] A further example, this time sponsored by William II, was the acquisition in the Cotentin of several churches by Robert fitz Humphrey de Vieilles.[39] Families of less exalted status were also involved: the Bertrands, originally from the Pays d'Auge, appear holding property at and in the vicinity of Bricquebec (Manche, chef–lieu du canton); the Broc, a much more humble family from the neighbourhood of Rouen, appear in the second half of the eleventh century as tenants of the *vicomtes* of the Bessin, both in the Bessin and in the north of the Cotentin.[40] A final example – one on the grand scale, and one which must be selected from among many cases such as the installation of the Taisson on ducal demesne to the south of Caen and in the Cotentin or the extension throughout Lower Normandy of the Goz estates – is the transfer of the *comté* of Mortain to William II's half-brother Robert. This brought about a series of links between his family's original property on the south bank of the Seine estuary and Lower Normandy: Robert's father, Herluin de Conteville, acquired an estate at Muneville-sur-Mer on the coast of the Cotentin peninsula, which he held from his son; Robert's sister Muriel married into a Lower Norman family; finally, Robert's religious foundation at Mortain received property near the original 'family seat' of Conteville, while the family's monastic house in central Normandy, the abbey of Grestain, gained lands in the Cotentin[41] (see Map 7).

It should also be stressed that the feuds and the extension of property holdings were in some respects a part of a struggle between families for 'a place in the sun'. Over the period as a whole some prospered consistently; others, however, faltered; while a few experienced a disastrous reverse of fortune. The Montgommerys' record of territorial gain is consistent from *c.* 1025 and the acquisition of monastic estates, through to the marriage of Roger II and Mabel de Bellême in *c.* 1050 and the following push to Sées and beyond. The Giffards similarly, starting from Bolbec in Richard II's time, obtained Montivilliers under Robert I, and then Longueville after the fall of William of Arques. On the other hand, the lineage of Goscelin the *vicomte*, which started well when Goscelin picked up the *vicomté* of the Talou in the 1020s along with a number of ecclesiastical estates, and then proceeded to consolidation through the establishment of the abbey of La Trinité-du-Mont at Rouen, fell on harder times after Goscelin's son-in-law Godfrey had been stripped of some of his lands in 1047 by count William of Arques and when Godfrey's son William failed to succeed to the *vicomté*.[42] It is no coincidence that the Montgommerys and the Giffards went on to immense fortunes in England, whereas William d'Arques cut very little ice indeed after 1066. A variation on the theme is that of the family of Haimo *Dentatus*, a *vicomte* in the 1030s, who fought on the losing side at Val-ès-Dunes, made very little impression in the 1050s, but whose sons Haimo and Robert were successful in England after 1066. The real catastrophes usually afflicted members of the ducal family, such as counts William of Arques or William Werlenc of Mortain, who lost all their lands as a result of acts of disobedience during William II's reign.

These changes also provided opportunities for the *milites*, the warriors who followed and benefited from the fortunes of the powerful. It seems probable that the extension of aristocratic estates enabled the *milites* to gain land as well. The installation of the Taisson in Lower Normandy in the last years of Richard II's reign was followed by the dismemberment of their former ducal demesne in favour of a number of tenants. Further clear examples are provided by the division of the large ducal domain of Fécamp during Robert I's reign in order to provide for a number of relatively insignificant families, or of Lillebonne at the same period in favour of the followers of Ralph the Chamberlain. The narrative of Godfrey the *vicomte*'s defeat at the hands of count William of Arques recorded that his father-in-law Goscelin had not developed the estate which he had received from the abbey of Fécamp, 'but rather had brought it to nothing, and, contrary to the agreement with the abbot and the monks, had divided it up among his dependents' (*atque suis hominibus contra statutum pactionem distribuit*).[43] This pattern of distribution of acquired estates to dependents is one which must have occurred throughout the province. The records of the encroachments on the estates of Bayeux and Coutances cathedrals describe them as the work mainly of men of obscure status.[44] It must be remembered that the feuds and the dispossession of the Church were the actions of bands of men, all, within their own social horizons, pursuing fortune. The developments of the 1030s and 1040s require much more of the careful research into local conditions which has started to be undertaken during the past decade. When completed, this work is likely to show not only the extension of the estates of the most powerful members of the leading families, but also an almost immediate dispersal of the newly acquired land into the hands of military dependents.

The dispossession of churches and the violence of the second quarter of the century must therefore be regarded as merely the symptoms of a profound process of social change. Its manifestations are various: a colonisation of western Normandy, the subjugation of formerly independent freemen who would often be among the warriors who benefited from this time of opportunity. The whole process was the sort of whirlwind which afflicted most regions of northern France, although at different times and with varying degrees of intensity. In Flanders, for example, there was a steady augmentation of the estates of the greater families, usually involving a colonisation of lands to the east of the county, during the reign of count Baldwin IV (988–1035).[45] Within the Ile de France, the dismemberment of ecclesiastical domains took place in the later tenth century.[46] The origins of the changes in Normandy can be tentatively related to a crisis which was whittling away the estates of powerful families: there is reason to think, for example, that the original Giffard possessions around Bolbec were becoming enfeebled by grants to dependents by the first decades of the eleventh century, and that partitions among heirs had left Humphrey de Vieilles with little property in the vicinity of the family's base at Pont-Audemer.[47] Whatever the reason, the clear similarities between what happened in Normandy and in other regions means that the structural elements of change can be analysed through techniques evolved and applied by French scholars such as Bloch, Duby and Lemarignier. The next section is, therefore, an exercise in sociology, a definition of the terms 'nobility' and 'knighthood' and a discussion of their relationship to the stability, or otherwise, of the social structure. The following section examines the changes in the organisation of aristocratic families and their property during the period and says something about their relationship to ducal government. The final part tackles the subject of the relations between the lords and their dependents, so called 'Norman feudalism'. The results will enable something to be said about the original features of Norman society, and will lead on to a discussion of ducal government and the character of the co-operation achieved between the dukes and their chief subjects.

Nobles and knights

The 'rise of the knights' was identified by Marc Bloch as a fundamental force for change in early medieval society. The knights emerged during the tenth and eleventh centuries to destroy the pre-eminence of the existing nobility and, in time, to form a new aristocracy themselves. This view is now completely rejected. Instead, the 'rise of the knights' is seen in terms of a contemporary sociology, defined through the opinions of the clerics who wrote the documents. The continuous existence of some sort of nobility throughout the whole period is allowed, with its view of its role in society and also of its way of life being steadily transformed during the eleventh century by the impact of the entirely military ethos of those who made a profession of war. The documents therefore represent, not the emergence of a new aristocracy, but a transformation in the way in which the existing one regarded its function in society. The study of this particular problem, which relies on an essentially semantic methodology, has produced remarkably varied results. What happened in some places at a very early date was often long delayed elsewhere – at the extremes are the Mâconnais, where the changes came in the eleventh century, and the region of Namur where they were postponed until the last years of the fourteenth.[48] What is generally agreed is that all regions were subject to the same processes of change. Older notions of authority, stressing the existence of a nobility distinct from, and superior to, knighthood, probably stood a better chance of survival where the fragmentation of the Carolingian structures was less severe and where the rule of territorial princes remained strong.

Terms of Carolingian origin, implying the existence of a noble élite, proliferate in Norman charters. The dedication of the abbey of La Trinité of Caen in 1066 took place in the presence of William II, his wife, and 'the chief men of our land' (*cum... terre nostre primatibus*), while a charter, dated 1051, for the abbey of St-Wandrille, was confirmed 'by the authority of the aforesaid princes and the witness of many nobles' (*auctoritate supra dictorum principum et multorum testi-*

monio nobilium).[49] These are two from many examples. Such usage indicates the opinion that the duchy was ruled by a duke and by a group of men who could be described by terms such as *nobiles, proceres, primates*, and their equivalents.

It is not at all clear, however, who qualified to be a member of this select band. The above-mentioned terms are rarely employed adjectivally. The two clear instances where *nobilis* is used to describe a specific individual occur in the cases of the largely unknown Odo fitz Losfred (*quidam nobilis homo*) and Hugh Talbot (*quidam nobilium*). Two members of the Goz family, who were *vicomtes* and one of whose number became earl of Chester after 1066, were styled *duo nobiles viri de Normannia* in 1080, but men such as Robert fitz Humphrey de Vieilles, Roger II de Montgommery, or bishop Hugh of Lisieux, who might be expected to merit the epithet *nobilis*, did not receive it and were all at some stage described as vassals (*fideles*) of duke William II.[50] Only in documents from the abbey of St-Wandrille does any attempt appear to classify status within this amorphous nobility. In the above-mentioned act of 1051, count William of Arques, a son of duke Richard II, was identified as a *princeps* and all other witnesses as *nobiles*. In another charter, the phrase 'and many other nobles' concludes the first part of a long witness-list, which contained the archbishop of Rouen and several *vicomtes*, and the description 'other witnesses' was given to those in the second part, which included four abbots and several citizens of Rouen.[51] With these exceptions, Norman documents employed *nobilis* and like terms in a non-specific way which seems to have been normal in many areas of northern France. The inference is that there was an awareness of a governing élite and by implication of an accepted continuity of authority since Carolingian times. The second conclusion must be that this group had scarcely begun to arrogate to itself the characteristics of an exclusive caste. There were nobles in eleventh-century Normandy, but there was not a nobility.

The peculiar circumstances of Normandy and the renowned cooperation of duke and aristocracy have meant that several qualifications have been made to this statement. The most plausible is the idea that kinship to the ducal house was a determinant of nobility.[52] Some basis for this view can be found in the blood relationship of many members of the aristocracy to the duke; the holders of the *comtés* are obvious examples, but there are others for whom the only evidence is the celebrated set of genealogies which Robert of Torigny interpolated into the *Gesta* of William of Jumièges in the mid-twelfth century. This twelfth-century idea of the origin of the Norman aristocracy brings us back to the 'Norman Myth', with a view of the development of Norman society which superimposes twelfth-century thinking on to the past.

Robert of Torigny's genealogies made the sisters and nieces of Gunnor, the second wife of Richard I, the ancestors of many of the most important families of the duchy.[53] Because there are so few tenth-century documents, it is impossible to check their accuracy. It is at least clear, however, that the idea of the descent from Gunnor's relatives was not of Torigny's invention. The same Montgommery genealogy, for example, appears in a letter of bishop Ivo of Chartres to king Henry I, dating from *c.* 1113, which includes the information that the record of the lineage had actually been supplied by the family.[54] Rather earlier, in either 1100–01 or 1105–09, St Anselm, archbishop of Canterbury, advised Henry against marrying an illegitimate daughter to William de Warenne, on the grounds of a relationship within the prohibited degrees of kinship, which corresponded exactly to the details supplied by Torigny's genealogy.[55] Torigny, therefore, was recording opinions which had been current in Norman society since at least the early twelfth century.

Historians have shown a great reluctance finally to dispense with this material, despite the mediocrity of much of its content, and despite the fact that genealogical literature, endowing numerous families with a fabulous ancestry, which connected them to an important dynasty, was a very common twelfth-century *genre*. A much studied example, the history of the counts of Guines, composed in the late twelfth century by Lambert of Ardres, traced the house's origin back to the early tenth century and to a Viking adventurer who had seduced a daughter of a count of Flanders.[56] For Normandy, the notion of a distant connection between the leading families and the ducal house was one which would have had a special appeal, and was also one which, on the general grounds of the dukes' immense achievements, might easily have appeared in the very early twelfth century: it was precisely at this time that more elaborate genealogical theories started to come into fashion elsewhere.[57] One very solid clue suggests that this was precisely the development which did take place in Normandy: a tract written in *c.* 1080 traced the ancestry of the Tosny family back to a certain Hugh de *Calvacamp*, a native of the French Vexin, but Ordericus, in his early-twelfth-century interpolations into the *Gesta* of William of Jumièges, announced that the lineage could be traced back to an uncle of Rollo's.[58] This seems to be evidence of a new notion, perhaps of a qualification for nobility, and of an idea which was, like so much else which was an aspect of the twelfth-century 'Myth', a result of achievement rather than a historical fact.

Torigny's theories on one side, there is little to suggest that females closely related to the ducal ménage did marry into the province's aristocracy. With the exception of two daughters of the short-reigned Richard III, who made rather ordinary matches, the dukes tended to marry their female offspring outside the duchy.[59] This, taken along with the evidence of the eleventh-century charters and evidence such as Roger de Montgommery's boast of *c.* 1080 that he was 'a Norman of Norman stock', suggests that no definition of nobility which stressed a connection by blood with the ducal house existed at that time. If Roger's assertion means anything, it suggests a pride in independent origins.

Although there is no sign of any strict definition of nobility, it is likely that, in practice, men had a rather clearer understanding of rank than the documents – the St-Wandrille examples excepted – imply. Aristocratic marriages, for example, show every indication of being confined within a recognised range of acceptable partners. Among numerous examples, William fitz Osbern married a daughter of Roger de Tosny, and count Robert of Mortain, one of Roger de Montgommery. A little down the social scale, Eudo, a *vicomte* of the Cotentin, married a daughter of Herluin de Conteville, who was also a *vicomte*. The more enterprising might seek a bride outside the duchy, as, for example, Roger de Beaumont, who married a daughter of Waleran I, count of Meulan. A thorough investigation of these links might reveal a good deal about the social attitudes of the Norman aristocracy. In general, however, there was nothing extraordinary about the marriages. Intermarriage of social 'equals' was the universal practice within the regionalised aristocratic groups of early medieval western Europe. It demonstrates a limited consciousness of rank and prestige, which had not yet evolved into any very definite notion of nobility. It does not affect the conclusion that the eleventh-century Norman aristocracy had not started to support its position with legal privileges. Nor had admission to the upper echelons of society begun to be dependent on social shibboleths. There was merely an awareness that there was a governing élite. Membership of this, if it was based on anything, was guaranteed by power.

This élite was certainly distinguished by Norman contemporaries from the lower social group, the knights. A clear view of their status depends on the meaning of the word *miles* in contemporary documents. This term appears in the Norman records from the earliest time, but with some suggestion of a devaluation in the social standing of those referred to from the later 1040s, since the number of occasions when it is employed as a generic term rises significantly.[60] There are traces in non-Norman documents, which relate to the duchy, as well as in records emanating from the abbeys of St-Ouen and La Trinité-du-Mont of Rouen, of usage signifying a very elevated social status. Thus, the castellan William de Moulins-la-Marche, a ducal steward (*dapifer*), and a *vicomte* could on occasion be described as *milites*, while a literary source compiled in the early 1050s could describe Erneis Taisson as both a *miles* and 'one of the leading men of the principality' (*unus magnatum regni*).[61] But, consistent with the continued employment of a Carolingian terminology indicative of an élite, the most usual meaning of *miles* seems to have been 'a soldier', generally one who was a personal dependent of someone else, and often someone holding mediocre possessions. The overwhelming majority of examples refer to a specified individual, someone who was basically a vassal expected to perform military service, in phrases of the kind 'X, the knight of Y'. This meaning is emphasised by its occasional use alongside such terms as *fidelis* or *homo*.[62] The most comprehensive description of such a *miles* occurs in a charter transcribed into the thirteenth-century cartulary of the abbey of St-Pierre of Préaux: 'Ralph, a *miles* from the Pays de Caux, came to Préaux along with William Malet, the man for whom he performed his military duties, and gave to St-Pierre his land, namely, the land of a *vavassor*'.[63] The relative insignificance of some *milites* is shown by their insertion in the charters among lists of resources such as woodland and mills, and alongside members of the peasantry, from whom they were, therefore, not differentiated.[64] In pre-1066 Normandy the term *miles* remained pre-eminently one which described function, rather than status.

Although nobility and knighthood obviously failed to fuse, it is also clear that the ethos of knighthood did make a considerable impact on Norman society during the second half of the eleventh century. Its occasional application to very powerful men is a sure sign that the aristocracy, whose very position in society obliged them to be warriors, did not disdain to be identified as knights. Some of the trappings of knighthood appear. The scene on the Bayeux Tapestry, *Hic Willelm dedit Haroldo arma*, suggests the ceremony of knighting, something to which there are no references in pre-1066 Norman charters. It was assumed by 1091 that the son of a baron would be knighted.[65] In short, the military ethos of knighthood was in the process of penetrating the highest levels of Norman society in the second half of the eleventh century. But it did so within a conservative terminology which stressed the existence of a distinct governing class, and, as in other regions where the fusion of nobility and knighthood came late, the survival of the traditional forms of authority.

Knighthood failed to transform the Norman aristocracy before 1066. Indeed, the survival of a Carolingian terminology is very much an argument against the fundamental reorganisation of the Norman aristocracy at any state of its eleventh-century history. The continued currency of a vague and fluid terminology militates against there having been any precise definition of nobility in eleventh-century Normandy: in a legal and social sense, Norman aristocratic society was open, devoid of any preconceptions about its own origins, and as yet unprepared to formulate barriers between itself and the rest of the people. Knighthood, too, was an ill-defined idea: there are distinct signs that the title *miles* conferred prestige, yet at the same time, there was some vulgarisation of the term from the disorders of the 1040s: Norman terminology was generally traditional; on occasions, it was becoming strained and ambiguous.[66]

Family, lineage, and property

It is now generally agreed that a crucial factor in the evolution of the political life of most regions is the adaptation of the structure of the families of castellan status towards lineal forms around the year 1000. It is also recognised that the significance of the change was not simply domestic, since the reorganisation was part and parcel of the way in which the aristocracy strove to maintain its power and status. The transformation, a very complex one, is normally seen as coinciding with a fresh challenge to the authority of the territorial princes and often with the final decomposition of the territorial circumscriptions of Carolingian authority, the *pagi* (see pp. 49–50). It was sometimes associated with the transfer of the formerly exclusive title of 'count' down to a new level of society and almost invariably by the assumption by the castle-holding families of powers and modes of behaviour which had previously been the preserve of kings and territorial princes.

The broad lines of this evolution have been observed in regions where the tenth-century documentation is relatively plentiful. Nevertheless, in spite of the weakness of the early Norman records, there is on one important point an exact correlation between the Norman evidence and the conclusions drawn elsewhere: it is the case that modern genealogical research, supported by the possibility of examining the full range of the documents and by the paraphernalia of index cards, can usually reach no further back in time than the memories of the families themselves. This is clearly so for the Montgommery family, whose genealogy, given to bishop Ivo of Chartres in *c.* 1113, could trace ancestry in the male line back only to Roger II de Montgommery (*c.* 1030–94), and in the female through Roger's mother, who was named as Joscelina, to her mother, Sofria or Sainfria, a sister of Richard I's wife Gunnor. Robert of Torigny's mid-twelfth-century genealogy of the same family named Roger's father incorrectly as Hugh de Montgommery and his mother as Joscelina, and her mother as Wevia, a sister of Gunnor's and Sainfria's. The eleventh-century documents allow us to disinter the descent back to Roger II's father, Roger I, who was alive in Robert I's reign.[67] This same pattern applies to others among Robert of Torigny's genealogies. He was not, for example, able to describe the Warenne ancestry beyond William I de Warenne who is scarcely known before the 1050s; the documents refer to William's father, Ralph de Warenne, who was alive in the 1040s.[68] Finally, in the case of the more complex Beaumont genealogy, Torigny 'knew' the male ancestry back not only to Humphrey de Vieilles, who appears in the documents from the last years of Richard II's reign, but also to his father Turold, his uncle Turchetil, and his grandfather Torf; it was Turold who had married Duvelina, the mythical relative of countess Gunnor. Some, if not all, of these men seem to be fictional: the uncle Turchetil may be a confusion with a known brother of Humphrey de Vieilles, while Turold is not mentioned before the early twelfth century.[69] On balance, it looks as if memory ended and myth began at Humphrey de Vieilles' generation. It is important that the same general conclusion can be drawn from an independent genealogy, that of the Crispin family compiled by Miles Crispin, a monk of Le Bec, in *c.* 1140, which could name no ancestor before Gilbert Crispin, who is known to have been alive in 1025.[70]

These examples suggest that Norman families did pass through the sort of structural changes which affected the aristocracies of other regions. The combined failure of memory and genealogical research at the period from *c.* 1020 to *c.* 1050 suggests that these were the crucial decades for Norman society. Change can therefore be associated roughly with the period of disruption and violence which followed Richard II's death. If the example of other regions is anything to go by, we should discover within Norman society a reaction on the part of the aristocracy which was both aggressive and defensive; an extension of estates and the acquisition of powers which had previously

Economy and social structure

belonged to the territorial prince, but also a consolidation of power around the strong-points of castle and monastery, as well as a tendency to organise the inheritance of the family property substantially in favour of one son. The whole process was one which was basically the transformation of any one family from a large amorphous kin-group, which identified itself with no fixed residence and did not think in terms of ancestry transmitted in a direct male line, into a lineage tenacious of its rights over generations. It had the effect of changing political relationships between such a family and the territorial prince.

The spread of the use of toponymics as a sign of the concentration of a family's power around one focal point is the simplest aspect of these changes. It is, none the less, a delicate subject because the material is particularly susceptible to anachronism. To take one example. A name such as Humphrey de 'Vieilles' is bandied around freely by both twelfth-century writers and by modern commentators, but cannot with confidence be assigned to any document written during the man's lifetime: two early charters copied into twelfth-century cartularies style Humphrey as 'de Vieilles' at a date before he had actually taken possession of the place, while the one likely contemporary example of the toponymic, an attestation to an original charter for Fécamp, includes it as an inter-lineation in what may be a later hand.[71] The trap for the unwary, the interpolation of a toponymic by a later scribe, is clearly demonstrated in an original eleventh-century St-Ouen charter which mentions 'count Rodulf' and its twelfth-century copy which calls him 'count Rodulf of Ivry'.[72] A similar danger stalks archaeologists who study Norman castles. A careful survey of the district of Le Cinglais to the south of Caen has disclosed a very large number of earthworks which it is tempting to attribute to the period from 1025 to 1050. Yet excavation of two of them has shown that they must be dated to the late eleventh or early twelfth centuries and that their military significance was in any case slight.[73] Similarly, a motte at Audrieu (Calvados), which was dated to the eleventh century until the 1960s, turned out after excavation to have been built in the late twelfth century on a site fortified only in the middle years of that century.[74]

These reservations in mind, and with all due caution, it can be suggested that the date at which toponymics appear for the leading families was the 1040s. A reference of 1014 for Tosny is exceptionally early.[75] Otherwise, there is *c*. 1040, 1046/47–48, ?1051, and 1054 for Beaumont;[76] 1042, 1043–1048, and 1046/47–48 for Montgommery;[77] 1049–66 for Montfort;[78] and *c*. 1047–53 and

113

c. 1050 for Warenne.[79] The pattern is the same for the *comtés* where localisation began to occur from the later 1040s.[80] The use of toponymics is very rare for Richard II's reign and not much more common for Robert I's. On occasions toponymics are attached to less prominent figures such as Roger de Fécamp or Berengar de Heudeboville, but it is only in the 1040s that they start to be used regularly by the chief families. Their use multiplies from 1050 onwards, and by 1066 they are frequently applied to the holders of dependent tenures, the *milites*, a sign that some aspects of lineage were spreading further down the social scale.[81] Their initial significance must be as a statement that a particular man's power was centred on a specific place. It would be wrong to see them as surnames in any modern sense, since they tended to change from generation to generation.

The proliferation of castles is specifically assigned to William II's minority by William of Jumièges, although his evidence for individual castles is not plentiful.[82] What is clear, however, is that before this period, the privilege of living in a fortified residence was largely confined to the duke and the holders of the *comtés*. The only region for which there is any evidence to suggest that this monopoly was insecure was on the southern frontier where, according to Ordericus Vitalis, there were private castles at Laigle and Echauffour. The great period of aristocratic castle-building obviously began in c. 1030. Montgommery, for example, was described as a *vicus* in a charter of 1027–35, but by c. 1040 it could withstand a siege. Le Plessis-Grimoult, which has been excavated, appears to have existed as a domestic residence from the later tenth century, being made militarily viable only shortly before it was abandoned in 1047. But the documents, even taking account of the vague terminology they employ, are not particularly helpful on the subject of castellation, supplying pre-1066 references to 'private' castles only at Vernon, Gaillefontaine, La Ferté-en-Bray, Breteuil, and Moulins-la-Marche. This cannot be a complete list: there is, for example, no pre-1066 record of duke William's new castle at Caen.

The sparseness of the literary sources is, however, receiving amplification and in some respects explanation from the efforts of the archaeologists. As already mentioned, excavation is tending to place the origins of many Norman castles at a later date than was once thought; the favoured period seems now to be the late eleventh or early twelfth centuries, the 'anarchy' of Robert Curthose's reign. The sort of work which is essential, namely, the combination of archaeological exploration and documentary research, has so far been undertaken systematically only for the Pays de Caux, a region near Rouen where ducal authority was strong. The result confirms that castle-building in pre-1066 Normandy was restricted to a small élite: the counts of Evreux had a castle at Gravenchon by the 1020s, the Giffards built one at Montivilliers after 1025, and there were others at Graville, Canouville, and Buchy – places which can all be connected with families possessing great landed wealth. The survey also shows that fortifications tended to be constructed within the existing social structures, usually on the site of a previously unfortified residence.[83] These are results which need to be tested throughout the whole of the duchy; the odds are, however, that they will not prove to be unrepresentative, at least to judge by excavations which have already taken place.

Archaeological research also suggests that it would be unwise to be too dogmatic about the way in which the castles were built. The weight of the evidence indicates that most of them were large earthwork enclosures, surrounded by a wooden palisade or, in exceptional instances such as the ducal residences at Fécamp and Caen or at Arques, by a stone curtain-wall with simple mural towers. The circumference would generally have been large and would have contained a hall and domestic buildings.[84] In all this the receding image is that of the once all-popular mound and wooden tower. Few of these structures can be confidently assigned to the pre-1066 period. A likely example is the Taisson castle at Grimboscq (Calvados), but the artistic representation on the Bayeux Tapestry of mottes as the typical form of fortification is still a strong caution against those who would claim that they have no place in pre-1066 Normandy.[85]

Other indications of change are the aristocracy's assumption of the role of founders of monasteries; up until *c.* 1030 this had been the monopoly of the dukes. Most aspects of this movement will be discussed at the appropriate point in Chapter Five. Suffice to say here that most of the leading Norman families established monasteries during the period from *c.* 1030 to *c.* 1070. The first came in the 1030s: La Trinité-du-Mont of Rouen, St-Pierre of Préaux, and Conches. A second and much larger wave developed from the late 1040s, with, among others, Lyre and Cormeilles founded by William fitz Osbern, Troarn, St-Martin of Sées, and the nunnery of Almenèches, by Roger II de Montgommery, Grestain by Herluin de Conteville, St-Sever by Richard *vicomte* of the Avranchin, and St-Sauveur of Evreux by count Richard of Evreux. Intermingled with this movement was one which had begun earlier and which was to continue through the eleventh century, the foundation of colleges of secular canons, often small communities with no more than three or four inmates.

Quite apart from their obvious religious significance, these churches were as much symbols of a family's power and prestige as any castle or *bourg*. They were the places where members of the family were buried, a function which the inmates of the religious institution appear to have taken seriously, to judge by Ordericus' macabre tale of the battle between the canons of Lisieux cathedral and the nuns of St-Désir to acquire the corpse of bishop Hugh (died 1077), who had governed the former church and founded the latter.[86] An abbey could also be a means of establishing beyond any doubt a family's right to hold a particular estate. Roger de Montgommery, for example, founded both Troarn and Almenèches on estates which had once belonged to the abbey of Fécamp, and set up St-Martin of Sées in a region over which he had recently gained control. The churches were also the focus of loyalty: the stories in Ordericus Vitalis' account of the early years of St-Evroult show the followers of the founding families giving lands to the monastery, sometimes sending relatives to become monks there, and asking to be buried at the church. These are patterns which receive copious confirmation in the charters of other institutions. The family monastery was a crucial element in the evolution of the eleventh-century aristocratic lineages; a reinforcement of status and domination, more subtle, but in its way just as effective as the castle. The way in which this fashion spread through a whole section of society in a relatively short time clearly associates it with the formation of lineages and with the fragmentation of formerly royal and princely prerogatives.[87]

The accumulation and retention by powerful families of the chief positions in ducal government was a further development which took place in the first half of the eleventh century. The pattern was set by the *comtés* awarded to members of the duke's family during Richard II's reign. Their holders were in general able to pass them on to their children, although the exchanges involving the *comtés* of Eu and Brionne do suggest that the count was still regarded as a removable official in Richard II's time. The breakthrough for the great non-ducal families came, however, mainly after Richard II's death in 1026. The charters of his reign reveal that most of the office-holders of the time were relatively obscure Upper Norman landholders. One among the five who are specifically named was an isolated figure called Odo the constable, who held some land near the mouth of the river Dives.[88] The other four, who are much more frequent in their charter attestations, were two chamberlains named Berengar and

Economy and social structure

Roscelin, Roger the butler, and Baldric *procurator*.[89] These four names, often admittedly without descriptive titles, appear from time to time in each other's company in witness-lists, suggesting a compact administrative group.[90] All four are obscure as landowners; a plausible identification would locate Berengar's, Roscelin's, and Roger's lands near Fécamp.[91] Despite the association of some powerful families with *vicomtés* in Lower Normandy, such as that of Thurstan Goz, or those of Anschetil and Nigel, who were respectively *vicomtes* of the Bessin and the Cotentin, the overwhelming impression is that Richard II's administration was largely a family and domestic affair. The most solid testimony to this is the convenient list of twelve *vicomtes* who attested a charter for the abbey of Bernay of 1025. It consists of characters such as Walter, Odo, Sihtric, and Wimund, who leave no subsequent trace in the sources.[92] Their disappearance after 1026 indicates that a drastic change occurred in the relations between a number of wealthy families and the organisation of the duke's government in the years immediately following Richard II's death. It scarcely needs emphasis that those involved were the very same families who were at the same time involved in the extension of their lands, the construction of castles, and on occasions the foundation of monasteries.

The irruption of these families into office is a process which can be fairly easily traced. So, too, can their retention of these positions, often through to 1066. A well-known case is the lineage of Roger I and Roger II de Montgommery, the former being first named as a *vicomte* in 1033 and the son being still in post in 1066. Others can be established by research. Hugh I de Montfort's earliest appearance as a *vicomte* is in 1027–33 and, despite his father's violent death, Hugh II succeeded and was still a *vicomte* in 1066.[93] Another case is the previously unrecognised dynasty of Roger and Robert, probably *vicomtes* of Caux, who were holding office in the 1030s and were still represented by Robert after 1068.[94] A further likely example is the Crispin family as hereditary *vicomtes* of the Norman Vexin, an acquisition which the family biographer dated to William II's reign, but one which may have come earlier, since a *vicomte* with the appropriate name, Gilbert, attests a charter in 1033.[95] If we take account of the three 'hereditary' *vicomtés* which had existed since Richard II's reign, then we have evidence of the appearance of most of the vicecomital families of the pre-1066 duchy during this short period. It is a list which becomes still more impressive if we add Goscelin and Godfrey, successively *vicomtes* of the Talou from *c.* 1025 to the late 1050s (see p. 104), and the household office of *dapifer* to which

Osbern fitz Arfast, a nephew of Richard I's widow Gunnor, acceded in duke Robert's time, to be followed by his son William fitz Osbern, who was still in post in 1066.[96] Other household lineages established at this time were those of Humphrey de Vieilles and Ralph the chamberlain.[97] The general argument loses nothing from the failure of at least one of the lineages which thrust itself forward in the late 1020s to hold on to its *vicomté*. This is the case of the *vicomte* named Richard de Lillebonne, who can be identified with the *vicomté* of Rouen in the 1030s, but whose son Lambert appears never to have held the *vicomté*. It may be that Lambert was pushed out by Roger de Beaumont, who appears as *vicomte* of Rouen in *c*. 1050 and that the family also lost a power struggle at Lillebonne against the family of Ralph the chamberlain.[98] In any event, Roger de Beaumont subsequently handed over the *vicomté* of Rouen to a certain Ansfrey, who may possibly have been a protégé.[99]

At the core of all these changes were an infinite number of decisions taken by the families themselves, as well as an aggressive, power-seeking mentality. The accepted view now is that the crucial underlying development was a concentration in each separate family of the rights of inheritance on one son, usually the eldest. This, a change which was basic to the evolution from large, shapeless, kin-group to lineage, connects with all the developments taking place in the second quarter of the eleventh century in Normandy.

The Norman evidence for aristocratic inheritance is not simple, partly because there is no indication of how the families operated before *c*. 1030, and partly because there is no contemporary eleventh-century description of the organisation of an inheritance. Sometimes we know only that a division between heirs had taken place, as was reported by Ordericus in the cases of the three sons of archbishop Robert of Rouen (died 1037) and the two sons of Robert I de Grandmesnil (killed in the 1040s).[100] The much fuller information about the estates held by Giroie (died 1033) shows that they were partitioned among four sons; the eldest, Arnold, receiving what may well have been his father's inheritance, the second son William apparently obtaining most of the land which his father had acquired, and the other two sons being given much smaller portions. Arnold's death in *c*. 1041 allowed William to reunite most of his father's lands.[101] A much more complicated division split the estates given by duke Richard II to Ralph Taisson between his two sons, Ralph and Erneis. The details which can be deduced from the earliest charters of the family's monastic foundation of St-Etienne of Fontenay demonstrate how a patrimony could be dismembered in a way which broke down previously unified estates: the two brothers each received, for example, a part of the churches of Fontenay and the forest of Le Cinglais. The eleventh-century history of these lands shows the break-up of what had once been a single domain held by the duke into smaller parts held by different branches of the family and by their vassals. It catches the moment at which the general interest of all sons in the family lands was transformed into an interest held by any one son in a particular piece of territory. The two brothers, Ralph and Erneis, might be considered initially as partners when they took over the inheritance, but the eventual result was a permanent division of the estates between the two branches.[102] In other cases, however, there are signs of a stronger determination to maintain the unity of the family lands. The tripartite division among the three sons of Humphrey de Vieilles gave the lion's share to two sons, Roger and Robert 'de Beaumont', with several instances of co-ownership of estates. A third son William received a much smaller portion. But the entire patrimony was reunited in Roger's hands after Robert was killed during the feud against the Tosnys in the 1040s.[103]

Some examples display a quite brutal favouritism on behalf of one son. The lands of Herluin de Conteville, who died in c. 1066, went almost in their entirety to one son, count Robert of Mortain, while the other son, Odo, received only a tiny estate. This settlement might have been affected by the fact that as early as 1049/50 Odo had embarked on a remarkable and often outrageous career as bishop of Bayeux. In the case of the two sons of Osbern the steward (murdered in c. 1040), there are signs of an acknowledged partnership in the estates during the 1040s. But in the end, one son, William fitz Osbern, received not only the paternal inheritance, but also the vast estates of his uncle, bishop Hugh of Bayeux (died 1049), with the other son, Osbern, emigrating to England to make his fortune at the court of king Edward the Confessor, eventually becoming bishop of Exeter after 1066.[104] But the commoner practice appears to have been for a division to be made giving a substantial, although rarely equal, provision for two sons. Walter I Giffard in the 1040s was another who made some sort of partition.[105] What is, however, clear is that all such arrangements resulted from decisions made by individual families. It is fruitless to look for regular inheritance customs in pre-1066 Normandy; when such customs do begin to crystallise and become amenable to definition in the early twelfth century, the formulation had still to be a permissive one. Similarly, there was no legal language applicable to inheritance before 1066.[106] There are several references to testamentary bequests whereby one man made another his heir; and on occasion instances whereby such a grant could take the property outside the family to a tenurial neighbour.[107] Such a case seems, however, to have been exceptional. In general, families reacted to the disturbed conditions of the second quarter of the century through a stricter organisation of their property. An effort was made to reconcile the conflict between the long-standing principle that all members possessed an interest in the patrimony and the more recent emphasis on the leadership of the family by one among its number who received the castle and the bulk of the property.

The associated changes of the period from 1025 to 1050 created many of the features of Norman society which were transported to England after 1066. Readily apparent are the symbols of power: the castle, the monastery, and the *bourg*. These years also conditioned the aristocracy's attitudes to the organisation of inheritances. In a more general way, the processes of the extension of estates and their fragmentation among collateral branches contributed to the pattern whereby all major families possessed lands dispersed throughout the duchy. To take one example to prove an invariable rule, the estates held by the counts of Evreux can be traced to the vicinity of Evreux, to the neighbourhood of the monasteries of Jumièges and St-Wandrille, to the Cotentin peninsula, and to the environs of Dieppe. These were conditions with roots deep in the past: such scattered estates were known in the Carolingian period. They also went far down the social scale, with the dispersal of the tenurial units of alods and benefices normal: an alod granted to the abbey of St-Etienne of Caen after 1066 was situated at St-Pierre-Azif (Calvados, cant. Dozulé) and in other places (*in aliis locis*), while a benefice (*beneficium*) awarded by duke Robert I lay on the Norman mainland at and near La Croix-Avranchin (Manche, cant. St-James) and on the island of Jersey.[108] This was a pattern deeply embedded in Norman society, yet one which could only grow more complex through transfers of property resulting from inheritances, marriages, forfeitures, and the like. But it was also one whose significance was to an extent modified by the tendency towards concentration in a particular region – the castles of the counts of Evreux, for example, show that the basis of their power lay at Evreux and at Gravenchon near St-Wandrille.[109]

The second quarter of the eleventh century also forged the relationship between duke and aristocracy to which Professor David Douglas has rightly drawn attention. In the years immediately prior

Economy and social structure

to 1066 this formed the basis for a remarkable co-operation. The immediate significance, however, of the developments which took place was to produce a great change in the nature of political relations within the ruling classes. The establishment of 'private' castles and monasteries were threats to some very basic aspects of ducal power. They heightened the physical capacity for defiance of ducal authority, since a disaffected lord could now retreat behind ramparts. They encouraged patrimonial attitudes which might weaken one of the chief attributes of ducal rule, his unique position as the protector of the Church. The new mentality which resulted from the changes is aptly illustrated by the respective monastic patronages of counts Rodulf of Ivry, William of Arques, and Robert of Mortain, all men of similar status. The grants made by the first two were directed entirely towards the established ducal monasteries such as St-Ouen of Rouen, Fécamp, and St-Wandrille, along with the cathedral church of Rouen.[110] Count Robert, however, despite his renowned loyalty to his half-brother duke William, adopted a much more self-centred attitude, supporting only churches founded either by his father or himself. His one gift to duke William's abbey at Caen was a bequest.[111] The changes as a whole cannot be regarded as anything other than a potential threat to ducal authority, since basic prerogatives had been infringed, a stranglehold obtained over the chief offices of government, and aristocratic families had consolidated local power in such a way as to direct some of their energies away from serving the duke. The formation of the new social structures had been accompanied by widespread instability and by conditions which had allowed some men to make extensive acquisitions. The whole process, as this section has suggested, has close analogies with changes which elsewhere wreaked havoc with traditional forms of authority.

Power

Fragmentation of authority of the kind widely prevalent elsewhere turns out to be almost unknown in eleventh-century Normandy. The appropriation by the owners of the castles of the exclusive power over all men on their lands (the *ban*) and the assumption of the supervision over the local churches (lay advocacy) appear only in the southern marches, where in 1063–66 William de Moulins-la-Marche was described as exercising the economic and jurisdictional rights of the *ban* and where count Robert of Mortain possessed something resembling lay advocacy in 1082.[112] But with these exceptions, the powers of the Norman aristocracy were kept within traditional limits. The authority of the duke had of course replaced that of the king, but otherwise the developments of the second quarter of the eleventh century did not disrupt the basic framework of government. Why this should have been the case is the theme of Chapter Four. Suffice to say here that while lordship in eleventh-century Normandy did entail immense powers of exploitation – the earliest record of Norman customs, the inquest of 1091, distinguished positively between those places where jurisdiction belonged to the duke, and where to the lord[113] – the aristocracy's powers within their territorial lordships were partially circumscribed by ill-documented prerogatives such as the ducal right to levy general taxes and to call out a universal levy of freemen. More significantly, it was normally acknowledged that certain types of power were held only by ducal licence and that the most fundamental features of the great families' strength could not escape supervision. Their castles, for example, could be taken over by ducal guardians and their monasteries remained subject to the duke's general protection of the Church. These ducal prerogatives were very forcefully exercised in the second half of the eleventh century. As a result, bannal lordship and lay advocacy were stillborn on Norman soil.[114]

A much more complex and controversial problem is the nature of the relationships between the lords and their dependents, above all, their military followers, the *milites*. This one subject, so-called Norman 'feudalism', looms large in any discussion of the institutions imported to conquered England. In spite of the relatively clear-cut character of these arrangements in England, most recent commentators agree that they were only just starting to assume this coherence in the duchy by 1066. The terminology of the relationships between lord and vassal was pre-eminently one which signified personal arrangements between the two parties, conditions characteristic of a fluid society and what Marc Bloch called 'The First Feudal Age'.[115]

The crux of the matter is the significance which can be attached to the words *beneficium* and *alodium* in the pre-1066 Norman texts. These two words, which appear in approximately equal numbers in the surviving records, are almost the only ones used to describe a piece of land which one man held of another. In the second half of the eleventh century, however, *beneficium* was steadily replaced by *feudum*, a term which recognised that most benefices were in fact transferred hereditarily. There may well have been an element of clerical conservatism which delays our knowledge that this change

Economy and social structure

had taken place: *feudum* was the exclusive word in documents written for the two Caen abbeys, which were founded in *c.* 1059 and *c.* 1063, whereas the older *beneficium* endured much longer in other longer established *scriptoria*. It is in any case very clear that *alodium* had a different meaning from *beneficium/feudum* in the eleventh-century texts, since the two were often contrasted in phrases like *non tantum alodos meos, sed etiam villam que dicitur Meslet quam de beneficio ejus tenebam* in a charter of 1015–26, or *tam in alodio quam in foedio* in one of 1080–82. There is also a clear example from 1066–77 of an alod being converted into a benefice.[116]

Among the many recorded examples of property held as a benefice, the number which actually specify the nature and extent of the services owed is very small. A typical form is 'the benefice which T. holds of the aforesaid R. in X'. The benefice held by Gilbert Crispin of duke William II at Hauville-en-Roumois is explicitly described as being his as a reward for military service already rendered, but the type, the amount, and whether Gilbert was expected to continue providing it are not specified.[117] To judge by the *eques* whose job it was to guard a meadow, the obligation might be of the most trivial kind.[118] In general, many benefices do appear in the possession of *milites*, but it was also the case that clerics, women, and cooks held *beneficia*, for purposes which were presumably non-military.[119] In one notable instance, a *beneficium* was described as an annual money payment, while another comprised a castle.[120] In 1085, Gilbert d'Auffay accepted a fief (*feudum*) from the abbey of Fécamp for the purpose of assisting the church in pleas held at Rouen.[121] It does not seem as if *beneficium*, or indeed its successor term *feudum*, had acquired any meaning more specialised than that of an estate held in order to provide some sort of service. Consistent with this non-technical meaning is the great variation in the size of Norman *beneficia*: the one held by Roger de Clères of Ralph de Tosny, and granted by them to the abbey of St-Ouen of Rouen, comprised several manors, whereas that given by the abbot of La Trinité-du-Mont of Rouen to Robert, son of Roger *Malpasnage*, consisted of no more than nine acres.[122] These *beneficia* of all sizes could be made up of the most varied resources: churches, tithes, even episcopal customs.[123]

In most regions of France the term *alodium* signified family land, by definition property transmitted from generation to generation, not subject to any lord, and therefore free of the burdens typical of the *beneficium*. In Normandy, although it might refer to an exceptionally free type of estate – 'that they should do with it whatever they might wish, as if it were their own alod' – and although on occasions its complete freedom from seigneurial control might be implied,[124] the *alodium* was sliding into the same category as *beneficium/feudum*, signifying an estate held by someone in a condition of personal dependence. In a charter of 1025, duke Richard II consented to a grant by a certain Drogo involving his 'paternal alod'.[125] Later documents provide an increasing number of references to services owed by the holders of alods. Thus, between 1043 and 1048 one Geoffrey fitz Goscelin *Stantuin* gave an alod to the abbey of Jumièges from which he had previously performed service to remain in the lordship of Roger de Montgommery.[126] It also seems that while the obligations owed by the holder of an alod were often of a non-military character as, for instance, was true of an alod held of the abbey of St-Wandrille, from which were rendered all tithes and an annual rent of 10s., the holders of such properties were being progressively sucked into dependent relationships requiring military service.[127] There are several examples of *milites* holding alods.[128] Two charters of the year 1025 give the most precise definition of the distinction between the alod and the benefice, as well as demonstrating how both were incorporated into lordship; both were types of property held by *fideles* (vassals), but the benefice was extracted from the lord's estates, whereas the other was the family's.[129]

These conditions can be contrasted with the 'classical feudalism' of the 'Second Feudal Age', in which the fief was the basic form of tenure from which a set of well-defined obligations, governed by custom, were owed. The holders of the fiefs, all obliged to perform military service, had emerged as an élite within the lord's entourage; they were the honorial barons, the constituent personnel of the honorial court. Such clear institutional forms are some distance removed from what existed in pre-1066 Normandy, where the use of terminology was extremely general and non-technical. The current usage of *beneficium/feudum* and *alodium* is indicative of a society very familiar with notions of personal dependence and with the reciprocal obligation to perform service. But it was a society in which these bonds catered, without much differentiation, for the various domestic and military demands of lordship. Such conditions are entirely consistent with the meaning established earlier for *miles*, which usually signified nothing more than a soldier, and certainly not the man who was obliged to turn out with specified equipment as in the twelfth century. They are also in accord with the persistence of the old Carolingian term *fidelis* to describe a vassal and with those occasions on which *milites* were inserted among the peasantry. The components of pre-1066 Norman feudalism were a loose and vague set of

Economy and social structure

arrangements which still emphasised the personal nature of dependence, a conclusion which means that the views propounded early in the twentieth century by the American historian Charles Homer Haskins must finally be abandoned. Haskins' demonstration that such customs as the 'forty-day service term' had a place in pre-1066 Normandy was achieved on the basis of a documentation which is impossibly precarious by modern standards of diplomatic.[130] While it is natural that the origins of many later tenures can be traced back into the earliest documented period – this has been achieved, for example, in the case of fiefs held of the abbey of Fécamp or of Bayeux cathedral[131] – this does not prove the existence of the full apparatus of twelfth-century Norman feudalism. Norman society in 1066 was one in which feudal forms were not far removed from the primitive phase when ties of obligation were spreading, one in which the holder of a dependent tenure was not a prestigious figure in a reasonably articulate hierarchy, but usually a simple soldier whose main responsibility was to fight.

The changes in the use of terminology and the general evidence for 'feudal' relationships in pre-1066 Normandy are consistent with a society in which lordship was already widespread and strong by the early eleventh century, in which many previously 'free' landowners were being pulled into dependent relationships, in which many among these men must have increased their property by accepting benefices, and in which a consolidation and institutionalisation of tenurial relationships began to take place in the 1050s. The strength of early eleventh-century lordship is suggested by the frequency with which the appropriate terminology occurs in the documents and by the way in which, even at this date, *alodium* was invariably used to describe an estate held of someone else. The definition supplied in the 1025 charters suggests the process by which men who were 'free' – the term is employed in the sense of 'unburdened by services to a lord' – were slipping into dependence. The same development is clearly implied in the Jumièges charter of 1043–48 which recorded how Geoffrey fitz Goscelin did service for Roger de Montgommery because the alod remained in his lordship (*et inde michi serviebat pro eo quod ipse alodus in mea ditione manebat*). It may also explain the career in the 1030s of Herluin, the later abbot of Le Bec, who, according to his early-twelfth-century biographer, continued to support his patron, count Gilbert of Brionne, despite the confiscation of his benefices.[132] Other aspects of this same extension of lordship, which must have been most widely prevalent during the second quarter of the eleventh century, appear in the widespread augmentation of estates by force, described earlier (pp. 99–105), and in the devaluation of the term *miles* towards a collective noun; the *milites* in the charters of Richard II's reign were always identifiable individuals, men who were singled out by name, which was not always the case later (see p. 111). The first signs of the subsequent consolidation in the 1050s are firstly a number of references suggestive of a reluctance to transfer land held by *milites* to the Church,[133] and secondly the earliest indications in the charters of the idea of a tenurial hierarchy, which appear in a new type of reference to the confirmation of a dependent's grants to the Church by both his lord and his lord's lord (see p. 107).

The consistent strength of lordship, something which must have evolved in the second half of the tenth century, suggests that we are dealing with a process of change in the eleventh century which was essentially the extension of the lordship of well-established stronger families over equally well-established weaker ones. This view is supported by the evidence for the inheritance of the properties of those holding in dependence. Especially impressive is the way in which *beneficia* appear to have assumed the heritable characteristics of *alodia* from the earliest documented period. Important in this respect is a remarkable original charter, dating from the time of abbot Henry of St-Ouen of Rouen (?1006–33), which describes how a *miles* named Gonduin was allowed to pass the *beneficium* which he held from the abbey on to his sons, who would continue to perform the same service.[134] That this represents a general pattern is suggested by the absence of references to *beneficia* resumed by the lords who must have granted them.[135] The prevalence and the strength of inheritance can be emphasised by the later history of a *beneficium* held by a *miles* named Gilbert as a dependent of Robert fitz Humphrey de Vieilles (killed in the 1040s), and subsequently of Roger de Beaumont, which he bequeathed to the abbey of St-Pierre of Préaux at a time when he had no heirs. The birth of a daughter, who married, meant that the abbey had to concede her claims to inherit by awarding a life-lease on the property to her and her husband.[136] Similarly, the opinion of a twelfth-century commentator, looking back on the grants of benefices made by bishop Robert of Coutances (1026–48), was that they had been granted 'in fee and in inheritance' (*in feudum et in hereditatem*).[137] The result was that by 1066 the archaic notion that benefices were in any sense precarious tenancies was being dissipated through the growing use of the term *feudum*, signifying inheritance.

Consolidation from the 1050s is demonstrated by the way in which ideas of lineage began to penetrate to the level of the *milites*.

Economy and social structure

The spread of toponymics in the second half of the century must be a sign that the same identification of one man with the family property was taking place, as had happened earlier with the most powerful families. In the early eleventh-century documents, it is common for inheritance by all sons to be mentioned: this seems to have been the case in the succession arranged by Gonduin, the *miles* of the abbey of St-Ouen of Rouen, and also in that of Roscelin, a canon of Rouen cathedral, who granted a mixture of alods and benefices to the same abbey between 1015 and 1017.[138] The developing influence of ideas of lineage must be behind the spread of references to benefices which were held by brothers, of whom only one was named.[139] An important demonstration of such clarification of responsibility within the family group appears in a text in the Préaux cartulary, which, in referring to arrangements which must have been made some time before 1072, identified one brother as being responsible for the service due from the benefice, an anticipation of the practice which would later be described by the technical term *parage*.[140] This document supplies the first clear reference to what was to become a cardinal feature of twelfth-century Norman law, the indivisibility of 'feudal' property. Its significance for the consolidation of tenurial relationships is entirely in conformity with a chronology whereby clear references to the institutions of lordship only start to appear after 1066. Although the witness-lists of charters suggest their existence from the 1050s, the earliest mentions of lords holding courts to adjudicate between their tenants come from the 1070s.[141] Similarly, characteristic terminology such as 'relief', 'homage', and 'liege homage' only begins to become current in the later eleventh century.[142] Likewise, the eleventh-century evidence for wardship is so ambiguous as to suggest that Normandy had not yet made up its mind between seigneurial wardship, which became customary in the twelfth century, and family wardship, which was normal in neighbouring regions: in the case of the two Taisson minorities during William II's reign, the duke protected the young heir on the first occasion and the family on the second.[143]

The evidence as a whole can surely only signify conditions in which a great extension of lordship and dependence accompanied the expansion of aristocratic estates in the first half of the eleventh century. Despite the turmoil, this process was basically a readjustment of relations between established landowning families. This view fits in with the opinion that the structure of landed power within Normandy was exceptionally stable, at least in comparison with neighbouring territories where the insistent alienation of benefices often brought about the dangerous break-up of lords' estates.[144] The details of change are, however, complex and require much deeper investigation. The example of a family such as the Broc who managed, from a base near Rouen, to build up estates throughout the entire duchy during the course of the period up until 1066 suggests that, although the structural changes in terms of the relative strength of families may not have been that great, the instability with regard to the possession of land certainly was. The careers of individual families supply plentiful evidence of those who successfully exploited the turbulent period between c. 1025 and c. 1050 and those who did not. In general, on the basis of what we know of the seizure of ecclesiastical estates and the colonisation of Lower Normandy, these years must have witnessed a significant redistribution of property and power and greatly affected the political role which particular individuals could play. In the end, however, the absence from Normandy of bannal lordship and lay advocacy, along with the sustained distinction between nobility and knighthood, and the continuity of the Norman *pagi*, indicate that social change was eventually confined within a traditional and in many respects Carolingian structure of authority. This must be the background to the precocious evolution in Normandy of institutions of military lordship with a much more authoritarian and hierarchical character than was the case elsewhere.[145] But we should beware giving too coherent a shape to the institutions of Norman lordship at too early a date. Their developed form, like the idea that nobility might be defined by reference to a blood relationship to the ducal house, was something which came into existence in the twelfth century, not the eleventh. In 1066 the powers of the Norman lords over their tenurial dependents were still in the process of definition after a period of turbulence and change.

THE TOWNS

Rouen and Bayeux are the only Norman towns which are known to have been of any importance in the tenth century. The two places were singled out by the two-pronged invasion of 944 led by king Louis IV and duke Hugh the Great, and both were sites of comital residences. They alone of the Norman towns possessed mints. In neither case is there a serious reason to regard the Scandinavian settlements as having been immediately or especially disruptive. Both were sacked during the ninth century, but the survival at Bayeux of the Roman street plan right on into the seventeenth century points to a basic continuity of urban life. Of the two, Rouen was unquestionably the more important. Its mint, for example, was the only one to use new dies during the tenth century; Bayeux's, as far as we can know from a very small number of coins, merely continued to produce coin in an archaic Carolingian style. Rouen indeed shows every sign of having profited enormously from its role as an emporium at which Viking booty was exchanged. By the year 1000 it was a busy town, frequented by people of many races. Dudo of St-Quentin mentions Greeks, Indians, Frisians, Bretons, Danes, English, Scots, and Irish – palpable exaggeration in all probability, yet a list which is demonstrably correct in some of its apparently more incredible suggestions.[146] The one group of notable commercial absentees, the Jews, arrived in the late eleventh century.

The two towns continued to prosper and grow in the eleventh century, despite the ending of the links with Scandinavia. Rouen was apparently so large as to need to import corn by sea from Lower Normandy, while its traders seem to have been well known in England. One of its leading merchant families was strong enough in the late eleventh century to take an important part in the struggles for the control of Normandy between Robert Curthose and William Rufus, an act of political presumption which was concluded when the later king Henry I dropped one of the family from the tower of the castle.[147] There are clear signs of the town's expansion by 1030, with the existence of the three parish churches of St-André-hors-Ville, St-Eloi, and St-Laurent, in the suburbs, suggesting a population spreading beyond the walls.[148]

Bayeux, too, was a developing community, although one which, because of a fuller documentation, also illuminates the strains and stresses of the times. New fangled church dedications to St George or St Mary Magdalene again suggest the creation of new parishes and a rising population. The appearance of either four or five satellite *burgi*, a kind of urban overspill, points to the same conclusion.[149] Our knowledge of the citizenry reveals several families whose fortunes were based on financial wealth and on the sale and acquisition of urban property. As early as Richard II's reign, a ducal chaplain named Arnold was renowned for his wealth in gold, silver, and real estate. From *c.* 1050 there seems to have been an intensification of contacts between such men and the developing organisations of the cathedral chapter and the duke's government. We can know a little of the careers of men such as Conan, treasurer of the cathedral in the last years of the eleventh century and the early twelfth, whose financial transactions extended as far as incurring large debts to king Henry I, and whose stone house was an object of wonder to contemporaries in what was already a city of fine buildings. His probable predecessor as treasurer, Samson, also a ducal chaplain, and subsequently bishop of Worcester (1096–1112), was the owner of a sizeable estate in the town which he was apparently increasing by purchases.[150] Two early-twelfth-century descriptions of the town survive. One, a brief record by a monk of St-Benoît-sur-Loire named Ralph Tortaire, emphasises the magnificence of the town and the cathedral, the shining roof-tops and the soaring towers.[151] The other, the turgid verse of a canon of the cathedral named Serlo, spoke of a male population of 3,000 and of at least ten parish churches, as well as of many splendid buildings, of which the cathedral, the episcopal palace, Conan's stone house, and the canons' dwellings were singled out. The purpose of Serlo's poem, however, was to describe and explain the catastrophe of 1105, when Henry I's invading army burnt down a large part of the city. He located the reasons for this in the evil ways of the citizens, who had engaged in canonically prohibited trade, counterfeiting, theft, and the dispossession of widows and orphans.[152] Through his vitriolic pen, we can perceive a prosperous and busy community, elevated a little above its station by the exuberant extravagance of bishop Odo (1049/50–97). Bayeux presents a clear example of active urban life in the early eleventh century, and, in the second half of the century, of the increasingly complex connections between urban wealth and the institutional development of both Church and ducal government.

The vitality of Norman urban life can be just as well illustrated from the history of other towns. *Burgi* outside the walls existed at a number of places: Sées, for example, possessed one as early as 1025. The most remarkable testimony of all is the establishment of whole new towns or greatly enlarged communities at Dieppe, Caen, Falaise, Alençon, St-Lô, Valognes, and Cherbourg. This burgeoning, which in the cases of Caen and Cherbourg was quite clearly a result of ducal encouragement, was a feature which distinguished Normandy from much of the rest of western Europe and placed it in that region of north-western Europe especially notable for urban growth, which included Flanders and England.[153] The documents which relate to Caen supply the most rounded picture possible for any of the Norman towns. First mentioned in *c.* 1025, the most obvious cause of the town's rapid growth was duke William II's and his wife Mathilda's foundation there of two abbeys in *c.* 1059 and *c.* 1063, coupled with the place's importance as a ducal residence. It

Economy and social structure

became so much a focal point for the duke's government that, by the later eleventh century, a great deal of property had passed to functionaries of the ducal court.[154] Two charters, dating respectively from 1082 and 1083, show clearly not only the effects of an expanding population but also the endeavours of the great landowners to regulate and control its growth. The charters refer to the construction of the new parish churches of St-Gilles and St-Nicholas to serve the communities which had grown up around the religious houses of La Trinité and St-Etienne. The associated expansion of the *bourg* belonging to the monks of St-Etienne was evidently so threatening that the duke was obliged to require them not to poach from among the inhabitants of his own *bourg*, while the nuns of La Trinité secured an agreement that parishioners attending their churches at St-Etienne-le-Vieux and St-Martin would not be seduced over to the monks' new church of St-Nicholas.[155] A unique list, at least in terms of the Norman documentation, supplies some clues to the occupations of the inhabitants of the *bourg* of the monks of St-Etienne, including, among others, five cobblers, two fullers, an iron-worker, and a leather-worker. It also suggests considerable social mobility, since two houses are mentioned as having recently changed hands and the personal names contain some which are manifestly Breton. The likelihood is that most urban populations did include a sizeable manufacturing element. Iron- and leather-work are also known at St-Lô and Falaise, while a brewer appears among the residents of the *bourg* sponsored by the bishops of Bayeux.[156] Before 1066, there is even an indication that at Rouen, some trades were associated with a particular part of the city.[157]

Nothing is known of the government of the eleventh-century Norman towns. Socially, however, those for which there is sufficient information give every appearance of being both thriving and expanding communities. Their life can never be entirely divorced from the dominant forces of ducal government, aristocratic lordship, and the Church. Caen can in one sense be seen specifically as a bastion of population developed by duke William II in order to provide a focus for the duke's government in Lower Normandy. The main ducal residences were invariably in large towns and it was there that the great men would congregate: bishop Odo of Bayeux, for example, is known to have possessed houses in both Caen and Rouen, to which one in London was added after 1066.[158] It also seems that those whose wealth was primarily urban and financial would gravitate into the institutional safe havens of ducal government and cathedral chapters and that townsmen who had made their fortunes might tend to invest their wealth in land: the dynasties of the ducal moneyer Rannulf and his son Waleran and the treasurer Conan and his son John both possessed a mixture of urban and rural properties.[159] Yet the chief towns also obviously possessed an economic and social momentum which was uniquely urban. Rouen and its neighbourhood may not have been self-sufficient in basic food supplies, while there and elsewhere there existed groups of merchants and artisans whose mode of life was firmly based in urban communities. Outside the big three of Rouen, Bayeux, and Caen, there are plentiful signs of similar developments to the ones which can be observed there, although naturally on a smaller scale: *burgi* were established outside Sées and Evreux, while Coutances had its *suburbium* and was embellished by an elaborate building programme undertaken under the aegis of bishop Geoffrey (1048–93); merchants were said to frequent the relatively insignificant centre of Trun.[160] In short, the towns of Normandy show every sign of a reasonably consistent prosperity throughout the eleventh century. The foundation of new towns can be dated back to the first quarter of the century. After 1050, the economies of many towns, and of Caen and Bayeux in particular, were evolving quickly, in broad conformity with the pattern of consolidation and more rapid evolution also apparent in the countryside.

SOME CONCLUSIONS

The features which stand out in Norman society as it evolved up until 1066 are firstly, its wealth, secondly, the enduring strength of the institutions of public authority, and thirdly, the extensive social changes which took place during the second quarter of the eleventh century and which were still very much in the process of consolidation in 1066. The first is attested by the active money economy, the growth of towns, and the widespread indications of initiatives which required confidence and what we would now call 'capital'; the second, by the failure of nobility and knighthood to fuse and by the maintenance of prerogatives once claimed by the Carolingian monarchy, a strength of continuity which, as we shall see, was unique in contemporary France. But the third point shows that it was none the less the case that immense changes had taken place in the structure of aristocratic power and that these were only in the process of coalescing into institutional forms by 1066.

Economy and social structure

It is crucial to recognise that in Normandy change was largely contained within the traditional framework of ducal authority and that lordship was starting to shape into a rough-and-ready hierarchy by 1066 which gave pre-eminence to the duke. The manner in which alodial property was becoming subject to lordship emphasised just how great was the dominance exercised by the most powerful families. It would probably be correct to argue that the final result of the events of the second quarter of the century was to make those families who were already strong, even stronger. Although most of them lost members in the feuding, in perspective most of them simply rose and fell on the swings of fortune and favour, and many maintained a steady pace of acquisition from the 1020s onwards. The probable restriction of castles to a relatively small group supports this general view. It is also likely that the general economic prosperity sustained the pre-eminence of this small number of families; it allowed the dukes to disburse money rather than land, and it created conditions in which the aristocracy could reasonably expect to increase their estates by purchase as well as by armed force.[161] The example of Normandy, despite the obvious profits made by townsmen and even peasantry, appears to support one of the basic truisms of an early medieval society; that is, that prosperity tended mainly to favour those with the greatest power to exploit it. Politically and economically Normandy was firmly part of that area of north-western Europe notable for its exceptional wealth and for the resilience of traditional forms of authority. The closest parallels are with the county of Flanders and, if we look further afield, with the kingdoms of Germany and England.

The technique of placing Normandy's development against its wider context suggests that we should be wary about pronouncing that pre-1066 Normandy was in some special sense a 'feudal society'. The way in which this classification was first used – with the significance that Normandy was a territorial principality in which clear institutions of lordship worked from a very early date to support a single source of authority – must be abandoned.[162] It is not just that the institutions of pre-1066 Normandy in many respects merit epithets such as 'old-fashioned' or 'Carolingian'; it is also the case that the consciously antiquarian terminology employed to describe the peasantry suggests the survival of a level of 'freedom' untypical of other regions of northern France where the brutal tripartite social categorisation into those who prayed, those who fought, and those who worked had become current.[163] In terms of the chronology of social change this survival of ancient forms of authority and social

133

organisation must be explained by the fact that the transformation of aristocratic families, with the associated phenomena such as castle-building, the plundering of ecclesiastical estates, and the spread of dependent tenures, arrived in Normandy at a date which was significantly later than elsewhere. The period of *c.* 1025 to *c.* 1050 must be set against one around the late tenth or early eleventh centuries for most neighbouring regions. Even in Flanders, where the counts kept such firm control that 'private' castles were unusual in *c.* 1050, lineages were starting to form around the year 1000.[164] The postponement of developments which came everywhere in response to failing judicial and peace-keeping institutions must be attributed to the consistent exercise of authority by the counts/dukes, and in particular to the strength of Richard II's rule. It must, however, have its foundations in the circumstances of the Scandinavian settlement period which endowed the counts/dukes with such immense landed resources.

Comparison with other regions also suggests that the idea of a 'new aristocracy' which arrived to dominate Norman society from the 1020s onwards is one which should be abandoned. To propose this is to do no more than to recognise the force of the arguments developed over the past two decades by French and German scholars who have studied the ruling classes of early medieval western Europe. The original thesis of a 'new aristocracy', propounded in a series of remarkable articles during the 1940s by Professor David Douglas, was in fact conceived within the then current historical orthodoxy of the rise of a new aristocracy throughout northern France.[165] The demonstration, through the work of Werner, Boussard, and others, that our inability to trace ancestry back before a certain point in time is a sign, not of the rise of a new aristocracy, but of a far-reaching transformation in the structure of long-established families, is a conclusion which must be applicable to Normandy. The idea of a new warrior aristocracy smashing its way upwards at the expense of an older nobility just cannot be reconciled with the massive continuities such as the Carolingian character of ducal government, the stability of estate boundaries and organisation through from the ninth century to the eleventh, the separation throughout the eleventh century of nobility and knighthood, and the inheritance of *alodia* and *beneficia* from the earliest documented period. In addition, no one has so far discovered the aristocracy who were superseded in the not so sparse records of Richard II's reign. What actually happened in Normandy was that the province, shedding most of its Scandinavian characteristics during the second half of the tenth century, evolved into an exceptionally stable territorial principality under duke Richard II. After his death, a process of social change, against which even Richard's regime had not been entirely invulnerable, swept forwards. Numerous powerful families, most of them established in the Scandinavian settlement period, expanded their estates, splintered into lineages, established domination over offices in ducal government and over weaker neighbours, and consolidated their power around castles. The process as a whole is one which demands extended investigation. Its main lines have been laid bare for the Pays de Caux by the important studies of Jacques Le Maho. The records of the early Beaumonts point in the same direction, as do the persistent innuendoes of undiscovered relationships between the lineages who appear in Robert of Torigny's genealogies, or between the Warennes and the family of bishop Hugh of Coutances (*c*. 989–1025), or between the two *vicomtes* Thurstan Goz and Haimo *Dentatus*.[166] The consolidation of these changes began only from *c*. 1050 with the return of stable conditions which encouraged the proliferation of *bourgs* and monasteries and the crystallisation of the institutions of lordship.

Comparison with other regions also highlights the coincidence between the evolution of new social structures and the change in the dukes' attitude towards 'foreign policy'. It was only after the unstable second quarter of the eleventh century that a Norman ruler launched out on a policy of systematic expansion, such as had been typical of other principalities for some time. A likely hypothesis is that the maintenance of internal peace under William II was in high degree dependent on external aggression, whereas Richard II's 'peace' does seem to have been grounded in what were by eleventh-century standards genuinely pacific attitudes. It certainly seems that the kinds of structural changes which took place in Normandy between *c*. 1025 and *c*. 1050 tended, when they occurred in other well-organised principalities, to produce a reflex of external aggression. Internal disorder, the formation of lineages, and eastwards expansion came together in Flanders during the reign of count Baldwin IV (988–1035).[167] In Aquitaine, a principality firmly governed by dukes William IV (*c*. 963–95) and William V (995–1030), the subsequent period of disorder, characterised by the formation of lineages, the spread of independent castellanries, and Angevin invasion, was followed by expansion into Gascony and even the Iberian peninsula under duke Guy-Geoffrey (1058–86).[168]

Within Normandy itself, the events which took place before 1050 were of a type very likely to stimulate external aggression. Duke

Normandy before 1066

William's campaigns after 1050 might well be represented as essentially a grander version of the localised actions of the Norman aristocracy before 1050. It might be suggested that the obvious licence allowed to Roger de Montgommery to press ahead against the Bellêmes merely legitimised the sort of behaviour which the family had been indulging in for twenty-five years. Similarly, the formation of lineages, which converted families from something resembling a corporation with a chief into one property owner and a number of less well-endowed, even rootless, young men, must, as elsewhere, have tended to turn these *juvenes* towards the only two careers open to them, the Church, and more especially, the profession of arms. Although the pre-1066 Norman documents supply little evidence for military households to place alongside the slender detail in the early-twelfth-century life of Herluin, abbot of Le Bec, who is said to have received a military training in c. 1030 in the entourage of count Gilbert of Brionne, the changes in family structure cannot – unless Normandy differed radically from the rest of western Europe – have had any effect other than to increase the brittleness of an already violent society.[169] We should probably connect the brutalisation of Norman society which undoubtedly took place between c. 1025 and c. 1050 with the general circumstances which have persuaded one commentator, Professor Jean Dhondt, to make an explicit connection between the all-pervading and chronic instability of northern French society and the insistent aggressive campaigns and the sometimes outrageous ambitions of the leading territorial princes.[170]

The final conclusion which can be drawn by comparative methods is the quite remarkable strength of ducal authority, especially as it developed under William II after 1050. There was in fact a sense in which the changes of the first half of the eleventh century encouraged authority to develop, although not necessarily that of the dukes. The introduction of inequalities within kin-groups, the territorialisation of power, and the establishment of literate, property-owning corporations called monasteries, were stimuli towards the production of written records to detail ownership of land. Such developments were also productive of disputes. The decision by bishop John of Avranches to bequeath property outside his family meant that the grant was disputed in turn by his nephew and his great-nephew.[171] A quarrel within the monastery of St-Evroult between the abbot and a member of the founding family, who also happened to be the prior, meant that external authority in the shape of both the duke and the papacy had to be called in.[172] It was duke William's achievement to create the conditions in which the responsibility for resolving such disputes remained largely with the dukes and to ensure that in any event they were resolved without recourse to arms. He was also able to turn the aristocracy's possession of control over offices of government into a remarkable alliance, whereas it might have spelt the end of effective ducal rule. His government not only sustained most of the powers exercised by his predecessors, but managed to weld a remarkable, if temporary, unity among most of the politically influential members of Norman society. It is his achievement which explains why a blood relationship – real or otherwise – did become a criterion for nobility in the twelfth-century duchy and why 'Anglo-Norman feudalism' became so markedly authoritarian. Chapter Four will consider the structure and development of ducal government.

NOTES

1. For references to slavery in Normandy, L. Musset, 'Actes inédits du XIe siècle. II. Une nouvelle charte de Robert le Magnifique pour Fécamp', *BSAN*, lii (1955, for 1952–54), 150–1. Also, R. Fossier, *La terre et les hommes en Picardie* (Paris and Louvain, 1968), 552–62.
2. L. Musset, 'Les domaines de l'époque franque et les destinées du régime domanial du IXe au XIe siècle', *BSAN*, xlix (1946, for 1942–45), 68–76.
3. *Miracula sancti Wulfranni, Acta Sanctorum*, March, iii, 151.
4. L. Musset, 'Foires et marchés en Normandie à l'époque ducale', *AN*, xxvi (1976), 6–10.
5. *Recueil*, no. 223 (= *AAC*, no. 1); *AAC*, no. 14.
6. L. Musset, 'Quelques notes sur les baleiniers normands du Xe au XIIIe siècle', *Revue d'histoire économique et sociale*, xlii (1964), 147–61. For wine-growing, see, for example, *Recueil*, p. 470, index *vinea*; E. de Certain, 'Raoul Tortaire', *Bibliothèque de l'école des chartes*, xvi (1854–55), 516.
7. *Recueil*, no. 83. For the Norman money economy, L. Musset, 'La vie économique de l'abbaye de Fécamp sous l'abbatiat de Jean de Ravenne (1028–1078)', in *L'abbaye bénédictine de Fécamp*, i (Fécamp, 1959), 67–79, 345–9; idem, 'A-t-il existé en Normandie au XI siècle une aristocratie d'argent?', *AN*, ix (1959), 285–8.
8. For a payment in kind consisting of a horse and a hauberk, both assigned a money value, *Recueil*, no. 113.
9. E.g. *datis denariorum probate monete sexaginta libris*, ibid., no. 83. For comment on payments by weight, T.N. Bisson, *Conservation of Coinage: Monetary Exploitation and its Restraint in France, Catalonia, and Aragon (c. A.D. 100–c. 1225)* (Oxford, 1979), 23–4.
10. *Recueil*, no. 45, an original charter. See also, *ejusdem ville villanorum cen-*

sus decimam, ibid., no. 120; *IIII censarios in Monasteriis qui reddunt XL solidos, AAC*, no. 12.

11. *Recueil*, no. 86; P. Le Cacheux, 'Une charte de Jumièges concernant l'épreuve par le fer chaud (fin du XIe siècle)', *SHN, Mélanges*, xi (1927), 215.
12. This point is well brought out in Richard II's charters for Fécamp and St-Ouen of Rouen, which describe the grants of earlier Norman rulers, *Recueil*, nos. 34, 53, and then by the foundation charter of La Trinité of Caen, *ibid.*, no. 231.
13. L. Musset, 'Recherches sur le tonlieu en Normandie à l'époque ducale', *RHDFE*, 4e série, xlvi (1968), 361–2.
14. See, for example, *Recueil*, nos. 64, 84, 197, 208. For *hospites*, who were usually settlers on new land, *ibid.*, nos. 187, 195.
15. L. Musset, 'Peuplement en bourgage et bourgs ruraux en Normandie du Xe au XIIIe siècle', *CCM*, ix (1966), 187–95. See also, Françoise Piletta, 'Les bourgs du sud du pays d'Auge du milieu du XIe au milieu du XIVe siècle', *AN*, xxx (1980), 211–30.
16. *GC*, xi, instr. col. 219.
17. *Documents de l'histoire de la Normandie*, ed. M. de Bouard (Toulouse, 1972), 66–7.
18. L. Musset, 'La Seine normande et le commerce maritime du IIIe au XIe siècle', *Revue de la société savante de la Haute-Normandie*, no. 53 (1969), 12.
19. L. Musset, 'Les conditions financières d'une réussite architecturale: les grandes églises romanes de Normandie', in *Mélanges offerts à René Crozet*, ed. P. Gallais and Y.-J. Riou (Poitiers, 1966), i, 307–13.
20. The main studies on the Norman aristocracy are, D. C. Douglas, *William the Conqueror* (London, 1964), 83–104; J. Le Patourel, *Norman Barons* (Hastings and Bexhill Branch of the Historical Association, 1966); L. Musset, 'L' aristocratie normande au XIe siècle', in *La noblesse au moyen âge XIe–XVe siècles. Essais à la mémoire de Robert Boutruche*, ed. P. Contamine (Paris, 1976), 71–96.
21. On the Norman *comtés*, the fundamental study is D. C. Douglas, 'The earliest Norman counts', *EHR*, lxi (1946), 129–54. The origins of Mortain are much clarified by *André de Fleury, Vie de Gauzlin, abbé de Fleury*, ed. R. -H. Bautier and G. Labory (Paris, 1969), 48–50; see also, *Recueil*, p. 25, note 28. For the descent of Ivry, D. R. Bates, 'Notes sur l'aristocratie normande. I. Hugues, évêque de Bayeux (1011-env.–1049). II. Herluin de Conteville et sa famille', *AN*, xxiii (1973), 10–15.
22. Douglas, *William the Conqueror*, 408–9.
23. *WJ*, 100–1, 102–3.
24. *Ibid.*, 100. Also, 'Inventio et Miracula sancti Wulfranni', ed. Dom J. Laporte, *SHN, Mélanges*, xiv (1938), 47.
25. *WJ*, 107–8.
26. Hugh of Flavigny, *Chronicon*, in *MGH, Scriptores*, viii, 401.
27. In general, Douglas, *William the Conqueror*, 90–1. For Humphrey, *Les annales de l'abbaye de St-Pierre de Jumièges*, ed. Dom J. Laporte (Rouen, 1954), 85.
28. *Ibid.*, 85; *Recueil*, no. 201.
29. *Ibid.*, no. 72; *Thesaurus Novus Anecdotorum*, ed. E. Martène and U.

Durand (Paris, 1717), i, col. 167; Rouen, Bibliothèque municipale, MS. 1193 (Y. 44), fo. 30v.

30. *Antiquus Cartularius ecclesiae Baiocensis (Livre Noir)*, ed. V. Bourrienne (Rouen, 1902–03), i, no. 21; *GC*, xi, instr. col. 218; *Recueil*, no. 148 (version A²); Avranches, Bibliothèque municipale, MS. 210, fo. 87rv.
31. For Gilbert and Eu, Douglas, 'The earliest Norman counts', 135–40.
32. Ordericus, interpolation in WJ, 157–8.
33. *Cartulaire de l'abbaye de St-Vincent du Mans*, ed. R. Charles and M. le vicomte Menjot d'Elbenne (Le Mans, 1913), no. 621; Cartulaire de St-Martin de Sées, fo. 95v (see chapter 2, note 92).
34. *Chartes de l'abbaye de Jumièges (v. 825 à 1204) conservées aux archives de la Seine-Inférieure*, ed. J. J. Vernier (Rouen and Paris, 1916), i, no. 42.
35. J. Le Maho, 'L' apparition des seigneuries châtelaines dans le Grand-Caux à l'époque ducale', *Arch. méd.*, vi (1976), 9–11, 18–19, 32–7.
36. For Turchetil: *GC*, xi, instr. col. 199; *Neustria Pia*, ed. A. du Monstier (Rouen, 1663), 522. Also, *GC*, xi, instr. col. 203; Cartulaire de St-Pierre de Préaux, A. D. Eure, H. 711, fo. 122r. On all matters relating to the Beaumont family I am deeply indebted to the research and the advice of my student Mr David Crouch.
37. L. Musset, 'Aux origines d'une classe dirigeante: les Tosny, grands barons normands du Xe au XIIIe siècle', *Francia*, v (1978, for 1977), 72–3.
38. F. Lot, *Etudes critiques sur l'abbaye de St-Wandrille* (Paris, 1913), pièces justificatives, no. 18.
39. *Recueil*, nos. 128, 129.
40. For the basic information on the Bertrands, *Recueil*, no. 205; *CTR*, no. 79; also the earliest text of the *pancarte* of the abbey of Grestain, see note 41 below. For the Broc, J. -M. Bouvris, 'Une famille de vassaux des vicomtes de Bayeux au XIe siècle: les Broc', *Revue du département de la Manche*, xix (1977), 11–24.
41. These connections are demonstrated in Bates, 'Notes sur l'aristocratie normande', 23–4, but need clarification in the light of the discovery of the earliest *pancarte* of the abbey of Grestain, of which there are three copies of the 17th–18th centuries, BN, collection du Vexin, iv, 141–5, 147–9; xi, fos. 158r–60v. The text will appear in my revision of *Regesta Regum Anglo-Normannorum*, vol. i, to be published by the Oxford University Press. Muriel's existence is confirmed by her attestation of the *pancarte* of the abbey of Lessay, printed with facsimile in *Musée des archives départementales* (Paris, 1878), 51–5, planche XVIII. The document itself was destroyed in 1944. The suggestion in *Regesta*, i, no. 198, that it is a forgery is groundless.
42. This story can be built up from *Recueil*, nos. 54, 61, 72, 85; *Thesaurus Novus Anecdotorum*, i, col. 167, *CTR*, no. 25, Rouen, Bibliothèque municipale, MS. 1193 (Y. 44), fo. 30v.
43. L. Musset, 'Actes inédits du XIe siècle. V. Autour des origines de St-Etienne de Fontenay', *BSAN*, lvi (1963, for 1961–62), 20–3; Le Maho, 'L' apparition des seigneuries châtelaines', 9–11, 18–19, 32–7; *Thesaurus Novus Anecdotorum*, i, col. 167.
44. *Antiquus Cartularius Ecclesiae Baiocensis*, i, no. 21; *GC*, xi, instr. col. 218.
45. E. Warlop, *The Flemish Nobility before 1300* (Kortrijk, 1975–76), i, 88.
46. Marie de la Motte-Collas, 'Les possessions territoriales de l'abbaye de

Saint-Germain-des-Prés, du début du IXe au début du XIIe siècle', *Revue d'histoire de l'église de France*, xliii (1957), 49–80.
47. Le Maho, 'L' apparition des seigneuries châtelaines', 32–7. I am grateful to Mr David Crouch for the second point.
48. Above, Chapter 2, notes 8, 9, and 17, for some references to a much studied subject. A good introduction, although inevitably a little dated, is G. Duby, 'The nobility in medieval France', in *idem, The Chivalrous Society* (London, 1977), 94–111. For some discussion of Normandy, Musset, 'L' aristocratie normande au XIe siècle', 85–94.
49. *Recueil*, nos. 231, 124.
50. *Ibid.*, nos. 93, 128, 140, 223; *CTR*, no. 56; L. Musset, 'Actes inédits du XIe siècle. I. Les plus anciennes chartes du prieuré de St-Gabriel (Calvados)', *BSAN*, lii (1955, for 1952–54), 140.
51. *Recueil*, nos, 124, 95.
52. This idea has recently been advanced tentatively in J. Le Patourel, *The Norman Empire* (Oxford, 1976), 289.
53. WJ, 320–9.
54. Ivo of Chartres, *Epistolae, PL*, clxii, col. 266 (*ep.* no. 112).
55. *S. Anselmi Cantuariensis Archiepiscopi Opera Omnia*, ed. Dom F.S. Schmitt (Edinburgh, 1938–61), v, 370, *ep.* no. 424.
56. Duby, in *The Chivalrous Society*, 144. See also K.F. Werner, 'Untersuchungen zur Frühzeit des französischen Fürstentums', *Die Welt als Geschichte*, xx (1960), 116–19.
57. G. Duby, 'French genealogical literature: the eleventh and twelfth centuries', in *The Chivalrous Society*, 154–7.
58. *Acta Archiepiscopum Rotomagensium, PL*, cxlvii, col. 277; Ordericus, interpolating WJ, 157.
59. The two daughters of Richard III are mentioned in *Chronique de Robert de Torigni, abbé du Mont-Saint-Michel*, ed. L. Delisle (Rouen, 1872–73), i, 33–4. See further, OV, iii, 252; v, 34; Bourvris, 'Une famille de vassaux', 9–10.
60. Thus, the phrases, *servitium militum, dominium cum militibus, Recueil*, no. 140. See also, *ibid.*, nos. 130, 147 (version C), 208, 229; *AAC*, nos. 7, 18; A. D. Eure, H. 711, fo. 137v. Before William II's reign, *miles* was always applied to a specific individual, except *ac militum meorum* (of count Robert of Mortain), *Recueil*, no. 16.
61. *Ibid.*, nos. 225, 43; 'Miracula Rotomagensie Sanctae Catarinae', ed. A. Poncelet, *Analecta Bollandiana*, xxii (1903), 432.
62. Thus, *Valselini militis Lisiacensis episcopi, Recueil*, no. 48; or, extravagantly, *quidam meus miles vehementer michi carissimus, nomine Rodulfus, Chartes de Jumièges*, i, no. 8. For synonymity, *quidam homines mei scilicet milites, Recueil*, no. 85; or *quidam miles homo Rogerii conestabuli*, A. D. Eure, H. 711, fo. 136r.
63. A. D. Eure, H. 711, fo. 145r. *Vavassor* seems to be used in its twelfth-century technical sense, suggesting that this section of the text has been rewritten. The remainder is acceptable 11th-century diplomatic form. See, J. Yver, '"Vavassor", note sur les premiers emplois du terme', *RHDFE*, 4e série, lii (1974), 548–9.
64. E.g. *Recueil*, nos. 130, 140, 147, 197, 205, 208, 229; *AAC*, no. 18; *Thesaurus Novus Anecdotorum*, i, cols. 167, 168. Also *terram unius carruacae et*

unum equitem et unum villanum et tres bordarios, BN, collection du Vexin, iv, 147. For England and the *miles* of 'Domesday Book', Sally Harvey, 'The knight and the knight's fee in medieval England', *Past and Present*, no. 49 (1970), 14–28.

65. *Consuetudines et Iusticie*, c. 5, in C. H. Haskins, *Norman Institutions* (Cambridge, Mass., 1918), 282.
66. N. B., *Milites vero mediae nobilitatis, atque gregarios*, WP, 232. For similar ambivalent uses, *Recueil*, no. 202; A. D. Eure, H. 711, fo. 100rv. Above, note 60.
67. *PL*, clxii, col. 266; WJ, 321; *Recueil*, nos. 69, 74.
68. WJ, 328; *Recueil*, no. 128.
69. WJ, 324. For Turchetil, see note 36 above. The earliest reference to Turold appears to be OV, ii, 12; iv, 206. He appears in none of the records of the two Préaux abbeys and Humphrey never employed the patronymic. Interestingly, some of the names mentioned by Robert of Torigny, such as Turold and Dunelina, appear in the 'beaumont' family in the mid-11th century, *GC*, xi, instr. col. 203; A. D. Eure, H. 711, fo. 112v; *Neustria Pia*, 522.
70. 'De nobili Crispinorum genere', in *Beati Lanfranci Cantuariensis archiepiscopi... Opera Omnia*, ed. L. d'Achery (Paris, 1648), *Appendix*, 53; *Recueil*, no. 35.
71. *Ibid.*, nos. 29 (version B), 50, 85.
72. *Ibid.*, no. 13 (version C).
73. M. Fixot, 'Les fortifications de terre et la naissance de la féodalité dans le Cinglais', *Château Gaillard*, iii (1966), 61–6; J. Decaens, 'Les enceintes d'Urville et de Bretteville-sur-Laize (Calvados)', *AN*, xviii (1968), 344–5, 363–8.
74. Annie Renoux, 'L' enceinte fortifiée d'Audrieu (Calvados) (XIIe–XIVe siècles)', *Arch. méd.*, ii (1972), 63–7.
75. *Recueil*, no. 15.
76. *Ibid.*, nos. 96, 106, 123, 133.
77. *Ibid.*, nos. 99, 105, 106, 107.
78. *Ibid.*, no. 190.
79. *Ibid.*, no. 128; A. D. Eure, H. 711, fo. 137r; *CTR*, no. 27.
80. *Ricardi comitis Ebroice civitatis*, *Recueil*, no. 92, from 1038 is the earliest certain example from an original charter. After this come the earliest references from Arques and Eu, which date from the late 1040s, *ibid.*, nos. 107, 108, 112, 123, 124, 191.
81. For other toponymics from Richard II's reign, *ibid.*, nos. 48, 54. On the spread of toponymics, Musset, 'L'aristocratie normande au XIe siècle', 94–5.
82. WJ, 115–16. In general, J. Yver, 'Les châteaux forts en Normandie jusqu'au milieu du XIIe siècle. Contribution à l'étude du pouvoir ducal', *BSAN*, liii (1957, for 1955–56), 52–7.
83. Le Maho, 'L' apparition des seigneuries châtelaines', 49, 83–7. Also *idem*, 'De la curtis au château: l'exemple du Pays de Caux', *Château Gaillard*, viii (1977), 171–83.
84. Annie Renoux, 'Le château des ducs de Normandie à Fécamp (Xe–XIIe s.). Quelques données archéologiques et topographiques', *Arch. méd.*, ix (1979), 17–19; M. de Bouard, *Le château de Caen* (Caen, 1979), 9–11,

30. See also, B. K. Davison, 'Early earthwork castles: a new model', *Château Gaillard*, iii (1966), 37–47; J. Decaens, 'L' enceinte fortifiée de Sébécourt (Eure)', *ibid.*, vii (1974), 49–60.
85. M. de Bouard, 'La motte d'Olivet', *Arch. méd.*, vi (1976), 355–8; viii (1978), 292–3.
86. OV, iii, 16–18.
87. In general, J. -F. Lemarignier, 'Aspects politiques des fondations de collégiales dans le royaume de France au XIe siècle', *La vita comune del clero nei secoli XI e XII* (Miscellanea del Centro di Studi Medioevali, i, Milan, 1962), 23–8.
88. *Recueil*, no. 36.
89. *Ibid.*, nos. 15, 44, 55, all original charters.
90. Berengar, Baldric, and Roscelin appear, *ibid.*, no. 21; Baldric, Roscelin, and Roger, *ibid.*, nos. 35, 55.
91. *Ibid.*, nos. 34, 53.
92. *Ibid.*, no. 35.
93. The numerous references to *vicomtes* named Hugh in pre-1066 charters can be brought together and assigned to Hugh I and Hugh II. Hugh the *vicomte*, son of Thurstan, who attests a charter of 1027–33, must be Hugh I, since his father's name is known from other sources to have been Thurstan, *Recueil*, no. 65. Hugh the *vicomte* and his son Hugh who appear in 1035–*c*. 1040 must be Hugh I and Hugh II, *ibid.*, no. 93. Hugh I was killed during duke William II's minority. Hugh II is definitely named as a *vicomte* in 1055, *ibid.*, no. 137. Finally, the Hugh the *vicomte* who received property at St-Philbert-sur-Risle in 1066 is conclusively identified as Hugh II by a reference to Hugh de Montfort having held property at St-Philbert in a copy of a lost Le Bec cartulary, BN, MS. latin 13905, fo. 83v.
94. The basic material appears in *Recueil*, no. 94, recording grants of 1035–*c*. 1040 and 1068–78. Roger the *vicomte* and his son Robert also appear in another pre-1066 Fécamp charter, BN, collection Moreau, vol. 21, fo. 22v. That Roger the *vicomte* and Robert the *vicomte* both attest the *pancarte* of the abbey of Montivilliers of 1068–76 might indicate that Roger was still alive in or after 1068, GC, xi, instr. col. 330. For other references to Robert, BN, collection Moreau, vol. 21, fos 20v, 27v.
95. 'De nobili Crispinorum genere', 53; *Recueil*, no. 69.
96. Osbern, *Recueil*, nos. 69, 79, 85.
97. Humphrey may well be the *Anfredi dapiferi* who attests *ibid.*, no. 69. His son Robert was certainly a *dapifer, ibid.*, nos. 105, 149. For Ralph, *ibid.*, no. 89.
98. It is difficult to distinguish between this *vicomte* Richard and Richard, son of Thurstan Goz. The earlier references, that is, from Thurstan's lifetime, are likely to be to Richard de Lillebonne, *Recueil*, nos. 35, 43, 49, 85, 89, 110. A Lambert, son of Richard the *vicomte*, attests an act of archbishop Malger for St-Ouen of Rouen, A. D. Seine-Maritime 14H, 189, and Robert of Torigny names Richard *vicomte* of Rouen as the father of Lambert de St-Saens, WJ, 328. This Lambert was the father of Helias de St-Saens, a devoted supporter of Robert Curthose and guardian of William Clito, OV, iv, 182; vi, 162–4, 286–8, 368.
99. A. D. Eure, H. 711, fos. 132v, 137r.

100. OV, ii, 40; iii, 84. For these problems in a more general context, J. C. Holt, 'Politics and property in early medieval England', *Past and Present*, no. 57 (1972), 3–52, and especially, 4–13, 40. Also, Le Patourel, *Norman Empire*, 191–4.
101. Marjorie Chibnall, 'Les droits d'héritage selon Orderic Vital', *RHDFE*, 4e série, xlviii (1970), 347.
102. Musset, 'Fontenay', 27.
103. For Robert and William's lands, A. D. Eure, H. 711, fos. 98r, 98rv, 102rv, 119v, 122v, 136r; *Neustria Pia*, 522; Bouvris, 'Une famille de vassaux', 13.
104. Bates, 'Notes sur l'aristocratie normande', 10–15, 29–30.
105. Le Maho, 'L' apparition des seigneuries châtelaines', 32–7.
106. Holt, 'Politics and property', 40.
107. E.g. Cartulaire de St-Martin de Sées, fos. 7v, 9r; *Cartulaire de Marmoutier pour le Perche*, ed. l'abbé Barret (Mortagne, 1894), no. 6; *Recueil*, no. 212; see, note 171 below.
108. *AAC*, no. 6; *Recueil*, no. 110. In general, Musset, 'L' aristocratie normande au XIe siècle', 87–8.
109. For the counts of Evreux, *Recueil*, nos. 10, 92, 208, 234; Lot, *St-Wandrille*, pièces justificatives, no. 18; Le Maho, 'L' apparition des seigneuries châtelaines', 26–9.
110. *Recueil*, nos. 13, 34, 36, 53, 100, 112, 234; Lot, *St-Wandrille*, pièces justificatives, no. 15; Rouen, Bibliothèque municipale, MS. 1193 (Y. 44), fos. 31r, 55v.
111. *AAC*, no. 7.
112. *Recueil*, no. 225. In a charter of 1082, count Robert is described as *ipse comes advocatus et guarantus sit illius elemosinae*, BN, collection Baluze, vol. 77, fo. 60r, no. 46 (*Regesta*, i, no. 145).
113. *Consuetudines et Iusticie*, c. 10, in Haskins, *Norman Institutions*, 282.
114. *Ibid.*, 27–31; J. Yver, 'Les premières institutions du duché de Normandie', *Settimane di Centro Italiano di Studi sull' Alto Medioevo*, xvi (Spoleto, 1969), 348–9.
115. Douglas, *William the Conqueror*, 96–8; Yver, 'Les premières institutions', 334–7. Very valuable is J. R. Strayer, review of *Recueil*, *Speculum*, xxxvii (1962), 608–10. See also, D. J. A. Matthew, *The Norman Conquest* (London, 1966), 57–68. At a late stage I learnt that Dr. Marjorie Chibnall, working independently, has reached similar general conclusions on pre-1066 Norman 'feudalism' to those here. I am grateful to her for sending me a copy of her paper which will appear in *Proceedings of the Battle Conference*, v, 1983.
116. *Recueil*, no. 43; *AAC*, nos. 6, 14.
117. *benefitium Alsvillam scilicet, quam a predicto meo domino militans obtineo*, *Recueil*, no. 188.
118. *unum equitem cum terra sua qui eadem prata custodit*, *AAC*, no. 7. The attempts to establish whether *miles* and *eques* were in fact equivalents merely demonstrate the non-technical nature of the terminology, Musset, 'L' aristocratie normande au XIe siècle', 89; J. Flori, 'Chevaliers et chevalerie au XIe siècle en France et dans l'Empire germanique', *Le Moyen Age*, lxxxii (1976), 127.
119. E.g. *Recueil*, nos. 43, 80, 122, 135, 197, 205.

120. *praeterea viginti solidi quos annuatim de sancto Petro et abbate in beneficio habebat*, A. D. Eure, H. 711, fo. 123v – the date seems to be mid-11th century; *Recueil*, no. 98.
121. P. Chevreux and J. J. Vernier, *Les archives de Normandie et de la Seine-Inférieure* (Rouen, 1911), planche no. 7.
122. *Recueil*, no. 191; *CTR*, no. 76.
123. *Recueil*, nos. 139, 191, 219; *CTR*, no. 50.
124. *Recueil*, no. 87. Also, *Hoc est terra que vocatur Marcisie et Morsalin, quod est alodum ex paterna hereditate. Terra vero Amblida dedit per auctoritatem comitis Willelmi*, BN, collection Moreau, vol. 30, fo. 190r. See, in general, L. Musset, 'Réflexions sur *alodium* et sa signification dans les textes normands', *RHDFE*, 4e série, xlvii (1969), 606. Also, R. Carabie, *La propriété foncière dans le très ancien droit normand (XIe–XIIIe siècles), I. La propriété domaniale* (Caen, 1943), 230–43; Matthew, *Norman Conquest*, 145–6.
125. *Recueil*, no. 36.
126. *Ibid.*, no. 113.
127. Lot, *St-Wandrille*, pièces justificatives, no. 34.
128. E.g. *Recueil*, nos. 85, 94.
129. *ea que fideles nostri, nostro consensu, aut precario vel beneficiis que nostri juris erant, vel de hereditatibus quas paterno jure possidebant, concesserunt*, ibid., no. 34. See also, *ibid.*, no. 36
130. Haskins, *Norman Institutions*, 5–24. See, Appendix B.
131. L. Musset, 'Notules fécampoises', *BSAN*, liv (1957–58), 586–9; Bates, 'Notes sur l'aristocratie normande', 17, note 70.
132. *Recueil*, no. 113; *Vita Herluini*, ed. J. Armitage Robinson, in *Gilbert Crispin, Abbot of Westminster* (Cambridge, 1911), 87–8. See, C. Harper-Bill, 'Herluin, Abbot of Bec, and his biographer', *Studies in Church History*, xv (1978), 15–17.
133. E.g. *Recueil*, nos. 147, 208; *Chartes de Jumièges*, i, no. 32; A. D. Eure, H. 711, fo. 137v.
134. *Ad hoc etiam Gunduinus supradictis gratis et sine precii taxatione dedit nobis X acros de meliori terra quam possidebat eo rationis tenore ut beneficium quod ex parte nostra habuit post mortem eius filiis filiis* [sic in MS.] *suis sub eodem servitutis respectu quo et ipse servivit consentiremus*, A. D. Seine-Maritime, 14H. 255..
135. On resumed *beneficia*, Carabie, 247, citing *Chartes de Jumièges*, i, no. 17; and *Cartulaire de St-Ymer-en-Auge*, ed. C. Bréard (Rouen, 1908), no. 1. Note also, *CTR*, no. 30.
136. A. D. Eure, H. 711, fo. 100rv.
137. *GC*, xi, instr. col. 218.
138. A. D. Seine-Maritime, 14 H. 255; *Recueil*, no. 21.
139. E.g. *Godeboldum militem et omnes fratres ejus, cum omni eorum alodo*, *Recueil*, no. 94.
140. *duo fratres prescripti Anschitilli, Gislebertus videlicet et Gaufridus petiverunt abbatem Ansfridum qui eo tempore proerat loco, ut in beneficium concederet illis tenere de se, ea tamen ratione ut Gaufridus solus inde redderet servitium*, A. D. Eure, H. 711, fo. 108rv.
141. For Robert of Mortain's *curia* in 1082, BN, collection Baluze, vol. 77, fo. 60r. For Roger de Montgommery's in 1083–89, Cartulaire de St-

Martin de Sées, fo. 61v. These are the earliest appropriate uses of the term that I have been able to find in a record source. The earliest pleas heard before Roger de Beaumont date from the 1070s, *GC*, xi, instr. cols. 61, 202–3; A. D. Eure, H. 711, fo. 100rv. Earlier mentions of the *curia* of Roger de Montgommery appear in a non-Norman source, *Cartulaire de l'abbaye de St-Vincent du Mans*, nos. 621, 769.

142. For some comment, Yver, 'Les premières institutions', 335, note 84; Musset, 'L' aristocratie normande au XIe siècle', 90, note 7. For relief, there is the early, clumsy, *les reiles des vavassoribus*, in an original charter of *c.* 1050–66, *Recueil*, no. 191. Other references date from well after 1066 and are rare before *c.*1080. See, *reddidit illi feodum suum sine relevamento, commandisam hominicatus abbati facio*, Cartulaire de l'abbaye de St-Wandrille, A. D. Seine-Maritime, 16H., non classé, fos. 320r, 324r; *domno Radulfo abbati hommagium fecit*, Cartulaire de St-Martin de Sées, fo. 16v; *pro relevatione terre quam de Sancto tenebant*, Lot, *St-Wandrille*, pièces justificatives, no. 46. For liege homage, *Antiquus Cartularius Ecclesiae Baiocensis*, i, no. 76; E. Deville, *Notices sur quelques manuscrits normands conservés à la Bibliothèque Sainte-Geneviève. IV. Analyse d'un ancien cartulaire de l'abbaye de Saint-Etienne de Caen* (Evreux, 1905), 24, 30.

143. Musset, 'Fontenay', 23. See, in general, J. Yver, 'Le "Très Ancien Coutumier" de Normandie, miroir de la législation ducale?', *Revue d'histoire du droit: Tijdschrift voor Rechtsgeschiedenis*, xxxix (1971), 354, note 63.

144. Musset, 'Les domaines', 52–60, 67–8.

145. This general point is made in the discussion by T. N. Bisson, 'The problem of feudal monarchy: Aragon, Catalonia, and France', *Speculum*, liii (1978), 470–7. See also, Fossier, *La terre et les hommes en Picardie*, 546–50; M. Bur, *La formation du comté de Champagne, v. 950–1150* (Nancy, 1977), 399–402.

146. L. Musset, 'Le satiriste Garnier de Rouen et son milieu (début du XIe siècle)', *Revue du moyen âge latin*, x (1954), 248–9.

147. Suzanne Deck, 'Les marchands de Rouen sous les ducs', *AN*, vi (1956), 246–8.

148. *Recueil*, nos. 36, 52, 61.

149. For the *bourgs*, Musset, 'Peuplement en bourgage', 184. For the churches, *idem*, 'Observations sur le culte de sainte Marie-Madeleine en Normandie et notamment à Bayeux', *BSAN*, lvi (1963, for 1961–62), 667–70; *Rouleaux des morts du IXe au XVe siècle*, ed. L. Delisle (Paris, 1866), 161.

150. For detail on these families, Musset, 'Aristocratie d'argent', 295–8.

151. De Certain, 'Raoul Tortaire', 516.

152. 'Versus Serlonis de capta Baiocensium civitate', in *Minor Anglo-Latin Satirical Poets and Epigrammists of the Twelfth Century*, ed. T. H. Wright (Rolls Series, 1872), ii, 242–3.

153. L. Musset, 'La renaissance urbaine des Xe et XIe siècles dans l' Ouest de France: problèmes et hypothèses de travail', in *Etudes de civilisation médiévale, IXe-XIIe siècles. Mélanges offerts à E.- R. Labande* (Poitiers, 1974), 570–1, 573–4.

154. L. Musset, 'Actes inédits du onzième siècle. VI. L'abbaye de Saint-Ouen de Rouen et la ville de Caen', *BSAN*, lviii (1967, for 1965–6), 122–3.

155. *AAC*, nos. 8, 12, 17.
156. *Ibid.*, pp. 46–7; no. 17.
157. *Recueil*, no. 158; cf. F. Barlow, M. Biddle, *et al., Winchester in the Early Middle Ages*, i (Oxford, 1976), 496.
158. Cartulaire de St-Martin de Troarn, BN, MS latin 10086, fo. 158v; H. Navel, 'L' enquête de 1133 sur les fiefs de l'évêché de Bayeux', *BSAN*, xlii (1935), 20; *Regesta*, ii, no. 646.
159. Musset, 'Aristocratie d'argent', 292–4, 296–7.
160. *Recueil*, no. 223 (= *AAC*, no. 1).
161. E.g. *Recueil*, no. 83; *Neustria Pia*, 521.
162. Cf. Haskins, *Norman Institutions*, 5.
163. Duby, *The Chivalrous Society*, 90–3.
164. In general, *ibid.*, 146–8. See also, J. -F. Lemarignier, *Le gouvernement royal aux premiers temps capétiens* (Paris, 1965), 69–70; Fossier, *La terre et les hommes en Picardie*, 480–8; O. Guillot, *Le comte d'Anjou et son entourage au XIe siècle* (Paris, 1972); i 456–65; Warlop, *The Flemish Nobility*, i, 43, 89. For Maine, there is R. Latouche, *Histoire du comté du Maine pendant le Xe et le XIe siècle* (Paris, 1910), 59–65.
165. See especially, Douglas, 'The earliest Norman counts', 148–9.
166. E.g. L. C. Loyd, 'The origin of the family of Warenne', *Yorkshire Archaeological Journal*, xxxi (1934), 102–3; Musset, 'St-Gabriel'. 126.
167. Warlop, *The Flemish Nobility*, i, 55.
168. C. Higounet, 'Le groupe aristocratique en Aquitaine et en Gascogne (fin Xe–début XIIe siècle)', *Annales du Midi*, lxxx (1968), 563–5, 571; Jane Martindale, 'The origins of the Duchy of Aquitaine and the government of the counts of Poitou (902–1137)' (Oxford University D. Phil. Thesis, 1965), 97–114, 123–8.
169. N.B., *transtuli ad militiam nostram,* and *cum magno comitatu militum, Recueil,* nos. 70, 149. Also, *Vita Herluini*, 87–8.
170. See chapter 2, note 19.
171. *Recueil*, no. 229; E. A. Pigeon, *Le diocèse d'Avranches* (Coutances, 1888), ii, 661.
172. OV, ii, 64–6, 90–2, 106–16.

CHAPTER FOUR
Ducal government

Dukes Richard II, Richard III, and Robert I are utterly obscure as personalities. All sources describe Richard II as a paragon of respectability, a firm guardian of the peace, and a generous benefactor to the Church. This colourless verdict hides a ruler who can only have been both extremely able and personally impressive. His two sons who followed him as duke both died young; Richard III in what some contemporaries regarded as suspicious circumstances in 1027, and Robert at Nicea on the return journey from a pilgrimage to the Holy Land. Robert's reputation for generosity was of a sort which a modern commentator might interpret as a sign of instability and weakness. For William II, too, we can know little, partly because eleventh-century chroniclers scarcely moved beyond stereotypes in their characterisations, and partly because he seems to have had none of the frailties which make a personality sympathetic. Any view of this remarkable man must be dominated by the famous, and still moving, obituary written by an anonymous Englishman; a regretful, yet dispassionate, epitaph to someone who had overwhelmed so much that the writer held dear:

This king William of whom we speak was a very wise man, and very powerful and more worshipful and stronger than any predecessor of his had been. He was gentle to the good men who loved God, and stern beyond all measure to those people who resisted his will. . . . Also, he was a very stern and violent man, so that none dared do anything contrary to his will. He expelled bishops from their sees, and abbots from their abbacies, and put thegns in prison, and finally he did not spare his own brother, who was called Odo; . . . Amongst other things the good security he made in this country is not to be forgotten – so that any honest man could travel over his kingdom without injury with his bosom full of gold: and no one dared injure another, however much wrong he had done him. Certainly in his time people had much oppression and very many injuries: he had castles built and poor men hard oppressed....[1]

William was a man who made others tremble. Several writers commented on his immense physical strength – he was probably just under six feet tall.[2] The details of his government and his relations with the Church indicate that he possessed an insight which set him apart from more ham-fisted counterparts such as count Geoffrey Martel of Anjou or the Capetian king Philip I. That Ordericus should have commented on his affability comes as a bit of a surprise. His jokes were of a brutal kind, such as his demonstration of the immutability of a grant to the abbey of La Trinité-du-Mont of Rouen by pretending to stick a knife through the abbot's hand.[3] We know of a prisoner who was being held on his orders and whose limbs were being steadily crushed; a late-eleventh-century commentator remarked that he treated those captured in war with a severity otherwise unknown in northern France.[4] He satisfied the requirements for successful rule in one of the rawest periods of western European history. Even so astringent a critic as pope Gregory VII (1073–85) thought him pre-eminent among contemporary princes.

THE DUKE

Although it is now customary to refer to the eleventh-century Norman rulers as dukes, this was neither their unique, nor indeed their most frequently used title before 1066. Commoner in the documents is the more humble 'count'. It must be said at the outset that no entirely satisfactory analysis of the relationship of the two terms is possible. Quantitative methods are vulnerable to the rate of documentary survival: the acta which survive, for example, from the abbey of Montvilliers use only 'count' as the Norman ruler's title; their relatively large number must obviously distort any statistical calculations. Twelfth-century attitudes can also be misleading, since 'duke' did become the unique title from Henry I's reign (1106–35) onwards and could often have been substituted for 'count' by scribes copying earlier charters. This point is well illustrated by two surviving copies from the abbey of St-Wandrille: the eleventh-century original of the document refers to the Norman ruler as a 'count'; the twelfth-century 'modernisation' makes him into a 'duke'.[5]

Richard II was beyond all doubt the first Norman ruler to style himself 'duke' (*dux*). There is impeccable evidence in the text of an original charter for the abbey of Fécamp, which dates from the year 1006.[6] Richard's assumption of the new title must be regarded as an attempt to push himself into a small élite of French territorial rulers which comprised the 'duke of the Franks', a title used by the Robertians/Capetians and which went into abeyance when its holder became king in 987, and the 'dukes' of the Burgundians and the Aquitanians, who had both taken the title in the second half of the tenth century, without thereafter using it with entire consistency. The Normans' presumption provoked on occasion an overt disapproval. A charter written at the Poitevin abbey of Bourgueil in 1012 mentioned William, duke of the Aquitanians (*Aquitanorum ducis*), and Richard, marquis of the Normans (*Normannorum marchionis*).[7] Bishop Fulbert of Chartres (1006–28), a copious letter-writer and a stickler for protocol, never referred to Richard as a duke, although he was careful to address him in more splendid language than was reserved for the count of Anjou. Non-Norman churches which received benefactions from the Norman rulers almost invariably called them counts.[8] Most significantly, after a moment of weakness in 1006, the Capetians refused to acknowledge the title until they themselves became 'dukes of Normandy' after 1204: in 1076 king Philip I's chancery acidly drew a contrast between Guy-Geoffrey (William), *duke* of the Aquitanians, and William, king of the English and *count* of the Normans.[9]

The writers of Norman charters used titles with a bewildering randomness. A remarkable effort in an original charter from the abbey of Jumièges styled William II as *principis Willelmi, ducis, Nortmannie comitis*.[10] Under Richard II, 'count' is the more frequent title, appearing in 29 acts, as opposed to 'duke' in 22, but this undervalues the greater prominence of 'count', since 'duke' is invariably combined with another title (*dux et princeps, marchio et dux*, etc.). Under Robert I, 'duke' is employed in 17 ducal charters, against 'count' in 15, but this proportion is again seriously modified by the use of 'duke' alongside other titles. Under William II 'count' appears on its own in 68 acts, 'duke' alone appears in 28 – the proportion is 13 to 5 in original charters – with the two titles together in a further 30. Although this looks like a reaction in favour of 'count', it may be significant that 'duke' appears as the sole title with much greater frequency under William II. Constitutional precision is impossible in this imbroglio. What is certain, however, is that a scarcely dimmed recollection was maintained right through until 1066 that the official basis of the Norman ruler's authority was that of a count whose power had been sanctioned by the French king; *comes* was the only title used in the foundation charter of the abbey of La Trinité of Caen, *princeps* appears in the first charter of St-Etienne, and *comes* was still used by William of Poitiers in *c.* 1077.[11] A testimony, both to the usurpation of the early eleventh century and to the future trend towards the new title of 'duke', is the suggestion in a papal bull forged at the abbey of Fécamp in the late eleventh century that Richard II had taken the ducal title with the authorisation of pope Benedict VIII (1012–24).[12]

Succession to the position which, for the sake of convenience, can still be called 'duke', moved along what were in theory well-defined lines. The normal pattern was for a reigning duke to designate his eldest son as his heir and to associate him in the ducal/comital title, usually in consultation with an assembly of magnates. Territorial provision was generally made for cadets, who normally received a *comté*, and who in both 996 and 1026 did homage to the prospective ruler.[13] After 1035 William II made arrangements for those younger sons of Richard II who had been too young to receive land in 1026. Almost invariably, the eldest surviving son succeeded to the ducal/comital title. The contrasting cases of 1027, when Robert I took over, perhaps by violence, against any claims which might have been advanced for a very young illegitimate son of Richard III who was placed in a monastery, and 1035, when Robert's bastard, the seven- or eight-year-old William, succeeded against older uncles, indicate that the arrangements were made *ad hoc* rather than according to any custom. This pattern of anticipatory association and territorial provision for cadets who did homage to the head of the house was a commonplace of most royal, princely, and aristocratic successions. In Normandy, as elsewhere, these arranged successions frequently did not work out in practice. Between 1026 and 1106, four successive dukes had to fight to maintain rights which had been bequeathed to them. Like Geoffrey the Bearded (1060–68) in Anjou, Richard III – possibly – and, after 1087, duke Robert Curthose, for certain, discovered that anticipatory designation was no substitute for force of character and martial prowess. Members of the ducal family seem consistently to have taken the view that their personal interest in the inheritance was more important than loyalty to any higher ideal of public order which might have existed.

With regard to the women in the lives of the Norman dukes, we tend to know more about their mistresses than their wives. Richard I was long outlived by his widow Gunnor (*c.* 950–*c.* 1030), who had previously been his mistress. She remained influential during her son's reign, during which her relatives, her brother Arfast and her nephew Osbern, laid the foundations of their family's later landed prosperity. Richard II married firstly Judith, a sister of Geoffrey, count of Rennes, and secondly, a Norman wife named Papia, with whom an earlier liaison might be suspected. Robert I may at one stage have been betrothed to a daughter of king Cnut, but the woman with whom he is always linked is Herleva, probably the daughter of Fulbert, a tanner of Falaise. Herleva was the Conqueror's mother.[14] Her subsequent marriage to Herluin de Conteville produced two sons, whom their half-brother advanced to positions of great wealth and power; namely, Odo, bishop of Bayeux (1049/50–97), and Robert, count of Mortain (c. 1060–90). William II himself married and was conspicuously faithful to Mathilda, a daughter of Baldwin V, count of Flanders. Like Gunnor, Mathilda seems to have been one of those women who could make her influence felt in a predominantly masculine world: she was given responsibility in Normandy after 1066 and in the late 1070s and early 1080s tried fruitlessly to intercede in the quarrels between her wayward eldest son and her unbending husband. Remarkably, she may have been no more than four feet three inches tall.[15]

THE STRUCTURE OF GOVERNMENT

Ducal government was itinerant. The duke moved around the province surrounded by his household and a group of familiars. It is impossible to gain any clear idea of the organisation of these travels – if indeed there was one. The exigencies of warfare and special occasions such as the dedication of an important church would probably predetermine many of the Norman rulers' movements. The most numerous set of references for any single year shows that between January and September 1066, William II visited Bayeux, Bonneville, Fécamp, and Rouen, as well as being with his invasion fleet in the estuary of the river Dives and then at St-Valéry-sur-Somme. If any year is likely to have been untypical, it is this one. A revealing story told in a document written for the monks of the abbey of St-Florent of Saumur gives some insight into William's movements after 1066. On 7 January 1080 the abbey was successful in a plea heard before William at Caen. The monk who had been present on behalf of St-Florent was then obliged to travel some thirty-five miles southwards to the abbey's priory at Briouze to collect a charter, which was then placed before William for confirmation on 31 January at Boscherville on the river Seine, some seventy miles north-east of Caen.[16] Again, we cannot know whether seventy miles in three and a half weeks, assuming that William travelled by the direct road, was a normal or abnormal rate of progress. It seems excessively slow. Such government 'on the road' could be very informal: in c. 1081, for example, William confirmed a grant 'while sitting on his carpet between the church and the forester's house' at Bernouville (Eure).[17]

The pre-1066 charters suggest that William II's travelling ranged much more widely throughout the duchy than that of his predecessors. Richard II is known to have authenticated charters only at Rouen and Fécamp, where he had palaces. Robert I, likewise, except for one visit to Préaux.[18] For William II the documents record visits to twelve places, of which the most remote was La Hougue in the north of the Cotentin.[19] Although the contrast between the separate reigns is impressive, it cannot be taken entirely at face value. A literary source shows that Richard II had a residence at Bayeux.[20] Given that the documents on which our knowledge of the ducal itineraries is based are generally charters written on behalf of monasteries, and that before c. 1050 most of these establishments were in Upper Normandy, the argument has something of a circular quality: because the documents come from a limited region, it is almost inevitable that they should show that the dukes visited only that area. On the other hand, the evidence for Richard II's time does positively suggest a 'palace' style of government. A high proportion of charters from the reign do indicate where the document was drawn up – 1 : 4 as opposed to 1 : 5 from William II's. In addition, when a church outside the duchy required confirmation of a grant, or when the monks of Mont-St-Michel wanted a new abbot, they almost invariably approached Richard II at Rouen, a town which Ralph Glaber, writing in the 1040s, could describe in terms of a capital.[21] The minimum conclusion is that the proliferation of monasteries, which followed on the social changes of the second quarter of the century, had the effect of multiplying the number of institutions whose existence required the duke's protection. This alone would prove an intensification of activity. More likely William's rule did encompass Lower Normandy much more positively than that of previous dukes; a conclusion supported by other evidence as well as by his development of Caen as a residence and centre of government (see p. 178).

The dukes' revenue was drawn from sources of a traditional kind, a mixture of wealth derived from the possession of land and from fiscal rights. Although no full survey of the ducal lands has ever been attempted, it is at least clear from the records of the dowries given to their wives by Richard II and Richard III that the demesne at that time consisted of numerous manors scattered throughout the entire duchy. Judith, Richard II's first wife, received an enormous landed endowment made up entirely of rural domains situated in three blocks in the vicinity of Bernay, in the district of Le Cinglais to the south of Caen, and between Valognes and the western coast of the Cotentin peninsula. A steady reduction in the extent of the ducal lands and a consequent reorientation in the basic sources of revenue is implied as early as 1027 when the dowry given by Richard III to his bride Adèle was composed of a mixture of rural estates, castles, and financial rights.[22] William II's grants to churches during the period before 1066 demonstrate in an extreme way what the increasingly westerly location of the dowries implies; namely, that the ducal demesne in Upper Normandy was being greatly reduced in the first half of the century, as a result of alienations and enfeoffments, and that by 1050 William II could grant only parcels of land and, increasingly, revenues or jurisdiction (see map 8).[23]

The character of the Norman rulers' exploitation of their lands and revenues appears to have changed somewhat over the period up until 1066. Richard II's and Robert I's reigns are typified by liberal alienations of the extensive lands inherited from the first counts of Rouen in favour of both immigrant and Norman families. Out of Judith's dowry, for example, St-Christophe-du-Foc in the Cotentin had passed to the Tosny family by *c.* 1020, much of the Cinglais was held by the Taisson before 1025, while Vieilles and Beaumont went to Humphrey de Vieilles by the early 1030s. Under William II, as has already been suggested, the aristocracy appear in general to have received lands only when they were made available by a forfeiture (see p. 101). Generosity changed into parsimony; complacency into firmness. At the same time William's rule is characterised by what looks like a more intensive exploitation of other revenues. The first references to the general taxes, the *bernagium* and the *gravarium*, occur in his reign. Since both have Carolingian antecedents – the *bernagium*, for instance, which was a levy taken in oats throughout the entire province, has clear analogies with the earlier *fodrum* – the appearance of the terms is more likely to indicate the time at which more intensive exploitation caused them to splinter away from the generic *consuetudines* rather than innovation. This suggestion is in accord with the growth in the number of references to tolls at about the same time and with duke William's renowned financial wealth (see p. 58).[24] But, alongside this greater firmness, what must also be emphasised is the essentially traditional nature of the revenues collected for duke William II up till and beyond 1066. The first novelty, and even this is one for which the evidence is entirely inferential, is the *monnéage*, a tax taken in lieu of a recoinage of the duke's money, which does not appear until the later years of William's reign.[25]

A shift towards a more intensive financial exploitation under William II is supported less by any change in the very rudimentary institutions of central government than by a rise in the number and importance of personnel. The chamber (*camera*), which was the centre of fiscal administration, is known from Richard II's time.[26] By the end of his reign its organisation was already sufficient to make simple payments out of the revenues, such as a tenth of the profits of coinage, or a tenth of the receipts from purchases and gifts, or a tenth of the tolls collected at Bayeux and Caen. The precision with which these payments are recorded may suggest a system of record-keeping of which all trace has been lost.[27] The only significant developments under William II were the obvious personal importance of Ralph the chamberlain, who witnesses many charters, and, as will be suggested in the next paragraph, the appearance of an extra chamberlain shortly before 1066. In like fashion, there is no clear evidence for an organised writing-office before 1066. Charters were invariably the work of a scribe employed by the beneficiaries; original documents as a result usually conform to the 'house' style of a particular monastery, rather than to any form imposed by ducal administration. Thus, to cite one example from many, a charter of archbishop Malger of Rouen, dating from 1037 to 1048, was written in the same hand as one of Odo, bishop of Bayeux, from 1070 to 1082; both were presumably composed in the abbey which received them, St-Ouen of Rouen.[28] Similarly, there is nothing to suggest that the sealing of charters was anything more than a very irregular and unsystematic practice in pre-1066 Normandy, if indeed it was done at all. References to a ducal seal in Richard II's and Robert I's reigns and an eighteenth-century 'facsimile' of the former's seal are all that there is to go on. One tantalising mention in a document written between 1081 and 1087 to the summons of the ducal army by writ (*per brevem*) implies administrative technique of a kind which, if any solid indication of what was meant could be obtained, would revolutionise our appreciation of the literacy of eleventh-century Norman government. As it is, the clumsiness of post-1066 attempts to seal Norman charters must be treated as demonstrating the primitive quality of ducal administration.[29] The most convincing signs of a ducal chancery and of some sort of organised secretariat come from Richard II's reign, in the form of a number of references to a chancellor, and in the central direction which gave common characteristics to four charters of the year 1025, which were drawn up in favour of four different abbeys.[30] If anything, therefore, this evidence, coupled with the form of the surviving documents, points to a deterioration in diplomatic practice after the end of Richard II's reign which had not been repaired by 1066.

The central administration, and particularly the household, appears to have grown considerably from the late 1040s onwards. In Richard II's time there had been a small group of familiars, including two chamberlains and a butler (see pp. 116–17). A formally organised household, with officials bearing the titles of steward, butler, constable, and chamberlain, after the Carolingian model, first appears in Robert I's time; Osbern and 'Ansfrey' (possibly Humphrey de Vieilles) are named as stewards, Robert as butler. Turold as constable, and Ralph as chamberlain.[31] In some cases there is a continuous family occupation up to and beyond 1066; Osbern was eventually followed as steward by his son William fitz Osbern, while Ralph, the first in the line of hereditary chamberlains from the Tancarville family, was still chamberlain in 1066. But numerous 'new men' occur from *c.* 1050; Hugh the butler first appears a little before 1050, Stigand *dapifer* (steward) in 1046/47–48, and Gerald the butler and steward in *c.* 1050 and again before 1054.[32] These men witness charter after charter and must have been in regular attendance on the duke. Shortly before 1066 they may well have been joined by other newly appointed household officers, such as Hubert the steward and Humphrey the chamberlain,[33] and also by a group of ducal chaplains. A further refinement which took place at about the same time was William fitz Osbern's title of 'count of the palace', an imitation of Carolingian nomenclature and an honorific dignity held at the Capetian court by the counts of Blois-Chartres.[34] The way in which all these executed their duties is entirely obscure. It is at least clear that tenure seems usually to have been for life, with sons often succeeding their fathers. The position of ducal chaplain, known from Richard II's time, but only uncertainly attested in the pre-1066 records, was one with a great future as men such as Arfast and Baldwin, both mentioned before 1066, acquired bishoprics in England and Normandy after 1066.[35] The transfer of household offices from Robert I's time onwards into the hands of members of powerful landed families is entirely in accord with the effects of the social changes which were taking place from the 1020s. From the base which was created at that time, an expansion in the number and the duties of the household offices in the years immediately prior to 1066 seems certain.

The chief local officials of ducal government were the counts and the *vicomtes*. The former, a small and privileged group, were established for a special purpose in Richard II's reign. All the counts appointed at this time were chosen from among the duke's close blood-relations, with his uncle Rodulf given Ivry, and his half-brothers, Eu, Evreux, Brionne, and Mortain. The base of their power was usually a castle, although in the cases of Evreux and the later *comté* of Arques (founded *c.* 1037), responsibility may have been for an entire *pagus*.[36] The original purpose of the *comtés* was undoubtedly military, since in addition to the tenure of castles there are early references to *milites* at Ivry and Mortain.[37] Each of them was located at a strategic point on the frontier, Brionne included, since on the river Risle in central Normandy, it lay on the extreme edge of the region in which Richard II's power was concentrated. As the *comtés* evolved, the counts came to possess an authority which was equivalent to the duke's, and which made their territories into specially privileged immunities. Their character of nascent castellanries was, however, firmly controlled and they remained integrated within the framework of ducal authority.[38] Under Richard II the counts may well have been removable officials; count William, for example, was moved from Exmes to Eu and an exchange involving Eu and Brionne followed. But the original families became entrenched after 1025, a process testified to by the prevalence of hereditary succession and the employment from the 1040s of territorial designations resembling toponymics. The result was to leave the duke only the two options of confiscation and suppression, the fate of Arques and Brionne in William II's reign. It looks very much as if, within the limitations of acceptable political action, there was a reaction against the institution of the *comté* under William. Not only did two disappear, but no new ones were created; even Robert, the duke's half-brother, a man of warlike temperament admirably suited to a frontier posting, had to wait until Mortain became vacant in *c.* 1060 after the expulsion of count William Werlenc. The *comté*, favoured by Richard II and Robert I as a means of endowing ducal relatives, appears to have lost ground under William II to the *vicomté*, an office founded on the stabler territorial base of the *pagus*.

The *vicomtés* were the rock on which local administration rested. The first reference is from *c.* 1014, although their origins were probably somewhat earlier. There must be a strong presumption that from the beginning the *vicomte* was responsible for a *pagus*, as his twelfth-century successor most certainly was, especially as the pre-1066 documents provide evidence of a direct connection between a *vicomte* and six of the twelve *pagi*. The appearance of twelve *vicomtes* in the witness-list of a charter of 1025, along with the frequent references to the *pagi*, might even be regarded as decisive proof of the identity of *vicomté* and *pagus*.[39] Yet there are a few pieces which do not fit. References to revenues from the *vicomtés* of Bayeux and Fécamp appear in charters from Richard II's reign onwards. Even more interesting is the contrast drawn between the *vicecomitatus* of the Cotentin, of Coutances, and of Gavray, in a charter of 1042 which may not, however, be altogether trustworthy.[40] In addition, the example of the twelve *vicomtes* who appear in 1025 is not straightforward either, since they do not include the name of Anschetil, who is known to have been in office before and after 1025.[41] The inference that there were more *vicomtes* than *pagi* is not weakened by the known existence of a total of twenty-one *vicomtes* between 1014 and 1026, a high rate of turnover, nor by the difficulties caused by the existence of two unrelated *vicomtes* of the Cotentin, Eudo and Nigel, who appear to have been in office from *c.* 1060.[42] It may be that before 1066 a *vicomte* was still essentially what the name implies, a deputy of the count of Normandy. The case of Richard de Lillebonne, a *vicomte* who was also the duke's leg-armour bearer in the 1030s, may suggest that at that stage the office was insufficiently specialised for it to be entirely distinct from a position in the ducal household.[43] These reservations made, and the possibility that there were always more *vicomtes* than *pagi* admitted, it is none the less clear that their responsibility for a *pagus* was an evolving and often an established one before 1066.

The *vicomtés* passed into the grasp of a number of powerful aristocratic lineages in the 1020s and 1030s. As has been shown above, this created a relationship between family power and office which endured largely unchanged through to 1066 (see p. 117). What can be known of the *vicomtes*' responsibilities shows why the position was such an attractive one; they controlled all the main aspects of local administration. It is clear from the references in the previous paragraph to revenues collected in the *vicomtés* of Bayeux and Fécamp that the *vicomtes* superintended finance. Their range of authority is occasionally alluded to in the documents by vague phraseology like *consuetudines vicecomitatus*, powers which a crucial text in the cartulary of the abbey of St-Pierre of Préaux equate with some of the most basic prerogatives of ducal authority. It can therefore be assumed that the *vicomtes* administered the ducal *consuetudines*, a set of powers which are described in the next sections (see pp. 162–7).[44] In addition, stray references such as William of Jumièges' account of Nigel, *vicomte* of the Cotentin, organising local military levies, or a mention of his son's responsibility for a ducal castle at Le Homme, suggest other duties. Finally, the *vicomtes* could be charged with commissions outside their *vicomté*; the same Nigel also appears as guardian of the castle of Tillières-sur-Avre in *c*. 1014; he and others are mentioned as hearing pleas from the 1030s onwards. William II's rejection of claims such as those which the younger Nigel of the Cotentin advanced to the ducal castle at Le Homme ensured that both the office and its powers were still substantially under the duke's control in 1066.[45]

The political focus of ducal government was the occasions on which the duke met with the chief men of the province. Ducal itineration meant that in some respects it was the duke who went to meet his people, not vice versa. As a result charters were often simply confirmed by the duke and those immediately concerned; namely the grantor and his relatives along with the recipient.[46] This does not of course prove that these were the only people present, nor that all the witnesses came together on one occasion. The evidence of the witness-lists does none the less demonstrate that there must have been many gatherings at which men of political and landed significance met for a deliberate purpose. One such occurred in August 1025 at Fécamp when duke Richard II, very probably aiming to publicise arrangements for the succession to the duchy, issued charters for the abbeys of Fécamp, Bernay, and Jumièges. The Bernay charter, attested by 7 bishops, 12 *vicomtes*, and 116 other names, shows just how large such a meeting might have been. Another obvious instance is the assembly reported by William of Poitiers which met to discuss the prospective invasion of 1066. More obscure, but undoubtedly much more typical, were occasions such as the agreement made between Hugh II de Montfort and the abbey of Fécamp at Brionne in the early years of William II's reign, which was concluded in the presence of the duke, count William of Arques, bishop Hugh of Avranches, Nigel *vicomte* of the Cotentin, Osbern the steward, Goscelin the *vicomte*, and others.[47] The simultaneous attendance of such a group cannot have been accidental.

The witness-lists of charters, which provide most of the information for such gatherings, suggest that important changes in the composition and significance of the entourage took place over the course of the period up until 1066. The documents from Richard II's reign are attested almost exclusively by the 'official' classes; immediate

Ducal government

family, the counts, the bishops, the *vicomtes*, and household familiars. Sometimes the witness-lists are very much family affairs of wife, mother, sons, archbishop Robert of Rouen, and bishop Hugh of Bayeux. The bishops were frequent attenders; several acta were witnessed by at least six out of the seven. There is also something of an Upper Norman domination of the entourage with the bishops of Sées and the counts of Mortain very irregular visitors.[48] A part of this general character was carried on into Robert I's reign. It was, however, much modified by the intrusion of the men whom we have seen in Chapter Three taking church lands and assuming office. The most prominent witnesses, a mixture of family and 'new men', are archbishop Robert, count Gilbert of Brionne, Goscelin the *vicomte*, Nigel the *vicomte*, Humphrey de Vieilles, and the bishops of Coutances and Lisieux. During William II's minority the entourage was usually composed of a small group, among whom count William of Arques, archbishop Malger of Rouen, the three *vicomtes* Thurstan Goz, Nigel, and Godfrey, Roger I and Roger II de Montgommery, and Ralph Taisson were outstanding.[49] Notably absent were bishop Hugh of Bayeux and the counts of Evreux and Mortain, who seem to have as good as deserted the company of the young duke.

Political recovery is clear in the ducal charters from the late 1040s onwards, which illustrate the great extension of authority achieved by duke William II; at some stage before 1066 almost everyone who held substantial power in the duchy attests. But these same documents also reveal two other important features. One is the domination of the entourage by a very small number of powerful men, most notably William fitz Osbern and Roger II de Montgommery, and by the household officers. At the same time, there is a noticeable reduction in the appearances of the 'officials', the counts and the bishops and, up to a point, of the *vicomtes* as well.[50] The other change is the great increase in the number of occasions on which the duke's confirmation was simply superimposed on to a local witness-list and to a gift of quite exceptional mediocrity.[51] It looks, therefore, as if the ducal entourage in Richard II's time comprised a small group of intimates who attested charters on account of their rank. It may be that they were not the only ones present when the charter was drawn up; what is important is that they were singled out as being especially worthy to attest. Thereafter there is deterioration in the sense that attestation ceased to be a restricted prerogative and that in William II's reign little dignity attached to a ducal confirmation. The charters of the period after *c.* 1050 demonstrate a weakening of institutional form. At the same time, however, the much increased range of personnel suggests a great increase in ducal power; and the pre-eminence of a small clique, that the duchy was to all intents and purposes controlled by William and a chosen group of favourites.

The role of the duke and his entourage in the settlement of disputes is documented from Richard II's time, although there are indications in the number of reports of trials which survive of much more intensive activity immediately prior to 1066. This increase may reflect the growth in record-keeping; more likely, it testifies to the growing range of ducal government. It must be significant that the appropriate technical term to describe the duke's court, *curia*, is rare in pre-1066 Norman documents; when used, it seems not only to have encompassed the meaning of a court which did justice, but also the entourage in general or the administration.[52] This institutional informality is sometimes alluded to in the documents; a charter of 1016–17 mentions those bishops and priests who were fortuitously present when duke Richard confirmed the grant, while a plea in 1080 was judged by those ecclesiastics 'who were there'.[53] It is only after 1066 that *curia* seems to evolve the more technical meaning of a court which did justice.[54] What is clear is that by 1066 William's court was established as the place where disputes between the mightiest of his vassals would be heard. Its standing was such that justice could apparently be done without the duke himself being present, although the court would seem under such circumstances to have still been identified as the duke's.[55]

Any conclusions about the function and procedure of the duke's court can only be drawn from plea reports composed by one of the parties involved, a type of record especially open to later editing.[56] No formal records kept by the court itself survive; given the general context of eleventh-century administration, it is extremely unlikely that any were ever kept. Although justice in the sense of deciding greater right was often necessary, a frequent result of a matter coming before the duke was a compromise. The decisive verdict of an ordeal was deliberately avoided and the two parties brought to an agreement; some reports actually specify that the court's role was to produce a settlement.[57] In the event of a compromise being unobtainable, both sides were apparently given the opportunity to present their arguments. If necessary, further evidence was sought from the memories of old men or, in a celebrated – and quite isolated – instance, dating from 1070 to 1079, through an inquest involving four elected representatives.[58] The information in the plea reports suggests that reliance was usually placed on human testimony, but that

Ducal government

especially difficult or controversial cases would be decided by the ordeal. Thus, a particularly complicated dispute involving the legitimacy of a child and the consequential inheritance was resolved after ordeal by hot-iron. Likewise, when William Pantulf was suspected of the murder of Mabel de Bellême in *c.* 1077, he was forced to clear himself through a similar ordeal, either because the evidence was inconclusive or because any other proof of innocence was unacceptable to her irate husband and family.[59] It may be that God was called in when men found a case too complex or too sensitive. The normal procedure, however, was to nominate judges from among those present, usually men of great experience.[60] If the judges disagreed, then the final word may have lain with the duke.[61]

The officials and the political relationships which have been discussed in this section were those at the most eminent levels of government. Administration was in practice much more complex than a general survey can suggest and involved relatively large numbers of personnel. The documents draw our attention to, among others, *gravatores* responsible for the collection of the *gravarium*, moneyers, and such worthies as the ducal swineherd.[62] That the moneyers, like the ducal chaplains, seem often to have been from wealthy urban families, is one more demonstration of the way in which the expanding net of government drew on a wider social range as 1066 approached (see pp. 129–32). Innovation was even possible at these lower levels; the *prepositus* (provost), for example, a revenue-collecting official based on the duke's demesne lands, first occurs in the 1030s. The office's development before 1066 is not altogether clear, mainly because it is usually impossible to distinguish between ducal and seigneurial *prepositi* in the documents. But the appearance from the 1060s of references to the *prepositura*, the area administered by a *prepositus*, must demonstrate that the office was securely established by that time.[63] In general, however, the evolution of eleventh-century ducal government is more apparent at a political than an institutional level. The most obvious signs of change are the duke's enlarged itinerary, the increase in the judicial functions of the *curia*, and the widening of the range of the entourage. Administration certainly intensified from the 1050s onwards, but it did so within a structure which remained characteristically Carolingian – the *pagus*, the *bernagium*, and so on. The cause of these developments, apart from the personal energy of duke William II, was the necessity of coming to terms with the effects of the social changes of the second quarter of the eleventh century. The efficient government of Richard II's time was transformed within its basic structure to accommodate aristocratic tenure of offices and the serious diminution of the landed resources available to the dukes.

THE DUKE AND HIS SUBJECTS

The major responsibility of any early medieval ruler towards his subjects was to maintain that social stability which guaranteed men's rights. That 'rights' in eleventh-century Normandy tended to be interpreted almost exclusively as being those of the Church and the military upper classes is in no way surprising. As everywhere else, these were the only groups who wielded significant power and whose actions could be construed as overtly political. None the less, the dukes are known from later surveys of Norman custom to have embraced the typically Carolingian philosophy that it was their duty to protect the weak, widows, orphans, and children. Above all it was their task to maintain peace and to curb internal warfare. They set out to do this amidst 'normal' conditions which were, in terms of modern understanding, almost unimaginably violent; in a society where the ethos of knighthood glorified the practice of arms and where the blood-feud was a respectable social convention. The desperate character of the struggle can be summed up by a legislative enactment of the ecclesiastical council held at Lisieux in 1064, which banned armed assault on a cleric, unless he deserved it, and then with the proviso that the bishop had been given reasonable advance warning.[64]

The earliest statement of the disciplinary powers of the duke appears in the results of the inquest of 1091, usually known as the *Consuetudines et Iusticie*, whose specific purpose was to describe powers exercised by duke William II.[65] The survey, which was on its own admission only a partial summary of the duke's rights, included the basic power of control over castle-building, through a prohibition on the construction of fortifications over a certain size and the ducal prerogative to occupy any man's castle at will. The inquest also asserted that money could not be produced outside the ducal mints at Rouen and Bayeux, that coins should be made of half silver and half alloy, and that they should be of the correct weight. The duke was permitted to seize the young sons of his leading subjects (*barones*) as a guarantee of good behaviour. He had the right to judge certain major crimes such as arson or rape. The general character of

Ducal government

the regulations is that of a set of misdeeds, any one of which constituted a breach of the peace. Thus, someone who attacked an enemy on a journey either to or from the duke's court, or assaulted anyone travelling to or from the duke's army, or injured a pilgrim or a merchant, was automatically at the mercy of the duke's will. It was forbidden to set fire to a house or a mill, or to pillage in a dispute over land. Violence as such was not condemned; but many forms of it were. The powers revealed by the *Consuetudines et Iusticie* had not attained the comprehensiveness of the 'dukes's peace' of the twelfth century, nor the clear definition of the later category of reserved ducal cases (the 'pleas of the sword') first recorded in an inquest of 1172–74, but they were, by contemporary standards, a group of far-reaching prohibitions of specific breaches of the peace.

Many features of the *Consuetudines et Iusticie* demonstrate a very strong continuity from Carolingian notions of authority. Despite adaptation over the intervening period, the duke's monopoly of fortification was an idea which went back in time at least to the legislation of Charles the Bald's Edict of Pitres (864), while the notion that the minting of coin was a regalian right existed under Charlemagne, and had been upheld by the tenth-century Norman rulers. Among other sections which betray a Carolingian spirit are those which dealt with assaults on travellers going to or from the court or on merchants and pilgrims, which echo the regalian power of jurisdiction over public roads, and the ducal control over the punishment of assaults in the forest, which appears to derive from an earlier jurisdiction over the forest. The most eloquent evidence of the survival of earlier public authority is the duke's exercise of the arbitrary power to pardon. This, defined as *harmiscara* in the ninth-century capitularies, is indicated in 1091 in references to the *misericordia domini Normannie*. The likelihood of institutional continuity is strengthened by one of ceremonial: William of Jumièges reported two incidents from the reigns of Richard II and Robert I where the duke's pardon was sought by a postulant placing a saddle on his shoulders.[66]

This essentially Carolingian legacy had been reinforced in the tenth century by a number of Scandinavian importations. The most notable of these were the protection accorded to agricultural implements and the duke's power to exile, which could still be described by its Scandinavian name of *ullac* in a document of *c*. 1050. The sum of these two sets of powers must have been the basis of Richard II's authority. The most important later addition was the Peace of God, introduced into the duchy at an uncertain date, which, despite insistent controversy, is now generally assigned to the last months of

1047.[67] In essence, the Norman Peace sought to limit violence by prohibiting fighting between Wednesday evening and Monday morning, and laying down penalties for those who infringed it. The inception of the Peace of God in Normandy has something of the ecclesiastical colouring present in those regions of southern France from which the Peace first emanated. Its proclamation took place in an assembly near Caen to which saints' relics were specially transported; its enforcement was initially made the responsibility of the bishops. But after a simple repetition at the council of Lisieux (1064), the Peace was steadily grafted on to the peace-keeping powers of ducal government. From the very beginning the duke's army had been exempted. At the council of Lillebonne (1080), it was announced that duke William himself had introduced the Peace into Normandy and that any frailties in the bishop's jurisdiction should be supplemented by recourse to the offender's lord and, if necessary, to the duke's *vicomte*.[68] This strengthening of the Peace appears to have been part of a wider policy of William II's later years. In 1075 William forbade private vengeance in a case of murder, unless the victim had been either a father or a son.[69] The 1080 Lillebonne decrees envisaged the duke's officials as assisting in the examination of married priests, and the duke's own court as a kind of supervisory tribunal over the relationship of secular and ecclesiastical jurisdiction.[70]

The effectiveness of such powers is hard to ascertain. As a general rule, it is always difficult to marry legislation, which usually exudes neatness and good organisation, with charter and chronicle evidence, which is disjointed and prone to record extraordinary events. The histories of William of Jumièges and William of Poitiers, for example, after extolling the firm peace maintained by the dukes of Normandy, proceed to devote a high percentage of space to warfare. Peace was harder to describe and much less glamorous. The claim of the 1091 inquest to record powers actually exercised is important. So, too, is the increasing precision of the ecclesiastical legislation of William II's reign and its generally realistic content. But, when all this has been said, the picture of ducal authority through the entire eleventh century is one with periods of unsteadiness and, notably, a serious weakening between 1026 and *c*. 1050. Zeal for peace and justice was frequently compromised by the exigencies of social change and political power.

This general vulnerability is well illustrated by the eleventh-century history of the dukes' coinage. The monopoly was one which can be traced back to William Longsword's time, the clearest demonstration that there is of the continuous exercise by the Norman rulers of a former Carolingian prerogative. Yet, despite the superficial continuity up until 1091, the carefully made pennies of the tenth century were displaced from about the 1020s by clumsy products. The trend throughout northern France was for the weight of coinage to decline, but this lightening assumed excessive proportions in Normandy.[71] An average weight of 1.20 grams in 980–85 had fallen to 0.96 grams by 1020–30, and to 0.80–0.84 grams by 1050–60; the ratio of silver to alloy content fell below a half from 1050 to 1060. Style became increasingly deformed and, from the second quarter of the eleventh century, the legends had become illiterate. There are signs of an attempt to pull things round under William II, with a simple but well-manufactured coin in *c.* 1050, and then with a new design reflecting English influence after 1066. In its early stages this effort was sufficient to leave its mark in the documents.[72] The initial deterioration in the 1020s could easily have been the result of the disarray into which ducal government was thrown after Richard II's death. But recovery under William II proved to be impossible; perhaps because an active market accustomed to the use of money would not have borne the consequences of the necessarily dramatic rise in the silver content. The periodic issue of new coin, which seems to have been well organised in the tenth century, was much less so in the eleventh: the hoards show that coin remained in circulation over a very long period, often into the twelfth century. In the end, the institution of the *monnéage* may well have been an admission that the dukes had nothing to gain from an organised, let alone a manipulated, coinage.

The right to control castles and to exile, as the two prerogatives which most directly affronted the aristocracy's freedom of action, show clearly the limitations and fluctuations of ducal authority. The first of the two, despite isolated exceptions on the frontiers, must have been very firmly enforced by Richard II. But the frequency of castle-building during the 1030s and 1040s must indicate that the duke's powers of supervision largely collapsed during these two decades. Le Plessis-Grimoult, for example, which has been meticulously excavated, having long remained unfortified, received a stone curtain-wall only a short time before it was abandoned in *c.* 1047.[73] The weakening of ducal control may have extended to his being in danger of losing power over some of his own castles. A charter written in the 1070s describes how Robert I had sold a ducal castle at Le Homme (now L'Isle-Marie) in the Cotentin to his sister Adeliza, from whom it had been forcefully taken by her son, count Guy of

Brionne. Guy in turn gave it to his associate in the conspiracy of 1047, the *vicomte* Nigel, who, after William II was securely in control, was obliged to recognise that he held the place as a guardian on Adeliza's behalf, and not as hereditary family property.[74] Duke William's reconstitution of authority had to acknowledge that changes of this kind had taken place. The reference in 1091 to the duke's absolute right to take over a castle is an admission that independent fortifications existed and that they could not be suppressed.[75] In spite of William of Poitiers' suggestion that illicit castles were destroyed, William's policy seems to have been to take over, or more often entrust to friends, places which might have been dangerous.[76] The *vicomte* Nigel retained Le Homme. Roger de Mortemer, who had given worthy service during the campaigns of 1053–54, but who had sheltered his non-Norman lord, count Ralph of Amiens-Valois-Vexin, lost the castle at Mortemer, which was given to William de Warenne. Ivry, once held by count Rodulf, and by all hereditary considerations the property of William fitz Osbern, was handed over to Roger de Beaumont. The extent of William's surveillance by 1087 is demonstrated by the passage in Ordericus' *Ecclesiastical History* describing the ejection of ducal custodians once the news of William's death became widely known. By this date the fortifications of Bellême, Tosny, the counts of Evreux, and others, the strongest families of the province, had succumbed to his authority.[77]

The history of the right to exile does not demonstrate the weakening of ducal authority in so forthright a way. Its application is, however, much more informative with regard to the limits to which political punishment could normally be taken. No duke, and especially William II, about whose use of the prerogative we know most, employed it as a means to break men or to attempt a radical amendment to the social structure. For Richard II's reign, there is the famous story of the Norman named Ralph (possibly Ralph de Tosny) who, having fled from the duke's wrath, organised intervention in southern Italy before finally returning to the duchy.[78] The most detailed account of an exile is Ordericus' report of Arnold d'Echauffour's banishment in the early 1060s. The salient features are that for Arnold, exile from Normandy meant residence at Courville (Eure-et-Loir), no more than twenty-five miles south of the established Norman frontier, and only ten miles from Thimert, whose castle duke William had captured in 1058. Arnold stayed with a kinsman, Giroie de Courville, and organised raids into Normandy. His exile lasted in all for three years and, although he visited southern Italy during that time, his behaviour was consistently that of a man who retained an interest in recovering his patrimony and probably expected to do so.[79] The normal pattern was for ducal displeasure to be temporary. This was even true of Nigel, *vicomte* of the Cotentin, prominent on the losing side at Val-ès-Dunes in 1047, who went no further away than Brittany, and had returned to Normandy by 1054 at the latest. The terms of reconciliation, which can be traced from charters, show that Nigel had to disgorge substantial property in favour of the abbey of Marmoutier.[80] A similar pattern of exile near Normandy and of restitution after a period of time is recorded for Adam de St-Brice, Hugh de Grandmesnil, Ralph de Tosny, and a certain Roger who had murdered a swineherd who served the abbey of Mont-St-Michel.[81] When a career was irrevocably broken, as in the case of archbishop Malger of Rouen, deposed in 1054, a refuge in the Channel Islands was provided.[82] Even so flagrant a malefactor as count Guy of Brionne was pardoned, but preferred to leave, according to both William of Jumièges and William of Poitiers.[83]

The history of these prerogatives, taken alongside the evidence for the loss of lands and the disruption of the entourage which was surveyed in the previous section, emphasises how severely ducal government was impaired during the second quarter of the eleventh century. It shows that, although the authority of the Norman rulers must in general be regarded as having been greater than that of other territorial princes, their power was still neither monolithic nor unshakeable. An exceptional man such as William II could on occasions get away with harsh actions, as in the cases of Grimoald du Plessis-Grimoult who is supposed to have languished in chains from 1047 until his death, or of his brother Odo who was imprisoned in 1082 with the manifest intention that he would never be released. But government had to be based on collaboration between duke and aristocracy; authority needed to be sufficiently firm, yet at the same time resilient, in order to maintain order. William II by and large accepted the results of the social changes of the 1030s and 1040s; castle-building and the removal of ecclesiastical property were admitted and forgiven. It is important that when William II rebuilt the prerogative control over fortification, he did so, not by entrusting castles to social upstarts, but by granting them to those members of the leading families whom he felt he could rely on. In like vein, in attending the dedication of the abbey of St-Martin of Troarn in 1059, William tacitly assented to Roger II de Montgommery's development of a property which duke Richard II had confirmed as a possession of the abbey of Fécamp in 1025. The reorganisation of the coinage after *c.* 1050 could only be taken as far as economic conditions would permit. The exceptional success of duke William's revival of ducal authority was achieved by adapting powers, most of which already existed, to suit prevailing conditions. There were innovations such as the Truce of God, but his achievement depended mainly on political skill and on a more energetic and intensive administration. One very significant result of this was the steady extension of the duke's powers of lordship.

The nature of ducal lordship must be interpreted in a way which is consistent with the earlier conclusions, that pre-1066 Norman 'feudalism' was characterised by bonds of obligation which were still essentially personal ties between individuals, and that a consolidation of the extension of lordship which had taken place in the second quarter of the century was only beginning to take place in 1066 (see pp. 122–7). For these reasons it cannot be correct to think of the dukes as drawing clearly defined services from their vassals before 1066, or of fixed terms of military service, or of regular wardships, reliefs, and aids. To say this is not to deny that military service was taken; it must have been asked for and provided both regularly and efficiently. Rather it is to argue that systematised institutions of lord–vassal relations were not present in pre-1066 Normandy and that they were not yet one of the fundamental features of ducal authority. As a result, the thesis, which was propounded by the American historian Charles Homer Haskins in the early twentieth century, that the eleventh-century dukes of Normandy were at the pinnacle of a well-organised 'feudal pyramid', must finally be abandoned.

Some among Haskins' arguments are unsound when set against rigorous modern standards of documentary criticism. The description of the barony of the abbey of St-Evroult, which appears in a charter of 1128, is likely to be relevant to that period, not to the time of the monastery's establishment in *c.* 1050; for conditions then, we should rely on the vaguer language of the abbey's foundation charter. Also, the argument that the honour of Le Plessis-Grimoult, which owed eight knights to Bayeux cathedral in 1133, must have owed ten knights up until the time that bishop Odo created seven prebends out of the honour, in or after 1074, is entirely inferential and has no documentary basis.[84] But the linchpin of Haskins' thesis, and the aspect of it which has been the most resistant to criticism, is the suggestion that fixed quotas of military service from certain cathedrals and monasteries must have been imposed at a date before 1030. This conclusion was deduced from observing that all the churches listed as owing knight-service to the duke in the earliest record of fiefs, the inquest returns of 1172, were either bishoprics, all of which had been re-established by the beginning of the eleventh century, or, with one or two insignificant exceptions, monasteries founded by the 1020s. Haskins therefore opined that unless the quotas had been definitively imposed by 1030, other later monasteries, such as Cerisy, would have had a similar service imposed on them. The most telling argument against this is a suggestion which Haskins himself made and dismissed; namely, that all the abbeys which owed service were ducal foundations, or, in the cases of St-Denis, La Trinité-du-Mont of Rouen, or St-Evroult, abbeys which came under the dukes' special protection.[85]

In fact, all the abbeys established and patronised by the dukes before 1066, with the strange and inexplicable omission of Cerisy (founded 1032) and also La Trinité of Caen (founded c. 1059), came to owe service to the duke. The date of their foundation was irrelevant. As in most regions at this time, a founding family took the opportunity to give church lands to their armed followers from whom they would then expect military service. It was this practice which eventually produced the fixed quotas once the impact of Gregorian reform in the later eleventh century had discredited this form of lay exploitation of the Church. That many abbeys were founded in pre-1066 Normandy which did not owe service to the duke is immaterial to the date by which fixed service quotas had evolved. Such monasteries, if they had received military tenancies, would perform service for their founders and their descendants; an arrangement which is clear in the cases of Troarn (a college of canons converted into a monastery in the late 1040s), Lyre (founded c. 1050), and Cormeilles (founded c. 1060).[86] The way is open to suggest that the dukes would naturally have drawn military service from the bishoprics and the monasteries of which they were patrons. But there is no reason at all to state that the obligation would have been converted into a fixed quota by 1066, let alone 1030. The vagueness of the terminology and the frequent references to the acquisition by these very same churches of *milites* and their lands right up until 1066 suggests that their 'baronies' were still in the process of formation; Avranches cathedral, for example, only received an important portion of its feudal endowment in 1066 itself.[87] If it is true that the military service owed from individual churches to the duke was only beginning to crystallise into institutional forms in 1066, the same is even more likely to be true of the lay aristocracy as a whole. Although some of the tenures which made up a 'barony' might have been held from an early date, their organisation into defined service-quotas had not taken place in 1066.

The development on which attention ought to be concentrated is the great extension of ducal lordship which took place during the eleventh century. An analysis of all references in the ducal charters to anyone who is described as a vassal (*fidelis, miles,* or *homo*) of the duke, or who acknowledged that the duke was his lord (*dominus, senior*), demonstrates firstly that the language employed to refer to the dukes' lordship was identical to that used for other lords. It also shows that there was a large geographical expansion of ducal lordship from Richard II's time through to William II's. In the latter's reign lordship encompassed all the most powerful men in the duchy in a way that it had not necessarily done under Richard II (see Map 9). Of fifty-two references in the charters to vassals of duke Richard II, only five appear as having held any property outside the Upper Norman *départements* of Eure and Seine-Maritime.[88] The duke often did dispose of properties in Lower Normandy to churches, but the charters usually refer to manors, rents, and rural churches, and only rarely to the holders of benefices.[89] In William II's reign the picture has changed completely. There are references to at least forty vassals whose property was scattered throughout the length and breadth of the duchy. Also, in comparison to Richard II's time when the *fideles, milites,* etc. were generally either obscure characters or ducal kinsmen, William II's *fideles* consisted of the likes of Robert and Hugh de Grandmesnil, Robert fitz Humphrey de Vieilles, Roger II de Montgommery, and bishop Hugh of Lisieux. Those who acknowledged William II as *dominus* included Ralph de Warenne, Thurstan Haldup, and William de Moulins-la-Marche.[90] A further observable change is the much heavier use of *dominus* with reference to William II, a shift away from the older terms such as *fidelis* – only used in four of the ducal charters from William II's reign – to the more authoritarian *dominus*, stressing that the duke was lord. This development was accompanied by the first signs of a tenurial hierarchy, in the form of examples of the duke giving his consent as the lord of another lord, who was himself agreeing that a grant be made.[91]

The objection which can be made to this argument for a great increase in the range of ducal lordship, that because before *c.* 1025 all the monasteries which produced documents, with the exception of Mont-St-Michel, were situated in Upper Normandy, and that as a result the evidence would only reveal ties of vassalage in that region, is not entirely convincing. It would be reasonable to expect vassals in all parts of the duchy to contribute benefactions to their lord's monastic houses, especially as these abbeys did receive land throughout the province. As was pointed out in the preceding paragraph, there is in fact a notable absence of references to vassals in Lower Normandy on those estates which the duke did dispose of. At the very least this suggests that the Lower Norman regions were not so firmly integrated into the structure of fidelity to the duke or so attached to the centres of religious devotion which were so much a part of his power. But the stronger argument for a restriction of Richard II's *fideles* to Upper Normandy is very feasible in the context of his itinerary, the establishment of a *comté* at Brionne, the recruitment of officials from among his kinsmen and among Upper Norman families, as well as, as we shall see, his appointment of bishops from these same groups. Similarly, an extension of ducal lordship into Lower Normandy from Robert I's time onwards fits in with the colonisation of the western parts of the province by leading families and by the Church, as well as with William II's enlarged itinerary and the more comprehensive character of the witness-lists of his charters. The consolidation of ducal lordship in Lower Normandy can reasonably be seen as a part of the expansion of the Upper Norman 'system' throughout the province.

These developments contain implications for our understanding of Norman military organisation and of the effectiveness of ducal government. References to a universal levy of freemen, the first from 1081 to 1087, suggest the maintenance through the tenth and eleventh centuries of another power of Carolingian origin.[92] But access to the military contingents which were being assembled by the great Norman families during the 1030s and 1040s came only as William II reimposed ducal rule. Richard II can be shown to have possessed only a socially and geographically limited group of *fideles*. Robert I's reign should be seen as an important transitional phase. His known vassals include powerful men such as the *vicomtes* Goscelin and Nigel, the second of whom appears to have held property only in Lower Normandy.[93] It may be that complacency on the duke's side towards the acquisition of ecclesiastical property was balanced on the part of the recipients by a willingness to acknowledge his lordship. But the overwhelming conclusion to be drawn from the charters of this reign is yet another sign of the serious deterioration of the power of government. The list of *fideles* which can be compiled for the reign is very short in comparison to that from Richard II's time or to that from the period after 1050. There looks to have been a dramatic decline in the Norman ruler's capacity to intervene in the donations by his subjects to the Church; most of the surviving acta either confirm Robert's own gifts or describe agreements or exchanges which in practice constituted a diminution of ecclesiastical property.[94]

Ducal lordship seems to have evolved rapidly once William II was securely in control. The corollary of this, the comparatively recent date in relation to 1066 at which powers of lordship had developed, is suggested by most of the evidence. It may be reflected, for example, in the derisory obligations owed by some of the baronies listed in the 1172 inquest returns; out of the 2,200 knights recorded in this incomplete survey, only 681 were available for ducal service; the bishopric of Bayeux, with 120 knights at its disposal, served the duke with a mere 20, while the honour of Montfort, with 44¾, provided 8½.[95] An interesting, but entirely speculative, comparison can be made with the late-twelfth-century register of fiefs for the county of Champagne, which shows that out of 2,036 vassals, over half were liegemen of the count.[96] But it is also clear that by 1066 the duke of Normandy was placing himself at the head of a tenurial hierarchy, within which the steady erosion of the freer alodial holdings would in time guarantee immense power to the superior lords. The readiness of the entire Norman aristocracy to enter into ties of vassalage with duke William II must reflect the intensification of government which has been apparent in so many aspects of this chapter. The willingness with which lordship was recognised must be a sign that at this stage the demands which the duke could make were slight ones; pre-1066 Norman 'feudalism' was probably not much more than a loose association in fidelity. The general development would also explain the growth in the activity of the ducal court in the second half of the century, something which only slightly prefaces the appearance of honorial courts. The history of military 'feudalism' in the duchy indicates that Normandy only became 'a society organised for war' in the years immediately prior to 1066. The bases of ducal authority had long been the traditional powers inherited from Carolingian ancestors; additions were only starting to be made when the expedition departed to conquer the English kingdom.

THE NORMAN POLITY

In the heyday of William II's reign ducal government had developed to such an extent as to have ramifications in all corners of the province. To gain any idea of its intimate workings, we have to turn to Ordericus Vitalis, most of whose adult life was lived in Henry I's reign (1106–35), but whose history none the less gives some hint of the intrigue, the pettiness, and the exploitation which must have existed around such a focus of power. He tells us of, for example, the rise of Rannulf Flambard, the supposed 'evil genius' of William Rufus' rule in England, who is said to have made his way among the 'parasites' of the Conqueror's court; the brawl between the followers of Robert Curthose and his two brothers when the entourage was at Laigle (Orne) on the southern frontier; or the same Robert Curthose's discomfiture when confronted with two children whose mother announced that they were his, and proved her case at the ordeal by hot-iron.[97] For Ordericus, a fierce critic of what he regarded as the effeminacy and immorality brought into the world in William Rufus' and Henry I's days, the Conqueror's reign represented 'the good old days' when men had kept their hair short and worn shoes which fitted their feet.[98] The extensive influence of William's government is also revealed in more prosaic contemporary material. Caen, like Winchester on the other side of the Channel, became so much a centre of administration that the distribution of property within the town was significantly affected.[99] The regime involved in one way or another many active men with rural or urban wealth. Sometimes imagination can take us a little way into the hive. Promotion on merit within the ducal service? – we know of a ducal cook whose son became a ducal moneyer. Or a paternal interest on the part of the duke in the doings of less important members of the entourage? – William II attended the dedication of the small priory of St-Martin-du-Bosc, which had developed from the decision of two otherwise unknown courtiers to live as hermits.[100]

The first three sections of this chapter all lead to the general conclusion that the government of the eleventh-century Norman dukes was able to preserve to a remarkable degree inherited Carolingian prerogatives. This said, it is also obvious that a very great change took place between Richard II's reign and William II's, under the impact of the violence and the social changes of the second quarter of the century. Government, heavily dependent on the personal qualities of the ruler, seems over time to have become even more reliant on the positive and individual leadership of the duke. A relationship of cause and effect surely existed between, on the one hand, the serious diminution of ducal resources in the first half of the century and the brutalisation of Norman society between *c.* 1025 and *c.* 1050, and, on the other, William II's more energetic administration and what was undoubtedly a conscious decision on his part to embark on a policy of aggressive war against his neighbours.

Normandy before 1066

Richard II's rule rested mainly on the firm application of powers of a traditional kind. That he was able to govern in this way must have been a consequence of the immense landed wealth inherited from his tenth-century predecessors, which is clearly evidenced in the charters of the reign, and which gave him the resources to reward *fideles* and to maintain the lavish monastic patronage for which he was famous among contemporaries. His rejection of the Peace of God in 1023 was a vote of confidence in the peace-keeping powers of his own regime, a proclamation that the Church had no place meddling in the responsibilities of the secular power. In duke Richard's view, Normandy had no need of newfangled devices which had been developed elsewhere to combat the fragmentation of authority.[101] His exertions in support of the Capetian kings, his unwillingness to encourage the disintegration of the kingdom by becoming involved in multiple vassalage relationships, and his aloofness from the ceaseless martial endeavours of other territorial princes, are all indications of an authority which remained resistant to the more anarchic features of early-eleventh-century French society. Government was mostly conducted from an Upper Norman base through the despatch of kinsmen or Upper Norman *fideles* to the more remote parts of the duchy, to act as counts or bishops. A special role was assigned to the ducal relatives who became counts, who were endowed with castles and extensive powers of jurisdiction, and, as we shall see, to the monasteries which were reformed under the aegis of William of Volpiano. Although cracks were undoubtedly developing by the 1020s, as a result of encroachments into the Norman lands, and because of the dissipation of ducal demesne by grants to Norman and non-Norman *fideles*, Richard deserves the high reputation he enjoyed among contemporaries. Within his territorial principality, authority remained far more resilient than in any other region of northern France. He clearly possessed a good opinion of his own importance, since he was the first Norman ruler to assume the title 'duke of the Normans'. In his time ducal authority was set above its subjects, allowing no one a place in government unless they had specifically been assigned one.

The twenty or so years after Richard II's death saw a serious weakening of the dukes' government. The nadir undoubtedly came during the years between William II's accession in 1035 and his victory at the battle of Val-ès-Dunes in 1047, a period when, because of the duke's youth and inexperience, there was no one to provide the Norman aristocracy with military leadership and no one to referee its internal feuds. All kinds of powers were undermined; from the duke's control over the construction of castles, to his right to nominate to vicecomital and household offices, to the quality of his coinage and his charters. It is too simple to take an extreme position and argue either that, because there was so much violence, ducal authority must have collapsed completely, or, on the other hand, that, because *vicomtes* continued to frequent the ducal entourage and to hold castles, government was still functioning. The predominant theme of these years was one of attempts to manipulate ducal authority and to consolidate local power. It was often in the great families' own interests to frequent the ducal court and to maintain some sort of local government. As in other regions the goal of most lineages was not wanton destruction; rather they were seeking what was basically self-preservation through a redefinition of political power. What the events of these years show is how public authority might be transferred to a lower level of society without the sustained control which only a strong and adult duke could provide. The idea that a 'new aristocracy' emerged during this difficult and confused period must be abandoned. The true significance of the disturbances lies in the changes which took place in the relationship between the duke and the existing aristocracy, consequent on the castle-building, the acquisition of office, and the subjugation of alodial landholders, which were typical of the time.

A definite effort was made during these years to sustain some sort of government. Duke Robert undoubtedly exerted himself, although he appears to have been unequal to the task of ruling firmly. He did at least organise military campaigns and he generally insisted on confirming the 'exchanges' which the aristocracy made with monasteries. In the last resort, it is impossible to judge whether his acquiescence in the transfer of ecclesiastical property and *vicomtés* to the Montgommerys, the Montforts, and their kind, was the result of a policy of involving the province's strongest families in the operation of ducal government or of extreme pliability and weakness. The clearest evidence that he was not entirely in control of events is his pacification, rather than adjudication, of feuds, and acts such as the sale of the ducal castle of Le Homme.[102] These suggest that he maintained more the form than the substance of authority.

Government was even more seriously impaired during William II's minority. Nevertheless, that William should at times have been in personal danger, and that a fair amount of the slaughter occurred in the vicinity of the ducal entourage, suggests that control of the ducal office was worth fighting for; a late source tells us that the young duke had sometimes to be hidden away at night from his enemies; Osbern the steward is known to have been killed in William's presence in 1040.[103] The group which emerged from this competition was far from being negligent or irresponsible. Its two leading figures, William's two uncles, count William of Arques and archbishop Malger of Rouen, have usually been treated with unjustifiable harshness by historians, presumably because their opposition to the duke in 1053–54 put them in line for character-assassination by William of Poitiers.[104] Yet count William's recorded actions display many of the qualities which had been typical of Richard II's government; he was a patron of most of the ducal monasteries, the force behind the restoration of some of the lands taken from the abbey of Fécamp in the early 1030s, and the sponsor of a very respectable appointment to the bishopric of Evreux from a family which had already supplied at least one bishop in the later years of Richard II's reign.[105] That count William should have built a stone castle of notably advanced design and should sometimes be described in charters in language normally reserved for the duke is, given the circumstances and his pre-eminence, only to be expected.[106] As for archbishop Malger, he assumed the role undertaken elsewhere by churchmen when the lay power was failing, organising an ecclesiastical council to condemn the seizure of church property, and probably being involved in an abortive attempt to introduce the Peace of God in $c.$ 1042.[107]

The early stages of William II's revival of ducal government revolved around a sequence of dramatic gestures. The promulgation of the Truce of God at an assembly near Caen in late 1047, to which saints' relics were brought from many parts of the province, was probably more significant as a symbolic display after the victory at Val-ès-Dunes than for any immediate and direct contribution to the strength of William's government. It was followed in the late 1040s and early 1050s by a series of actions which, in the context of the time, appear to have been extremely provocative; sufficient, for example, to end the century-old alliance between the Norman rulers and the Capetians, and to produce an active anti-Norman coalition organised by the former enemies, king Henry I and the count of Anjou (see pp. 76–7). Given the relative weakness, in comparison to Richard II's time, of the landed base supporting ducal authority, and the militarisation of Norman society which undoubtedly took place from the 1020s onwards, it is likely that drastic action of some kind was essential to the restoration of the power of ducal government. What is certain is that William's actions during these years led rapidly to closer and more co-operative relations between the duke and the

Ducal government

aristocracy. The battle of Val-ès-Dunes crushed the hopes of the pretender count Guy of Brionne and brought to heel the predominantly Lower Norman magnates from whom he had drawn support. By the early 1050s, the association between the small group of powerful men on whom William was to rely for much of his life was starting to form; in 1051–52 William fitz Osbern and Roger II de Montgommery, the two outstanding figures in the pre-1066 ducal entourage, appear acting together at the siege of Domfront,[108] while the duke's half-brother Odo was thrust into the see of Bayeux in either late 1049 or early 1050. These developments suggest that William II's methods must have been endowed with remarkable healing powers; Roger de Montgommery's father had killed William fitz Osbern's. They also show how the duke was surrounding himself with a group of men of similar age, and presumably, a similar outlook, to his own.

William's government during the 1050s and 1060s combined aggressive war, an astute management of individuals, and an efficient exploitation of financial and landed resources. His achievement is in many ways a classic demonstration of how power can be increased through seeming to give others a share in the rewards. Those in whom William had the greatest trust were apparently allowed to pursue ambitions of their own. The clearest example of this is Roger de Montgommery's push southwards into the regions of Sees and Bellême. It was as if William and Roger had struck up an agreement that, in tackling the problems of this sensitive southern frontier, Roger should be responsible for infiltrating Bellême, while the duke would face count Geoffrey Martel and his ally the Capetian king.[109] Similar freedom may have been given to count Robert of Mortain after his appointment in *c*. 1060 to push southwards, and probably to those others who were the beneficiaries of a general policy of increasing the number of castles on the frontier; we know that Hugh de Grandmesnil, who received the castle of Neufmarché, raided eastwards into the Beauvaisis and that William de Vernon and William Crispin, who were granted castles looking across from the Norman to the French Vexin before 1066, may have behaved likewise in their localities.[110] Another side to collaboration was the rise of William de Warenne, who profited out of the confiscated estates of count William of Arques, and who seems to have made a career with duke William as what a later age would have described as a commander of household troops.[111] Finally, and very significantly, co-operation extended to the organisation of the internal government of the duchy, with Roger de Beaumont being especially important both as a custodian of castles and as a judge in the duke's court, and both Roger de Montgommery and William fitz Osbern sharing in the organisation of the duke's protection of monastic houses (see p. 207).[112] From William's point of view, the aim must have been to create a group of followers of unshakeable loyalty and with such wealth and influence as to enable him to beat down any opposition.

William's methods gave him a direct authority throughout his duchy of a kind which none of his predecessors had possessed. His relationship with the most powerful lineages enabled him to check the results of the social changes of the second quarter of the century and in many respects to turn them to the duke's advantage; the men who had built up great power during that troubled period were by and large persuaded that their best interests were served by collaboration with the duke. What is particularly interesting is how this relationship supported a steady consolidation of the duke's power. In a remarkable way, William was able to compensate for the weakening of ducal landed resources, to develop effectively existing sources of revenue, and to re-establish the foundations of ducal authority as they had existed in Richard II's reign. Unlike in Richard's time, however, when the duke had been in a position simply to prohibit castle-building or the emergence of lay advocacy over churches, Willim had to operate within a changed political and social framework to impose control over the fortifications and monasteries which had appeared in the second quarter of the century. Although it is clear that this was done through the agency of William's inner circle of magnates, what is notable is that these men were themselves willing to accept the disciplines of William's regime and were usually willing to work for their rewards; the duke abandoned the generosity to *fideles* which had been a feature of previous reigns, and generally granted away land only when a forfeiture had made it available (see p. 101). The most dramatic symbol of duke William's political achievement must be the town of Caen, where he was eventually to be buried in the abbey church of St-Etienne which he had founded. Caen was not just a 'new town' with a large castle and two abbeys. It was a deliberately created conurbation in a region which dukes before William had scarcely visited. It highlighted the way in which ducal government could draw on the potential inherent in economic prosperity and a rising population to organise an enlarged community as a bastion of authority. This, on the grand scale, typified the sort of consolidation which many members of the aristocracy were effecting over their own men and within their own estates (see pp. 101–2). Yet, despite all the evidence for governmental development, what ultimately gave William II's Normandy its stability must surely be the one feature in which his rule differed radically from that of his forerunners: the constant and generally successful prosecution of war against the duchy's neighbours. This, a focus for the ambitions of lineages who had fought among themselves before c. 1050, along with the duke's remarkable personality, must be seen as underpinning the cohesion of the Norman polity which had been created by the year 1066.

The original qualities of the government of the Norman rulers can be more fully appreciated through a comparison with other principalities. That the dukes operated to so large an extent within an inherited Carolingian framework means that there are close similarities with other units of power, since all the territorial rulers had taken over and had sought to maintain what were fundamentally the same prerogatives. The counts of Anjou, Champagne, and Flanders, for example, each upheld with varying degrees of success a control over castle-building in the tradition of Charles the Bald's Edict of Pîtres. The counts of Anjou collected the *fodrum*, the tax from which the Norman *bernagium* was descended, and exercised rights over public roads and forest. The counts of Champagne also received the *fodrum*, controlled coinage, and had prevented the spread of lay advocacy. The counts of Flanders possessed a monopoly of the right to mint money and the right to levy tolls.[113] It also appears as if all the leading territorial rulers proceeded along what were by and large the same lines in their attempts to reinforce their authority. All introduced formal households; the Capetians from 1043, the counts of Anjou from 1056, and the counts of Flanders in the last third of the century.[114] The appearance of the *prepositus* was also a universal development, with the counts of Anjou and the counts of Blois-Chartres seemingly leading the way from the early eleventh century.[115] The Peace of God, although rejected by Normandy in 1023, was eventually established in a form very similar to the second stage of the Flanders' Peace as promulgated in 1042–43; that is, with a prohibition of fighting between Wednesday evening and Monday morning and exemption for the count's army.[116] It can be added that the construction of castles at the limits of a ruler's territorial power was an extremely widespread practice.[117] Finally, the example of Caen's development by William II is paralleled in Flanders, where towns such as Lille and Ypres were planted in the middle years of the century by the counts to strengthen their power in regions where their authority was weak.[118]

It is a fruitless exercise to try to establish chronological priority in order to decide which principalities were innovatory in either administration or policy. Developments would take place at particular times in response to the conditions which existed in the principality concerned. Innovation might indeed be a sign of a weakening of authority, rather than an increase. The establishment of *prepositi*, for example, essentially a demesne official based where a prince had lands, reflects an inability to uphold any higher notion of authority than that which could be sustained by an immediate presence. In Normandy this new official was overshadowed by the *vicomte*, demonstrating the durability of the *pagus*, whereas in Anjou and Flanders new units of authority called respectively *prepositura* and castellanries were set up to supersede the dismembered *pagi*.[119] What is important is that the rudimentary character of eleventh-century Norman institutions was entirely typical of what was prevalent elsewhere. Only the Capetians, for example, possessed any sort of organised chancery, and very evidently no territorial prince felt under any particular pressure to develop one, with the counts of Anjou, for instance, having a chancery from 1047 to 1060, but then needing to re-create it in 1085.[120] It is in fact impossible to discover any method of government before 1066 which was fundamentally unique to eleventh-century Normandy. Such extra powers as had been gained in the tenth century from Scandinavian sources certainly contributed to the strength of eleventh-century ducal rule, but by 1050 they were incorporated into a single apparatus of authority which was administered through institutions which were totally Frankish; the earliest list of a selection of the dukes' powers, which appears in a text of *c*. 1050, arranges Scandinavian and Carolingian elements without distinction (*consuetudines, . . . scilicet hainfaram, ullac, rat, incendium, bernagium, bellum*).[121] It is only after 1066, in items such as William the Conqueror's peace legislation or in some of the provisions of the ecclesiastical council held at Lillebonne in 1080, that Norman government starts to branch out into channels which were truly original (see p. 248).

The special quality of the government of the eleventh-century dukes of Normandy is their success in maintaining a traditional base for their authority. This is something which has been demonstrated over and over again during this and the preceding chapters: the resilience of duke Richard II's regime and the late date for territorial fragmentation within the duchy; the failure of nobility and knighthood to fuse; the near-exclusion of lay advocacy and bannal lordship from the duchy; the survival of the *pagus* as a unit of administration; these are merely some illustrations of this very important general theme.

The result was a principality which was by contemporary standards very highly centralised. To anyone who reads the now numerous monographs devoted to the various regions and principalities of early medieval France, the contrast in the structure of political power is a stark and powerful one.

The cohesion which existed in Normandy in 1066 was built around the relationship between the duke and the aristocracy, since in Normandy the dominant families had not to any extent dismantled the apparatus of government; rather they had been integrated into its operation. This was the result of the acquisition by the province's powerful lineages of the chief offices of ducal government during the second quarter of the eleventh century, followed by William II's reassertion of ducal authority. If the evolution of the witness-lists of the ducal charters is compared with similar processes elsewhere, the significance of this development becomes clearer (for Normandy, see pp. 158–60). In the Capetian demesne, for example, the witness-lists suggest strong analogies between the essentially 'official' entourages of duke Richard II and king Robert the Pious. But from 1028 there began a progressive decline in the quality of the Capetian entourage, reflecting the emergence of the castellanries, the desertion of the entourage by the more powerful families, and the decay of royal power. No member of a castellan family appears holding a household office before 1091.[122] In Anjou Geoffrey Martel appears to have sustained a regime similar to Richard II's right up until his death in 1060, rigorously excluding the chief families from office. This policy of bleak confrontation can only have been sustained by Geoffrey's prestige and military achievements; his death was followed by the proliferation of independent castellanries and a decrease in the number and quality of the count's vassals.[123] It is only in Flanders, where the administrative castellanries set up by the counts and the household offices went to the most powerful families and where the count remained in control, that there are any parallels with Normandy.[124]

The foundation of ducal authority was the base established by the tenth-century counts of Rouen. This was threatened seriously on several occasions in the eleventh century, both by the encroachments of neighbouring powers and by the disturbances of the second quarter of the century. The way in which William II rebuilt ducal authority can only be traced, as has been attempted in the preceding chapters, through a close examination of his campaigns and of the structure of his government. These both point to the importance of aggressive warfare and of ambitions such as that to gain the English kingdom as a crucial device to sustain internal stability. It is as if the expansionist ambitions of the aristocratic families who had dominated in the second quarter of the eleventh century were moulded into a single outward drive with the duke at its head. The result, the duchy over which William ruled in 1066, was a polity which was well organised, administratively traditional, and politically centralised and coherent to a remarkable degree. One very impressive demonstration of this achievement was the clarity of the Norman frontier in the 1060s. Another is the organisation of the Norman Church.

NOTES

1. *Anglo-Saxon Chronicle*, 'E', 1086 (*recte* 1087), in *English Historical Documents*, ii, ed. D. C. Douglas and G. W. Greenaway (London, 1953), 163–4.
2. D. C. Douglas, *William the Conqueror* (London, 1964), 369.
3. *CTR*, no. 67.
4. *Sancti Anselmi Cantuariensis Archiepiscopi Opera Omnia*, ed. Dom F. S. Schmitt (Edinburgh, 1938–61), iii, *ep.* no. 27; *Self and Society in Medieval France. The Memoirs of Abbot Guibert of Nogent*, trans. J. F. Benton (New York and Evanston, 1970), 69.
5. *Recueil*, no. 52.
6. *Ibid.*, no. 9. On the whole problem, fundamental is, K. F. Werner, 'Quelques observations au sujet des débuts du "duché" de Normandie', in *Etudes . . . Yver*, 691–709. Also, J. Yver, 'Les premières institutions du duché de Normandie', *Settimane di Centro Italiano sull' Alto Medioevo*, xvi (Spoleto, 1969), 312–16; F. L. Ganshof, 'A propos de ducs et de duchés au Haut Moyen Age', *Journal des Savants* (1972), 13–24; W. Kienast, *Der Herzogstitel in Frankreich und Deutschland (9.bis 12. Jahrhundert)* (Munich and Vienna, 1968), 107–30.
7. *Recueil*, no. 14.
8. *The Letters and Poems of Fulbert of Chartres*, ed. F. Behrends (Oxford, 1976), 116, 150, 152, 178. Non-Norman charters in which Richard II and William II are styled duke are *Recueil*, nos. 20, 137, 156, 199, 227, 230. Of these, only no. 199 is an original charter. Also, no. 227, although in favour of the abbey of Beaumont-lès-Tours, was probably written by an archdeacon of Bayeux cathedral. There are no examples from Robert I's reign.
9. *Recueil des actes de Philippe Ier, roi de France (1059–1108)*, ed. M. Prou (Paris, 1908), no. 84.
10. *Recueil*, no. 188.
11. *Ibid.*, nos. 223, 231; WP, 23, note 4.
12. . . . *Richardo gratia Dei illustrissimo comiti, quem apostolica auctoritas ducem Normannorum ex hoc iam appellari constituit, Acta Pontificum Romanorum Inedita*, ed. J. von Pflugk-Harttung (Tübingen and Stuttgart, 1881–86), i, no. 13.

13. Dudo of St-Quentin, *De moribus et actis primorum Normanniae Ducum*, ed. J. Lair (Caen, 1865), 297; WJ, 72, 97, 100, 111–12. See in general, J. Le Patourel, 'The Norman succession, 996–1135', *EHR*, lxxxvi (1971), 234–40; A. W. Lewis, 'Anticipatory association of the heir in early Capetian France', *American Historical Review*, lxxxiii (1978), 911–21. Richard II and Richard III both witness an original charter for St-Wandrille as 'duke' in 1025–26, *Recueil*, no. 55.
14. The *pancarte* of the abbey of Grestain provides an 11th-century reference to Herleva's name, see Chapter 3, note 41, for the manuscripts.
15. Douglas, *William the Conqueror*, 369–70.
16. *Chartes normandes de l'abbaye de St-Florent près Saumur*, ed. P. Marchegay (Caen, 1879), no. 15.
17. L. Delisle, *Histoire du château et des sires de Saint-Sauveur-le-Vicomte* (Valognes, 1867), pièces-justificatives, no. 42; *Regesta*, i, no. 133.
18. For Richard II, *Recueil*, nos. 9, 12, 13, 15, 18, 20, 25, 26, 34, 35, 36, 41. For Robert I, *ibid.*, nos. 64, 71, 89, 90.
19. *Ibid.*, no. 151.
20. *Translatio S. Dadonis vel Audoeni episcopi*, *Acta Sanctorum*, August, iv, 824.
21. *Recueil*, no. 12; *Raoul Glaber, Les cinq livres de ses histoires (990–1044)*, ed. M. Prou (Paris, 1886), 20.
22. *Recueil*, nos. 11, 58. See, L. Musset, 'Actes inédits du XIe siècle. III. Les plus anciennes chartes normandes de l'abbaye de Bourgueil', *BSAN*, liv (1959, for 1957–58), 32–5.
23. These conclusions are based on a careful survey of the William II charters in *Recueil*. There is nothing in the charters of 1066–87 to modify this opinion. Note too that most of William's grants of Upper Norman lands occurred very early in his reign, see especially *Recueil*, no. 94.
24. In general, L. Musset, 'Que peut-on savoir de la fiscalité publique en Normandie à l'époque ducale?', *RHDFE*, 4e série, xxxviii (1960), 483–4.
25. The complex evidence is set out by T. N. Bisson, *Conservation of Coinage: Monetary Exploitation and its Restraint in France, Catalonia, and Aragon, (c. A.D. 1000–c. 1225)* (Oxford, 1979), 14–28.
26. *Recueil*, no. 34. The document exists in a late-11th-century copy.
27. *Ibid.*, nos. 34, 36. See, C. H. Haskins, *Norman Institutions* (Cambridge, Mass., 1918), 42–4.
28. A.D. Seine-Maritime, 14H, 160, 14H, 189; *Recueil*, p. 273, note 2. On the subject as a whole, *ibid.*, pp. 41–7; P. Chaplais, 'The Anglo-Saxon chancery: from the diploma to the writ', *Journal of the Society of Archivists*, iii (1965–69), 160–1.
29. *AAC*, no. 4*bis*. For sealing after 1066, below, p. 248.
30. *Recueil*, pp. 41–3, nos. 34–6, 53.
31. *Recueil*, nos. 65, 69, 73, 79, 82, 85, 89.
32. For Hugh, *ibid.*, no. 116. For Stigand, *ibid.*, no. 107. For Gerald, A. D. Eure, H. 711, fo. 137r; *Cartulaire de l'abbaye de St-Père de Chartres*, ed. B. E. C. Guérard (Paris, 1840), i, 176.
33. *Recueil*, nos. 204, 204*bis*, 231.
34. *CTR*, no. 67; cf. J. -F. Lemarignier, *Le gouvernement royal aux premiers temps capétiens* (Paris, 1965), 129.

35. *Recueil*, no. 141. See, L. Musset, 'Chapelles et chapelains du duc de Normandie au XIe siècle', *RHDFE*, 4e série, liii (1975), 171–2.
36. D. C. Douglas, 'The earliest Norman counts', *EHR*, lxi (1946), 149–50. Yver, 'Les premières institutions', 323–5, is rightly much more sceptical about the identity of *comté* and *pagus*. Count William of Arques is described once as *comes territorii quod Talohu nuncupatur* in an original charter, *Recueil*, no. 100, but he is usually 'count of Arques', *ibid.*, nos. 100, 107, 108, 112, 124, 131, 142.
37. *Ibid.*, nos. 13, 16.
38. For the powers of jurisdiction of the counts, J. Yver, 'Contribution à l'étude du développement de la compétence ducale en Normandie', *AN*, viii (1958), 153–4; J. Le Patourel, 'Henri Beauclerc, comte du Cotentin, 1088', *RHDFE*, 4e série, liii (1975), 167–8. For ducal supervision, note, *omnes consuetudines que ad comitatum pertinent, quas ipse ex nostro jure possidebat,* and *electione Ricardi senioris avi mei Normannorum principis Ebroicae civitatis comes electus et constitutus, Recueil*, nos. 36, 208.
39. *Ibid.*, no. 35; Yver, 'Les premières institutions', 325.
40. *Recueil*, nos. 36, 99, 203. The 1042 charter for Cerisy contains financial information of a remarkably detailed and sophisticated kind. Interpolation or rewriting must be suspected.
41. For Anschetil, *ibid.*, nos. 17, 65, 69, 80.
42. Delisle, *Saint-Sauveur*, 22–4.
43. *Recueil*, no. 89; BN, MS. latin 1939, fo. 171v.
44. *Recueil*, no. 121; p. 286, note 1.
45. WJ, 76–7, 84; *AAC*, no. 21. For pleas, *Antiquus Cartularius Ecclesiae Baiocensis*, ed. V. Bourrienne (Rouen, 1902–03), i, no. 21; Delisle, *St-Sauveur*, pièces-justificatives, no. 42; *GC*, xi, instr. col. 65.
46. E.g. *Recueil*, nos. 119, 170.
47. *Ibid.*, no. 93.
48. *Ibid.*, pp. 58–62; nos. 16, 17, 23, 33, 35, 49, 51. A good proportion of the attestations of the bishops of Sées and the count of Mortain occur in charters for Sées cathedral itself (no. 33) or in connection with Lower Normandy (nos. 16, 17, 23, 49).
49. The relevant attestations appear in *ibid.*, nos. 93, 94, 95, 98, 99, 100, 102–8, 110, 112, 113, 115.
50. *Ibid.*, pp. 59–62.
51. E.g. *ibid.*, no. 170.
52. See, *duas reclamationes in mea corte vel curia faciant, ibid.*, no. 71; *intra ejus curiam fuerant observati, ibid.*, no. 218; *decem auri libras curie pro tanta temeritate persolvat, ibid.*, no. 219. Most pre-1066 examples of *curia* appear in non-Norman documents.
53. *Ibid.*, no. 20; *Chartes normandes de l'abbaye de St-Florent près Saumur*, no. 15. Note also, *Recueil*, no. 157. See, in general, L. Musset, 'Gouvernès et gouvernants dans le monde scandinave et dans le monde normand (XIe-XIIe siècles)', in *Recueils de la société Jean Bodin*, xvii (1968), 462–3.
54. Examples are frequent, e.g., *CTR*, no. 82; Rouen, Bibliothèque municipale, MS. 1193 (Y. 44), fo. 30v.
55. For a pre-1066 example of the duke delegating a plea, *Recueil*, no. 209. On institutional status, ... *iudicio curiae regis Anglorum coram episcopis*

Gaufrido videlicet Constantiensis, Michaele Abrincensis, Gisleberto Luxoviensi, et Eudone vicecomite, quibus idem rex judicium illud praecepit, Delisle, *St-Sauveur,* pièces-justificatives, no. 42.
56. See recently, D. R. Bates, 'The land pleas of William I's reign: Penenden Heath revisited', *BIHR*, li (1978), 4–5, 11–12.
57. See the comments by L. Musset, 'Actes inédits du XIe siècle. VI. L'abbaye de Saint-Ouen de Rouen et la ville de Caen', *BSAN*, lviii (1967, for 1965–66), 124. Among many examples, ... *ne causa ecclesie determinaretur humano sanguine ... taliter feci pacem et concordiam ..*, F. Lot, *Etudes critiques sur l'abbaye de St-Wandrille* (Paris, 1913), pièces-justificatives, no. 37. Or, even more explicitly, in 1086 Robert de Bellême, *volens pacem facere inter barones suos,* Cartulaire de St-Martin de Sées, fo. 34v (see Chapter 2, note 92).
58. *GC*, xi, instr. col. 65. For the testimony of old men, *Cartulaire de Marmoutier pour le Perche*, ed. l'abbé Barret (Mortagne, 1894), no. 3.
59. P. Le Cacheux, 'Une charte de Jumièges concernant l'épreuve par le fer chaud (fin du XIe siècle)', *SHN, Mélanges*, xi (1927), 213–16; OV, iii, 160–2.
60. For examples of William nominating judges, *Chartes normandes de l'abbaye de St-Florent près Saumur,* no. 15; *Cartulaire de Marmoutier pour le Perche,* no. 3.
61. *Recueil,* no. 159.
62. *Ibid.,* no. 197.
63. Promising for examples of pre-1066 ducal *prepositi* are *Gisleberti prepositi de Usmis* (Exmes) and *Unfridus prepositus de Badvento* (Bavent: Calvados: cant. Troarn, which was ducal demesne, *Recueil,* no. 231; *AAC,* no. 8), *Recueil,* nos. 146, 156. For *prepositura* and *prefectura, ibid.,* nos. 174, 231; *AAC,* nos. 11, 12, 14.
64. L. Delisle, 'Canons du concile tenu à Lisieux en 1064', *Journal des Savants* (1901), c. 5.
65. Printed, Haskins, *Norman Institutions,* 281–4. Fundamental to any discussion of their content is Yver, 'Les premières institutions', 340–3, 349–63.
66. WJ, 96, 101; Yver, 'Les premières institutions', 353–5.
67. On the Peace and Truce of God in Normandy, M. de Bouard, 'Sur les origines de la trêve de Dieu en Normandie', *AN,* ix (1959), 169–89; J. -F. Lemarignier, 'Paix et réforme monastique en Flandre et en Normandie autour de l'année 1023', in *Etudes ... Yver,* 458–61. The latest affirmation of 1047 is by J. -C. Richard, 'Les "miracles" composés en Normandie aux XIe et XIIe siècles', *Ecole des Chartes. Position des Thèses* (1975), 184–5.
68. OV, iii, 26.
69. This was reported in 'Annales Uticenses', in Orderic Vitalis, *Historia Ecclesiastica,* ed. A. Le Prévost (Paris, 1838–55), v, 158; 'Annalis Historia Brevis in Monasterio S. Stephani Cadomensis conscriptae', in A. Duchesne, *Historiae Normannorum Scriptores Antiqui* (Paris, 1619), 1017. The two sets of annals are not independent at this point.
70. OV, iii, 26, 34.
71. For this section, Françoise Dumas, 'Les monnaies normandes du Xe-XIIe siècle', *Bulletin de la société française de numismatique* (1978), 389–94.

72. William's recoinage is presumably referred to in the text of a pre-1066 charter, *acceptis ab eo vi libras denariorum nove monete*, BN, collection Moreau, vol. 21, fo. 22v; see, L. Musset, 'Sur les mutations de la monnaie ducale normande au XIe siècle', *Revue numisnatique*, 6e série, xi (1969), 292.
73. Elisabeth Zadora-Rio, 'L'enceinte fortifiée du Plessis-Grimoult, résidence seigneuriale du XIe siècle', *Château Gaillard*, v (1970) 237–9.
74. *AAC*, no. 21.
75. But the 1091 text may have represented only a section of the ducal powers, C. L. H. Coulson, 'Rendability and castellation in medieval France', *Château Gaillard*, vii (1972), 59.
76. WP, 20. In general, J. Yver, 'Les châteaux forts en Normandie jusqu'au milieu du XIIe siècle. Contribution à l'étude du pouvoir ducal', *BSAN*, liii (1957, for 1955–56), 42–63.
77. OV, iv, 88, 114.
78. *Raoul Glaber*, 52–5.
79. OV, ii, 90–2, 106, 122–4. For some general comment, L. Musset, 'Autour des modalités juridiques de l'expansion normande au XIe siècle: le droit d'exil', *RHDFE*, 4e série, li (1972), 561–2.
80. Delisle, *St-Sauveur*, 19–21.
81. OV, ii, 106; *Recueil*, nos. 142, 156, 232.
82. *Acta Archiepiscoporum Rotomagensium, PL,* cxlvii, col. 278.
83. WJ, 124; WP, 20.
84. See Haskins, *Norman Institutions*, 5–24. For further comments on the documents on which his conclusions were based, see Appendix B.
85. For the ducal protection of La Trinité-du-Mont and St-Evroult, J. Yver, 'Autour de l'absence d'avouerie en Normandie', *BSAN*, lvii (1965, for 1963–64), 202–7.
86. For Troarn, . . . *concessit etiam ipse abbas ut quando faceret ipse Sanson guardam in castellis domini ipsius abbatie, haberet conveniens adjutorium de hominibus ipsius terre sicut de ceteris hominibus quos habet de feudo comitis Rogerii, et hoc semel in anno, . . .*, BN, MS. latin 10086, fo. 180rv, a report of a plea heard before Robert de Bellême at Fourches in 1101. See also the early-13th-century registers of king Philip Augustus, *RHF*, xxiii, 715. For Lyre and Cormeilles, which owed service to the honour of Breteuil, *ibid.*, 617, 714, 715; A.D. Eure, H. 438, for a *vidimus* containing a text of a charter of Robert IV, earl of Leicester, recording that Lyre owed castle-guard at Breteuil.
87. *Recueil*, no. 229.
88. *Ibid.*, nos. 34, 36, 53.
89. E.g. *ibid.*, no. 23.
90. *Ibid.*, nos. 122, 128, 135, 140, 167, 223 (= *AAC*, no. 1), 225.
91. In dealing with such confirmations the language of the charters is often clumsy, a likely sign of a new development which is not apparent in Richard II's or Robert I's charters. See, for example, *ibid.*, nos. 107, 113, 122, 169, 191, 211.
92. *AAC*, no. 4*bis*; Yver, 'Les premières institutions', 336, note 88.
93. *Recueil*, nos. 61, 73.
94. Clear references to duke Robert's lordship appear only in *ibid.*, nos. 61,

72, 73, 80, 84, 85, 86. For exchanges and encroachments, *ibid.*, nos. 70, 71, 72, 74, 85.
95. J. Boussard, 'L'enquête de 1172 sur les services de chevalier en Normandie', *Recueil... Clovis Brunel* (Paris, 1955), 205–8.
96. M. Bur, *La formation du comté de Champagne, v. 950–v. 1150* (Nancy, 1977), 398.
97. OV, ii, 356–8; iv, 170–2; v, 282.
98. *Ibid.*, iv, 186–92.
99. Musset, 'L'abbaye de Saint-Ouen', 119–20, 122–3; cf., F. Barlow, M. Biddle, *et al., Winchester in the Early Middle Ages*, i (Oxford, 1976), 474–6, 479–80.
100. *CTR*, no. 60; *Recueil*, no. 218.
101. The point is well made by Lemarignier, in *Etudes... Yver*, 457–61.
102. *AAC*, no. 21. For the feuds, see p. 101.
103. OV, iv, 82; WJ, 156.
104. WP, 50–4, 130–2.
105. For count William's benefactions, *Recueil*, nos. 100, 112, 234; Lot, *St-Wandrille*, pièces justificatives, no. 15. For the Fécamp restoration, *Thesaurus Novus Anecdotorum*, ed. E. Martène and U. Durand (Paris, 1717), i, cols. 166–8. Bishop William of Evreux (c. 1046–66) was a vassal of count William, and was probably helped into office by him, Cartulaire de l'abbaye de St-Wandrille, A.D. Seine-Maritime, 16 H, non classé, fo. 319r; printed, D. Gurney, *The Record of the House of Gournay* (London, 1848), 56–7.
106. For the select treatment of William of Arques in charters, *Recueil*, no. 124; *Thesaurus Novus Anecdotorum*, i, col. 166.
107. For a justified 'rehabilitation' of Malger, Margaret Gibson, *Lanfranc of Bec* (Oxford, 1978), 106–7; see also, De Bouard, 'La trêve de Dieu', 175–6.
108. WP, 38. For the date, see Appendix A.
109. For developments on this frontier, see pp. 78–81
110. OV, ii, 130. See also, 'De nobili Crispinorum genere', in *Beati Lanfranci Cantuariensis archiepiscopi... Opera Omnia*, ed. L. d'Achery (Paris, 1648), *Appendix*, 53; Douglas, *William the Conqueror*, 87–8.
111. J. O. Prestwich, 'The military household of the Norman kings', *EHR*, xcvi (1981), 14–15.
112. For Roger de Beaumont as a judge, D. R. Bates, 'The origins of the justiciarship', *Proceedings of the Battle Conference*, iv (1982), forthcoming.
113. O. Guillot, *Le comte d'Anjou et son entourage au XIe siècle* (Paris, 1972), i, 301–17, 379–81, 391–6; Bur, *Champagne*, 390–2, 494–7; E. Warlop, *The Flemish Nobility before 1300* (Kortrijk, 1975–76), i, 89–90. See also, Coulson, 'Rendability and castellation', 59–62; F. L. Ganshof, *La Flandre sous les premiers comtes* (3rd edn., Brussels, 1949), 97–111.
114. Lemarignier, *Gouvernement royal*, 148–9; Guillot, *Le comte d'Anjou*, i, 417–29; Warlop, *The Flemish Nobility*, i, 157–78.
115. K. F. Werner, 'Kingdom and principality in twelfth-century France', in *The Medieval Nobility*, ed. T. Reuter (Amsterdam, New York, and Oxford, 1978), 256–58.
116. See, E. I. Strubbe, 'La paix de Dieu dans le nord de la France', *Recueils*

de la société Jean Bodin, xiv (1961), 496–8; H. Platelle, 'La violence et ses remèdes en Flandre au XIe siècle', *Sacris Erudiri*, xx (1971), 116–19.
117. A general point well made by R. Aubenas, 'Les châteaux-forts des Xe et XIe siècles. Contribution à l'étude des origines de la féodalité', *RHDFE*, 4e série, xvii (1938), 562–8.
118. J. Dhondt, 'Développement urbain et initiative comtale en Flandre au XIe siècle', *Revue du Nord*, xxx (1948), 151–6; J. -F. Lemarignier, 'L'origine de Lille et de Caen', *Revue du moyen âge latin*, iv (1948), 191–6.
119. See now, Warlop, *The Flemish Nobility*, i, 105–36; Guillot, *Le comte d'Anjou*, i, 398–415.
120. Guillot, *Le comte d'Anjou*, i, 418–22.
121. *Recueil*, no. 121.
122. Lemarignier, *Gouvernement royal, passim*, and especially, 153–7.
123. Guillot, *Le comte d'Anjou*, i, 417–29.
124. Warlop, *The Flemish Nobility*, i, 108–74.

CHAPTER FIVE
The Church

In 990, for the first time for over a century, it is possible to name a bishop for each one of the seven Norman dioceses. At this same date, there were five monasteries in existence, of which four, including the recently refounded abbey of Fécamp, were within the traditional centre of ducal power in Upper Normandy, and the fifth, Mont-St-Michel, was in the extreme West. By 1066 this elementary organisation had been transformed out of all recognition. After 990 the succession to bishoprics seems to have been continuous, and by the second half of the century all were securely established with new cathedrals in the course of construction and embryonic chapters and diocesan administration evolving everywhere. Monasteries and religious houses had become both numerous and prosperous.

The sources for the history of the Norman Church are, as might be expected, more plentiful than for other aspects of this book. The charters record gifts of property to the Church. We can also draw on the testimony of chronicles, and most especially on the work of Ordericus Vitalis with its vivid record of the first years of the abbey of St-Evroult. Then there are the decrees of ecclesiastical councils, historical tracts produced by several of the Norman churches, the survivals from monastic libraries, and the buildings. For all this relative wealth, there are, however, snags, both of a general and particular kind. The received version of the negotiations connected with William II's supposedly incestuous marriage, for example, rests entirely on one very dubious source written at the earliest in 1140, while our acceptance of another 'old chestnut', the papal banner which Alexander II is supposed to have despatched to William in 1066, relies mostly on the faith which we are prepared to place in William of Poitiers.

Then there is the extreme sparseness of the records from the bishoprics; Evreux plumbs the depths with no surviving episcopal charter from before the year 1100. A particularly active monastic *scriptorium* can as a result give a possibly misleading impression of the precocity of a bishopric's development; Rouen and Sées are much better covered than, say, Bayeux, about which little is known before the development of the two abbeys at Caen from the 1060s.

A difficulty of a more general kind is that much of the material on which we depend was written in the twelfth century and therefore reflects the ideas and attitudes which became current with the Gregorian Reform Movement of the later eleventh century. Such late sources often condemn as voluptuaries and illiterates prelates who were both respectable and industrious by eleventh-century standards; they stand censured by the moral and educational requirements of a later and very different age. Nowhere indeed is the truism that a historian reflects the attitudes of his own time more apt than in this period, when views on the role of secular authority in a Christian society and on the standards of behaviour expected of churchmen were changing so rapidly. It has recently been pointed out how far the early-twelfth-century accounts of the origins in the 1030s of the famous abbey of Le Bec reflect the contemporary interest in primitive monasticism; when a former member of what had become a renowned and wealthy monastery compiled a biography of its first abbot, he felt obliged, as a result of changing fashions in monastic ideals, to present its earliest years as a desperate struggle for survival.[1] Ordericus Vitalis, who usually did his best to be fair, demonstrated his own place in the cosmos by his ambivalent treatment of Odo of Bayeux, a warrior prelate who kept a mistress but who was also generous to the Church and an efficient diocesan, and by his careful scrutiny of the early Cistercians and Savignacs, whose literal interpretation of the Rule of St Benedict and excessive emphasis on manual work he found discomfiting, but whose profound commitment and respect for monastic obedience he thought praiseworthy.[2]

THE DUKES AND THE CHURCH

The eleventh-century Norman dukes treated the Church within their duchy as an aspect of government. Normandy was structurally an ideal place for a close alliance of secular and ecclesiastical administration, since the territorial boundaries of the two almost coincided; the metropolitan province of the archbishops of Rouen, with their supervision of six suffragan bishops, covered an area which was slightly larger than that of the duchy. Both Richard II and William II were renowned in their day for their active support for ecclesiastical reform and their concern for the welfare of the Church. Both were associated with religious advisers who achieved European reputations: duke Richard with the monastic reformer William of Volpiano (or Dijon), who became abbot of Fécamp; William II with the Italian Lanfranc, successively prior of the monastery of Le Bec, abbot of St-Etienne of Caen (c. 1063–70), and archbishop of Canterbury (1070–89). The only blemish in this history of benevolence was the period of Robert I's reign and William II's minority, when ecclesiastical property was secularised in large quantities and the Church in general was exposed to despoliation at the hands of laymen. The ducal office itself possessed strong religious connotations at the height of William II's power, and may well have done so before that time; like kings, the Norman rulers were acclaimed by the singing of ritual *laudes* on special feast-days. The Norman version of the *laudes*, which survives in an eleventh-century manuscript, is another sign of the self-esteem and prestige of the dukes; typically Frankish in form, it included prayers for the French king, but none the less praised the Norman ruler in a style which was notably ornate and indeed almost regal.[3]

Such quasi-religious authority embodied a well-established tradition of 'lay theocracy' of the kind exercised by the Carolingian and Ottonian emperors and by the pre-1066 English kings. It represented centuries-old arrangements by which a unitary Christian society, within which the papacy maintained an easygoing oversight in matters of doctrine, was in practice governed by lay rulers. In France in the early eleventh century, these notions were still upheld by the Capetian kings. Robert the Pious (996–1031), for example, was the subject of a semi-hagiographical biography by Helgaud, a monk of the abbey of Fleury-sur-Loire, in which he described the king as 'set in the bosom of Mother Church, having assumed the duty of God's servant', and as the critic of an archbishop's speculations on the real presence in the eucharist.[4] The fragmentation of royal authority meant that this organisational and doctrinal role came to be assumed by the territorial princes within their principalities. Thus, bishop Fulbert of Chartres could allude to the bishops within the territory of duke William V of Aquitaine (995–1030) as '*his* [i.e. William's] bishops' (*episcopis eius*), and duke William, like Robert the Pious, could preside at ecclesiastical synods.[5] In some regions the disintegration of authority allowed control over bishoprics to pass into the hands of the aristocracy, with the office becoming as much an adjunct of local power as a pastoral responsibility. Immediately to the south of Normandy, for example, the see of Le Mans became a possession of the Bellême family during the first decades of the eleventh century. This was a state of affairs of which some churchmen were becoming increasingly critical, and which provided the ammunition for the propagandists of the 1050s and 1060s who elaborated the programme of reform which was applied during the pontificate of pope Gregory VII (1073–85). It was their conclusion that, despite the manifest merits of some lay rulers, the root of all the Church's problems was its subjection to lay domination. But such ideas only became a challenge to the established order in the last third of the eleventh century. The pre-1066 Norman dukes succeeded in untroubled confidence to a role in ecclesiastical government which, like so many other aspects of their regime, had its origins deeply embedded in the Carolingian past.

The existence of this 'lay theocracy' means that in many respects the development of the Church in Normandy mirrors that of society and government. The peace of Richard II's reign was a time when a monastically organised reform was attempted and when the foundation of monasteries remained a ducal prerogative. The novel practice by which aristocratic families started to establish monasteries from *c.* 1030 onwards was an infringement of this monopoly and a consolidation of local power closely associated with the other changes which took place during the troubled period between *c.* 1025 and *c.* 1050. With William II securely in power, the Norman Church acted much more purposefully as a unit, through the inauguration of regular meetings of synods attended by all the Norman bishops and presided over by duke William himself, and through the colonisation of most of the recently founded monasteries from the pre-existing ducal abbeys. There are, however, additional dimensions to the history of the Norman Church, some of which were peculiar to Normandy, and some of which were a result of the Church's own mission and organisation. Normandy was unusual, for example, in that the bishoprics, with the partial exception of Rouen, had been ruined during the settlement period in the early tenth century and had not been the subject of any sort of revival until the closing years of that century. There could not be the same continuity of organisation as in other regions. It is important, too, that the Norman Church was in theory part of a universal organisation with the papacy at its head, a consideration which was insignificant until the middle years of the eleventh century, but which assumed greater importance thereafter, as successive popes threw the weight of papal authority behind a campaign to improve the moral and spiritual quality of the clergy and to discipline where necessary the conduct of the laity. Finally, because so many developments were concentrated in the 1060s and 1070s, and because the legislation of the council of Lillebonne (1080) is so vital a source for ecclesiastical government, it is often neater and necessary to continue many aspects of the history of the Church in Normandy on for a few years beyond 1066.

Richard II's treatment of the Church in Normandy built upon the one existing solid foundation, the monasteries which had become well-established communities in Richard I's time. This involved co-operation with William of Volpiano, and, more particularly, with his principal Norman agent, Thierry, a man who, according to a late source, was related to the Montgommery family who supposedly emerged among the 'new aristocracy' of the 1020s and 1030s.[6] William of Volpiano became abbot of Fécamp in 1001, installing a small company of monastic disciples in the abbey which had been refounded by Richard I in 990. William himself had been trained at Cluny under abbot St Mayeul in the late tenth century, and was subsequently sent to reform the abbey of St-Bénigne of Dijon. During his lifetime, he built up the sort of monastic confederation typical of the age; at his death in 1031, he was abbot of over forty monasteries, including not only Fécamp, and St-Bénigne of Dijon, but also abbeys in the Ile de France, Lorraine, and northern Italy. Thierry, who became prior at Fécamp, was abbot of Jumièges and Mont-St-Michel from 1017 and 1023 respectively, and was also guardian (*custos*) of the abbey of Bernay, which had been founded in *c.* 1017 out of the dowry of duke Richard's first wife Judith. It seems likely that St-Ouen of Rouen was also reformed from Fécamp, possibly in 1006. The result, quite deliberately sought, was to give a unity and stability to Norman monasticism which it had not previously possessed.

The monastery at Fécamp was the pivot for a scheme with far-reaching implications. Duke Richard's charters in favour of the abbey show not only that it was given what was in effect a complete exemption from all forms of external authority, both ducal and ecclesiastical, but that it also received a large number of rural churches and the right to organise the ordination of priests – something which was normally reserved to the diocesan bishop.[7] So endowed, Fécamp became a training-centre for priests as well as something of a base for evangelisation. Schools were set up in the monastery under abbot William which, so we are told, were open to all.[8] The location of the churches granted to Fécamp shows that most of them were situated near the monastery in the *pagi* of Caux and Le Talou, but that there were others on the west bank of the Seine above Rouen near Le Vaudreuil and Pont de l'Arche, and some in Lower Normandy at and around Caen. It would probably be expected that the monastery would involve itself in the construction of new churches in other settlements, particularly in Lower Normandy, where it received substantial grants of land during Richard's reign.[9] It is also clear from the group of confirmation charters drawn up in 1025 that the other Upper Norman monasteries were also part of the plan; both Jumièges and St-Ouen of Rouen were exempted from secular jurisdiction, and, although neither was as obviously free from the authority of the diocesan bishop as Fécamp, both were assigned zones in which they were responsible for the reform of the local clergy (see Map 10). A similar role was clearly envisaged for newly founded Bernay and for some non-Norman churches; Chartres cathedral, for example, which at this date was ruled by the celebrated bishop Fulbert, received six churches in 1014, four of which lay in a block in the immediate vicinity of Bonneville-sur-Touque (Calvados, cant. Pont-l'Evêque) in central Normandy, and over which the church was exempted from ducal jurisdiction.[10] An aspect of the scheme's operation appears to be illustrated in a particularly explicit text from the abbey of St-Père of Chartres, which describes the suppression of a church at Breteuil (Eure) because of damage sustained during a war, and its amalgamation with another church at neighbouring St-Georges-Motel, where the monks had organised the construction of a new building in stone and cement. An original charter from the middle years of the eleventh century mentions a priest who had been trained at the Fécamp school.[11]

This concentration of religious and secular authority around selected monasteries is in some respects closely akin to the earlier English tenth-century reform, sponsored by Dunstan, Aethelwold, and others. It also has similarities with the policies developed in Germany by the tenth-century Ottonian emperors. The aim was undoubtedly to use to the utmost the available resources for religious organisation in order to impose a more positive direction on churches in the Norman countryside, many of which must have survived in the ownership of laymen throughout the tenth century.[12] The scheme also tried to supplement the deficiencies of ducal government by a wholesale transfer of power over defined territories to monastic institutions, an arrangement which in many ways parallels the contemporary creation of *comtés* for ducal relatives. It seems, like so many other aspects of Richard's government, to have been largely restricted to Upper Normandy; no comparable organisation of rural churches around the abbey of Mont-St-Michel is known before Robert I's reign, and, while Richard did approve the appointment of abbot Hildebert I in 1009, no nominee of William of Volpiano's was installed at the monastery until 1023.[13] It cannot be shown that Richard and abbot William were also seeking the moral and spiritual regeneration of the episcopate, although this must be a strong possibility, if only by an analogy with the English reform; the Upper Norman origins of many Norman bishops of the first half of the eleventh century and several appearances by bishop Hugh of Avranches (1028–60) in Fécamp documents is the best evidence available for a connection between the monastic schools and the early-eleventh-century episcopate.[14] The overall scheme may not have been entirely satisfactory, since it did detract from the powers of what were in theory at least the established sources of authority; the canons of Chartres cathedral, for example, had to protest, in the first case ineffectually, against encroachments on their exemption by the bishops of Lisieux and by Baldric, one of duke Richard's *curiales*.[15] None the less, given the plight, Rouen excepted, of the bishoprics, the arrangements made by Richard and William of Volpiano must have been the course of action most likely to establish a modicum of religious education and organisation.[16]

The remarkable confirmation charters of the year 1025 for the duchy's chief monasteries provide the most lucid commentary on duke Richard's generosity to the Church and his achievement in guaranteeing the security of ecclesiastical property. His willingness to alienate portions of church lands in favour of the new *comtés* is only a small qualification to this general protection; more than anything, it reflects the typically proprietorial attitudes of any early medieval ruler and the co-ordination of secular and religious authority during Richard's reign. A demonstration of the Church's confidence in duke Richard's rule is provided by the embassy which attended the meeting with king Robert and the count of Flanders at Compiègne in 1023 to discuss the introduction of the Peace of God into northern France. Its leaders were the duke himself, his brother archbishop Robert, and finally abbot Thierry, William of Volpiano's representative. These three were in the last resort responsible for the decision that the Peace movement, which gave the support of ecclesiastical sanctions to the peace-preserving role of lay government, was not needed in Normandy. Their action supported the continuation, basically unchanged, of a relationship between ecclesiastical and

Normandy before 1066

lay authority which was entirely traditional and Carolingian.[17]

Duke Robert I's reputation, based on the comments of William of Jumièges and others, is primarily that of a ruler who was prepared to grant away church land, but who reformed in the later years of his reign, made some restitution, and eventually undertook the pilgrimage to Jerusalem. This verdict is one which is amply confirmed by charter evidence; in 1034, for example, we find Robert sponsoring an exchange between the abbey of Fécamp and bishop Hugh of Bayeux, which, as an aside typical of a number of Fécamp charters of this period tells us, was detrimental to the abbey's interests.[18] It is not, however, the whole story of Robert I's reign. The duke is known to have had contacts with important non-Norman ecclesiastical reformers, such as Richard de St-Vanne, abbot of Verdun. Despite Thierry's death in 1027 and William of Volpiano's own in 1031, their monastic reform held firm under a second generation of disciples. William's nephew, John of Ravenna, became abbot of Fécamp in 1028 and the other monasteries passed into the government of their protégés. Only the newly founded Bernay faltered during this difficult period.[19] Consistent with what had been done in his father's reign, duke Robert extended exemption from secular jurisdiction to Mont-St-Michel and reacted against any weakening of his own and the reformers' authority there by introducing an Italian monk named Suppo from Fécamp into the abbacy.[20] He was also willing to confirm grants to the new monastic foundations of the aristocracy, showing that he was not unsympathetic to this extension of religious organisation, or at least that he did his best to stress a ducal supervision of the development.[21] The dismemberment of ecclesiastical estates during the reign is best understood, as in other principalities, as a symptom of the wider processes of social change and the fragmentation of authority; the connection is especially clear in Normandy where the chief beneficiaries at the Church's expense were the same families who were building castles and acquiring offices in ducal government. Duke Robert's own role is inevitably ambiguous. He can be portrayed as one of many early medieval rulers from Merovingian times onwards who succumbed to the temptation to 'bash the Church' to provide for their military followers. On the other hand, the basis of his father's programme of reform was maintained and extended.

A constructive and original side to Robert's treatment of the Church in Normandy was his foundation of two new religious communities, one a house for Benedictine nuns at Montivilliers near Fécamp and the other a monastery at Cerisy on the western limits of the Bessin. The second of these was an aspect of the extension of ducal authority into Lower Normandy. At the same time, however, the arrangements made for the endowment of both institutions demonstrate a new concern to reinforce episcopal authority; instead of the far-reaching exemptions granted to Fécamp and other monasteries, both received only the 'episcopal customs' over the churches which came into their possession. This meant that they obtained only the right to the revenues which the bishop would have received and to judge such cases as the bishop would have judged. The definition of monastic privilege in terms of episcopal authority was the first explicit recognition in eleventh-century Normandy that the ultimate responsibility for ecclesiastical discipline rested with the diocesan bishop.[22] This must reflect changes, notably the construction of new cathedrals and the recovery of lands, which had begun in the 1020s and in which Robert himself participated. The duke, for example, confirmed his uncle Robert's reconstitution of the estates of Rouen cathedral, an event which presaged a similar reorganisation at Bayeux in 1035–37.[23] This beginning of a revival – it certainly did not extend to all the dioceses – must be a development out of the foundations laid by Richard II and William of Volpiano. Like everything else connected with ecclesiastical organisation, it cannot have benefited much from the disorders of William II's minority.

The period when William II was incapable of exercising effective authority is a time when the fortunes of the Norman Church were at a low ebb. The efforts of count William of Arques provide the one sign of any endeavour to sustain the stability of ecclesiastical property (see p. 176). The simony through which bishop Geoffrey of Coutances (1048–93) received his office suggests a considerable falling-away from previous standards; his relationship to Nigel, *vicomte* of the Cotentin, might even indicate that a local family had taken over the bishopric, something which had already happened at Sées in the later years of Robert I's reign and which elsewhere was another of the symptoms of the fragmentation of royal and princely authority.[24] The disruption of these years was so serious that monasteries were obliged to counter persecution by bribing lay protectors and by the use of excommunications.[25] Some sectors of the Norman Church did at least try to assert their influence against the violence. Archbishop Malger of Rouen (1037–54), at a date before 1046, held a synod to protest against lay appropriation of ecclesiastical property. The legislation of this council, attended by only two of Rouen's six suffragans, shows the Norman Church to have been capable of the sort of action which lay at the origin of the Peace of God movement in other regions, but it is otherwise a grim catalogue of the deficiencies of episcopal organisation in Normandy and of the disruption which had taken place over a period of more than a decade. The canons condemned the sale of Holy Orders, the purchase of archdeaconries, and the alienation by bishops of property, which was supposed to support clergy, to laymen. Bishops were forbidden to usurp the authority of other bishops; archdeacons, likewise.[26] Any reader of these canons cannot fail but be struck by their intellectual mediocrity; they compare badly, for example, with the legislation of the two councils of Bourges and Limoges of 1031, and inevitably with what is known of the papal council of Rheims of 1049.[27] They demonstrate what a thankless task ecclesiastical government could become without the backing of the secular power. But they also testify to the poor standard of the Norman episcopate and, in this aspect of Norman life, to the enduring damage inflicted by the tenth-century invasions. An attempt to introduce the Peace of God into Normandy in 1041–42, sponsored by Richard de St-Vanne, failed.[28] The Peace was only established after duke William's victory at Val-ès-Dunes.

The revived ducal government of William II had to grapple with problems more complex than those which had confronted its predecessors. Val-ès-Dunes, for instance, almost coincided with the first *démarche* of the reformed papacy in northern France, Leo IX's council of Rheims (1049). The commitment of papal authority to a campaign whose aim was the improvement of the condition of the Church in the localities introduced a new factor into the task of governing the province. Since 991, when a legate appointed by pope John XV had arranged a treaty between Richard I and king Aethelred of England, the only mentions of papal authority in Normandy had been a possible confirmation of Fécamp's privileges in 1016 and a bull sanctioning an exchange between the abbeys of Jumièges and St-Vaast of Arras in 1023.[29] At Rheims, however, the conduct of two Norman bishops came under attack; bishop Ivo of Sées was censured for allowing his cathedral church to be damaged during a skirmish, while Geoffrey of Coutances was accused of simony, a charge which was rebutted only with the excuse that the see had been bought for him without his knowledge. More seriously still, the duke's marriage plans were criticised and condemned on the grounds of his and his prospective bride's consanguinity.

William's eventual organisation of the Norman Church bears all the hallmarks of the political acumen which assisted his dominance over the aristocracy. The clearest testimony to his achievement is the praise heaped on him over his lifetime by a succession of popes, some among them vigorous critics of lay involvement in ecclesiastical affairs. The zealot Gregory VII (1073–85) described him as pre-eminent among kings: 'with God's help you have well merited the title of "jewel of princes"'; 'without doubt you are destined to be the chief of princes in future glory'.[30] These plaudits were gained in response to William's government of the Norman Church over the period from the late 1040s until his death, which was constructed around a combination of carefully conducted relations with the papacy and a firm central direction of the Church in Normandy. The chief instrument in the latter was the regular holding of synods of the ecclesiastical province of Rouen, usually attended by all the Norman bishops, and over which William himself presided. Such meetings are known to have taken place at Brionne in 1050, Lisieux in 1054, Caen in 1061, Rouen in 1063, Lisieux in 1064, Rouen in 1070, 1072, and 1074, and at Lillebonne in 1080. The work of these councils was supported by a revitalisation of episcopal authority, a process which came to fruition in the 1060s and 1070s. In its early stages, this revival drew heavily on the second and third generations of the reformers organised by William of Volpiano, who provided leadership in the difficult period around 1050, and who must have been deeply involved in the colonisation of the new monastic houses founded by the aristocracy. But in time, William and his advisers were able to assert authority over all essential features of the life of the Norman Church through the creation of firm institutional structures of a kind which had not previously existed, which emphasised the authority of the bishops in their dioceses.

The warmth of papal praise, which is consistent up until the time of William's brushes with Gregory VII in *c.* 1080, seems somewhat out of place in the light of the received version of events. William, so we are told, married Mathilda, the daughter of count Baldwin V of Flanders, in defiance of the papal ban and maintained the illicit union until it was legitimised by pope Nicholas II (1059–61) at the Rome Easter council of 1059. This settlement, as we are led to believe, was negotiated in person by Lanfranc, prior of Le Bec, and came only after Nicholas had imposed an interdict on the duchy. Forgiveness involved a penance by which William and Mathilda agreed to found two abbeys at Caen. Given that most of the popes of the 1050s, especially Leo IX (1049–54) and Nicholas II, were scarcely renowned for their acquiescence in abuse, the consistent eulogies addressed to a man who had defied the papacy for almost ten years seem a little odd.

Clarification begins to emerge once it is recognised that almost all of this particular story rests on the insecure foundations of the *Vita Lanfranci* ('The Life of Lanfranc'), an account attributed to Miles Crispin, precentor of Le Bec, and written, possibly between 1130 and 1150, but more probably between *c.* 1140 and 1156.[31] The one solid fact in the accepted story is the threatened prohibition at the Rheims council, which was recorded in a contemporary source.[32] But, otherwise, none of the main elements in its sequence of events stand up to scrutiny. The story in the *Vita Lanfranci* that Lanfranc was almost banished from the duchy because he expressed disapproval of the marriage is an embellishment on an anecdote in the earlier 'Life of Herluin, abbot of Le Bec', written between 1109 and 1117, which also described how Lanfranc was almost exiled, but which did not connect the incident with any particular indiscretion on his part.[33] This episode seems to have baffled all who tried to make something out of it; William of Malmesbury, for example, writing between 1120 and 1125, attributed Lanfranc's temporary disgrace to the intrigues of a chaplain named Arfast, a version which was most likely worked up from knowledge of Lanfranc's scathing attack on Arfast's lack of learning after the latter had become bishop of Thetford.[34] The author of *Vita Lanfranci* himself admitted that it was only hearsay which made him relate Lanfranc's troubles to his opposition to the marriage.[35] He need not, therefore, be believed. A second problem is that the suggestion in the *Vita* that the two Caen abbeys were founded as a penance has no documentary support earlier than the interpolations made into the *Gesta* of William of Jumièges by Ordericus Vitalis in the early twelfth century. It is mildly surprising that no allusion was made to the penance in a papal privilege for St-Etienne of 1068 or in Gregory VII's letter of 1074 about the abbey's exemption.[36] A third point is that the weight of evidence is against Lanfranc's having visited Rome during Nicholas II's pontificate (1059–61). Verbal similarities between the *Vita Lanfranci*'s statement that Lanfranc negotiated on William's behalf at the 1059 Easter council and the tract which Lanfranc himself wrote in *c.* 1063 to refute the eucharistic speculations of Berengar of Tours suggest that the now accepted story derives from a slovenly reading of his source by the *Vita*'s author; Lanfranc described the events of the council without indicating that he was actually present; the author of the *Vita* says that he was.[37] The most damning piece of evidence against this part of the narrative in the *Vita Lanfranci* is a letter written by pope Nicholas II, in which he expresses regret that Lanfranc had not been able to visit Rome because of his studies, and which

The Church

then proceeds to speak warmly of duke William as a friend and as someone who was, through Lanfranc's guidance, acquiring grace. This is hardly the language of an irate pontiff who had recently imposed an interdict.[38] Relevant, too, is Berengar of Tours' reply to Lanfranc's arguments, in which he also indicates that Lanfranc had not attended the 1059 Easter council.[39] But it is Nicholas' letter which rules out the possibility that Lanfranc ever visited Rome during that pope's brief pontificate. It appears, therefore, that the version of events presented in the *Vita Lanfranci* is simply untrue. Its author built up his story from earlier sources in a way which was not very intelligent, and which was, as far as we are concerned, misleading. All that we can accept as reliable fact is the threat of a ban against the marriage made at the Rheims council (1049).

In all probability the matter of the 'incestuous' marriage was resolved fairly speedily. There was a lively traffic between Normandy and Rome in 1050. Bishop Geoffrey of Coutances attended the Rome synod of April 1050, while Lanfranc, who had fallen under suspicion of heresy, was in Leo IX's company for almost a year from the end of 1049. In addition, abbot John of Fécamp acted as a papal legate in *c.* 1050; his somewhat hysterical report on a mission dogged by accidents mentioned the friendship between the Normans and the papacy.[40] It is likely that a settlement, which may have involved an agreement to build the two abbeys, was made during one of these journeys. The tradition that there was opposition within the Norman Church to the marriage seems to have been a twelfth-century invention; Lanfranc's quarrel with the duke seems unrelated to it, while the suggestion that archbishop Malger protested and that this was a cause of his deposition in 1054 is incredible, since he was removed with the consent of a papal legate.[41] On the principle that if there is smoke, there must be fire, then it is likely that there was a fair amount of ecclesiastical breast-beating about the time that the marriage took place. It may be significant that the earliest and simplest account of the affair, Ordericus' interpolation in William of Jumièges, mentions criticism after the marriage had taken place, an embassy to Rome which was despatched on William's initiative, and the penance. This could easily be interpreted as suggesting that there was an early and amicable settlement. The marriage actually took place in either 1050 or 1051. It is interesting, in the context of the course of events proposed above, that no one, either then or since, has ever been able to say precisely what the rumoured degree of consanguinity was.

After this matter had been settled, relations with Rome were good up to and beyond 1066. The papacy was indeed treated with considerable reverence. When, for example, the question arose of deposing archbishop Malger in 1054, or of transferring bishop John from Avranches to Rouen in 1067–68, papal approbation was sought, as was canonically proper. William does not appear to have been opposed to all direct papal intervention in the Norman Church's organisation, since, in 1068, for example, he was quite willing to allow any disputes which might arise between the abbey of St-Etienne of Caen, which he had founded, and any bishop whatsoever, to be settled by the pope.[42] The important principle would seem to have been that the essential decisions about the government of the Norman Church should be taken in Normandy. When abbot Robert fled from St-Evroult in c. 1061, the duke consulted ecclesiastical advisers, selected and installed a new abbot, and threatened violence against a papal legate who tried to take up the case.[43] The near-autonomy of the Norman Church was condoned under Alexander II (1061–73), who was prepared to acknowledge openly that duke William chose the archbishop of Rouen.[44] This harmony owed most to William's sympathy with the cause of church reform. Lanfranc's presence in Normandy from the 1040s must also have made a considerable contribution; he was personally acquainted with most of the influential figures in Rome, and by c. 1060 possessed so great a reputation as a teacher that both Nicholas II and Alexander II sent him pupils. Abbot John of Fécamp, although a member of a fading generation by the 1050s, was also a figure of European stature who had acted as a papal legate. Given the consistent good relations between duke William and a succession of reforming popes and the weight of the allusions in one of Gregory VII's letters, it is likely that we should accept William of Poitiers' unsupported testimony that Alexander II despatched a papal banner in 1066 in support of William II's war against king Harold.[45]

William was given a marvellous opportunity to assert his authority over the Norman Church when the dioceses of Bayeux and Lisieux fell vacant in the years immediately after Val-ès-Dunes. They were conferred respectively on the duke's half-brother Odo and on his second cousin, Hugh, the son of count William of Eu. The dominant motive – transparently so – was to install two close relatives in strategic positions; Odo was little more than a boy at the time of his appointment and Hugh was in all probability some way below the canonically required age of thirty for promotion to a bishopric. Their personal influence cannot have been very great at this stage. The thorny problem which preoccupied Norman churchmen around the year 1050, the dissemination of the eucharistic opinions of Berengar of Tours, shows above all the continuing importance of William of Volpiano's disciples in the government of the Norman Church.

Berengar, a pupil of Fulbert of Chartres, and, from *c.* 1040, a member of the cathedral chapter at Angers, had veered towards a denial of the real presence at the Mass. His abrasive personality, love of self-publicity, and predilection for what were then novel methods of theological enquiry, involving close attention to the meaning of individual words, may well have posed a greater immediate threat than his ideas. These, in the midst of a labyrinthine Latin prose style, tended to suggest that, although the sacrament was visible, Christ's presence was not.[46] With the undoubted aim of canvassing support, Berengar came to Normandy in 1050, visited abbot Ansfrey of Préaux who had already expressed reservations, subsequently called on abbot Durand of Troarn, and finally placed his theories before an assembly which met at Brionne under the duke's presidency. There the Norman Church made its first rejection of Berengar's views.

The Norman Church's reaction to Berengar's speculations was from the first carefully orchestrated, culminating in a united denunciation of their validity. The theological arguments employed against him were cautious and conservative. Among those Norman churchmen who wrote to attack Berengar in the 1050s, abbot Durand of Troarn replied with the sort of synthesis of biblical and patristic authorities against which Berengar and his kind were reacting, and as good as accused his opponent of threatening the moral fabric of society.[47] The doyen of the Norman Church, abbot John of Fécamp, by this time well into his sixties, although far from unversed in the new methods of enquiry, announced in his *Confessio Fidei* that in the last resort the whole question was a matter of faith rather than of reason. The *Confessio* was indeed a work of such traditional excellence that it was for centuries included among the authentic writings of St Augustine.[48] Another Fécamp disciple, archbishop Maurilius of Rouen (1054–67), converted this condemnation of Berengar's ideas into the unanimous opinion of the Norman Church through a eucharistic profession, enacted at a date before 1059 at a synod of the entire province of Rouen, and repeated on subsequent occasions.[49] As a result of this concerted reaction at an early stage, the Norman Church sheltered in a secure rectitude as the dispute ground its way through the Church Universal, via the attempt at compromise at Tours in 1054 and Berengar's condemnation at the Rome council of 1059. The whole affair demonstrates the important contribution which William of Volpiano's followers made towards the first stages of duke William's revival of ducal authority within the Church. It also shows the theological conservatism in the 1050s of what was still very much a monastically dominated Church. A firm base was laid on which to build the later attempts to refute the still unrepentant Berengar on his own terms: those of Lanfranc, who had himself fallen under the suspicion of heresy in *c.* 1050 and who had kept quiet during the first decade of the dispute, and of Guitmund of La Croix-St-Leuffroy, in *c.* 1063 and *c.* 1073–75 respectively. Finally, the co-ordination between the actions of these Norman churchmen in the 1050s shows the continued existence of a strong sense of the need for organisation, which must have survived through from Richard II's reign, and which must have been of invaluable assistance to the young duke William.

From this point the government of the Norman Church evolved rapidly. The immense organisational strides made over the period between *c.* 1050 and 1080 can be demonstrated by the increasingly detailed content of the legislation which survives from the ecclesiastical councils which were held during this time. From archbishop Malger's council in the early 1040s, which offered little more than slogans against simony, the usurpation of bishoprics and archdeaconries, and the alienation of ecclesiastical property, we pass to the Lisieux canons of 1064, which were at least a recitation of a wider range of the principles held dear by eleventh-century ecclesiastical reformers, to the much more sophisticated Rouen (1072) and Lillebonne (1080) legislation. It is only in the decrees of these last two councils that we encounter a Church able to take its basic organisation for granted. The Lisieux canons simply rehearsed such general principles as the prohibition of marriage and concubinage by rural clergy, which had been the subject of legislation at an earlier Rouen council which had met either in the late 1050s or in 1063, the Truce of God, and a ban on clerics carrying weapons or engaging in usury. The 1072 Rouen decrees, however, along with the usual acts against marriage and simony, made extensive provision for the correct performance of the sacraments – chrism was to be regularly distributed by the bishop, the marriage ceremony should follow fasting, no one should celebrate Mass without himself taking communion, and the bread should not be consecrated a second time.[50] The Lillebonne legislation, a monument to the achievement of the eleventh-century Norman Church, provided a thorough survey of the bishop's pecuniary rights and some comment on his powers of jurisdiction.

The guiding force behind these developments was the revival of episcopal authority, something which built on initiatives taken during the 1020s and 1030s, but which only started to come fully to fruition in the 1060s and 1070s. The reliance on a group of enthusiasts, which had been so much a feature of Richard II's regime, was replaced in William II's time by support for the institutionalised authority of the diocesan bishop. The Lillebonne canons reveal that monks no longer enjoyed their former predominance and privilege; they were ordered to make a sufficient contribution to support priests serving churches in their possession, and to present new appointees to the bishop for examination and consecration.[51] Likewise, the exemption organised for William's own monastic foundation of St-Etienne of Caen – conclusive evidence surely of the duke's personal views on the subject – was granted, not in a ducal charter, but in one of the diocesan, bishop Odo of Bayeux. Although the abbey received extensive financial rights, the final hearing of what were described as 'criminal' cases was reserved to the bishop, and the priests serving churches in the monastery's possession were ordered to attend the diocesan synod.[52] The result of this policy was that all monasteries founded after the late 1040s were much more firmly integrated into the structure of episcopal authority. In broader terms, the development signified the evolution out of the vague 'episcopal *consuetudines*', referred to in the 1030s, of an episcopal jurisdiction which assigned a distinct and numerous range of cases to the bishop's court – the Lillebonne canons, which are not a complete survey, mention marriage within the prohibited degrees, divorce, and clerical marriage.

In spite of these changes, this ecclesiastical jurisdiction was in the 1070s still a part of the traditional world inherited from Richard II's time and before, in which secular and religious competence frequently overlapped. The duke could still intervene directly to support the Church's authority, as in the Lillebonne decrees which made his power available to buttress the Truce of God and the campaign against clerical marriage. Likewise, the Church had its part to play in upholding ducal authority; the possession of an ordeal-iron was restricted at Lillebonne to cathedral churches, and earlier, in 1068–70, a plea in the duke's court was correctly adjourned so that the ordeal could be held before two archdeacons at Bayeux.[53] What the twelfth century would have described as an ecclesiastical court would at this stage have been an indiscriminate gathering of clergy and laity, such as in the case heard in the court (*curia*) of archbishop John of Rouen in 1070, in which Roger de Beaumont was one of the judges.[54] This intermingling of jurisdictions was accepted and exploited by all; in

1058–60, the monks of Mont-St-Michel tried to assign the right of correction over a negligent abbot to the duke, rather than to the bishop of Avranches.[55] When, at Lillebonne in 1080, the Norman Church felt it necessary to consider for the first time the possibility that lay and ecclesiastical jurisdiction might clash, the solution, one utterly in the spirit of the eleventh-century Norman Church, was to assign the power of decision to the duke's court.

The duke's protection provided the generally peaceful conditions under which the Church could develop its organisation and seek to improve the standard of the clergy. It must not be overlooked, however, that this ducal supervision was an aspect of authority. This is already apparent in the way in which Richard II might transfer ecclesiastical property to the *comtés*; it becomes much more so in the better documented times of William II's reign. Charters might announce that the protection of the Church was a divinely ordained responsibility, but it could never be entirely disinterested, and it might not always be benevolent. A remarkable letter, written on behalf of the monks of Fécamp after 1066, shows that, while William's protection might, in general terms, have been effective, it was not necessarily kind to all. The monks complained of the depredations of the *vicomte* of Arques, against whom they could obtain no justice. They listed a number of estates which had been removed. In conclusion, the letter pleaded for protection – the abbey is the duke's – 'either protect it as if it is yours, or transfer it to the guardianship of another'.[56] When William imprisoned his half-brother, bishop Odo, in 1082, he allowed the abbey of St-Vigor, which Odo had founded just outside his episcopal city, to disband, and his bishopric to be plundered.[57]

William's rule of the Norman Church gives every impression of having been a carefully calculated operation. A survey of the pre-1066 charters for the monasteries founded by the aristocracy from the 1030s onwards shows that the duke often gave them no property at all, or at most very little; only St-Michel-du-Tréport actually seems to have received a grant of land, while St-Martin-du-Bosc was given land which had been purchased, and St-Georges of Boscherville, an estate which had once been a possession of the abbey of Bernay.[58] After 1066, the abbey of Notre-Dame of Grestain, which had been founded by William's step-father and in which his mother was buried, received the land of one peasant and exemption from tolls throughout England and Normandy, this latter a revenue which William would not have received before the abbey came into existence.[59] William undoubtedly deserves his reputation as 'one of the last of the great lay patrons of the Church in the descent through Charlemagne and the German emperors from Constantine'.[60] He could be notably generous, as in his grants to his own foundation of St-Etienne of Caen, or towards the restoration of the shattered bishopric of Coutances. But his attitudes were those of a proprietor, not a benefactor. It should not be overlooked that his first instinct in England after 1066 was to rob the Church.

In general, ducal guardianship operated to maintain stability and internal respectability within the component institutions of the Norman Church. As William's power grew, he was able to assert a protectorate over churches founded by aristocratic families. This must have been built up steadily in the 1050s and involved co-operation with the same men who assisted his control over castles. In a charter, dating from 1068, for the abbey of St-Martin of Troarn, established in the late 1040s by Roger II de Montgommery on an estate which had formerly belonged to the abbey of Fécamp, we find a recognition by Roger that the monastery should remain in the duke's protection, as was customary.[61] But in a charter for a college of secular canons founded in *c.* 1063–66 by Stigand de Mézidon, some few miles south of Troarn, we find the duke's duty to protect delegated to none other than Roger de Montgommery. William fitz Osbern had a similar responsibility for the Norman property of the abbey of St-Denis near Paris.[62] The ducal protection so established would appear to have had the character of a general oversight rather than that of direct control. Most of the business of a monastery which involved contact with the outside world would be conducted by the head of the founding family; he would represent his monastic protégés in the course of any pleas in which they might become involved, and would resolve any property disputes between his church and their mutual tenants.[63] The duke would take a hand only when other protection failed, as at St-Etienne of Fontenay in 1070–79, when, during the minority of Ralph III Taisson, the monastery's estates were plundered. As a Fontenay charter succinctly put it: the church was left 'without a patron, without advice, or assistance, except what remained from God and king William'.[64]

The duke would intervene in the internal life of a monastery only in the event of serious irregularities. At St-Evroult, for example, he followed up the denunciation of abbot Robert's involvement in a hostile conspiracy by substituting a new abbot. In the same monastery in 1066, he overruled the monks' two nominations for abbot, and chose instead the prior to take over. Likewise, when the monks of St-Ouen of Rouen were party to a brawl with the archbishop's entourage, the duke intervened to banish some of the miscreants to other monasteries.[65] He would expect to nominate the abbot of a ducal monastery himself but, as the correspondence in *c.* 1076 with abbot John of Fécamp about transferring one of his monks to the abbacy of Bernay shows, would at least go through the motions required by the Rule of St Benedict of consulting the abbot concerned when he wanted to transfer a monk from another monastery.[66] Evidence from St-Evroult and Le Bec in the 1060s and 1070s suggests that in both ducal and aristocratic monasteries abbatial elections were in principle 'free', that is, conducted by the monks without outside interference; the duke would examine the election procedure and the nominee, invest him with his office, and then pass him to the diocesan bishop for consecration.[67] At the height of his power William would also expect to be consulted when it was proposed to create a new abbey, a regulation made clear in an important agreement of the year 1080 between Richard and Thurstan de Creully and the abbot of Fécamp, about the status of the priory of St-Gabriel-sur-Seulles, which they had founded.[68]

There are three clear phases to the evolution of the pre-1066 Church in Normandy: the 'monastic' period dominated by Richard II and William of Volpiano, the disintegration of the second quarter of the century, and the revival of episcopal and ducal authority under William II. The strength of the dukes' supervision over the Church naturally varied in much the same way as did the powers of their government. It is obvious that there was a serious weakening in the second quarter of the eleventh century. Likewise, despite William II's successes, the bishop of Sées was a consistent absentee from the ducal entourage during the 1050s, simply because the duke had lost control in that southerly region. But certain trends run through all these phases. William of Volpiano's reform had the effect of setting Norman monasticism on a firm footing, which made a considerable contribution to the recovery after 1050. The period of disintegration led in the long run to the expansion and diversification of the Norman Church as more monasteries were founded. In Richard II's and William II's reigns the Norman Church, despite the grave weaknesses in the early-eleventh-century bishoprics, conformed to the highest reasonable standards that contemporaries could impose. It is time now to examine the internal development of the Norman bishoprics and monasteries.

ORGANISATION AND STRUCTURE

The bishoprics

Several basic points can be made about the history of the eleventh-century Norman bishoprics.[69] The first is the dukes' almost unbroken control over appointments. The second is the steady increase in the authority of the bishops, through from the 1020s, which saw the start of the construction of new cathedrals, to the 1060s and 1070s, which provide the first clear references to a wide range of jurisdiction and to organised cathedral chapters. A third is the considerable influence of reform on the episcopate. The majority of the bishops of Richard II's time had been married men, thoroughly imbued with the sort of patrimonial attitudes which led at least one among them to pass ecclesiastical lands on to a son.[70] By 1066 there had been a considerable change; a bishop such as Odo of Bayeux, who kept a mistress, was exceptional. Whatever the deficiencies of the Norman episcopate in 1066 – they can be overstated – idleness and a general disregard for the principles of reform were not among them.

The archbishopric of Rouen was always a special position, since its incumbent was titular head of the Norman Church. From 989 until 1054 the post was reserved for ducal relatives: Robert (989–1037) was a son of Richard I, and Malger (1037–54), one of Richard II. Both having committed what the later age regarded as the grave faults of marrying and fathering children and of wasting ecclesiastical property, neither received a favourable write-up in the tract on the history of the archbishops compiled in *c.* 1070.[71] In the context of a time when these 'vices' were widely prevalent, their respective records appear less blameworthy. Robert is known to have collected manuscripts, to have organised a school, to have started the construction of a new cathedral, and to have been on good terms with bishop Fulbert of Chartres. Malger governed the Church at a difficult time, but can be credited with the convocation of the first reforming synod, the continued organisation of the cathedral chapter, as well as a serious effort to keep the peace. A long list of charges, from sexual incontinence through to his having omitted to obtain a *pallium* from the pope, were subsequently offered to justify his deposition in 1054, but it is probable that his main offence was collaboration in his brother's, count William of Arques', rebellion in 1053–54.[72]

Malger's successor, Maurilius (1054–67), was, none the less, a great contrast. A native of Rheims educated in the then renowned schools at Liège, he had been an aspiring hermit, an unsuccessful abbot of an Italian monastery, and a monk of Fécamp before and after his Italian débâcle. Maurilius brought a range of experience to his office far beyond that of any of his predecessors. His archiepiscopate was notable for the first effective Norman reforming councils, along with the first prohibitions in the province of clerical marriage. His personal interests seem to have been in liturgical reorganisation, and his prejudices were essentially monastic; he was, for example, prepared to join his mentor, abbot John of Fécamp, in a protest when the bishop of Evreux exiled a monk who had breached the Truce of God.[73] The next archbishop, John (1068–79), was a different type again. He had been bishop of Avranches from 1061 and was a son of count Rodulf of Ivry and, therefore, the brother of bishop Hugh of Bayeux (c. 1011–49). His prime recommendations seem to have been energy, a scholarly interest in liturgical matters, and a zeal for reform which led him into a number of scrapes. On the one hand, while bishop of Avranches, he had composed an important treatise on church services through which he and Maurilius hoped to regularise worship throughout the province; on the other, he was stoned for the severity of his legislation against married clergy. Ordericus' story that he refused to bury bishop Hugh of Lisieux (1049–77), whom he disliked, is indicative of a passionate, unbending, nature. Ordericus attributed the paralytic stroke which crippled the last eighteen months of his archiepiscopate to divine punishment for this act of malice. The character which emerges from the extant correspondence with archbishop Lanfranc is one of extremes; a disciplinarian a little short on charity; someone in regular need of reassurance.[74] John may not have been a very nice man, but his career at least shows that the dukes consistently aimed to have a man of either high birth or, especially under William II, outstanding abilities at the head of the Norman Church.

The bishops appointed in Richard II's time tended to be from social circles similar to those which made up his secular administration. Members of his immediate family might be pushed either into a bishopric or a *comté*; archbishop Robert of Rouen and bishop Hugh of Bayeux held both. Of those bishops about whom anything can be known, all appear to have come from Upper Norman families. Bishop Hugh of Coutances (c. 989–1021) had a son named Roger whose estates lay in the immediate vicinity of Rouen and in the Pays de Talou.[75] Radbod, bishop of Sées (1025–32), was related to Gerard

Flaitel, another Upper Norman landowner, a benefactor of the abbey of St-Wandrille, and the father of bishop William of Evreux (c. 1046–66).[76] Finally, bishop Hugh of Avranches (1028–60) shows every sign of having had strong connections with the district around Fécamp, being chosen to consecrate abbot John in 1028, attesting three 'life-leases' arranged by the abbey between 1027 and 1040, and himself negotiating a lease on a piece of Fécamp property at Ryes-en-Bessin (Calvados) (see p. 195).

The character of the episcopate changed markedly once William II was firmly in power. After the fortuitous circumstances which allowed him in the late 1040s to give Bayeux and Lisieux to two relatives, William was consistently concerned to appoint men who had received an adequate ecclesiastical training. Often his bishops were clerks who had served as ducal chaplains. Baldwin of Evreux (1066–70), Gilbert Maminot of Lisieux (1077–1102), and the Italian Michael of Avranches (c. 1068–c. 1094) all gained promotion by this route, while bishop Gilbert of Evreux (1071–1112) had been an archdeacon at Lisieux. Most of these were good appointments. Odo of Bayeux, although scandalous in many respects, was a man of prodigious abilities, who greatly enriched his diocese, was an outstanding patron of learning, and a consistent supporter of monasticism.[77] Hugh of Lisieux was the subject of a eulogy by William of Poitiers, who was his archdeacon, and who praised his humility, chastity, sense of justice, industry, generosity, and balance. There is no hint in the sketch of either personal austerity or any special learning; Hugh was cheerful and enjoyed company; he entertained his guests with good food. His reputation, unlike Odo's, remained untarnished in the twelfth century, except that Ordericus, who consistently praised him, also felt obliged to mention a rustic priest's vision in which Hugh appeared among the cortège of the damned.[78] Of the others, Gilbert of Evreux and Michael of Avranches appear to have been excellent diocesan bishops. Gilbert Maminot was able but lazy, an inspiring teacher and priest, but an addicted gambler and huntsman.[79]

That episcopal authority in the early eleventh century still laboured under the devastating effects of the Scandinavian invasion and settlement is shown primarily by the evidence of terminology.[80] The phrase *consuetudines episcopales* ('customs exercised by the bishop') was extremely widely used in documents written in the duchy, a practice which is suggestive of the sort of devaluation of authority which affected secular government everywhere else. In most other parts of northern France, the powers of the bishops remained sufficiently intact for the two fundamental words of Carolingian vocabulary, *synodus* and *circada*, signifying respectively that the bishop held a diocesan synod and conducted a visitation of his diocese, to continue to be current. In Normandy, however, they were scarcely used before 1080. Likewise, the distinction between a church and its altar, a device which enabled the bishop to sustain authority in the face of lay or monastic ownership and which evolved in most regions in the late tenth century, is hardly known in Normandy before the late eleventh. The personnel of the Norman episcopate is another sign that the recovery after the settlement period was an extremely slow one. In contrast to neighbouring regions, where bishops were invariably drawn from the most powerful aristocratic families, the pre-1050 Norman bishops were frequently mediocrities from obscure backgrounds. There is no evidence to suggest that they had received a training appropriate to their office, a stark contrast to what is known about many of their contemporary equivalents such as the bishops appointed by the early Capetian kings. The assumption, made in other parts of northern France, that a bishop was pre-eminently someone with status and power, had only a small impact in Normandy before the late 1040s; the opinion that he should be educated, little if any. The exceptions to the first were the ducal relatives appointed to Rouen and Bayeux and the transfer in the mid-1030s of Sées out of ducal control and into the hands of Ivo de Bellême, who was the sort of figure associated everywhere else with episcopal rank. Duke William's ability to appoint his own chaplains, men of obvious ability and education, from *c.* 1060 onwards, therefore, marks a dramatic and significant development. In conformity with the remarkable sophistication of the 1080 Lillebonne decrees, the Norman episcopate had by that date acquired a professional quality which was outstanding in contemporary northern France.[81] The Norman bishoprics appear to have advanced rapidly and decisively from about the year 1050 onwards.

The first quarter of the eleventh century provides only isolated examples of attempts to exercise episcopal authority. Bishop Fulbert and the canons of Chartres protested that both bishops Roger (*c.* 985–1021) and Herbert (1022–49) of Lisieux were collecting synodal and visitation dues from churches which had been given to Chartres in 1014. The supplicating tone of their letters does not seem to have softened the hearts of the two bishops.[82] It is, however, the diocese of Rouen which is the only one to provide evidence of any consistent literary and pastoral activity. Archbishop Robert can be shown to have supervised a group whose members included Dudo of St-Quentin and a poet, known as Garnier of Rouen, who seems to have been strongly influenced by the school at Winchester organised by St Aethelwold. Such contacts with English ecclesiastical circles were a continuation of arrangements which had existed in the second half of the tenth century (see p. 33).[83] Diocesan administration was likewise maintained at Rouen; a charter from 1026 to 1028 refers to a dean and two archdeacons, a small core of officials who seem to have been sustained through Malger's archiepiscopate, when there are references to a dean named Osbern and an archdeacon named Hugh (see p. 209).[84] But the picture for the seven Norman dioceses taken together is one of considerable disorganisation. A famous story in Ordericus' history records how, when Giroie acquired estates at Montreuil and Echauffour in *c.* 1020, he asked the local people for the name of the diocesan bishop. Informed that there was none, Giroie submitted the churches to Roger, bishop of Lisieux, who promptly granted exemption from episcopal customs.[85] Legendary or not, this anecdote explains why a part of the diocese of Sées was transferred to Lisieux. The problem of uncertain diocesan boundaries appears to have been a subject of concern at archbishop Malger's council in the early 1040s.[86] That the difficulty should have been so prevalent was probably inevitable in the context of widespread inattention to pastoral responsibilities; the bishops of Coutances seem rarely to have visited their westerly diocese before the time of bishop Geoffrey (1048–93) – bishop Hugh (*c.* 989–1021) is even recorded to have moved seven canons back from Coutances to the college at St-Lô of Rouen where the bishops had resided during the tenth century – while most of the acts of bishops Hugh of Avranches and Hugh of Bayeux are connected with their personal landed estates rather than with their dioceses.[87] In contrast to the territorial *pagi*, to which there are numerous references in pre-1066 documents, there is only one mention in a charter of a diocese as a geographical unit.[88] Their eventual revival, largely within their Carolingian boundaries, probably owed rather more to the fact that these usually coincided with the limits of the *pagi* than to the efforts of the early eleventh-century bishops.

The first steps towards recovery were usually a reorganisation of lands and the start of the construction of a new cathedral church. The first of these came at varying dates in each of the seven bishoprics; the 1020s and 1030s for Rouen, Sées, and Bayeux, but the 1050s for Coutances, and possibly even the 1060s for Avranches.[89] The beginning of the work on new cathedrals can usually be placed in the 1020s or a little later; Rouen was started by archbishop Robert (died 1037); Coutances before 1030, since Richard I's widow Gunnor laid the foundation-stone; Avranches before 1028; and Lisieux under bishop Herbert (1022–49).[90] Although not much can now be deduced about their style and date of completion – unfortunately for our purposes, all were superseded in the twelfth and thirteenth centuries by Gothic churches and Avranches was actually pulled down in the late eighteenth century – all, with the exception of Rouen, while they may have been started in the 1020s or 1030s, appear to have been buildings essentially of the second half of the eleventh century. Rouen, from literary testimony, was begun by archbishop Robert and completed by Maurilius.[91] Bayeux, however, on the evidence of the crypt, which survives intact, and of the design of the capitals at the crossing, which were discovered beneath the Gothic masonry in the 1850s, was substantially the work of bishop Odo's episcopate (1049/50–97), despite a solid Bayeux tradition that a fair amount had been achieved under his predecessor.[92] In the case of the other churches, Lisieux, which may have been completed and damaged by fire before 1077, has recently been described as a building of the last third of the eleventh century; Coutances required an injection of funds from southern Italy in *c.* 1050 and was still being built well on into bishop Geoffrey's episcopate (1048–93), while Avranches was not even consecrated until the 1120s.[93]

In a similar pattern of development, the vague references to the episcopal *consuetudines*, apparent from *c.* 1030, are only transformed into solid evidence for effective jurisdiction exercised through archdeacons and for a cathedral staffed by a fully organised chapter in the 1060s and 1070s. The earliest indication of active jurisdiction comes from the diocese of Avranches, through the record of the first of a series of test-cases in which bishops tried their developing muscle against the pretensions of the monasteries in their dioceses. In 1061, bishop John, reacting promptly against a claim to exemption from episcopal jurisdiction on their island, which the monks of Mont-St-Michel had recently interpolated into a charter of duke Richard II, made a treaty with the monastery, by which the monks were allowed the authority of an archdeacon on the Mount, but with the right to correct their judgements, to hear matrimonial and criminal cases, to lift excommunications, to ordain and degrade clerics, and to administer the ordeal by hot-iron, reserved to the bishop of Avranches. This detailed agreement presaged in its general outlines the sort of arrangements subsequently made between the abbey of St-Etienne of Caen and the bishop of Bayeux (see p. 205).[94] It was also the first of a number of contests which took place during the next few years, and which must be indicative of the greater weight of episcopal authority within each diocese: the archbishop of Rouen and the abbey of St-Wandrille argued over the possession of an ordeal-iron and jurisdiction in four parishes; the bishop of Sées and the canons of St-Léonard of Bellême over altar offerings.[95] The settlement in all such cases tended to confirm monastic privilege while underpinning episcopal authority; the monks of St-Wandrille, for example, were awarded jurisdiction over their parishes, but their priests were ordered to attend the diocesan synod. The Lillebonne canons (1080), although disappointing in that they take for granted most of the kinds of case which a bishop's court would have heard, emphasise development by stating clearly many of the obligations which were owed to the diocesan by his clergy. It was announced that attendance at the diocesan synod was compulsory; archdeacons were reminded that they were obliged to make annual inspections of the vestments, altar vessels, and books of each priest under their supervision; laymen were forbidden to present priests to churches in their possession without having sought the bishop's consent; and the bishop's jurisdiction over cases of marriage within the prohibited degrees, divorce, and clerical marriage or concubinage, was mentioned.

The rapid growth and evolution of cathedral chapters is another development of the 1060s and 1070s. The diocese of Rouen anticipated what happened elsewhere, although here, too, the number of references to archdeacons suggests great expansion in the 1060s and 1070s; the small group known from the late 1020s expanded to include dignitaries such as a cantor, for whom there is evidence at a date before 1067 and in *c.* 1070, and probably four archdeacons.[96] Sées appears to have been the other progressive Norman diocese with a remarkable reference to five archdeacons before 1057, and a unique mention, although admittedly in the non-Norman part of the diocese, of a territorial archdeaconry before 1064.[97] It may be that Sées' apparent precocity resulted from its orientation away from Normandy during the twenty-five years from the mid-1030s when it was governed by Ivo de Bellême. It is interesting that the chapter appears to have been scaled down when the Norman, bishop Robert, was appointed in *c.* 1072.[98] As regards Normandy as a whole, it is clear that, although the office of archdeacon was known by the early 1040s, since it is referred to in the decrees of archbishop Malger's council, its organisation was extremely irregular and remained so for some considerable time.[99] While there may have been an archdeacon at Lisieux in *c.* 1050, the evidence for this and other officials in most of the Norman dioceses is invariably post-1066. Even at Bayeux, which had evolved an extravagantly large chapter by the time of bishop Odo's death in 1097, there is no evidence for any chapter dignitary before 1066; one archdeacon is named in 1066, two appear in 1068–70, and three in the 1070s alongside several other officials. Where anything can be known for the other dioceses, it confirms this pattern.[100] What is also interesting is that the pre-1066 evidence for the holding of individual prebends by the canons of all the Norman cathedrals scarcely exists; there are occasional references to *beneficia*, but the likelihood is that most of the Norman cathedrals before 1066 were served by a small number of canons, holding their property in common.[101]

The Norman bishoprics in the 1060s and 1070s continued to bear many marks from their long spell of disorganisation. With the exception of Rouen, many of the dioceses struggled to set up schools, and often had to call on outside help to do so. Odo of Bayeux, for example, is known to have organised bursaries to send promising students to Liège and may even have sent one of his best protégés, Thomas, who became archbishop of York in 1070, to sit at Lanfranc's feet at Le Bec.[102] The historian William of Poitiers, who became an archdeacon at Lisieux in the 1070s, received his training outside the duchy, while, at an earlier date, Fulk de Guernanville, who became dean at Evreux, had been a pupil of bishop Fulbert at Chartres.[103] It cannot be an accident that no schools are known at Coutances before bishop Geoffrey's time, or that references to the chapter dignitary, the 'master of the schools' (*magister scolarum*), did not occur elsewhere before the 1070s.[104] Another theme, one which can be illustrated anecdotally, was a sometimes desperate attempt to restock reliquaries denuded of their contents during the settlement period. One story, which must have been told with some relish in many northern French cathedral chapters, shows a Norman bishop resorting to underhand methods and receiving just retribution. Bishop Odo of Bayeux, so we are told, bribed the sacristan of the church of Corbeil, in order to procure the lost relics of St Exupère, the first bishop of his diocese. On the discovery that the sacristan had delivered the wrong bones, Odo's no doubt vehement protests were countered by a remark that, although the relics were undoubtedly those of someone named Exupère, not everyone who had borne that name had achieved sanctity.[105] Finally, the extent to which church property had passed into the hands of laymen during the tenth century is reflected in the tolerance shown in the eleventh-century Norman conciliar legislation towards lay possession of ecclesiastical *consuetudines*. This had been the subject of a blunt prohibition at Leo IX's council of Rheims in 1049, but the lead was not followed in Normandy until 1096. The first Norman council even to consider the problem, Lillebonne (1080), barred the laity from receiving altar and burial dues, but otherwise affirmed the *status quo* by forbidding bishops to usurp rights held by laymen. Along similar lines, the organisation of tithes within the duchy also mirrors heavy secularisation.[106] Extensive lay possession of ecclesiastical rights and the poverty of the prebends of all the Norman dioceses, with the exception of Bayeux, were the subject of comment in twelfth-century papal letters.[107]

The period from *c*. 1050, and above all the 1060s and 1070s, was the time when the Norman bishoprics began to be fully organised. The uncertainties which such rapid growth must have engendered are occasionally visible in the records. The question of the structure of a cathedral chapter seems to have been very much in the melting-pot at the time that a short tract, usually attributed to archbishop Maurilius (1054–67), was written on their organisation; it describes the office of chancellor, then unknown in Normandy. In like fashion, the bishops of Bayeux and Coutances are known to have treated the archidiaconate as an order rather than an office during the 1070s; putting appointees through a wholly uncanonical process analogous to an ordination.[108] None the less, the Norman cathedrals had become solidly placed at the heart of their dioceses by the time of the conquest of England; by the 1070s, for example, all priests were obliged to lead their flock in procession to the mother church every Whitsun.[109] The general evolution is one which runs parallel to William II's reconstitution of ducal government; the organisation of the one must have benefited and stimulated the other. It was also assisted by remarkable initiatives such as the visits to southern Italy made by bishops Geoffrey of Coutances and Ivo of Sées in the early 1050s to obtain funds. As well, the development of the cathedral chapters must be related to the growth of the towns and to the generally buoyant economy; the Bayeux chapter recruited heavily from wealthy urban families, as also in all probability did that of Coutances which contained family groupings similar to those at Bayeux.[110] What must finally be emphasised, however, is that the reorganisation of the Norman bishoprics was well under way by 1066 and in essence, as opposed to scale, owed little to the effects of the Conquest. It is clear that after 1066 the Bayeux chapter, which was in many respects unique, did become exceptionally large and was a training-centre for a career in English government. But an early-twelfth-century writer at Coutances went out of his way to point out that bishop Geoffrey had accomplished the important work within the diocese before 1066 and that the chapter was never a focus for *curiales*.[111] Over the period as a whole, the points to stress are the remarkable organisation of the Norman episcopate by 1066 through the synod of the province of Rouen, the late date of the reformation of most of the dioceses, and the great progress made during the 1060s and 1070s.

Monasticism

The eleventh century was a time of rapid growth in the numbers of monasteries in most regions of western Europe. Normandy was no exception; the six abbeys which had existed by 1026 had multiplied to about thirty-three by 1070, of which twenty-six were houses of Benedictine monks, and seven, convents for nuns.[112] As was normal in northern France in this pre-Investiture Contest period, the spread of monasticism was closely associated with social and political changes among the land-owning classes. The monasteries existing in Normandy in 1026 were all ducal foundations; after 1026, in conjunction with the fragmentation of authority and the extension of estates, the habit was taken up by the aristocracy. Almost all these new churches were established by members of the most powerful families in the duchy; the only known instances of a community developing out of the spontaneous religious impulses of one or more of its inmates are the small Fécamp priory of St-Martin-du-Bosc, which eventually failed, and Le Bec, which lacked a consistent lay provider and might well also have foundered but for the fortuitous arrival there of the brilliant teacher Lanfranc. Norman monasticism was, however, in a contemporary context, highly unusual in the exceptionally coherent way in which it evolved. Almost invariably, the monastic houses established by the aristocracy drew their original organisation and personnel from one of the abbeys already existing in the duchy. To a very large extent, Norman monasticism flourished from the base established by William of Volpiano and his followers in the early years of the eleventh century and without much direct contact with any of the foremost contemporary monastic confederations, such as Cluny. It should also be said that, in the second half of the century, these monasteries went on to produce a style of architecture in churches such as Cerisy or the two Caen abbeys, which was not only beautiful, but, in many respects, original.

Outside the great ducal abbeys re-established in the tenth century,

The Church

and subsequently reformed by William of Volpiano and his disciples, the earliest signs of development in the eleventh-century Norman Church were the appearance of small colleges of secular canons. The important pioneering role which these must have played is now almost lost to us, largely because the canons were usually replaced at a later date by monks, and because monastic propaganda invariably emphasised the loose-living proclivities of the canons.[113] Many of the Norman monasteries had their origins in haphazardly organised colleges, in which each individual canon was supported by a piece of property known as a prebend, and whose rules did not require a permanent withdrawal from the outside world. Both Mont-St-Michel before 966 and Fécamp before 990 had been served by communities of canons. The early eleventh century saw the appearance of a number of such foundations, mostly sponsored by Upper Norman families, at places such as Auchy-lès-Aumale, Eu, and La Ferté-en-Bray, and the second quarter of the century was marked by the multiplication and the spread of communities of this kind into Lower Normandy. They tended to be small, with, for example, four canons at Bohon, five at Néhou, and six at Auffay and Auchy. Often they were closely linked to a seigneurial residence and might be outrageously disorganised – one of the canons of Auchy actually resided in the castle at Auchy and a new recruit was expected to pay to obtain his prebend. These simple communities, vulnerable to a deterioration in the morals of the canons, were rapidly overtaken from the 1030s by the new fashion of founding monasteries, whose life was subject to a much more regular discipline. Yet it should not be overlooked that the foundation of colleges such as St-Sauveur-le-Vicomte, Bohon, and St-Fromond, all in the diocese of Coutances, prefaced the arrival of monasticism in these regions by some years. They represent a phase of Norman ecclesiastical history which passed fairly quickly, although in some respects they anticipate the much larger canonical foundations which started to be made in Normandy in the 1080s (see Map 11).

The reform achieved by William of Volpiano provided the source from which most of the later monasteries acquired their manpower and organisation. Thus, Fécamp itself supplied the first two abbots for Conches (founded c. 1035), the first at Troarn (founded in the later 1040s), and the second at the restored Bernay; Jumièges provided abbots for St-Evroult, St-Sauveur-le-Vicomte, and St-Sever. Norman monasticism can be visualised as a tree sprouting branches; La Trinité-du-Mont of Rouen, established in c. 1030 with an abbot and monks from St-Ouen of Rouen, itself subsequently gave abbots to Cormeilles, St-Pierre-sur-Dives, and Le Tréport. It was in fact highly unusual for a Norman monastery to receive its first abbot from a non-Norman abbey; Grestain's came from St-Serge of Angers, but even in this case the first monks were drawn from St-Pierre of Préaux and St-Wandrille.[114]

The whole process can also be seen in terms of a territorial colonisation, a movement which not only had as its core monks from a small number of ducal abbeys, but also one which spread monasticism throughout a province in which it had for a long time been almost wholly confined to the north-east. Thus, Fécamp, which had begun to acquire property in Lower Normandy in the late tenth century, only contemplated the foundation of priories there after c. 1050.[115] Similarly, the foundation, by either the duke or aristocratic families, of monasteries such as Caen, Fontenay, and Troarn in central and western Normandy, filled gaps in the religious organisation of the countryside, since their patrons generally endowed them with an allocation of rural churches and, according to the pattern outlined in the preceding sections, they usually acquired some share in episcopal authority (see p. 205).

In its early stages, the revitalisation of Norman monasticism relied heavily on the endeavours of 'foreigners' and on imported ideas and models. Both William of Volpiano and his nephew and successor at Fécamp, John of Ravenna, hailed from northern Italy; Mont-St-Michel was also ruled by an Italian and former monk of Fécamp, named Suppo, between 1033 and 1048; the first abbot of La Trinité-du-Mont of Rouen, Isembard (c. 1030–51), was a German, who had previously been a monk at St-Ouen of Rouen. Likewise, St-Wandrille, which remained outside William of Volpiano's circle, drew abbot Gerard (c. 1008–29) from the Ile de France. Below the level of abbatial government, we know of, among others, a Venetian named Anastasius, who possessed an exceptional knowledge of Greek, and who spent some time at Mont-St-Michel, and an Englishman named Clement, who eventually left Fécamp for St-Bénigne of Dijon, because his peace was constantly disturbed by visits from his countrymen.[116] The architectural and artistic legacy of these years also highlights the immense debt which the Norman Church at this stage owed to imported ideas. The abbey church at Bernay, built between c. 1020 and c. 1070, and now marvellously restored after centuries of neglect, is the one direct link with William of Volpiano's time, and reveals, in, for example, the carving of the capitals on the nave piers, close links with St-Bénigne of Dijon and Italy. The nave has close affinities with the remains of the late-tenth-century church of St-Pierre at Jumièges, itself built in a style which was purely Carolingian. The abbey church of Jumièges too (usually dated to *c.* 1040–67, but surely started at an earlier date) was probably influenced by St-Bénigne of Dijon for the alternating round and square shapes of the nave piers, and certainly draws on Rhineland models for the western towers and narthex, and sometimes on English manuscript illumination for the capital sculpture.[117] Similarly, the early-eleventh-century manuscripts surviving from Mont-St-Michel, now preserved in the Public Library at Avranches and meticulously studied by Dr Alexander, reveal in their decoration an eclectic borrowing and a knowledge of a large variety of sources.[118]

The early history of many of the monasteries founded by the aristocracy may have been somewhat precarious. What we know about their origins is usually indicative of difficult beginnings and a gradual consolidation. The fullest surviving accounts of the first years of an individual house, those from Le Bec and St-Evroult, reveal initial vicissitudes, the choice of a poor site, and the necessity of moving to a new one. A project to establish a house for nuns at St-Pierre-sur-Dives in the 1040s failed because of the violence of the times; as a result, they were transferred to the greater safety of Lisieux and a monastery subsequently founded at St-Pierre.[119] The first evidence for the abbey of St-Etienne of Fontenay occurs in the 1040s, but no abbot was appointed until *c.* 1066.[120] The assistance given by the ducal monasteries towards the establishment of these new abbeys seems to indicate a considerable adaptability and capacity for forgiveness. Troarn, for example, received an abbot from Fécamp in 1059, despite the fact that the monastery stood on land which had once belonged to the latter church. The Montgommerys, having also removed land at Almenèches from Fécamp's patrimony and set up a nunnery there, appear to have reached an agreement to perform military service from the property for Fécamp's benefit.[121] One sign of the sort of negotiation which must have taken place is the disagreement in the 1040s between the abbey of St-Wandrille and the founders of St-Pierre-sur-Dives, about whether the new church should be a priory of St-Wandrille or an independent abbey, which led to the responsibility for St-Pierre's development being transferred to La Trinité-du-Mont of Rouen.[122]

These new monasteries kept close contacts with the outside world. After receiving an initial endowment of property from their founders, they were thereafter left to do a great deal to make their own way in the property market. The charters of the abbey of Fécamp during the rule of abbot John (1028–78) show him disbursing vast sums of money to buy land; five transactions alone involved a total of almost £700.[123] Monasteries were an important element in oiling the economy, often making loans against pledges of land, and stimulating the circulation of coin by their financial activities. In so far as a conclusion on such a matter is possible on limited evidence, it seems that monasteries used their money predominantly to acquire land, rather than churches; the ratio of expenditure appears to have been about two to one in favour of the former.[124] All monasteries remained closely integrated with the fortunes of their founding family and of their chief patrons. The strength of the bond between lay benefactor and monastery is vividly demonstrated by the threat in the late eleventh century by three prominent families that they would repossess their gifts to the abbey of Le Bec, if Robert, count of Meulan, succeeded in establishing his domination over the church.[125] A founding family might offer privileges to its tenants who gave property to its monastery, and in an extreme instance, the Taisson actually forbade their vassals to patronise any abbey other than St-Etienne of Fontenay.[126] The landed endowments of most monasteries followed the geographical pattern of their founders' lands, suggesting a role in consolidating property; the church's location was often determined by strategic considerations which were more political then religious.[127] The monasteries were the burial-places for their patrons, they were expected to provide benefices for knights and to organise military service for their lords, the monks prayed for their founders' souls, and their abbots were often in attendance at the gatherings which evolved into honorial courts.[128] Such contact with the world may have contributed to instability within the monastic communities. The murder of abbot Gerard of St-Wandrille by one of his monks in 1029 is an extreme manifestation of the tensions which afflict any group of men who are constantly in each other's company. Ordericus' history provides several stories of men who sought the monastic habit during a period of illness, but who subsequently regretted the decision.[129]

All this said, it is clear that the internal condition of most Norman monastic communities was, in a religious sense, essentially vigorous and prosperous. Le Bec, which was unique because of Lanfranc's presence from the 1040s, supplies a remarkable example of how a church could rocket from obscurity to European fame in a single generation. The surviving illuminated manuscripts from Mont-St-Michel provide convincing evidence of an extremely active *scriptorium*, in touch with all the main European centres and capable of evolving its own house style from the middle years of the century.

The Church

The liturgical customs of the various Norman monasteries drew on sources which were, in western European terms, up-to-date, and in the mainstream of prevalent monastic fashion. What is especially significant, and a particular indication of an active internal life, is the readiness of the Norman houses to adapt, and even to innovate, to suit their own requirements. There was something of a reaction against the strongest of all contemporary forces, Cluny. William of Volpiano's Fécamp, for example, drew mostly on Frutturia, while Le Bec, and subsequently its daughter-house of St-Etienne of Caen, evolved an eclectic set of customs which derived from sources which were mainly non-Cluniac. Norman monasticism, with the exception of St-Evroult, which developed direct connections with Cluny, tended to reject the heavily ritual emphasis of Cluniac liturgy.[130] The records of monastic libraries also suggest a positive attention to the acquisition of the essential educational requirements; an eleventh-century catalogue from Fécamp demonstrates, for example, that the abbey possessed eighty-seven volumes in the time of abbot John (1028–78). At St-Evroult, the first abbot, Thierry, who had a particular interest in calligraphy, ensured that his monastery obtained the basic biblical and patristic texts within the first ten years of its existence.[131] The task of supplying adequate bibliographical resources was, none the less, an arduous one. Even Le Bec, of all places, could not muster a scribe to copy several books required in England by archbishop Lanfranc.[132] But St Anselm, as prior and then abbot after 1078–79, did at least busy himself in both borrowing and lending books. It is this strong drive towards the acquisition of the fundamentals which distinguishes the pre-1066 Norman Church from its pre-1066 English counterpart. While the Norman monastic houses may not have possessed the traditions and the ancient manuscripts extant in English abbeys, there did exist a well-nigh universal ambition to fill gaps and to keep abreast of contemporary ideas, which was not necessarily present across the Channel.

By 1066 the Norman Church possessed the distinctiveness which emanates from a lively and well-organised Church. The point is well made by what we know of the careers of 'foreigners' who became resident in the duchy. William of Volpiano, so we are told, perhaps for effect, came reluctantly. He and his followers must have been attracted, partly by the challenge of rebuilding a shattered Church, and partly by the remarkable peace of Richard II's Normandy, which abbot William appears to have praised so unreservedly to the historian Ralph Glaber. Forty years later, Lanfranc came to Normandy, so an early tradition maintains, because the province lacked teachers and because he hoped to make a career. Soon after his arrival in Normandy, however, he underwent a spiritual crisis and shut himself away inside Le Bec, before being persuaded to teach by abbot Herluin. When we come to Anselm, however, who reached Normandy in *c*. 1059, we are told that he was a pupil searching for a master, a wanderer who journeyed for three years before finding Lanfranc.[133] This same evolution from cultural dependence to confidence and originality has been observed in the manuscript art of Mont-St-Michel. There, by the middle of the eleventh century, the monastic scribes were worthy of the description of 'pioneers at the start of a new movement, not feeble copiers in the decadence of an old one'.[134] Achievement is above all apparent in the architecture of the Norman monastic churches of the second half of the century. The two Caen abbeys, and especially St-Etienne, are churches of immense grandeur and beauty. The enlargement of the tribune galleries at St-Etienne into large, in appearance empty, spaces and the plain symmetrical facade, were important developments. It was in all probability at Cerisy in *c*. 1070 where the first use of chevron ornamentation of a type which became extremely popular in England occurred. The massive capitals at the crossing in the eleventh-century cathedral at Bayeux, although not regarded as being of any special artistic originality, possess an astonishing monumentality. In the north tower of the same church, there is a strange prototype of a vault, with the ribs rising from the centre of the walls, rather than from the corners. Finally, it was in the very late eleventh century at Lessay that the first attempt to vault an entire church appears to have been made.

The history of Norman monasticism captures both the depth of the continuity from the Carolingian period, as well as the remarkable unity of the eleventh-century duchy. Ordericus' account of the history of St-Evroult adds an important strand to the way in which the tenth- and eleventh-century Normans maintained their Carolingian heritage, by making it clear that the abbey was in fact a restoration on a site abandoned in the 940s.[135] Many of the Norman monasteries were either direct refoundations of an ancient community or were endowed with lands and churches which had been in ecclesiastical hands up until the early tenth century. St-Pierre of Préaux, St-Martin of Sées, and Fontenay, for example, were all refoundations, while Cerisy picked up property which had belonged to the former monasteries of Deux-Jumeaux and St-Marcouf, and subsequently acquired St-Fromond, which was another old site, as a priory. Quite how the recognition and restoration of this land was accomplished is a process now utterly lost to us.[136] That it should have been possible on so large a scale is another argument for the stability of many aspects of Norman society through the second half of the tenth and the early eleventh centuries. This created the framework within which the remarkable unity of Norman monasticism evolved. Its self-contained growth within the duchy is superbly demonstrated by the distribution of the priories subject to the abbey of Marmoutier, which was an extensive monastic confederation, with dependencies throughout most of northern France, but one which made almost no impact within Normandy.[137] This concentration within Normandy was reinforced by the way in which the ducal monasteries, which had been restored in the tenth century, shed their non-Norman property in the first half of the eleventh century (see p. 58). The devotion of William of Volpiano's disciples to the specific task of reorganising the Church in Normandy was an important, if immeasurable, contribution towards the duchy's political cohesion.

The role of monasticism within the Norman Church none the less changed considerably over the years from $c.$ 1000 to 1066. The outward-looking character of William of Volpiano's reform, with its interest in education and the regeneration of the Church in the countryside, continued to be expressed throughout the eleventh century in, for example, the unusual architectural feature of passages at tribune level covering a whole bay and sometimes the entire transept. The purpose was presumably to accommodate processions by the laity on saints' days.[138] By 1066, however, the monasteries were becoming increasingly incorporated into the structure of episcopal authority, and their activities were being channelled into courses which were much more characteristically monastic. Apart from the two archbishops of Rouen, Maurilius and William Bonne-Ame, monks did not play an especially active role in the Norman episcopate. Until the conquest of England created a crisis of manpower, bishops were generally chosen from ducal family or chaplains. It could even be argued that secular clergy were employed to stiffen monasticism after 1066, since two of the abbots of important abbeys, William of Fécamp (1079–1107) and Gontard of Jumièges (1078–95), had been respectively dean and archdeacon of Bayeux and a ducal chaplain. The specific contribution of monks to the development of the Church in Normandy was, in the early eleventh century, to bring in ideas, techniques, and organisation from neighbouring regions. They assembled the foundations out of which the scholastic and architectural originality and much of the province's drive towards ecclesiastical organisation grew in the second half of the eleventh century.

Normandy before 1066

THE NORMAN CHURCH

The outstanding features of the Norman Church in 1066 were the close interrelationship between ecclesiastical and secular authority and the recent date at which much of its structure had evolved. The crucial underlying factor was the destructive effect of the Scandinavian raids and the slow recovery after 911. The bishoprics only began to revive in the later years of Richard I's reign. A small number of monasteries had supplied a base in the tenth century, which was reinforced by William of Volpiano's reform, which itself played an important political and organisational role through to the 1050s. The vital decades were, however, those between *c.* 1030 and *c.* 1070, when the spread of monasticism, and the reorganisation of the bishoprics eventually started to produce a coherent structure of authority under the presiding eye of duke William II. The Norman Church, as it existed in 1066, was still in the midst of rapid evolution and change, a process which was attracting fresh minds and ideas to the province, and which, since *c.* 1050, had given the Church an extremely strong sense of its own corporate existence. The result was shown in several distinctive elements of organisational and artistic originality.

The evolution of the eleventh-century Norman Church has much in common with ducal government. In Richard II's time, its organisation was mainly concentrated, both territorially and socially, in Upper Normandy. Personnel were despatched to the undeveloped region of Lower Normandy, lands there were handed over to Upper Norman, and indeed non-Norman, churches, and the chief impetus was towards the improvement of those churches which were in the vicinity of the few great monasteries. The disorders of the second quarter of the century threatened the dukes' role in the Church just as they attacked others of his prerogatives; the foundation of the new monasteries brought with it the possibility of lay advocacy and the attachment of rural churches to these abbeys, in a way which could have dissolved such authority as belonged to the diocesan bishop. Under these circumstances the helpful response of the established ducal monasteries was crucial, since it was their acquiescence in change which, in conjunction with the policies of duke William, made possible the new developments of the 1050s. Thereafter the Church in Normandy was pushed towards incorporation within the firm institutional structure of ducal authority and towards the organisation of its own internal government.

It must be correct to think in terms of the Norman Church acquiring most of its individuality from *c.* 1050 onwards. Up until that time, despite the immense efforts of duke Richard II and the likes of William of Volpiano, the direction of both ducal and ecclesiastical policy had been towards limited objectives and had relied on the efforts of a few high-minded individuals. It is particularly misleading, for example, to think that the Norman Church launched itself on what was, in western European terms, a precocious campaign of moral reform. The point, which is often made, that archbishop Malger's council of the 1040s, with its legislative pronouncements against simony and encroachments on ecclesiastical property, anticipated by several years the earliest papal decrees on the same subjects, misrepresents the course of historical development. Leo IX's council of Rheims in fact marked the papacy's adoption of a campaign which had already been proceeding for several decades in synods organised by the German kings, by French territorial princes, and, in some parts of France, by individual bishops. Malger's council was the blundering initiative of a Church unaccustomed to episcopal organisation and a brave protest against disruptive violence. The characteristic attitudes among the best of the Norman churchmen who were Malger's contemporaries were essentially monastic and generally conservative. Those who took the lead against Berengar of Tours did so from a traditional standpoint, stressing authority and the Church's integrity, and dismissing the need for speculative thought. The interest of the leading figures of this time lay mostly in music, spirituality, and liturgy; the contributions of abbot Isembard of La Trinité-du-Mont of Rouen to the first and of abbot John of Fécamp to the second were notable ones. The organisational and educational achievements of these men were in the context of the times massive, and should certainly not be belittled. But a strong case can be made out for the institutional backwardness of the Norman Church for much of its pre-1066 history. What is also important, however, is the sustained application which was directed towards rescuing the Church from the effects of its tenth-century sufferings. As a result the Norman Church from *c.* 1050 entirely reflects the political achievements of the dukes.

The 'lay theocracy' of the Norman rulers was given a theoretical justification in the course of the early-twelfth-century treatise composed by the so-called Norman Anonymous. The author's purpose was to justify a state of affairs which had massive historical support, a unitary Christian society within which the local churches were governed mainly by lay rulers. For him, kings 'reign over the Church, which is the kingdom of God; they reign together with

Christ in order to rule, protect, and defend her'.[139] He was defending a local hierarchical organisation with effective ecclesiastical authority exercised by an archbishop and his suffragan bishops, under the direction of a benevolent king or territorial prince, against what he saw as the ravages of the popes from Gregory VII (1073–85) onwards. What impressed the Anonymous was the steady reforming endeavour of organisations like the Norman Church, of which he was a member. He might have argued the practical aspects of his case from the careful adaptation of reform to local conditions typical of the approach taken by many Norman ecclesiastic and by their conciliar legislation. In Normandy, a reformer such as John of Fécamp would take tolerance as far as granting a church to a married priest, while taking precautions against hereditary succession.[140] The decrees of the Rouen (1072) and Lillebonne councils obviously tailored their attack on the lay possession of churches and clerical marriage to distinctive Norman conditions. In both cases ducal authority was to be called in when it was thought necessary. Had he been writing in more modern times, the Anonymous might also have added the more original of the achievements of the later eleventh-century Norman Church to bolster his case. As it was, he had the wit to perceive that the varying character and abilities of lay rulers was one of the chief weaknesses of his argument. Some thirty or forty years earlier, few can have guessed that it would even be necessary to write such a defence of a long-established system.

NOTES

1. Margaret Gibson, *Lanfranc of Bec* (Oxford, 1978), 23–5.
2. D. R. Bates, 'The character and career of Odo, Bishop of Bayeux (1049/50–97)', *Speculum*, 1 (1975), 2–4; OV, iv, 310–16.
3. E. H. Kantorowicz, *Laudes Regiae. A Study in Liturgical Acclamations and Medieval Ruler Worship* (Berkeley and Los Angeles, 1946), 166–71. See now, H. E. J. Cowdrey, 'The Anglo-Norman *Laudes Regiae*', *Viator*, xii (1981), 37–78, especially, 48–50, 68–69.
4. *Helgaud de Fleury, Vie de Robert le Pieux*, ed. R. H. Bautier and G. Labory (Paris, 1965), 64–6.
5. *The Letters and Poems of Fulbert of Chartres*, ed. F. Behrends (Oxford, 1976), no. 92. See in general, K. F. Werner, 'Kingdom and principality in twelfth-century France', in *The Medieval Nobility*, ed. T. Reuter (Amsterdam, New York, and Oxford, 1978), 252–4; Elizabeth Hallam, 'The king and the princes in eleventh-century France', *BIHR*, liii (1980), 156.
6. Robert of Torigny. 'De immutatione ordinis monachorum', in *Chro-*

nique de Robert de Torigni, abbé du Mont-Saint-Michel, ed. L. Delisle (Rouen, 1872–73), ii, 194.
7. *Recueil*, nos. 9, 34. Fundamental for what follows is, J. -F. Lemarignier, 'Le monachisme et l'encadrement religieux des campagnes du royaume de France situées au nord de la Loire, de la fin du Xe à la fin du XIe siècle', in *Le istituzioni ecclesiastiche della "societas Christiana" dei secoli XI–XII: Diocesi, pievi e parrocchie, La Mendola, 1974* (Milan, 1978), 357–94, especially 384–94. See also, N. Bulst *Untersuchungen zu der Klosterreform Wilhelms von Dijon (962–1031)* (Paris, 1973), 147–85.
8. N. Bulst, 'Rodulfus Glabers Vita domni Willelmi abbatis. Neue Edition nach einer Handschrift des 11. Jahrhunderts (Paris, Bibl. nat., lat. 5390)', *Deutsches Archiv*, xxx (1974), 472.
9. L. Musset, 'La contribution de Fécamp à la reconquête monastique de la Basse-Normandie', in *L'abbaye bénédictine de Fécamp*, i (Fécamp, 1959), 60–2.
10. *Recueil*, nos. 15, 35, 36, 53. The Bernay charter is rather imprecise, but note that there were twenty-one churches on the vills around Bernay, which Richard II gave to his wife Judith in 996–1008, and which later formed the basis of Bernay's endowment, *ibid.*, no. 11.
11. *Ibid.*, no. 29; A.D. Seine-Maritime, 7H, 2143.
12. Continuity of rural churches has been suggested for the Pays de Caux, an area of heavy Scandinavian settlement, J. Le Maho, 'De la curtis au château: l'exemple du Pays de Caux', *Château Gaillard*, viii (1977), 171. There is also the interesting case of the church of Querqueville in the far north of the Cotentin, whose construction is now dated to *c*. 900. The first element of the place-name is Scandinavian for 'church'. Laymen did, of course, sponsor the building of churches, e.g. F. Lot, *Etudes critiques sur l'abbaye de St-Wandrille* (Paris, 1913), pièces-justificatives, no. 16.
13. *Recueil*, no. 12.
14. On the recruitment of bishops, below, pp. 210–11. For Hugh of Avranches and Fécamp, 'Appendix ex Ms. Codice Cellae S. Gabrielis', in L. Musset, 'Notules fécampoises', *BSAN*, liv (1959, for 1957–58), 596; *Recueil*, nos. 72, 93, 145; BN, collection Moreau, vol. 21, fo. 25rv.
15. *The Letters and Poems of Fulbert of Chartres*, nos. 39, 66, 83. For Baldric, see p. 117.
16. For the early 11th-century Norman bishoprics, see pp. 212–3.
17. J. -F. Lemarignier, 'Paix et réforme monastique en Flandre et en Normandie autour de l'année 1023', in *Etudes . . . Yver*, 454–7.
18. *Recueil*, no. 71.
19. Bulst, *Wilhelms von Dijon*, 161–76.
20. *Recueil*, no. 73; J. J. G. Alexander, *Norman Illumination at Mont-St-Michel, 996–1100* (Oxford, 1970), 10–11.
21. *Recueil*, nos. 61, 89.
22. *Ibid.*, nos. 64, 90; J. -F. Lemarignier, *Etude sur les privilèges d'exemption et de juridiction ecclésiastique des abbayes normandes depuis les origines jusqu'en 1140* (Paris, 1937), 44–50.
23. *Recueil*, nos. 66, 67; *Antiquus cartularius ecclesiae Baiocensis*, ed. V. Bourrienne (Rouen, 1902–03), i, no. 21.
24. *GC*, xi, instr. col. 222. For Sées, see pp. 69–70.

25. *Chartes de l'abbaye de Jumièges (v. 825 à 1204) conservées aux archives de la Seine-Inférieure*, ed. J. J. Vernier (Rouen and Paris, 1916), i, no. 42; A.D. Eure, H. 711, fo. 137v.
26. For the canons, J. D. Mansi, *Sacrorum conciliorum nova et amplissima collectio*, xix (Venice, 1774), cols. 751–4.
27. *Ibid.*, xix, cols. 503–6.
28. Hugh of Flavigny, *Chronicon*, in *MGH, Scriptores*, viii, 403.
29. *Recueil*, p. 22; *Acta Pontificum Romanorum Inedita*, ed. J. von Pflugk-Harttung (Tübingen and Stuttgart, 1881–86), i, no. 13; *Regesta Pontificum Romanorum*, ed. P. Jaffé and G. Wattenbach (Leipzig, 1885–88), no. 4056. The authenticity of the Fécamp bull, which survives only in an 18th-century copy, has been endlessly discussed. K. F. Werner, 'Quelques observations au sujet des débuts du "duché" de Normandie', *Etudes . . . Yver*, 709, note 49, rejects it out of hand. St-Ouen of Rouen may once have possessed a bull of Benedict IX, dated 1044, Dom Toussaint Duplessis, *Description géographique et historique de la Haute-Normandie* (Paris, 1760), i, 379.
30. *Das Register Gregors VII*, ed. E. Caspar, *MGH, Epistolae*, iv (*Epistolae Selectae*, ii, Berlin, 1955), 500–1; *English Historical Documents*, ed. D. C. Douglas and G. W. Greenaway (London, 1953), ii, 645.
31. *Vita Lanfranci, PL*, cl, cols. 29–58, especially, cols. 34–7. The critique here draws heavily on Gibson, *Lanfranc*, 25–6, 31, 69, 196–7. Note that F. Barlow, 'A view of archbishop Lanfranc', *Journal of Ecclesiastical History*, xvi (1965), 171, describes the received view of events as 'inexplicable'.
32. *Historia dedicationis ecclesiae S. Remigii*, in Mansi, *Concilia*, xix, col. 742.
33. *Vita Herluini*, ed. J. Armitage Robinson, in *Gilbert Crispin, Abbot of Westminster* (Cambridge, 1911), 97–8. The incident should probably be connected with the siege of Brionne, Gibson, *Lanfranc*, 31.
34. *Willelmi Malmesbiriensis monachi Gesta Pontificum Anglorum*, ed. N. E. S. A. Hamilton (Rolls Series, 1870), 38, 150–1. See, *The Letters of Lanfranc, Archbishop of Canterbury*, ed. Helen Clover and Margaret Gibson (Oxford, 1979), no. 47.
35. *Hujus tam improvidae jussionis causam aiunt, Vita Lanfranci, PL*, cl, col. 35.
36. WJ, 181–2.
37. *Liber de corpore et sanguine Domini, PL*, cl, col. 409.
38. *Ibid.*, cxliii, cols. 1349–50.
39. *Berengarii Turonensis de Sacra Coena adversus Lanfrancum*, ed. W. H. Beekenkamp (The Hague, 1941), l.
40. *Histoire des conciles d'après les documents originaux*, ed. C. J. Hefele and Dom H. Leclercq, iv, 2 (Paris, 1911), 1040; Gibson, *Lanfranc*, 67; *PL*, cxliii, cols. 797–800.
41. *Willelmi Malmesbiriensis monachi, De Gestis Regum Anglorum*, ed. W. Stubbs (Rolls Series, 1887–89), ii, 327.
42. Lemarignier, *Privilèges d'exemption*, 143–6, with the text at 144, note 43.
43. OV, ii, 90–4.
44. 'Acta archiepiscopum Rotomagensium', in J. Mabillon, *Vetera Analecta* (Paris, 1723), i, 224.
45. Arguments to the contrary have been put by Catherine Morton, 'Pope

Alexander II and the Norman Conquest', *Latomus: Revue d'études latines*, xxxiv (1975), 362-82.
46. On the controversy, see now, Gibson, *Lanfranc*, 63-97. Also, although dated, R. W. Southern, 'Lanfranc of Bec and Berengar of Tours', in *Studies in Medieval History presented to Frederick Maurice Powicke*, ed. R. W. Hunt, et al. (Oxford, 1948), 27-48.
47. E.g. 'Liber de corpore et sanguine Christi', *PL*, cxlix, col. 1392. See, R. Heurtevent, *Durand de Troarn et les origines de l'hérésie bérengarienne* (Paris, 1912), 217-51.
48. Thus, *Fide capiendum est, non ratione quaerendum aut inveniendum*, 'Confessio fidei', *PL*, ci, col. 1087. See, G. Mathon, 'Jean de Fécamp, théologien monastique?', in *La Normandie bénédictine au temps de Guillaume le Conquérant*, ed. J. Daoust (Lille, 1967), 490-1.
49. *PL*, cxliii, cols. 1382-3; L. Delisle, *Canons du concile tenu à Lisieux* (Paris, 1901), 1.
50. *Ibid.*, 1-2; OV, ii, 286-92. See, in general, Raymonde Foreville, 'The synod of the province of Rouen in the eleventh and twelfth centuries', in *Church and Government in the Middle Ages: Essays presented to C. R. Cheney*, ed. C. N. L. Brooke, et al. (Cambridge, 1976), 19-39.
51. OV, iii, 30. All references to the Lillebonne decrees are to this convenient edition.
52. *AAC*, no. 13; Lemarignier, *Privilèges d'exemption*, 156-76.
53. OV, iii, 26, 34; P. Le Cacheux, 'Une charte de Jumièges concernant l'épreuve par le fer chaud (fin du XIe siècle)', *SHN, Mélanges*, xi (1927), 213-14.
54. BN, collection Baluze, vol. 77, fo. 48r; MS. latin 12878, fo. 231v.
55. *Recueil*, no. 49.
56. *Aut enim ut vestra custodite, aut alterius ditioni subrogate*, *Thesaurus Novus Anecdotorum*, ed. E. Martène and U. Durand (Paris, 1717), i, col. 198. In general, C. N. L. Brooke, 'Princes and kings as patrons of monasteries: Normandy and England', *Il monachesimo e la riforma ecclesiastica (1049-1122), La Mendola, 1968* (Milan, 1971), 125-44.
57. Bates, 'Character and career of Odo', 19.
58. See, *Recueil*, nos. 97, 99, 121, 142, 156, 197, 208, 215, 218, 227.
59. BN, collection du Vexin, iv, 147.
60. F. Barlow, *The English Church, 1066-1154* (London, 1979), 56.
61. ... *maneant sub defensione mea et heredum meorum sicut debent esse elemosine fidelium et bonorum christianorum*, R. -N. Sauvage, *L'abbaye de St-Martin de Troarn* (Caen, 1911), *preuves*, no. 2. On the whole subject of ducal protection, J. Yver, 'Autour de l'absence d'avouerie en Normandie', *BSAN*, lvii (1965, for 1963-64), 194-213. To the references there cited, add *Recueil*, nos. 115, 142, 199, 227.
62. *Ibid.*, no. 222; Cartulaire de l'abbaye de St-Denis, Archives nationales, LL, 1158, p. 590.
63. E.g. *Cartulaire de Marmoutier pour le Perche*, ed. l'abbé Barret (Mortagne, 1894). no. 3; Sauvage, *Troarn, preuves*, no. 6; *GC*, xi, instr. cols. 202-3.
64. L. Musset, 'Actes inédits du XIe siècle. V. Autour des origines de St-Etienne de Fontenay', *BSAN*, lvi (1963, for 1961-62), 40; *GC*, xi, instr. col. 65.

65. OV, ii, 90–2, 146; 'Acta archiepiscopum Rotomagensium', in Mabillon, *Vetera Analecta*, i, 225. For the latter incident, see also the annals of St-Etienne of Caen, *Historiae Normannorum Scriptores Antiqui*, ed. A. Duchesne (Paris, 1619), 1017–18.
66. Mabillon, *Vetera Analecta*, i, 450.
67. *Recueil*, no. 122; 'De libertate Beccensis monasterii', in *RHF*, xiv, 271–2; Marjorie Chibnall, 'Le privilège de libre élection dans les chartes de Saint-Evroult', *AN*, xxviii (1978), 341–2.
68. L. Musset, 'Actes inédits du XIe siècle. I. Les plus anciennes chartes du prieuré de St-Gabriel (Calvados)', *BSAN*, lii (1955, for 1952–54), 140.
69. See, in general, D. C. Douglas, 'The Norman episcopate before the Norman Conquest', *Cambridge Historical Journal*, xiii (1957), 101–15; Rosalind B. Brooke and C. N. L. Brooke, 'I vescovi di Inghilterra e Normandia nel secolo XI: Contrasti', *Le istituzioni ecclesiastiche della 'societas christiana' dei secoli XI–XII: Diocesi, pievi e parrocchie, La Mendola, 1974* (Milan, 1978), 536–45.
70. E.g. *Recueil*, no. 10; D. R. Bates, 'Notes sur l'aristocratie normande. I. Hugues, évêque de Bayeux (1011–env. -1049). II. Herluin de Conteville et sa famille', *AN*, xxiii (1973), 12–13.
71. 'Acta archiepiscopum Rotomagensium', *PL*, cxlvii, cols. 277–8.
72. *Ibid.*, col. 278; WP, 130–2. For the date of the deposition, see now, O. Guillot, *Le comte d'Anjou et son entourage au XIe siècle* (Paris, 1972), i, 186, note 232.
73. *PL*, cl, cols. 1387–90. For his liturgical interests, see especially, *Le 'De Officiis Ecclesiasticis' de Jean d'Avranches, archevêque de Rouen (1067–79)*, ed. R. Delamare (Paris, 1923), 3.
74. OV, iii, 18; *The Letters of Lanfranc*, nos. 14–17.
75. *Recueil*, nos. 135, 186; *CTR*, nos. 36, 40.
76. OV, ii, 254.
77. In general, Bates, 'Character and career of Odo', 1–20.
78. WP, 136–42; OV, iii, 14–18; iv, 240.
79. *Ibid.*, iii, 20–2.
80. J. -F. Lemarignier, 'Les institutions ecclésiastiques en France de la fin du Xe au milieu du XIIe siècle', in *Histoire des institutions françaises au Moyen Age*, iii, *Institutions ecclésiastiques*, 71–2; idem, 'Le monachisme et l'encadrement religieux', 391–4.
81. In general, J. Boussard, 'Les évêques en Neustrie avant la réforme grégorienne', *Journal des Savants* (1970), 161–96; B. Guillemain, 'Les origines des évêques en France aux XIe et XIIe siècles', in *Le istituzioni ecclesiastiche della 'societas christiana' dei secoli XI–XII: Papato, cardinalato ed episcopato, La Mendola, 1971* (Milan, 1974), 374–402, especially 380–3, 396–7.
82. *The Letters and Poems of Fulbert of Chartres*, nos. 39, 66. For the only other early Norman example of *synodalia* and *circada*, which occurs in a late text with very uncertain transmission, L. Musset, 'Les origines du prieuré de Saint-Fromond: un acte négligé de Richard II', *BSAN*, liii (1957, for 1955–56), 484.
83. L. Musset, 'Le satiriste Garnier de Rouen et son milieu (début du XIe siècle)', *Revue du moyen âge latin*, x (1954), 241–2. Also, M. Lapidge, 'Three Latin poems from Aethelwold's school at Winchester', in *Anglo-*

Saxon England, i (1972), 101–2; L. Musset, 'Rouen et l'Angleterre vers l'an mil. De nouveau sur le satiriste Garnier de Rouen et l'école littéraire de Rouen au temps de Richard II', AN, xxiv (1974), 287–90.

84. See, Cartulaire de l'abbaye de St-Père de Chartres, ed. B. E. C. Guérard (Paris, 1840), i, 116, 176; Neustria Pia, ed. A. du Monstier (Rouen, 1663), 521; 'Inventio et Miracula Sancti Wulfranni', ed. Dom J. Laporte, SHN, Mélanges, xiv (1938), 56–9; Recueil, nos. 103, 107.
85. OV, ii, 26.
86. Rouen, c. 5: *Ut nullus episcopus, sive abbas, alterius episcopi vel abbatis honorem supplantare praesumat*, Mansi, Concilia, xix, cols. 752–3.
87. Coutances: GC, xi, instr. col. 218; J. Le Patourel, 'Geoffrey of Montbray, bishop of Coutances, 1049–1093', EHR, lix (1944), 134–5. Avranches: see p. 195. Bayeux: Bates, 'Notes sur l'aristocratie normande', 10–15.
88. *in episcopatu Lisiacensi*, Recueil, no. 138. See also, *usque ad pontellum qui dividit Baiocensem episcopatum a Luxoviensi*, AAC, no. 13.
89. Recueil, nos. 33, 66, 67, 214; p. 24, note 24; Antiquus Cartularius Ecclesiae Baiocensis, i, no. 21.
90. PL, cxlvii, col. 278; GC, xi, instr. col. 218; OV, iii, 16; E. A. Pigeon, Le diocèse d'Avranches (Coutances, 1888), 328, 679.
91. PL, cxlvii, cols. 277–8; OV, iii, 84, 92.
92. Historia translationis SS. Ravenni et Rasiphi, Acta Sanctorum, July, v, 393; Bates, 'Notes sur l'aristocratie normande', 18–20. Above all, see now, J. Thirion, 'La cathédrale de Bayeux', in Congrès archéologique de France, 132e session (1974), Bessin et Pays d'Auge (Paris, 1978), 240–6.
93. Lisieux: OV, iii, 14; A. Erlande-Brandenburg, 'La cathédrale de Lisieux: les campagnes de construction', Congrès archéologique de France... (1974), 139–45. Coutances: GC, xi, instr. cols. 218–19; 'Miracula Ecclesiae Constantiensis', in E. A. Pigeon, Histoire de la cathédrale de Coutances (Coutances, 1876), 372.
94. PL, cxlvii, col. 265; Lemarignier, Privilèges d'exemption, 158–60.
95. Lot, St-Wandrille, pièces-justificatives, no. 39; Cartulaire de Marmoutier pour le Perche, no. 3.
96. Stigand *cantor*, Cartulaire de l'abbaye de St-Père de Chartres, i, 177; John the sub-cantor, BN, MS. latin 12878, fo. 232v. For archdeacons, see Appendix C.
97. Cartulaire de l'abbaye de St-Vincent du Mans, ed. R. Charles and M. le vicomte d'Elbenne (Le Mans, 1913), no. 545. For Odone archidiacono de Mauritonia (i.e. Mortagne) in 1050–64, Cartulaire de Marmoutier pour le Perche, no. 7. The editor overlooked the survival of this text in an original charter, A.D. Orne, H. 2561.
98. See, Cartulaire de Marmoutier pour le Perche, no. 12.
99. Rouen, c. 11: *Ut nullus archidiaconus alterius archidiaconatum supplantare praesumat*, Mansi, Concilia, xix, col. 753.
100. Lisieux: OV, ii, 18. Bayeux: Recueil, no. 227; Le Cacheux, 'Une charte de Jumièges', 214; A.D. Seine-Maritime, 14 H. 160. In general, see Appendix C.
101. For Bayeux, there is late evidence that seven prebends were created in 1074, H. Navel, 'L'enquête de 1133 sur les fiefs de l'évêché de Bayeux', BSAN, xlii (1935), 16, 21. For Rouen, Anne Brinkworth, 'The

archbishops of Rouen, 1037–1110' (University of Bristol M. Litt. Thesis, 1966), 265–7.
102. *Hugh the Chantor: The History of the Church of York, 1066–1127*, ed. C. Johnson (London, 1961), 2. On Odo's patronage of scholars, Bates, 'Character and career of Odo', 13–15.
103. OV, iii, 120.
104. Coutances: GC, xi, instr. col. 220. Avranches: Avranches, Bibliothèque municipale, MS. 210, fo. 83v. Bayeux: A.D. Seine-Maritime, 14H, 160. Sées: *Cartulaire de Marmoutier pour le Perche*, no. 12.
105. Guibert of Nogent, *De Pignoribus Sanctorum, PL*, clvi, col. 625.
106. OV, iii, 34; L. Musset, 'Aperçus sur la dîme ecclésiastique en Normandie au XIe siècle', *RHDFE*, 4e série, lii (1974), 544–5.
107. R. Génestal, 'La patrimonalité de l'archidiaconat dans la province ecclésiastique de Rouen', *Mélanges Paul Fournier* (Paris, 1929), 287–90; Cartulaire de la cathédrale d'Evreux, A.D. Eure, G. 122, fo.4v.
108. *Le 'De Officiis Ecclesiasticis' de Jean d'Avranches*, p. LIII; *The Letters of Lanfranc*, no. 41.
109. *AAC*, no. 13; 'Miracula Ecclesiae Constantiensis', 370.
110. For Bayeux, Bates, 'Character and career of Odo', 12–13; for full details, *idem*, 'Odo, Bishop of Bayeux, 1049/50–1097' (Exeter University Ph.D. Thesis, 1970), 180–4, 204–8. For Coutances, note the reference to *quidam juvenis praesumptuosus, majorum ecclesiae personarum consanguineus*,'Miracula Ecclesiae Constantiensis', 367. John, the author of the 'Miracula', was the son of Peter, dean and chamberlain in bishop Geoffrey's time.
111. GC, xi, instr. cols. 220–1.
112. A convenient list is provided in Barlow, *The English Church, 1066–1154*, 179, note 8. St-Vigor of Bayeux, which failed, could be added. The author omits to note that La Croix-St-Leuffroy, St-Pierre of Préaux, and St-Martin of Sées were refoundations. The main general account of Norman monasticism is Dom D. Knowles, *The Monastic Order in England* (Cambridge, 1941), 83–99.
113. For this paragraph, L. Musset, 'Recherches sur les communautés de clercs séculiers en Normandie au XIe siècle', *BSAN*, lv (1961, for 1959–60), 5–38.
114. See, Robert of Torigny, 'De immutatione ordinis monachorum', in *Chronique de Robert de Torigni*, ii, 191–203. Ordericus is also exceptionally valuable for the early history of the Norman monasteries.
115. L. Musset, 'La contribution de Fécamp à la reconquête monastique de la Basse-Normandie', in *L'abbaye bénédictine de Fécamp*, i (Fécamp, 1959), 64–6.
116. Alexander, *Norman Illumination at Mont-St-Michel*, 13; 'Altera vita sancti Guillelmi, ex chronico sancti Benigni Divionensis excerpta', *PL*, cxli, col. 864.
117. For Norman monastic architecture, see, especially, L. Musset, *La Normandie romane*, i. *La Basse-Normandie*, ii. *La Haute-Normandie* (Zodiaque, 1967–74). Also, G. Zarnecki, 'Romanesque sculpture in Normandy and England in the eleventh century', in *Proceedings of the Battle Conference*, i (1978), 168–89.
118. Alexander, *Norman Illumination at Mont-St-Michel*, 44–126.

119. GC, xi, instr. col. 154.
120. Musset, 'Fontenay', 15–19.
121. L. Musset, 'Les premiers temps de l'abbaye d'Almenèches des origines au XIIe siècle', in *L'abbaye d'Almenèches-Argentan et sainte Opportune. Sa vie et son culte*, ed. Dom Y. Chaussy (Paris, 1970), 21, note 50.
122. GC, xi, instr. col. 154.
123. Musset, in *L'abbaye bénédictine de Fécamp*, i, 67–79. See also, AAC, no. 20.
124. L. Musset, 'Actes inédits du XIe siècle: un nouveau document sur la fortune de St-Martin de Sées', *Bulletin de la société historique et archéologique de l'Orne*, lxxviii (1960), 24.
125. 'De libertate Beccensis monasterii', RHF, xiv, 272.
126. GC, xi, instr. col. 63.
127. See, Musset, 'Almenèches', 22–9; *idem*, 'Les origines et le patrimoine de l'abbaye de Saint-Sever', in *La Normandie bénédictine au temps de Guillaume le Conquérant*, 364–5, 367.
128. For military service, see p. 169. On the status of one college, see the remarkable, *hec autem omnia predicta ita honorifice habenda et tenenda sicut et ceteris baronibus suis*, Recueil, no. 222. The attendance of abbots at 'honorial courts' is illustrated by the Montgommery-Bellême evidence, e.g. Cartulaire de St-Martin de Sées, fos. 4r, 15v, 25v (see chapter 2, note 92).
129. OV, ii, 42–6.
130. *Consuetudines Beccenses*, ed. Marie Pascal Dickson (*Corpus consuetudinum monasticarum*, iv, Sigeburg, 1967), xxix–liii.
131. OV, ii, 48–50. See, in general, Geneviève Nortier, 'Les bibliothèques médiévales des abbayes bénédictines de Normandie', *Revue Mabillon*, xlvii (1957), 9–11, 26–30.
132. *Sancti Anselmi archiepiscopi Opera Omnia*, ed. Dom F. S. Schmitt (Edinburgh, 1938–61), iii, *epp.* nos. 23, 25.
133. *The Life of St. Anselm, Archbishop of Canterbury, by Eadmer*, ed. R. W. Southern (Oxford, 1972), 7.
134. Alexander, *Norman Illumination at Mont-St-Michel*, 126.
135. OV, ii, 14–16; iii, pp. xvi–xviii.
136. See, L. Musset, 'Les destins de la propriété monastique durant les invasions normandes (IXe–XIe s.). L'exemple de Jumièges', in *Jumièges. Congrès scientifique du XIIIe centenaire* (Rouen, 1955), 54.
137. Odile Gantier, 'Rôle économique et social de l'abbaye de Marmoutier aux XIe et XIIe siècles', *Bulletin philologique et historique du comité des travaux historiques et scientifiques* (1971, for 1968), 531–43, *carte*.
138. J.-Y. Canouville, 'Architecture et liturgie en Normandie au XIe siècle: les transepts', *Etudes normandes*, nos. 1–2 (1978), 115–19.
139. See the convenient translation in *English Historical Documents*, ii, 676–7. For a succinct appreciation of the Anonymous' ideas, Barlow, *The English Church, 1066–1154*, 292–7.
140. BN, collection Moreau, vol. 21, fo. 22rv.

CHAPTER SIX
Achievement

The emphasis throughout this book has been on the structure of social, political, and ecclesiastical change, and on an attempt to give context to the 'Norman Achievement'. The natural result of such an approach is to place narrative and the deeds of men somewhat in the background. There cannot in fact be any doubt that the Norman eleventh century was an exciting time, a period of dramatic exploits and positive endeavour. Even if the conquests are left on one side, there remains the widespread church- and castle-building and the abundant signs of economic initiative. Were such a thing possible, the best illustration of the fast rate of man-made change would be a series of aerial photographs of the entire province, taken at intervals of, say, twenty years. The most easily noticeable development would be the renewal of the Church, demonstrated by a large number of construction projects, driven forward at a relentless pace. But the landscape would also show signs of fresh habitation, the clearance of woodland, and new concentrations of aristocratic power around palisaded earthworks. The literary testimony to all this enterprise is in the pages of Ordericus Vitalis' *Ecclesiastical History*, a book which makes marvellous reading largely because its author could not select his material systematically, and because he never lost that sense of wonder before his subject which is essential to all outstanding historical writing. Ordericus informs us of the deeds of kings and princes, the visions of rustics, and the daily round of his monastery. It is from him that we learn of the career in southern Italy of William de Montreuil, 'the good Norman', or of Arnold d'Echauffour's brief visit to the South during a period of temporary exile from the duchy. Ordericus' work is therefore a sharp contrast to the limited panegyrics produced by Dudo of St-Quentin, William of Jumièges,

Achievement

and William of Poitiers. It is no surprise that, with his inexhaustible interest in the deeds of his fellow men, Ordericus should have so readily soaked up twelfth-century romance, and portrayed the Normans as a people capable of prodigious feats. When he wrote, the material for 'the Norman Myth' was to hand, awaiting its compiler. It is only by recognising his work for what it is, that we can acknowledge that the origins of Norman achievement must be found, not in some preconceived Norman *machismo*, but in the obscure recesses of the social and political structure of pre-1066 Normandy.

The trends underlying the history of pre-1066 Normandy, as they have been described in the previous chapters, suggest that the whole subject is best understood in terms of four distinct phases. The first, a period from 911 to *c.* 960, was characterised by heavy Scandinavian immigration and hostile Frankish intervention, but also by the counts of Rouen taking a firm grasp on the existing levers of power, and by the spasmodic, but effective, recovery of some sections of the Church. The second phase, from *c.* 960 to *c.* 1025, was a period of relative stability and consolidation. For much of it, Normandy remained in contact with Scandinavia through economic and political connections which contributed to Rouen's prosperity and permitted the counts/dukes to call in Scandinavian auxiliaries against threats to their power. At the same time, however, the province became more and more thoroughly absorbed into its Frankish environment to the extent that, by the early eleventh century, Scandinavian language had largely disappeared, and government, social structure, and Church, despite organisational limitations, conformed to types which were essentially Frankish. The third phase, from *c.* 1025 to *c.* 1050, was characterised by the final and complete rupture with Scandinavia, by the disintegration of ducal government, and by a complex transformation in the powers and organisation of the aristocracy. The fourth phase, from *c.* 1050 onwards, was dominated by William II's rehabilitation of ducal authority, a consolidation of the changes in social structure which had taken place during the previous phase, and a belated revival of the bishoprics. It also differed from preceding phases, with the obvious exception of the first, in that the maintenance of the power and prestige of a Norman ruler was tied directly to a policy of sustained aggression against the duchy's neighbours.

This periodisation is not inflexible; such schemes rarely are. In this case there are overlaps from one phase to another, like the evidence for some fragmentation of ducal authority before 1025, or for the precocious development of the archdiocese of Rouen in comparison with the other bishoprics. Such exceptions are mostly anticipations in an earlier phase of more general changes which came later. The scheme as a whole is one which draws attention to the main changes in the relationships within the ruling classes, and, more speculatively, to the attitudes which those changes provoked. It is likely, as a result, to identify the dynamic causes of the Norman expansion of the eleventh century. It suggests, through a comparison with what is known about other territorial principalities, that the period of decisive change in Normandy's internal history lay, not in the first half of the tenth century when the Scandinavians settled, but in the first half of the eleventh. The third phase, the period of instability from *c.* 1025 to *c.* 1050, should be regarded as a time which witnessed events and changes in social structure in general terms equivalent to those associated elsewhere with the breakdown of authority and with expansionist schemes on the part of territorial princes. These were the chief cause of an explosion within Norman society which galvanised the exodus to southern Italy. They also provided the basis for the forms of social organisation which were involved in the conquest and colonisation of Britain.

This view of the course of Norman history is one which abandons what can for convenience be termed the 'Norman Myth', and instead seeks to explain achievement in terms of attitudes and changes which were common to northern French society as a whole. Such an approach is justified by the essentially Frankish character of Norman government and society in the eleventh century. It does not in the last resort deny remarkable achievements to the Normans, nor does it necessarily argue that the people who ruled eleventh-century Normandy were not in some respects distinct from their neighbours – the fact that they resided within a defined political unit, and that their unusual origins continued to gain some recognition, ensured that this was the case even in the eleventh century. What this argument does do, however, is suggest that the eleventh-century military expansion should not be seen as a demonstration of one people's exceptional prowess in war, but rather as a part of wider changes which were taking place in northern French society. This means that any idea of a continuity of warlike enterprise from 911 through to 1066 and beyond, with the 1020s and 1030s representing, not a time of initiation into military expansion, but a redirection of activity, has to be rejected. To put the matter excessively simply: the third phase (*c.* 1025 – *c.* 1050) did not transform Viking pirates into Norman knights; it was the base from which all the aggressive expansion undertaken by the eleventh-century Normans evolved.

Achievement

The evidence from later tenth-century 'Normandy' is firmly opposed to any extensive Norman participation in Viking-style activity. The steady demise of the Scandinavian language and the absence of any second phase of place-name formation resembling the English '-bys' are solid points against any reinvigoration of the original settlement through the immigration of fresh raiding-parties. The overwhelming preponderance of continental coins over those from the Scandinavian sea-routes in the massive Fécamp hoard is utterly against any heavy Norman involvement in either raiding or trade. Two English pennies in a collection of over 8,000 coins hardly indicate dynamic relations with the political and economic life of the northern seas. The coin hoards which have been found on Scandinavian routes and in Scandinavia itself confirm this conclusion. The treasure buried at Terslev (Denmark) in *c.* 960 contained a single Norman coin, a rare William Longsword piece, among 1,708 coins; that at Vaalse (Denmark) in *c.* 1000, 1 out of about 700.[1] From the western British Isles, the proportions are 3 out of 338 at Iona (*c.* 980) and 1 out of 34 in the substantially dispersed Inchkenneth hoard (*c.* 990–*c.* 1010). Small finds have been made in Ireland and a batch of four coins may have been part of a treasure from Tiree in the Western Isles of Scotland. Two Norman pennies were included among the 860 coins found at Halton Moor (Lancashire), and 21 in a nineteenth-century discovery of several hundred coins, most of which were English, at a place which was not recorded.[2] Another, undoubtedly early-eleventh-century and therefore later, dimension is provided by the single eleventh-century Norman penny found during the recent excavations at Winchester, and by a further 22 Norman coins of *c.* 1030 discovered on their own in isolation from any other pieces at Southampton.[3]

In the context of the general rarity of Frankish coins on Scandinavian routes, Norman coins and, to a lesser extent, those from the now lost site of Quentovic in Picardy, appear more regularly than the products of any other late-tenth-century French mint. But their quantity does not compare with the thousands of English, and also German, coins which occur in the same hoards and in Scandinavia itself. The vast disparity is one which can up to a point be explained by the attractions of the relative excellence, in comparison with the universally prevalent deterioration of the Frankish currencies, of the English money after Edgar's reform (973) and of the German coinages which followed the opening of the silver mines in the Harz mountains. Account must also be taken of the heavy Danegelds levied in England and taken back to Scandinavia.[4] In the end, however, the presence of a few Norman coins in the hoards in the western British Isles cannot be regarded as proving anything more than contacts which were irregular and essentially superficial. Given that the Fécamp hoard has now shown that Norman pennies were made in considerable quantities at Rouen in the late tenth century, their relatively infrequent occurrence in north-western Europe must show that ties with the Scandinavian world were slender.

'Normandy' in the concluding three or four decades of the tenth century should be thought of as an increasingly stable territorial principality which maintained only some connection with the mobile Scandinavian bands and with the other Scandinavian settlements. The likely course of events within tenth-century 'Normandy' is one of substantial Scandinavian colonisation in the first half of the century, followed by the organisation of a remarkably firm control by count Richard I. In its early stages this process of consolidation was upported by sympathetic Frankish rulers such as duke Hugh the Great and, probably less significantly, by the Scandinavian auxiliaries who intervened in the early 960s. An intensification of contacts between the Norman rulers and the Scandinavians probably went along with the revival of the latters' interest in western Europe from c. 980. But the relationship must have been essentially one which, at the same time that it made the province available as a supply base for the war-bands, did not threaten the good order which the count of Rouen had established. Paradoxically, given the Vikings' popular reputation for 'rape and pillage', events such as the campaign against count Odo of Blois-Chartres in 1013–14 suggest that the intervention of the Scandinavian warriors to an extent guaranteed the strength of Richard II's rule and the stable conditions within the duchy. They must also have contributed to the town of Rouen's exceptional prosperity at this time.

This general picture of 'Normandy's' development conforms closely to the opinions of Ralph Glaber, who wrote in the 1030s and 1040s, and who probably derived his information from William of Volpiano. Glaber noted the excellent qualities of the Norman rulers from William Longsword onwards, their friendship with many Frankish territorial princes, the peace which they maintained within their lands, and the way in which their alliance with men from overseas allowed them to reinforce their armies when threatened. As a result they were more feared by their neighbours than fearful of them.[5] A relationship of this kind would fully explain such things as the discovery of a late-tenth-century Viking axe in the province, the slurs on the 'Norman' character made by a writer like Richer of Rheims,

Achievement

or Richard II's ability to negotiate the release of hostages such as the *vicomtesse* of Limoges (see p. xvi).[6] It is ironical that the family most clearly associated with the earliest expeditions to southern Europe, the Tosnys, were men who had recently emigrated from 'France' to Normandy. If Roger de Tosny did engage in cannibalism during his campaign against the Moslems in Spain in *c*. 1020, he did not do so under the influence of any Viking blood in his veins, since this was non-existent.[7] The breakdown of Richard II's regime was eventually brought on by pressure on the Norman frontiers from within 'France' and by the arrival in the province of immigrants, most of whom were French. The end of the Scandinavian connection was signalled by Richard II's ambivalence towards Cnut's ambitions in England (see p. 37). The beginnings of a substantial exodus towards southern Europe resulted from the collapse of an order which these relations with the Scandinavian world had in some part upheld.

The eleventh-century Norman expansion should be seen as evolving out of the disturbances which engulfed the duchy from the 1020s onwards. The coin evidence may even suggest that Normans were already travelling southwards from the late tenth century; a single Norman penny appears in a miscellaneous hoard buried in *c*. 990 at Soleure in Switzerland, and three occur at Le Puy (998–1002).[8] The combined southern Italian and French sources do, however, indicate that the arrival of Normans in southern Italy in any numbers must be placed a year or two before 1020. They also show that they were not sufficiently strong to make any significant impact as an independent force before the early 1040s; this was pointed out long ago by Chalandon.[9] If the sources which purport to describe the origins of Norman immigration into southern Italy, namely the early sections of the histories of Amatus of Monte Cassino and William of Apulia, are dismissed, as they should be, as worthless legends, then the principal record is that supplied by Ralph Glaber.[10] Glaber describes an initial intervention against the Byzantine rulers of southern Italy by an exiled Norman named Ralph, which was encouraged by pope Benedict VIII, and which should be dated to *c*. 1020. This force was subsequently joined by another one despatched and organised by duke Richard II himself. It fought several actions against the Greeks which ended indecisively, so that Ralph eventually decided that his troops were too weakened to continue alone and so merged his efforts with those of the emperor Henry II. The brief, but independent, account by the Aquitanian chronicler Adhemar of Chabannes supports the general outline of Glaber's story, but takes the view that the Norman enterprise failed.[11] After this, we learn, principally from the late-eleventh- and early-twelfth-century writers, Leo of Ostia and, to a lesser extent, Amatus of Monte Cassino, that the remaining Normans took service with local potentates and participated in their wars.[12] An important moment for the extension of Norman interests must have been the establishment, sponsored by duke Sergius IV of Naples, of the colony at Aversa in *c.* 1030. The settlers, according to William of Apulia, immediately sought reinforcements from Normandy.[13] It was not, however, until the later 1030s that the disturbances caused by the Normans began to attract outside attention, to the extent that the German ruler Conrad II tried to make peace between them and the natives; this coincided with the time at which the eldest sons of Tancred de Hauteville are known to have arrived in the South.[14] The event which seems to have made the strongest impression on contemporaries was, however, the support which the Normans in Aversa gave to the Lombard Arduinus in 1040–41 in his rebellion against the Byzantines. This was the first action of the Normans to be mentioned in the brief but contemporary source, the annals of Bari.[15] It was also the real beginning of the Norman story for later writers such as William of Apulia, since it was followed by the territorial conquests made by Rainulf of Aversa and other Normans such as William 'Iron-Arm'. The above is a broad chronology – an organised expedition in Richard II's time which fizzled out, followed by a steady but haphazard migration – which fits neatly into the pattern of Normandy's history from *c.* 1020 to *c.* 1050.

The driving-force behind the conquest of southern Italy should be located in the effects of social changes which occurred throughout most of northern France. It is clear that the movement south was not the sole preserve of the inhabitants of Normandy, and that it had nothing to do with any specifically Norman characteristics. The evidence in eleventh-century northern French charters for departures to the South, which has been collected by Professor Musset, provides ten names, of which five are Norman, three are men from the region of Chartres, one is from Maine, and one from Anjou.[16] The Giroie, one of the best known of the immigrant families because they figure so largely in Ordericus' account, were scarcely Norman at all, having moved from Brittany to the southern confines of the duchy in the early years of the eleventh century. Their history, as well as their racial origin, shows clearly that in their case the decision to go south was not motivated by some innate Norman drive towards conquest, but by the pressure of immediate circumstances; Arnold d'Echauffour, for example, made a visit to southern Italy in the early 1060s during a period when he had been banished from Normandy; Robert

Achievement

Giroie, the son of Robert fitz Giroie who had died in 1060 while at war against duke William, settled in the South for a long time, but returned to the North in 1089 to claim the castle of Ballon in Maine from duke Robert Curthose.[17]

The eleventh-century evidence, taken along with Ordericus' narrative, demonstrates over and over again that those who travelled to southern Italy usually did so for specific reasons. These were often connected with political problems in Normandy itself and with the presence of family already established in the South; they frequently had nothing to do with either conquest or settlement. The charters are inevitably not very eloquent. Ralph fitz Avenie is known to have sold his alod at Billemont (Eure, cant. Routot, comm. La Haye-Aubrée) to Humphrey de Vieilles in *c.* 1040, at what the document describes as a high price, and to have gone to Apulia; the land lay to the south of the forest of Brotonne, a region in which Humphrey is known from other sources to have expanded his estates.[18] Herluin de Fierville, who left Normandy in the mid-eleventh century, was an important tenant of the originally non-Norman Taissons; he may have travelled to join a younger member of the Taisson family in the South.[19] The motives of the ducal vassal, Nigel fitz Constantin, who departed at about the same time, are unknown.[20] Finally, and more interestingly, there is Hugh the clerk, son of Olivier du Mêle-sur-Sarthe, who set out in 1094, and who made arrangements in case he wanted to return home.[21] Ordericus' history shows that one reason for journeying south was the prospect of gain; in retrospect, it is obvious that a journey to southern Italy could lead rapidly to both wealth and power. William de Montreuil, who went in *c.* 1050, and William de Grandmesnil, who left Normandy in *c.* 1080, reaped enormous rewards. The latter was even able to marry a daughter of Robert Guiscard. Both subsequently displayed their essentially opportunist attitudes by acts of treachery against the men who had made their fortunes.[22] But political difficulties and family connections frequently explain the decision of the Giroies and others to leave Normandy. A serious disagreement with duke William accounts for the departure of abbot Robert of Grandmesnil and the monks of St-Evroult who left the abbey in *c.* 1061; a complex mixture of family and political circumstances seems to lie behind the two trips made in 1077 and 1092 by William Pantulf, the first being in all likelihood on account of having fallen under suspicion of the murder of Mabel de Bellême, the second to collect a tooth of St Nicholas for the priory of Noron.[23] Grave political problems explain the journeys of Hugh Bunel, Mabel's actual murderer, and of William Werlenc, the former count of Mortain.[24] It is clear from Ordericus that a visit to southern Italy was an attractive prospect; the lure was such that it could even tempt nuns to renounce their vows and join members of their families.[25] It is also obvious, however, that many who travelled south later returned to Normandy. The evidence as a whole shows that, as in any age, men generally made long journeys because they were personally restless or because they believed that circumstances obliged them to do so.

The infiltration of southern Italy should therefore be seen as part of a wider demographic movement, which began in the later tenth century. A hundred years after, much of this type of far-flung endeavour was concentrated into the First Crusade. During the eleventh century, it resulted, not only in the establishment of the Norman principalities, but also in the participation of numerous warriors, mostly from central and south-western France, in wars against the Moslems in Spain, a migration which intensified from c. 1060. The earliest manifestation of this explosion in northern France can be found in the careers of soldiers of fortune, often from Brittany, who exploited the aspirations of the more ambitious territorial princes by offering their services in return for reward. The immigration into Normandy from the later years of Richard II's reign of families such as the Giroie and the Taisson was one small section of the whole. At this early date, the chief target appears to have been the lands of the most successful among the territorial princes, the counts of Anjou; some among those who took part were, like the Giroies later, political exiles from their own lands.[26] The dramatic phase of specifically Norman expansion began when the same type of territorial fragmentation and reorganisation of family structures, which lay behind the developments elsewhere, became pronounced within Norman society. The relative stability of the late tenth and early eleventh centuries broke down, and attempts by individual magnates to enlarge their lands within the duchy, by the dukes to extend their territory around its borders, and by some to make their fortunes in distant lands, followed.

The chronology of the settlement in southern Italy, together with what is known of the pattern of social change in eleventh-century northern France, suggests that the evolution of the Norman movement of expansion can be traced in a direct line through from the disintegration of the relative good order of Richard II's time to duke William II's harnessing of the forces of disruption into a policy of external aggression. There is therefore no need at all to become entangled in ideas such as Amatus of Monte Cassino's exotic theory of

Achievement

over-population or to think that the Normans possessed any remarkable or outstanding prowess in war or love of adventure.[27] Recruits for southern Italy were drawn from much of northern France. Their strength must indeed have been further increased in the South itself; a famous passage in the 'Deeds of Robert Guiscard' written by William of Apulia describes how the 'Normans' recruited 'Italians', taught them their language, and instructed them in their customs.[28] The list of participants provided by Ordericus Vitalis, to an extent reinforced by the charter evidence, would suggest that the main areas of emigration were in the extremely unstable regions in and beyond the southern marches of Normandy. The domination of Normans within the movement can probably be explained by the fact that the kinship ties which appear to have been so influential would inevitably work to reinforce the settlement made by the remnants of the force despatched in *c*. 1020. The severity of the breakdown of Norman society between *c*. 1025 and *c*. 1050 provided the conditions to encourage further heavy migration. The sheer size of the Norman principality – much larger than any other in northern France – must also have worked to ensure a preponderance of migrants from the duchy and, hence, the Norman control over the whole movement. The varied geographical origins of the participants would help to explain why so little that survives from the conquests in the South in the way of art and architecture is demonstrably 'Norman'.[29]

The view that the Norman expansion was part of a wider northern French movement requires the rejection of the specific notion that the Normans possessed a special and exceptional aptitude for war. This widely held opinion, an integral part of the 'Norman Myth', is illogical in the context of the essentially Frankish structure of Norman society and government, and untenable in the absence of any contemporary Norman reputation for martial prowess. It ought to disappear without trace. Dukes Richard I and Richard II have no outstanding military successes to their credit, while Robert I struggled to hold his own against neighbouring powers. It was only in the second half of the eleventh century, after the victories obtained in William II's largely defensive campaigns in the 1050s, that significant territorial gains started to be made. The battle of Hastings itself was not won by a force of superhuman military geniuses, practising previously unheard-of tactics; merely by a large army, drawing on men and expertise from much of northern France, and dominated by a core of Normans hardened by twenty years' accumulated experience of fighting under an extremely good general. Their methods were founded in the common techniques of contemporary northern French warfare. A recent study has drawn attention to the considerable resemblances between the formation described in the late-tenth-century account by Richer of Rheims of the battle of Montpensier (892) and the way in which duke William is supposed to have deployed his troops at Hastings. The author concludes from this and other evidence that William relied on well-tried methods in 1066 and that tactically he did not innovate.[30] Similarly, it has also been emphasised that, as far back as the late tenth century, armies like the Norman force of 1066 were being employed in the wars between the counts of Anjou and the counts of Blois-Chartres.[31] It is particularly interesting, in the light of what we know about the battle of Hastings, that the Breton tactics against count Fulk Nerra of Anjou at the battle of Conquereil in 992 included, according to Ralph Glaber, a feigned retreat which lured the Angevins into an ambush.[32] In the wider perspective of the Normans' supposed love of travel and adventure, it is worth noting the opinion of one early-twelfth-century Norman writer that the Jerusalem pilgrimage was rarely undertaken before the middle years of the eleventh century;[33] also, the statement by two of the more sober southern Italian writers, Leo of Ostia and William of Apulia, that the Normans who were granted lands by the abbot of Monte Cassino in the 1020s settled peacefully, and that in 1040–41 the Normans in Aversa had to be persuaded to fight by the Lombard Arduinus.[34]

It follows, too, that the ruthless methods of colonisation practised by the Normans in England after 1066 were not in their general character original ones. The castles at the centre of the *comtés* established at the limits of the duchy in Richard II's reign, and subsequent examples such as Cherrueix beyond the frontier with Brittany, show that the Norman rulers were familiar with the territorial potential of castles located and garrisoned with aggressive intent. Such practices had, however, obvious precedent in, for instance, the way in which Theobald I and Odo I, counts of Blois-Chartres, had fastened their grip on northern Berry in the second half of the tenth century through the eviction of the previous tenants, the establishment of castles, and the installation of groups of loyal vassals with no previous stake in the region.[35] Similar colonisation was also organised in a most purposeful manner by the counts of Anjou, Fulk Nerra and Geoffrey Martel, in their wars against the dukes of Aquitaine and in the occupation of the Touraine after 1044.[36] It was also in this Loire valley region that the important developments in the construction of fortifications in stone, the evolution from the former Carolingian palace at Doué-la-Fontaine to the great *donjons* such as Langeais and

Achievement

Montbazon built for count Fulk Nerra, have been located by Professor Pierre Héliot. This same study comments that the Norman contribution to this type of architecture was 'negligible, if not nil'.[37] The recent, exhaustive, excavations at the ducal palaces at Fécamp and Caen have shown that these were magnificent buildings intended as demonstrations of political power. Their development testifies to the egocentricity of the individual dukes, since Fécamp was vastly extended in Richard II's reign and Caen was built virtually in its entirety for William II. But their style, a large enclosure, encircled by a stone curtain-wall, containing a hall and numerous other buildings, had little about it that had not been anticipated in other northern French princely residences.[38] It looks as if the great keeps built in conquered England, like Colchester, or the White Tower of London, were, like Fulk Nerra's *donjons*, the result of specific circumstances stimulating architectural and technological advance.

What did set eleventh-century Normandy apart from other territorial principalities was the depth of the continuity of a Carolingian institutional structure and the level of co-operation achieved between duke and aristocracy in the years immediately before 1066. Although the origins of this overall political coherence and institutional strength lie in the conditions created during the settlement period in the first half of the tenth century, their preservation through to 1066 resulted from the success of the governments of Richard I and Richard II and, above all, from the remarkable political achievement of duke William II. The great strength of ducal authority in Normandy owed much to the landed resources acquired by the first counts of Rouen and to the fact that a rupture occurred in the personnel of the ruling classes in 'Normandy' during the early tenth century, which did not happen in neighbouring regions. But the force which moulded the potential strength deriving from this institutional continuity into effective political power was William II's personal skill and authority. The sheer size and the varied composition of the army which crossed the Channel in September 1066 is a massive tribute to William's prestige and to what must have been a widespread belief in the likelihood of victory, the force not only contained representatives of most of the families who had benefited from the disorders of the second quarter of the century, but also men from a very wide area of northern France. By 1066, too, William's regime was in the process of creating the conditions in which were to evolve and flourish what can in retrospect be identified as the exceptional features of Norman society: the well-marked frontier, the clear definition of a Norman as someone who resided in the duchy, the authoritarian feudal institutions, the unity and near-autonomy of the ecclesiastical province of Rouen, the Norman 'school' of Romanesque architecture, and so on. If Norman military expansion must now be seen as evolving out of the military ethos which was general throughout the aristocracy of northern France, out of the sheer violence of social conditions, and out of a widely prevalent pattern of social change; then, another supposedly innate Norman characteristic, the capacity to organise their conquests, must be regarded as the product of long experience of living in the best organised and most stable of the northern French territorial principalities. It is surely one of the stranger among historical paradoxes that a settlement of parasitical, heathen pirates in the first half of the tenth century should have produced, in the second half of the eleventh, a remarkably centralised political community and a notably successful Church.

The postscript to the history of Normandy before 1066, the period from the conquest of England until William II's death in 1087, ought to have been a 'golden age' in the history of ducal Normandy. On the surface, there is much to justify this view. Few doubts are likely to be entertained, for example, by anyone who has visited William's castle and monastic foundation at Caen. It can reasonably be claimed that one effect of the conquest of England was to reinforce still further ducal authority in Normandy.[39] Government and administration certainly continued to evolve. William's peace legislation has evoked the comment – admittedly in an early work – from the most distinguished modern authority on the duchy's legal institutions, that 'by the Conqueror's death, Normandy was several centuries ahead of the rest of France'.[40] In the context of their time, the canons of the council of Lillebonne are a remarkably sophisticated text. The political relationship of duke and aristocracy developed further; it is not always appreciated how far the post-1066 government of Normandy relied on delegation, and notably on the consistent work of Roger de Beaumont in the ducal courts (see Ch. 4, note 112). Administration, too, began to be influenced by the more highly developed techniques of the Anglo-Saxon chancery, although it must be said that the known attempts to prepare charters for sealing are little more than the ham-fisted blunderings of beginners.[41] Yet, for all these signs of development, it cannot be denied that at a political level the flaws in duke William's regime were becoming obvious by the later years of his reign. By the time of his death in 1087, much that the duke and his associates had built up before 1066 was starting to crumble.

The immediate aftermath of the conquest of England was a trium-

Achievement

phal progress down the Seine valley in the first nine months of 1067. But the subjugation of the kingdom came to require extensive campaigning, mostly in the North, which continued into the early 1070s. At the same time, the balance of power in northern France shifted against the Normans. The Capetian king Philip I, on reaching manhood, proved to be a formidable opponent, until weakened in his later years by an excessive partiality for food and slumber. After 1068, Angevin fortunes also revived under the physically repellent count Fulk Rechin. Flanders, after Robert the Frisian's *coup d'état* in 1071, became a hostile power. William's preoccupation with northern England meant that the Norman grip on Maine steadily loosened between 1069 and 1072, to the benefit first of all of Geoffrey de Mayenne, and then to that of count Fulk Rechin. Although William successfully recaptured Le Mans in 1073, the count of Anjou was again able to penetrate Maine in 1077 and 1081. The appointment of a Norman client to the bishopric of Le Mans in 1081 was accomplished only with sympathetic support from pope Gregory VII. In 1085, a local revolt in Maine, which centred on the castle of Ste-Suzanne, proved hard to dislodge. On the Breton frontier, some of the security which derived from a local clientele disintegrated, when, in 1076, William failed to capture the castle of Dol, held against him by the nominal count of Brittany, Hoel, count of Cornouailles, and by the rebel Ralph de Gael, sometime earl of Norfolk. In 1077, the retirement of Simon de Crépy, count of Amiens-Valois-Vexin, allowed Philip I to assert his personal lordship over the French Vexin and from there to launch cross-border raids into Normandy during William's last years. In 1079 William suffered what William of Malmesbury described as the greatest humiliation of his career when he was defeated, and almost killed, in an engagement against his own son Robert, who had been installed in the castle of Gerberoi in the Beauvaisis by king Philip. Between 1066 and 1087 the menace of invasions, such as those of the 1050s, had subsided. But the dominant impression obtained from events after 1066 is that duke William remained mostly on the defensive.

The war against Robert Curthose represents a further strand of disintegration; namely, the quarrels within the royal/ducal family and within the upper reaches of the aristocracy. Robert's first open breach with his father took place in 1077–79; his second began in the later months of 1083 and was still smouldering in 1087, when he was summoned back to Normandy as his father was dying. The cause of contention, so Ordericus informs us, was Robert's demand that real authority be made over to him in Normandy and Maine.[42] Historians of the Anglo-Norman realm have generally been too ready to condemn Robert as a disobedient son who should have bent before his father's will, thereby missing the point that Robert, whatever his deficiencies of character, represents a common eleventh-century type, the wilful heir, anxious to acquire power and sometimes capable of taking it. Geoffrey Martel's defiance of Fulk Nerra in the 1030s, count Baldwin V's of count Baldwin IV at the same period, and Louis VI's assumption of responsibilities in the late eleventh century from a prematurely senile Philip I, are all cases to the point. Robert had been assigned Normandy before 1066, may have exercised some sort of authority there in the immediate post-Conquest years, and could only watch as some among his young contemporaries received a share in their fathers' estates.[43] These quarrels can be associated with a weakening of the unity of the ducal family; Mathilda is said to have supported her son against her husband, while in 1082, for reasons which are obscure, bishop Odo of Bayeux prepared to desert and was arrested and imprisoned by his half-brother. The revolts attracted support among the children of some of duke William's closest associates, such as Robert de Bellême, the son of Roger de Montgommery, a clear indication of the extent to which William's security and Normandy's peace depended on the personal ties between a small number of men.

Duke William II died at Rouen on 9 September 1087 and was buried in the abbey he had built at Caen. The circumstances in which the fatal injury, an intestinal rupture consequent on a fall from a horse, was sustained – in the course of a retaliatory raid into the French Vexin – indicate the constant vigilance and energetic activity which effective rule demanded from someone approaching sixty years of age. The humiliating events at his burial, with a local landowner haggling for payment for the ground before the high altar of St-Etienne in which the duke was to be laid to rest, and with the too corpulent body refusing to fit into the tomb, might prompt reflection on the transient nature of all wordly power. What followed were certainly the signs of the disintegration of a regime, of a relaxation on the transient nature of all worldly power. What followed source of authority had been removed. The career after 1087 of Roger de Montgommery's son, Robert de Bellême, including, for example, his claim to have a hereditary right to the bishopric of Sées and the extraction of Bellême from the Norman orbit of authority, shows the impermanence of the duke of Normandy's power in this always difficult region. Within Normandy, the renewed proliferation of 'private' castles, the assertion of patrimonial rights over monasteries, the intrusion of direct papal jurisdiction, and even the assumption of the right to mint money by some of the *vicomtes*,[44] indicate that the tight control which William had exercised was in danger of falling to pieces. The historian of eleventh-century Normandy also does well to ponder the opinion that Gerald of Wales attributed to Henry II's justiciar, Rannulf de Glanville, which was that Normandy rose to greatness when 'France' was weak.[45] This idea, formulated as the independent duchy was sliding towards the terminal disasters of 1203–04, contains an important grain of truth. It also reflects the fact that, despite his immense achievements in governing Normandy and conquering England, even William II had not been able to detach the duchy from the political framework which was eventually to be turned into feudal dependence on the French king.

A final estimate of the Norman achievement within Normandy must take account of all these weaknesses. Yet it should also bear in mind that Henry I, between 1106 and 1135, restored peace and stable government to Normandy. Recent work is emphasising the extent to which his reign should be seen as re-establishing the political relationships between king-duke and aristocracy along lines very like those which had existed in his father William II's time.[46] In the broader span of time, in which 'empires' rise and fall, the Norman achievement was long-lasting and in many respects splendid. The efforts of the tenth- and eleventh-century Norman rulers gave to the inhabitants of the place which came to be known as Normandy their clear identity as a separate people and provided the province with a political and governmental organisation and coherence unparalleled in the other French territorial principalities. The successful conquests of southern Italy and England provided the bases for two very different kinds of political achievement, both of which reached their fulfilment in the twelfth century. It was the mixture of eleventh-century successes and the twelfth-century view of the past which formed the 'Norman Myth'. It is surely proper that the achievements of the eleventh-century Normans should be celebrated in legend by their twelfth-century descendants. They built well and, from the foundations of the pre-1066 principality, achieved notable military and political success. Their history requires, and deserves, some reassessment.

NOTES

1. See, in general, J. Lafaurie, 'Le trésor monétaire du Puy (Haute-Loire). Contribution à l'étude de la monnaie de la fin du Xe siècle', *Revue numismatique*, xiv (1952), 93–6, 109–19; Françoise Dumas-Dubourg, *Le trésor de Fécamp et le monnayage en Francie occidentale pendant la seconde moitié du Xe siècle* (Paris, 1971), 55–60; L. Musset, 'Les relations extérieures de la Normandie du IXe au XIe siècle, d'après quelques trouvailles monétaires récentes', *AN*, iv (1954), 32, 35.
2. In general, M. Dolley and K. F. Morrison, 'Finds of Carolingian coins from Great Britain and Ireland', *British Numismatic Journal*, xxxii (1963), 83–5; Dumas–Dubourg, *Le trésor de Fécamp*, 59, note 1. See also, M. Dolley, 'The Continental coins in the Halton Moor find and other Norman *deniers* found in the British Isles', *Hamburger Beiträge für Numismatik* (1958–59), 53–7; R. B. K. Stevenson, *Sylloge of Coins of the British Isles. VI. National Museum of Antiquities of Scotland* (London, 1966), xiv–xv, xxiii, plate XXIX.
3. M. Dolley and C. E. Blunt, 'Coins from the Winchester excavations 1961–1973', *British Numismatic Journal*, xlvii (1977), 138; M. Dolley, 'The coins and jettons', in *Excavations at Medieval Southampton 1953–1969*, ed. C. Platt et al. (Leicester, 1975), ii, 326–8.
4. K. Skaare, *Coins and Coinage in Viking-Age Norway* (Oslo, Bergen, and Tromsö, 1976), 54–7. I am grateful to Professor H. R. Loyn for bringing this book to my attention.
5. *Raoul Glaber, Les cinq livres de ses histoires (990–1044)*, ed. M. Prou (Paris, 1886), 19–20, 29–30.
6. *Adhémar de Chabannes, Chronique*, ed. J. Chavanon (Paris, 1897), 167.
7. *Ibid.*, 178.
8. Lafaurie, 'Le trésor monétaire du Puy', 122.
9. F. Chalandon, *Histoire de la domination normande en Italie et en Sicile* (Paris, 1907), i, 76, 104–5.
10. *Raoul Glaber*, 52–5. See, on the fabulous nature of later accounts of the Normans' arrival, E. Joranson, 'The inception of the career of the Normans in Italy – legend and history', *Speculum*, xxiii (1948), 364–70; R. H. C. Davis, *The Normans and Their Myth* (London, 1976), 88–92; OV, ii, pp. xxx–xxxi. To these should now be added, G. A. Loud, 'How "Norman" was the Norman Conquest of Southern Italy?', *Nottingham Medieval Studies*, xxv (1981), forthcoming. This article explores in greater depth some of the suggestions made here. I am grateful to Dr. Loud for giving me a typescript of his article.
11. *Adhémar de Chabannes, Chronique*, 178.
12. See mainly, Leo of Ostia, *Chronicon Monasterii Casinensis*, in *MGH, Scriptores*, vii, 653; Chalandon, *Domination normande*, i, 57–76.
13. *Guillaume de Pouille: La geste de Robert Guiscard*, ed. Marguerite Mathieu (Palermo, 1961), 108, lines 180–7.
14. Wipo, *Gesta Chuonradi Imperatoris*, in *MGH, Scriptores*, xi, 273.
15. *Annales Barenses*, in *MGH, Scriptores*, v, 54–5. For a similar pattern, see the *Annales Beneventani* and *Annales Cavenses*, as well as the continuation of the annals of Bari attributed to Lupus Protospatarius, *ibid.*, iii, 178–9, 189; v, 57–8.

16. L. Musset, 'Actes inédits du XIe siècle. V. Autour des origines de St-Etienne de Fontenay', *BSAN*, lvi (1963, for 1961–62), 29–31.
17. OV, ii, 122; iv, 154.
18. *Neustria Pia*, ed. A. du Monstier (Rouen, 1663), 521. See p. 100.
19. Musset, 'Fontenay', 29, 39.
20. *Recueil*, no. 224.
21. . . . *donavit et in perpetuum, solute ac quiete dimisit, si ab Apulia non rediret,* . . ., Cartulaire de St-Martin de Sées, fo. 51v (see chapter 2, note 92).
22. OV, ii, 58; iv, 16, 338.
23. *Ibid.*, iii, 160; iv, 72.
24. *Ibid.*, v, 156–8; WJ, 172.
25. OV, ii, 102.
26. A. Chédeville, 'L'immigration bretonne dans le royaume de France du XIe au début du XIVe siècle', *Annales de Bretagne*, lxxxi (1974), 315–21.
27. *Storia de' Normanni di Amato di Montecassino*, ed. V. de Bartholomeis (Rome, 1935), 10.
28. *Guillaume de Pouille*, 108, lines 165–9.
29. Davis, *Normans and Their Myth*, 82–6, 93–100.
30. J. France, 'La guerre dans la France féodale à la fin du IXe et au Xe siècle', *Revue belge d'histoire militaire*, xxiii (1979), 195–6, and, in general, 185–96. I am grateful to Dr France for an illuminating and extremely helpful discussion of this and related problems. It is worth noting also that the book of which Dr France's article is critical makes no mention of any special Norman contribution to the development of warfare, J. F. Verbruggen, *The Art of Warfare in Western Europe during the Middle Ages*, trans. S. Willard and S. C. M. Southern (Amsterdam, New York, and Oxford, 1977), *passim*.
31. J. Boussard, 'Services féodaux, milices et mercenaires dans les armées, en France, aux Xe et XIe siècles', *Settimane di Centro Italiano*, xv (1968), 148–51, 158–63.
32. Raoul Glaber, 30–2.
33. 'Miracula Ecclesiae Constantiensis', in E. A. Pigeon, *Histoire de la cathédrale de Coutances* (Coutances, 1876), 376.
34. *Chronicon Monasterii Casinensis*, in *MGH, Scriptores*, vii, 653; *Guillaume de Pouille*, 110–12.
35. G. Devailly, *Le Berry du Xe siècle au milieu du XIIIe siècle* (Paris, 1973), 133–4.
36. J. Boussard, 'L'éviction des tenants de Thibaud de Blois par Geoffrey Martel comte d'Anjou en 1044', *Le Moyen Age*, lxix (1963), 141–9. See also, B. S. Bachrach, 'A study in feudal politics: relations between Fulk Nerra and William the Great, 995–1030', *Viator*, vii (1976), 111–21.
37. P. Héliot, 'Les origines du donjon résidentiel et des donjons-palais romans de France et d'Angleterre', *CCM*, xvii (1974), 229–32. See also, R. Allen Brown, 'The Norman Conquest and the genesis of English castles', *Château Gaillard*, iii (1966), 12–14.
38. Annie Renoux, 'Le château des ducs de Normandie à Fécamp. Quelques données archéologiques et topographiques', *Arch. méd.*, ix (1979), 17–19; M. de Bouard, *Le château de Caen* (Caen, 1979), 10–11.
39. D. C. Douglas, *William the Conqueror* (London, 1964), 283–4.
40. J. Yver, 'L'interdiction de la guerre privée dans le très ancien droit nor-

mand', in *Travaux de la semaine du droit normand tenue à Guernesey du 26 au 30 Mai 1927* (Caen, 1928), 323.

41. For early attempts at sealing, P. Chaplais, 'Une charte originale de Guillaume le Conquérant pour l'abbaye de Fécamp: la donation de Steyning et de Bury (1085)', in *L'abbaye bénédictine de Fécamp* i (Fécamp, 1959), 93–104, 355–7. See also, A. D. Calvados, H. 1830, no. 1 (*AAC* no. 4), H. 1832. A supposed original charter of king William for St-Ouen of Rouen, which has arrangements for sealing by parchment tag, is a mid-12th-century rescript, A. D. Seine-Maritime, 14H, 331.
42. See, C. W. David, *Robert Curthose, Duke Of Normandy* (Harvard University Press, 1920), 17–41; (1980), R. H. C. Davis, 'William of Jumièges, Robert Curthose and the Norman Succession', *EHR, scv* (1980), 597–606.
43. The obvious examples are Robert de Bellême and, in all likelihood, his younger brother Roger 'of Poitou'; also the two sons of Roger de Beaumont.
44. Françoise Dumas, 'Les monnaies normandes du Xe-XIIe siècle', *Bulletin de la société française de numismatique* (1978), 390.
45. 'De principis instructione liber', in *Giraldi Cambrensis Opera*, viii, ed. G. F. Warner (Rolls Series, 1891), 257–8.
46. See especially, C. W. Hollister, 'Henry I and the Anglo-Norman magnates', in *Proceedings of the Battle Conference,* ii (1979), 93–107.

APPENDIX A
The dates of William II's campaigns against Geoffrey Martel, 1048–52

The latest attempt to date these campaigns has been made by Olivier Guillot, who has resurrected the broad lines of the older chronology, proposed by Louis Halphen, against the amendments suggested by Professor David Douglas.[1] Guillot argues that Geoffrey Martel must have taken the castles of Alençon and Domfront in 1048–49, that duke William's expedition against the two castles took place in 1049, and that the duke then joined a large royal army which besieged and captured the castle of Mouliherne, near Angers, in late 1049. Douglas, however, had dated the siege of Mouliherne to 1051, and Geoffrey Martel's capture of the two castles and William's reaction to 1051–52. Any attempt to date these events rests on the extremely fragile basis of William of Poitiers' narrative.

It seems to me that Douglas is too dismissive of the, admittedly allusive, reference by Anselm, a monk of St-Rémi of Rheims, to a general expedition of the kingdom under Henry I's command which was being prepared at the time of the council of Rheims (September 1049): 'quibusdam viris potentibus dominationis ejus jugum detrectantibus, terrasque et castella quaelibet ab ipsius ditione abalienantibus. Quapropter regiae dignitati ferunt conguere utilitati reipublicae sua sapientia consulere potius quam synodis intendere; principes suos et totius exercitus sui potentiam commovere in rebelles, . . .'[2] This must refer to the Mouliherne campaign, in which Henry I, duke William, and Theobald III, count of Blois-Chartres, are known to have taken part.[3] The siege of Mouliherne should, therefore, be dated to late 1049.[4]

Guillot's suggested dating of William's campaign against Alençon and Domfront does not, however, overcome all of Douglas' arguments for 1051–52. Guillot reasonably points out that the filched castles mentioned by the monk Anselm could well have been Alençon and Domfront, especially since their likely owners, the Bellême family, were essentially royal vassals at this stage. On the other hand, it could be that Geoffrey only seized the castles after he had acquired a firm grip in Maine, that is, in or after 1051. From here, much depends on the interpretations placed on William of Poitiers' vague phrasing. Guillot is impressed by the statement that Geoffrey Martel had become complacent at the time of the Alençon–Domfront campaign because he had never suffered a military reverse. This, taken literally, would place the war before the Mouliherne campaign, in which Geoffrey was also worsted.[5] But Poitiers also remarks that Normandy was at peace when William moved against Alençon and Domfront. Douglas' argument that this must place the campaign after the fall of Brionne also seems to place too strict a meaning on some loose phraseology: the evidence for a three-year siege of Brionne (1047–50) is both late and ambiguous; it is in any case inconceivable that William would have spent three years staring at the ramparts of Brionne, so his departure to fight Geoffrey is not inconceivable.[6] But Douglas' point that Poitiers specifically assigns count William of Arques' defection to the siege of Domfront is harder to dismiss.[7] Count William attests surviving ducal charters up until 1051.[8] Guillot, relying on count William's attestation of another ducal charter, dated 1053, rejects this argument. Here his logic is seriously flawed. The document concerned, a grant to the abbey of St-Julien of Tours, exists only in a mediocre eighteenth-century copy by Roger de Gaignières, and has a blatantly suspect witness-list, including the name, of all people, of count Guy of Brionne. This very same witness-list appears, with equal improbability, at the foot of another St-Julien charter, copied by Gaignières, and dated 1059.[9] On balance, the evidence favours 1051–52 for the campaign. Among Poitiers' three vague phrases, only that concerning William of Arques supplies a hard fact; one which is to an extent confirmed by charter evidence. For this reason, I have placed the Mouliherne campaign in late 1049 and the Alençon–Domfront expedition in 1051–52. But it would be very unwise to make categorical assertions on such flimsy material. The suggestion that Poitiers treated his material selectively and telescoped several campaigns has merit.[10]

Appendix A

NOTES

1. O. Guillot, *Le comte d'Anjou et son entourage au XIe siècle* (Paris, 1972), i, 69–72; D. C. Douglas, *William the Conqueror* (London, 1964), 383–90.
2. Anselm, *Historia dedicationis ecclesiae sancti Remigii*, in *RHF*, xi, 465.
3. WP, 22–6.
4. This dating is also accepted by M. Bur, *La formation du comté de Champagne, v. 950–v. 1150* (Nancy, 1977), 200.
5. WP, 34.
6. *Ibid.*, 32; see. p. 75 and Chapter 2, note 78
7. WP, 52.
8. *Recueil*, nos. 124–6.
9. *Ibid.*, nos. 131, 142.
10. OV, ii, 365.

APPENDIX B
Two supposed 'feudal' documents of William II's Reign

It has been argued above that Haskins placed the appearance of clearly defined institutions of lordship and vassalage at too early a date in the duchy's history. An important part of his case rested on two documents, one a charter from the archives of the convent of St-Amand of Rouen datable only to 1066–87, the other a report of an agreement made before queen Mathilda at Bayeux between William Paganel and the abbey of Mont-St-Michel. Both were so vital to Haskins' thesis that he printed them in full.[1] From them he argued that the limit of forty days on a vassal's service, the distinction between full equipment and 'plain arms', and the types of aid due to a lord, all basic features of twelfth-century lord-vassal relations, otherwise unrecorded before the 1133 Bayeux inquest, were known in the duchy shortly after 1066.

It is suggested here that neither of these documents can be trusted as an accurate guide to eleventh-century conditions. Their manuscript traditions are insufficiently sound to be convincing and the fact that they employ terminology which is normally associated with the twelfth century indicates that they are at best texts heavily rewritten at that time. The St-Amand act survives only in a late confirmation of early St-Amand charters by king Philip IV dated 1313.[2] Its text is somewhat corrupt. In addition to the doubtful terminology, other aspects are suspicious; phrases like *clamo... quietum* and *de feudo Bascheville* are highly unusual in eleventh-century documents, as is the identification of the money by its mint (*xxx libras Rodesinorum*); finally, the clause relating to *totis armis*, etc. placed after the witnesses, has all the appearances of a later addition. The Mont-St-Michel report is known from the mid-twelfth-century cartulary of the abbey, a crucial source for early Norman history, but one notorious for the

Appendix B

many interpolations contained in otherwise authentic documents.[3] It uses freely terms such as *curia* and *revelatio* which were just becoming current in Normandy in the later eleventh century. Language such as *de septem paribus de honore* is, however, utterly unacceptable in an eleventh-century record. The use of the term *parage* in what seems to be a technical sense otherwise unknown in Normandy before the middle of the twelfth century is also very suspicious (*similiter faciet si in parage terram suam tenuerit*); the phrase *in paragio* is greatly used in the Domesday accounts for Hampshire, Dorset, and Somerset, but it is not clear that it had any meaning more technical than 'joint tenure by co-heirs', the sense which seems to have been implied in the rare eleventh-century use of the term in the lands to the south of Normandy.[4]

NOTES

1. C. H. Haskins, *Norman Institutions* (Cambridge, Mass, 1918), 20–2. For other comments, see pp. 168–9.
2. The original of this confirmation survives, A. D. Seine-Maritime, 55 H, fonds de St-Amand de Rouen, non classé. Its text is substantially reproduced by M. -J. Le Cacheux, 'Histoire de l'abbaye de St-Amand de Rouen', *BSAN*, xliv (1936), 244–53, as textual variations to the abbey's late-eleventh-century *pancarte*. Haskins' anxieties about the reading of the important word *plainas* are removed by references to the register copy, Archives nationales, JJ 49, fo. 26r, no. 46.
3. Avranches, Bibliothèque municipale, MS. 210, fos. 95r–96v.
4. See, in general, J. C. Holt, 'Politics and property in early medieval England', *Past and Present*, no. 57 (1972), 44–5. The early example from 1070–81 whose discovery Professor Holt attributes to H. Navel is in fact the text printed by Haskins. See also, H. Legohérel, 'Le parage en Touraine-Anjou au moyen age', *RHDFE*, 4e série, xliii (1965), 222–34; see p. 127.

APPENDIX C
A list of Norman archdeacons to c. 1080

The purpose of this list is to illustrate the development of the Norman Church up to and beyond 1066, with particular reference to the time of rapid growth in the 1060s and 1070s. Although it is intended to be complete for the period under consideration, it cannot always be taken as a comprehensive guide to an individual's career. Thus, for example, Goscelin of Bayeux lived on into at least the 1090s and Benedict of Rouen into the first decade of the twelfth century. Also, few details of a biographical nature are given, although some among those listed could be so treated; William de Rots, for instance, became a distinguished abbot of Fécamp in 1079, while the second Fulbert of Rouen is among the candidates to be the Norman Anonymous.

Rouen[1]
1. Wascelin — Before 1028[2]
2. Baldwin — Before 1028[2]
3. Hugh — 1037–c. 1045[3], 1037–54[4], 1046–47/48[5], 1050–54[6], 1053[7], 1055[8]
4. William 'Bona Anima' — 1054–c. 1057[9]
5. Fulbert[10] — 1046–47/48[5], 1068–79[11], 1084[12]
6. Gother — 1051–77[13], 1070[14], c. 1070[15]
7. Benedict — 1054–67[16], 1075[17], 1079[18], 1084[12]
8. Robert — 1066–83[19], 1070[14], c. 1070[15]
9. Ursel — 1068–79[11]
10. 'Gothenus'/Goscelin — c. 1070[15], 1075[17]
11. Fulk — c. 1070[15]
12. Osmund — 1079[18]
13. Bernard fitz Ospac — c. 1080[20]

Avranches
No references.

Bayeux

1. (?) Richard — 1066[21]
2. William de Rots — 1068–70[22], before 1078[23]
3. Goscelin — 1068–70[22], c. 1075–82[24]
4. Bernard — c. 1075–82[24]
5. Ralph — c. 1075–82[24]
6. Samson — c. 1080[20]

Coutances

1. Norman — 1066–87 (c. 1080?)[25], c. 1080[20]
2. Ralph — c. 1080[20]

Evreux

1. Robert — c. 1070 (?)[26]

Lisieux

1. Osbern — c. 1050[27]
2. Gilbert — 1066[28]
3. William of Poitiers — 1060s and 1070s[29]
4. Richard de Angerville — c. 1077[30]

Sées

1. Baldwin fitz 'Etvald' — 1041–57[31]
2. Roger de Mortagne — 1041–57[31]
3. Lambert de Bellême — 1041–57[31]
4. Hermer — 1041–57[31]
5. Fulcoin — 1041–57[31]
6. Odo — 1050–64[32], before 1064[33]
7. Norman — 1056–60[34], 1072–82[35]
8. Baldwin — 1072–82[35]

NOTES

1. The list in Anne Brinkworth. 'The archbishops of Rouen, 1037–1110' (University of Bristol M. Litt. Thesis, 1966), 342–4, is extremely helpful for Rouen.
2. *Cartulaire de St-Père de Chartres*, ed. B. E. C. Guérard (Paris, 1840), i, 116.
3. *Recueil*, no. 103.
4. *Cartulaire de St-Père de Chartres*, i. 176.
5. *Recueil*, no. 107.
6. *Neustria Pia*, ed. A. du Monstier (Rouen, 1663), 521.
7. 'Inventio et Miracula sancti Wulfranni', ed. Dom J. Laporte, *SHN, Mélanges*, xiv (1938), 58–9.
8. *Recueil*, no. 137.
9. OV, ii, 254. William was archbishop from 1080 to 1110.
10. References to an archdeacon named Fulbert occur from 1046–47/48 to

c. 1126 (OV, iv, 310). They must represent more than one man, but since they are almost continuous, it is hard to break them down. The first Fulbert may well have died in the late 1060s or early 1070s, since the name is uncommon in the relatively plentiful charters of the 1070s. For this first Fulbert as *sophista consiliarius* to Maurilius and *cancellarius*, OV, ii, 66; *Cartulaire de St-Père de Chartres*, i, 176.
11. M. -J. Le Cacheux, 'Histoire de l'abbaye de St-Amand de Rouen', *BSAN*, xliv (1936), 251, note 123. This reference only occurs in the Philip IV *vidimus*, see p. 258.
12. *Chartes de l'abbaye de Jumièges (v. 825 à 1204) conservées aux archives de la Seine-Inférieure,* ed. J. J. Vernier (Rouen and Paris, 1916), i, no. 33.
13. *CTR*, no. 45.
14. BN, collection Baluze, vol. 77, fo. 48r.
15. BN, MS. latin 12878, fo. 232v.
16. *Cartulaire de St-Père de Chartres*, i. 177.
17. BN, n.a.lat., MS. 1243, fo. 161r.
18. *Chartes de Jumièges*, i, no. 32.
19. A. D. Seine-Maritime, 14 H, 327.
20. L. Delisle, *Histoire du château et des sires de Saint-Sauveur-le-Vicomte* (Valognes, 1867), pièces-justificatives, no. 42 (*Regesta*, i, no. 132).
21. *Recueil*, no. 227. For a possible mention, *Rouleaux des morts du IXe au XVe siècle*, ed. L. Delisle (Paris, 1886), 185.
22. P. Le Cacheux, 'Une charte de Jumièges concernant l'épreuve par le fer chaud (fin du XIe siècle)', *SHN, Mélanges*, xi (1929), 214.
23. OV, ii, 150.
24. A. D. Seine-Maritime, 14 H, 160.
25. *Musée des archives départementales* (Paris, 1878), planche XVIII. For this Norman, also 'Miracula Ecclesiae Constantiensis', in E. A. Pigeon, *Histoire de la cathédrale de Coutances* (Coutances, 1876), 377.
26. *Chartes de Jumièges*, i, no. 40.
27. OV, ii, 18.
28. OV, ii, 142, 254.
29. OV, ii, 258; iii, 20.
30. OV, iii, 20.
31. *Cartulaire de l'abbaye de St-Vincent du Mans*, ed. R. Charles and M. le vicomte d'Elbenne (Le Mans, 1913), no. 545; O. Guillot, *Le comte d'Anjou et son entourage au XIe siècle* (Paris, 1972), ii, C268. For the terminal date above, pp. 79–80.
32. *Cartulaire de Marmoutier pour le Perche*, ed. l'abbé Barret (Mortagne, 1894), no. 5.
33. A. D. Orne, H. 2561.
34. Cartulaire de St-Martin de Sées, fo. 4r (see chapter 2, note 92).
35. *Cartulaire de Marmoutier pour le Perche*, no. 12.

Maps

Normandy before 1066

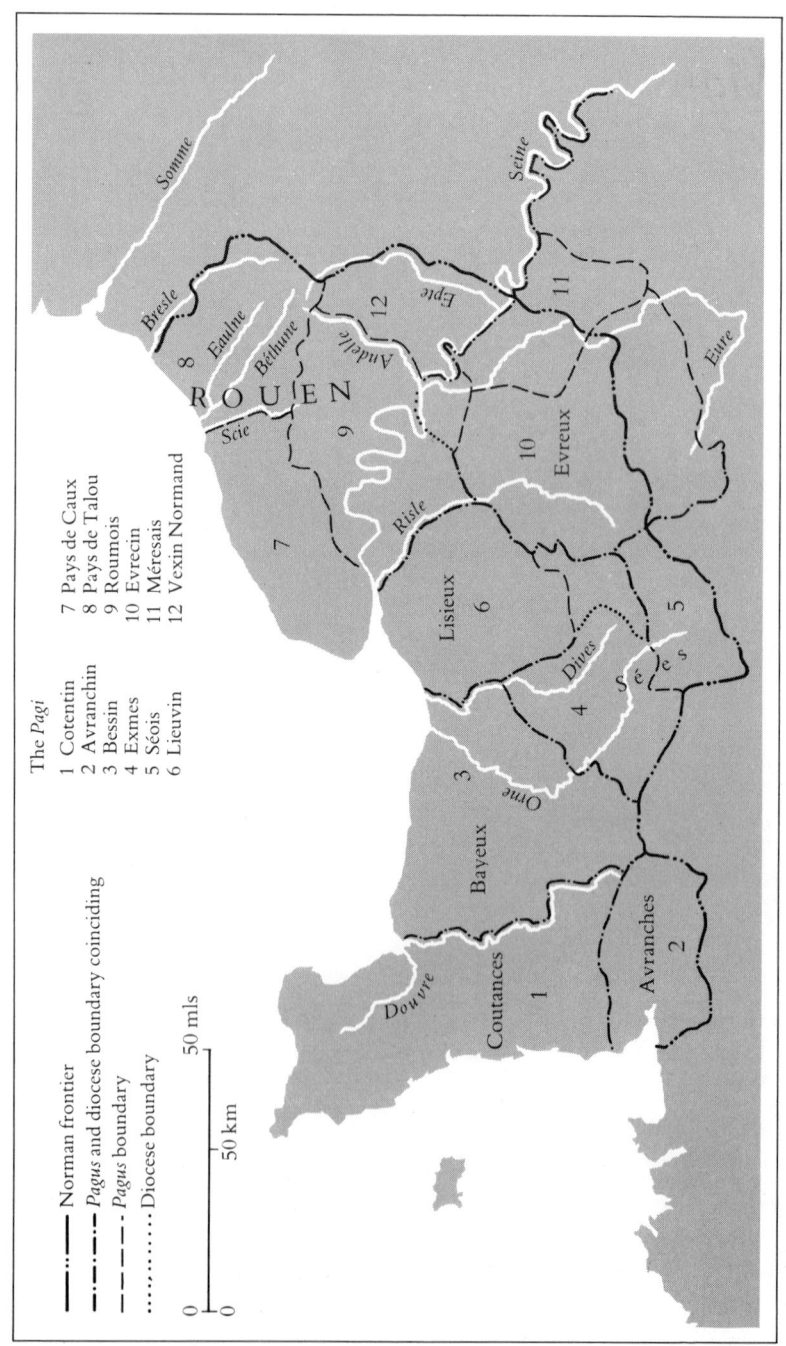

Map 1. *Pagi* and dioceses

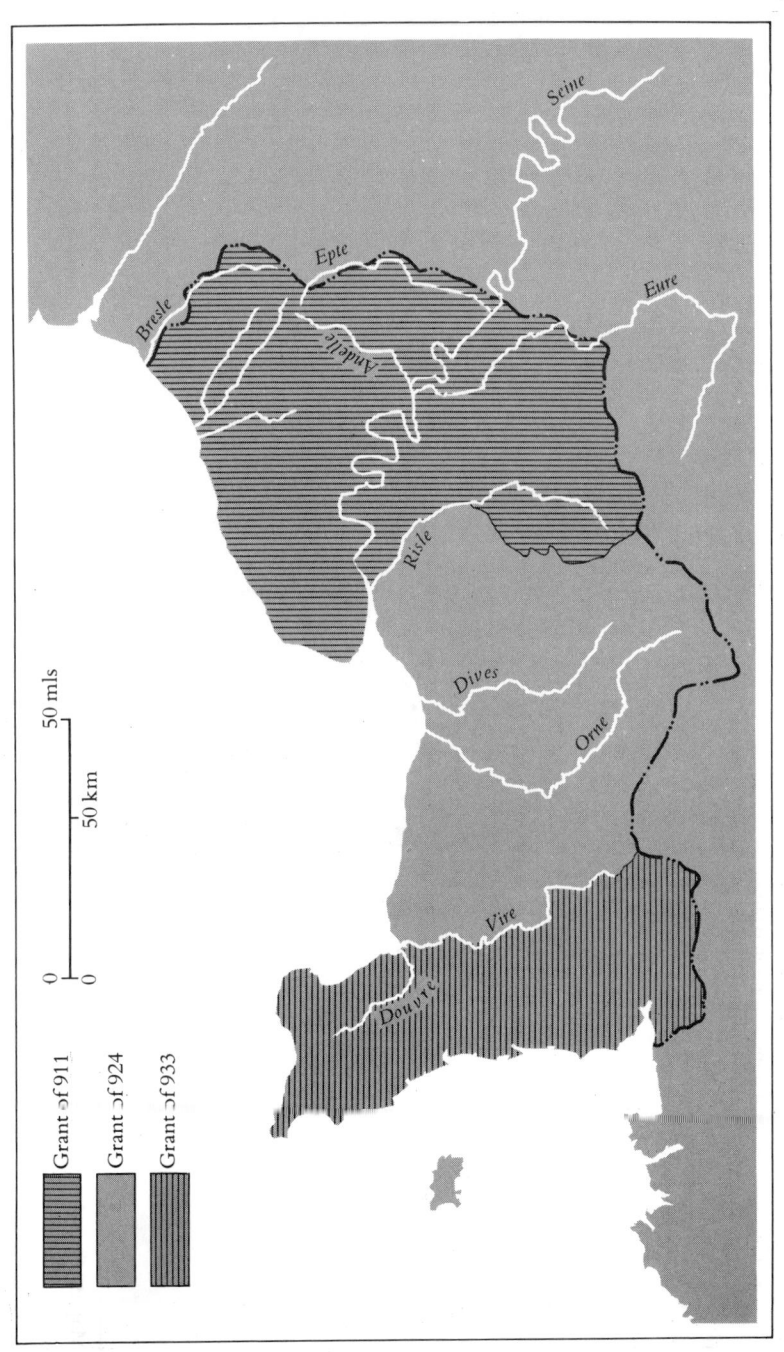

Map 2. The probable stages of the Norman settlement

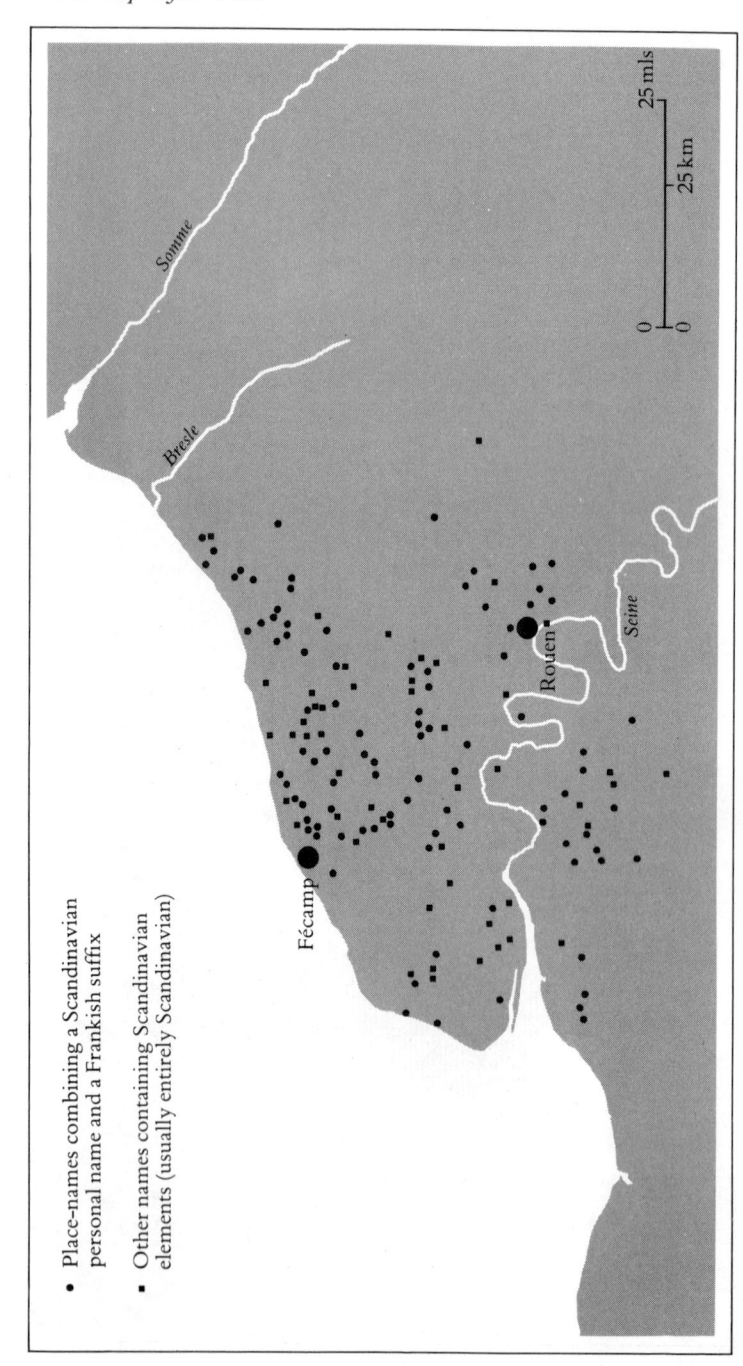

Map 3. Scandinavian place-names in Upper Normandy (material from Adigard des Gautries, *Noms de personnes scandinaves*, 373–435; *idem*, in *AN*, ii–ix, 1952–59)

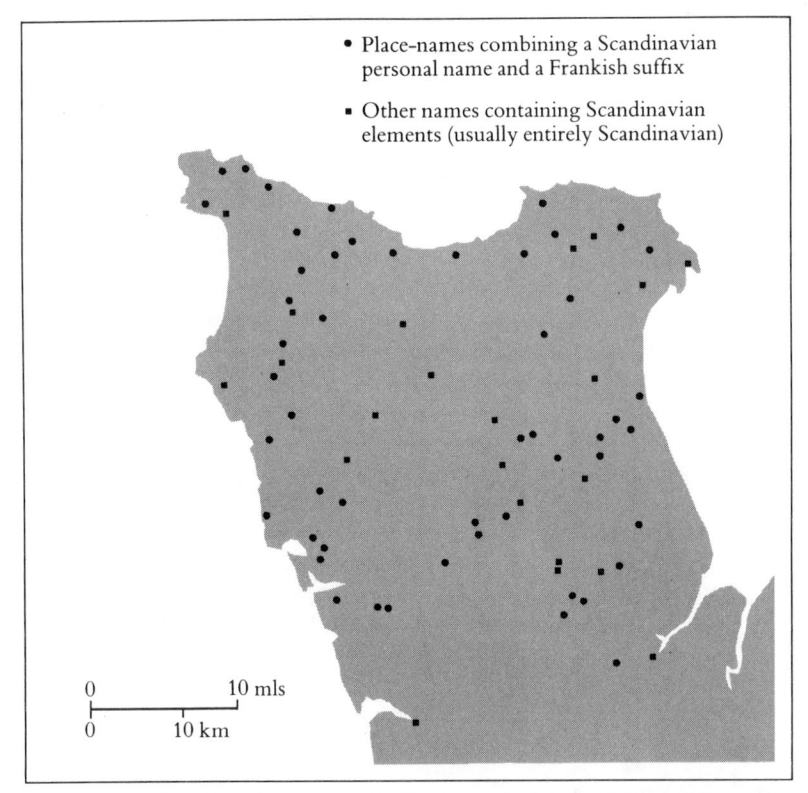

Map 4. Scandinavian place-names in the Cotentin (material from Adigard des Gautries, *Noms de personnes scandinaves*, 373–435; *idem*, in *AN*, i, 1951)

Normandy before 1066

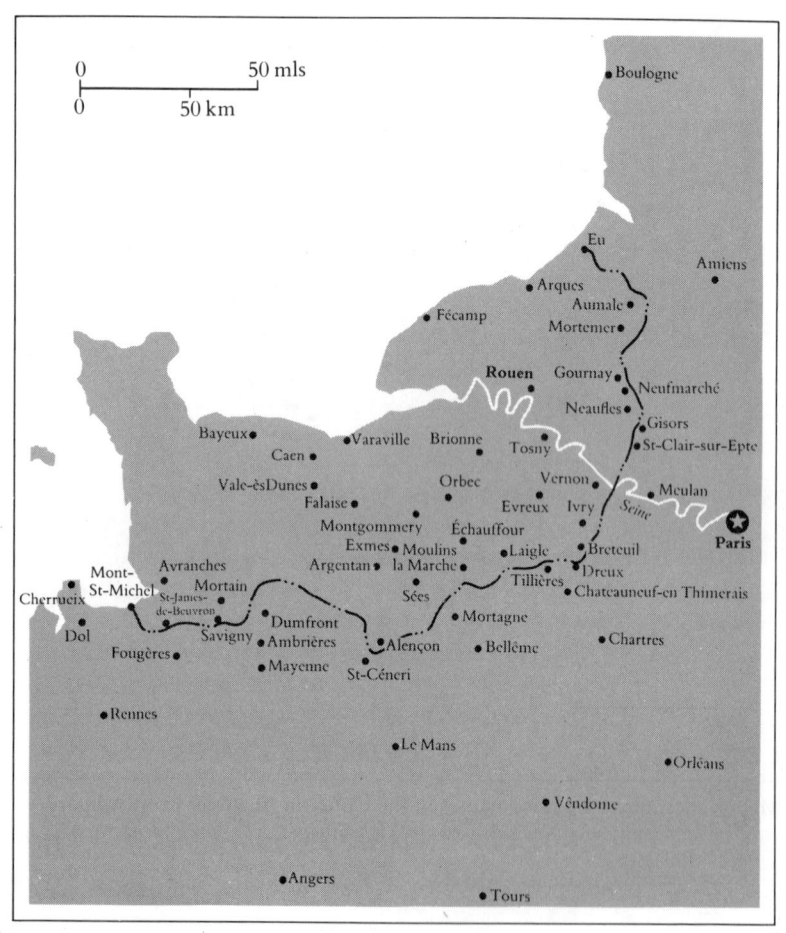

Map 5. Normandy and the surrounding regions

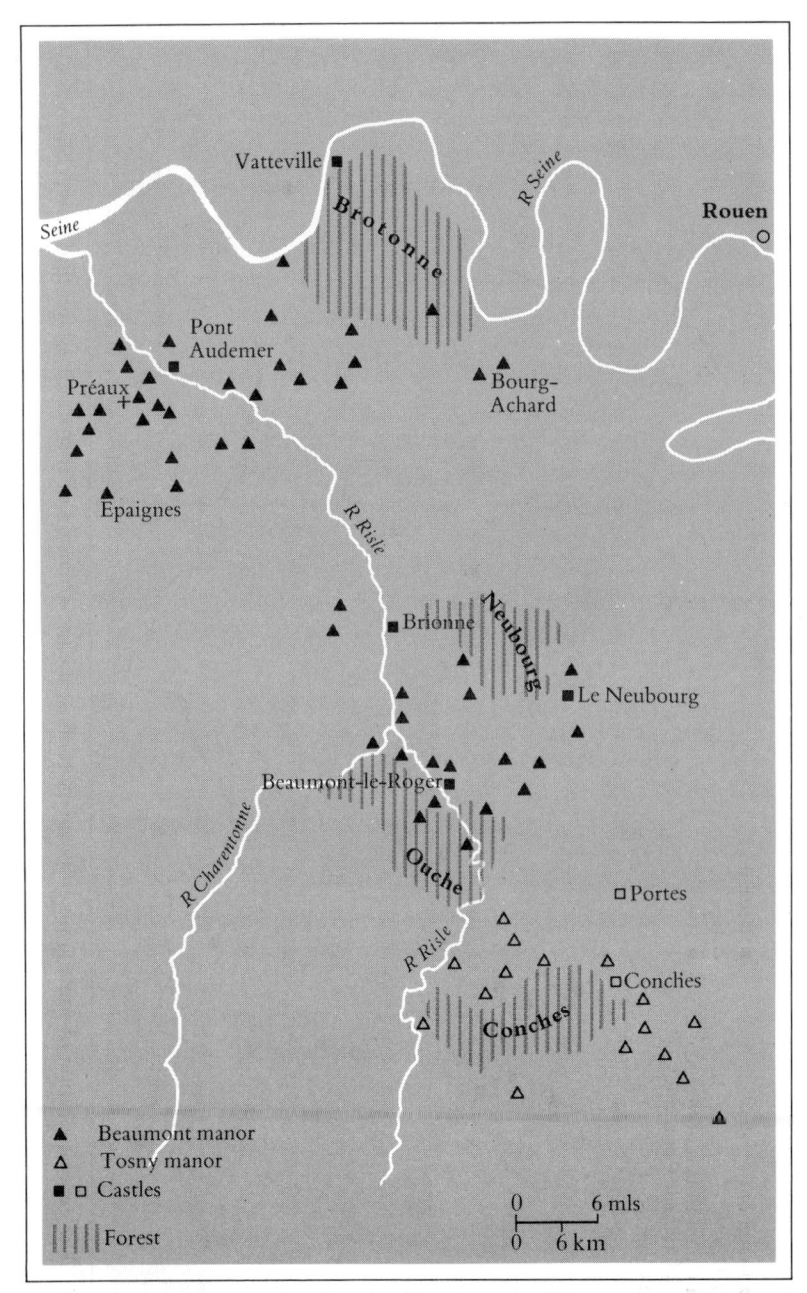

Map 6. Central Normandy, showing Beaumont and Tosny possessions
(with acknowledgement to Mr David Crouch)

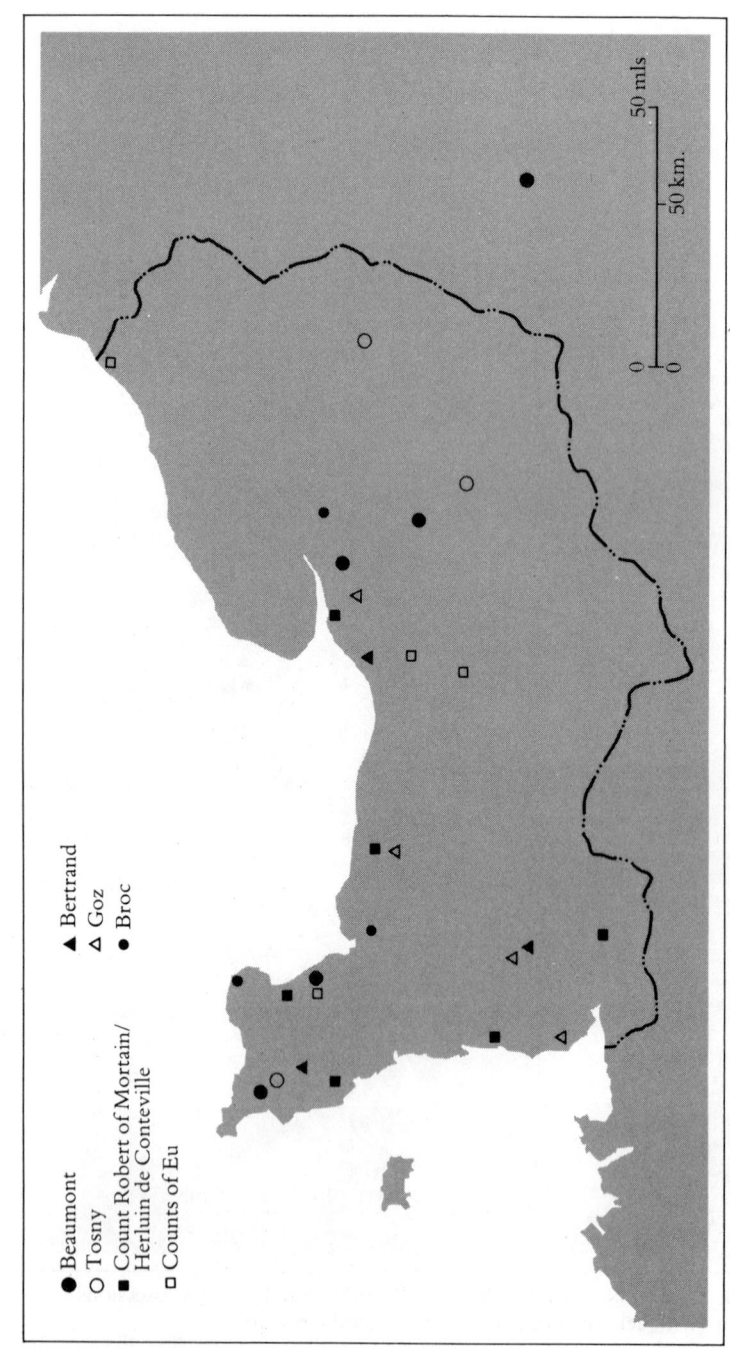

Map 7. The general location of some families' property to illustrate the extension of aristocratic estates into Lower Normandy

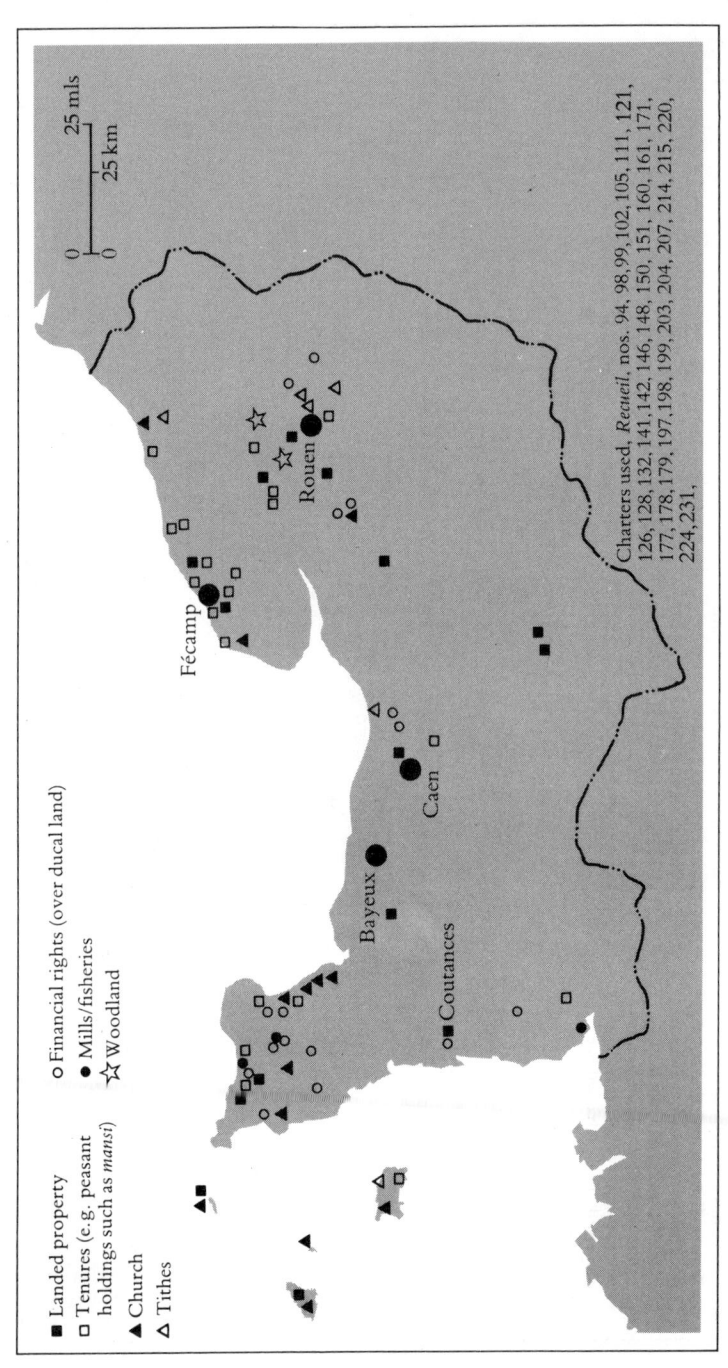

Map 8. Location of property granted to the Church by William II before 1066

Normandy before 1066

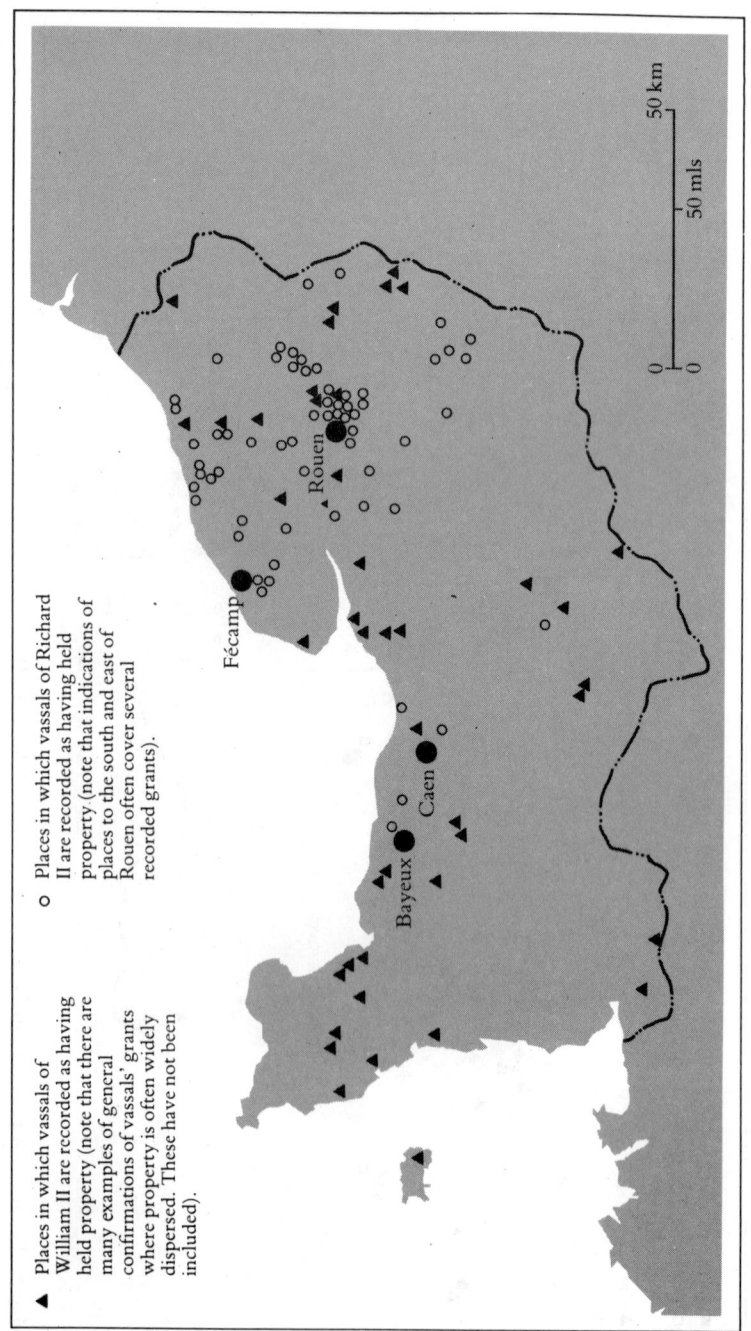

▲ Places in which vassals of William II are recorded as having held property (note that there are many examples of general confirmations of vassals' grants where property is often widely dispersed. These have not been included).

○ Places in which vassals of Richard II are recorded as having held property (note that indications of places to the south and east of Rouen often cover several recorded grants).

Map 9. The property of ducal vassals in pre-1066 charters

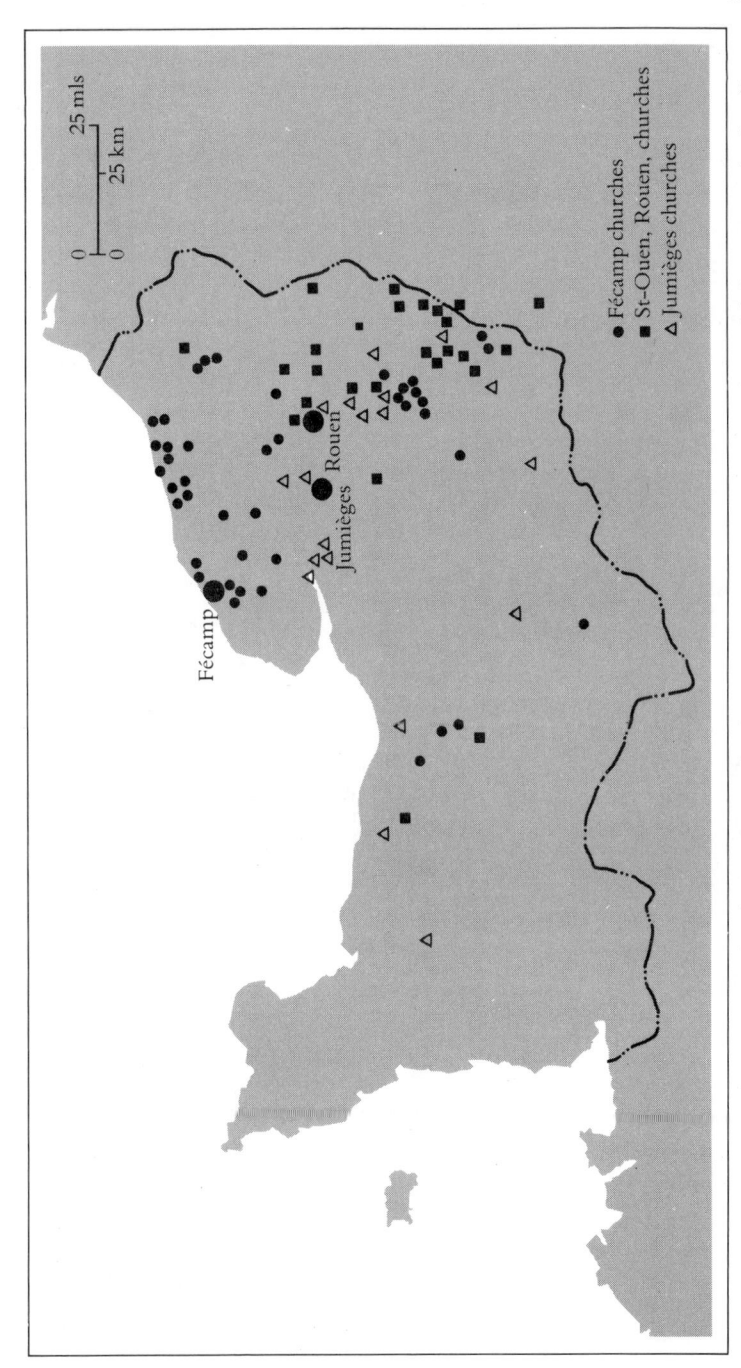

Map 10. Rural churches granted in Richard II's reign to the three main Norman monasteries (material from Lemarignier, 'Le monachisme et l'encadrement...', carte 1)

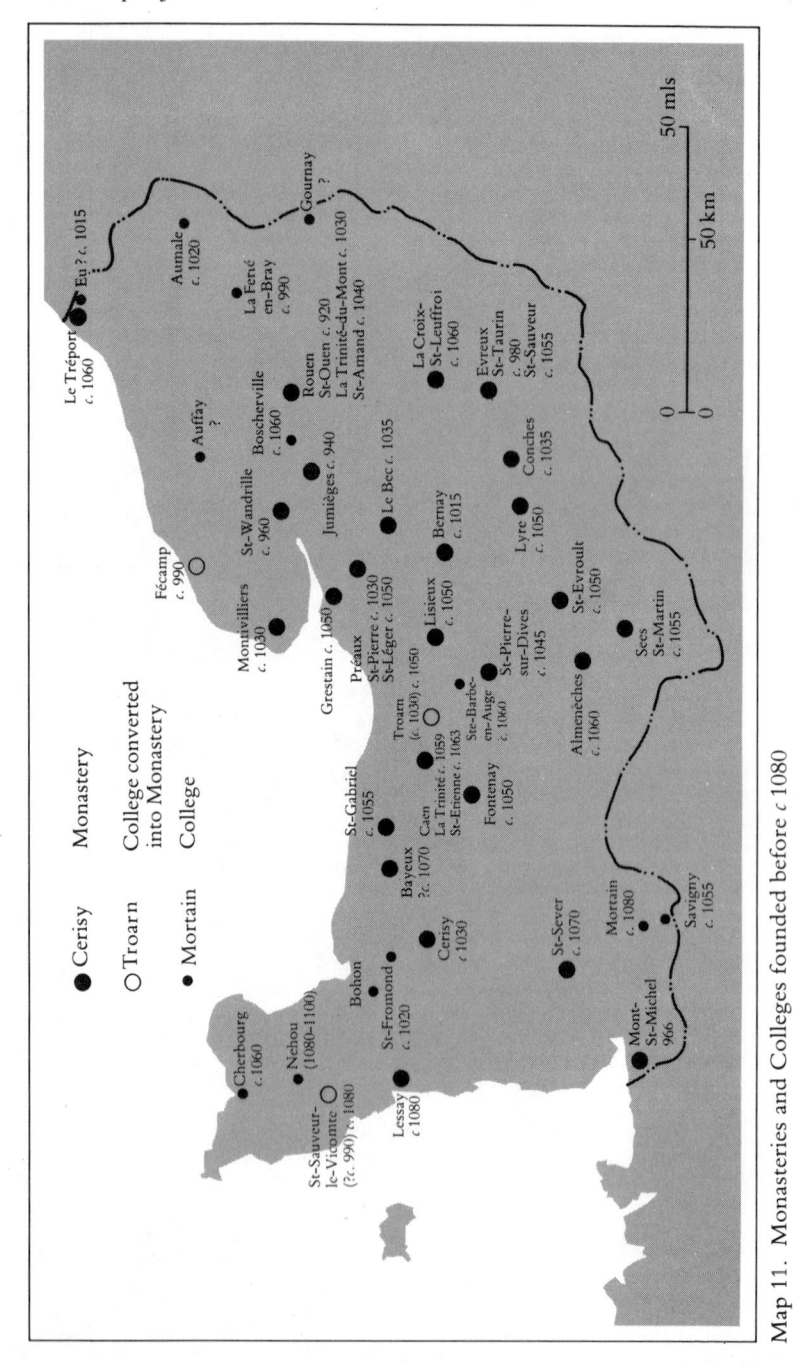

Normandy before 1066

Map 11. Monasteries and Colleges founded before *c* 1080

Index

Note: People identified by a title are indexed in the alphabetical sequence of their titles, e.g. Benedict, archdeacon of Rouen *before* Benedict VIII, pope; William of Volpiano, abbot of Fécamp *before* William of Jumièges. *Abbreviations used*: abp, archbishop; abt, abbot; archd, archdeacon; bp, bishop; ct, count; d, duke; k, king.

Adam de St-Brice, 167
Adelaide, sister of d William II, wife of ct Enguerrand I of Ponthieu, 77
Adèle, wife of d Richard III, 153
Adeline, wife of Roger de Beaumont, 71
Adeliza, sister of d Robert I, 165–6
Adhemar, 102
Adhemar of Chabannes, 13, 21, 241
Adigard des Gautries, J., 16
advocacy, 121–2, 180
Aethelred II the Unready, k of England, 7, 37, 67, 68, 198
Aethelstan, k of England, 22
Aethelwold, bp of Winchester, 194, 212
Ailred of Rievaulx, xv
Alan III, ct of Brittany, 68, 69, 70–1, 72, 74, 83
Alan the Red, ct in Brittany, 83
Alcuin of York, 2
Alençon, 130
    castle, 69, 76, 79, 255–6
Alexander II, pope, 189, 202
Alexander, J. J. G., 221
Alfred, brother of k Edward the Confessor, 67, 68
Alfred, k of Wessex, 3, 4

Almenèches, 100
    abbey, 115, 116, 221
Almod, abt of Mont-St-Michel, 70–1
alodium, 122–3, 123–4
Amatus of Monte Cassino, xvii, 241, 242, 245
Ambrières, castle, 78
Amiens, 9, 56
Anastasius the Venetian, monk of Mont-St-Michel, 220
Angers
    abbey of St-Aubin, 79, 80
    abbey of St-Serge, 78, 220
    cathedral chapter, 203
Anjou, counts and county, xviii, 6, 14, 27, 28, 47, 48, 49, 50, 54, 59, 62, 67, 73–4, 83, 85, 99, 149, 176, 179, 180, 181, 242, 244, 246; *see also* Fulk III; Fulk IV; Geoffrey II; Geoffrey III
Anno, abt of Jumièges, 35
Anschetil, *vicomte* of the Bessin, 117, 157
Anselm, monk of St-Rémi, Rheims, 255–6
Anselm, St, abp of Canterbury, 108, 223, 224
Ansfrey, abt of St-Pierre, Préaux, 203
Ansfrey, ducal *dapifer*, 155
Ansfrey, *vicomte*, 118
Anslech, 10th-century Norman noble, 34
Aquitaine, dukes and duchy, 27, 47, 72, 73, 135, 149, 246; *see also* Guy-Geoffrey; William IV; William V; William VI
Arduinus, Lombard rebel, 242, 246
Arfast, brother of countess Gunnor, 151

275

Arfast, ducal chaplain, bp of Thetford, 155, 200
Argentan, 74
Arles, 26
Arnold, ducal chaplain, 129
Arnold d'Echauffour, 166, 236, 242
Arnold fitz Giroie, 118
Arnulf I, ct of Flanders, 6, 10
Arnulf III, ct of Flanders, 61
Arques
  castle, 75, 115
  comté, 156; *see also* William
  vicomte, 206; *see also*
    Godfrey; Goscelin
Arras, 9
  abbey of St-Vaast, 198
Atto the Mad, 97
Auchy
  castle, 219
  college, 219
Audrieu, castle, 113
Augustine, St, 203
Aumale, 56, 72, 73
Auxerre, 66
Aversa, 242, 246
Avesgaud de Bellême, bp of Le Mans, 69
Avranches
  bishops and bishopric, xii, 11, 30, 169
    206, 213, 214, 260; *see also*
    Hugh; John; Michael
  cathedral, 214
Avranchin, *pagus*, xii, 5, 9, 10, 70
Avre, river, xii, 26, 65

Baldric, ducal *procurator*, 117, 195
Baldric, father of Baldric de Bocquencé, 99
Baldwin, archd of Rouen, 260
Baldwin, archd of Sées, 261
Baldwin fitz *Etvald*, archd of Sées, 261
Baldwin IV, ct of Flanders, 68, 105, 135, 250
Baldwin V, ct of Flanders, 47, 68, 76, 81, 151, 199, 250
Baldwin, ducal chaplain, bp of Evreux, 155, 211
Baldwin, monk of Jumièges, 32
Ballon, castle, 69, 243
bannal lordship, 64, 121–2, 180
Bar, battle, 74
Bari, annals of, 242
Bayeux, 9, 10, 13, 14, 19, 21, 96, 97, 128–30, 131, 132, 151, 152, 154, 205, 206, 211
  abbey of St-Vigor, 206

bishops and bishopric, xii, 11, 61, 100, 105, 125, 131, 168, 172, 190, 197, 202, 212, 213, 214, 215–6, 217, 261; *see also* Hugh; Odo
  cathedral, 214, 224
  cathedral chapter, 216, 217
  mint, 29, 129, 162
  vicomté, 157
Bayeux Tapestry, 84, 110, 115
Beaumont, 100, 153
  family, 71, 74, 101, 103, 112, 113, 135; *see also* Adeline; Duvelina; Humphrey de Vieilles; Robert, ct of Meulan; Robert de Beaumont; Roger de Beaumont; Torf; Turchetil; Turold; William
Beaumontel, 100
Beauvais
  region, 9, 10, 177
  smith from, 100
Bec, Le, abbey, 63, 81, 190, 208, 216, 218, 221, 222, 223, 224
  abbots, *see* Anselm, abp of Canterbury; Herluin; *see also* Lanfranc, abp of Canterbury
Bellême, 63, 70, 99, 177, 250
  college of St-Léonard, 215
  family, 48, 54, 63, 64, 69, 72, 76, 78–81, 136, 166, 192, 256; *see also* Avesgaud, bp of Le Mans; Ivo, bp of Sées; Mabel; Robert; William; William Talvas
  priory of St-Martin-du-Vieux, 81
Benedict, archd of Rouen, 260
Benedict VIII, pope, 150, 241
beneficium, 122–3, 126
Berengar, ducal chamberlain, 116–17
Berengar de Heudeboville, 114
Berengar of Tours, 200, 201, 203–4, 227
bernagium, 153, 161, 179, 180
Bernard, archd of Bayeux, 261
Bernard fitz Ospac, archd of Rouen, 260
Bernard, 10th-century Norman noble, 34
Bernay, 153
  abbey, 100, 117, 158, 193, 194, 196, 206, 208, 219, 220
Bernouville, 152
Berry, 49, 51, 246
Bertrand, family, 103
Bessin
  pagus, xii, 16, 103
  vicomtes of, 103, 117; *see also* Anschetil

Index

Billemont, 243
Bloch, M., 51, 105, 106, 122
Blois-Chartres
   counts and county, 6, 23, 27, 47, 48, 49, 50, 54, 59, 67, 73–4, 85, 155, 179, 246; *see also* Odo I; Odo II; Theobald I; Theobald III
   counts' coinage, 29
Bohon, college, later priory, 219
Bolbec, 104, 105
Bonneville-sur-Touques, 151, 194
Boscherville, 152
   college of St-Georges, 206
Botho, 10th century Norman noble, 34
Boulogne
   counts and county, 49; *see also* Eustace
Bourges, council (1031), 198
Bourgueil, abbey, 149
Boussard, J., 134
Bresle, river, xii
Breteuil, 57, 114, 194
Bretons, 5, 10
Bricquebec, 103
Brionne, 158
   castle, 75
   comté, 99, 116, 156, 171; *see also* Gilbert; Guy
   council (1050), 199, 203
   siege, 256
Briouze, 151
Brittany, 4, 8, 9–10, 33, 47, 63, 70, 82–3, 99, 167, 242, 244
   counts and county, 64; *see also* Alan III; Conan I; Conan II; Geoffrey I
Broc, family, 103, 128
Brotonne, forest, 100, 243
Burgundy
   duchy, 5, 49, 57, 66, 84, 149
   kingdom, 49, 55, 72, 84; *see also* Ralph III

Caen, 96, 130–2, 151, 152, 154, 164, 175, 176, 178, 179, 194
   abbey of St-Etienne, 96, 120, 121, 131, 150, 178, 199, 200, 202, 205, 207, 214, 218, 220, 223, 224, 250
   abbey of La Trinité, 106, 131, 150, 169, 199, 200, 218
   castle, 114, 115, 247
   church of St-Etienne-le-Vieux, 131
   church of St-Gilles, 131
   church of St-Martin, 131
   church of St-Nicholas, 131
   council (1061), 199
Canouville, castle, 115
Capetian monarchy, 55, 71, 149, 155, 174, 179, 180; *see also* Henry I; Hugh Capet; Louis VI; Philip I; Robert II
   Norman rulers as vassals of, 58–62
Capetian principality, 47, 51, 54, 181; *see also* Ile de France
castles, 49, 54, 57, 113, 114–15, 122, 162, 163, 165–6, 167, 179, 246–7
cathedral chapters, 215–16
Caux, *pagus*, xii, 7, 8, 16, 17, 22, 62, 110, 115, 117, 135, 194
Cerisy, abbey, 71, 169, 196, 218, 224
Chalandon, F., 241
Champagne, counts and county, 47, 48, 55, 172, 179; *see also* Odo III
chamber, ducal, 154
chancery, ducal, 154–5, 180, 248
chaplains, ducal, 155, 211, 212
Charles I (Charlemagne), emperor, 2, 163
Charles II the Bald, k of France, 5, 9, 29, 163, 179
Charles III the Simple, k of France, 2, 4, 5, 6, 8, 9, 10
Chartres, 66, 242
   abbey of St-Pere, 194
   cathedral and canons, 194, 195
Cherbourg, 130
Cherrueix, castle, 71, 246
Cinglais, Le, 113, 119, 153
Clement, monk of Fécamp, 220
Clontarf, battle, 7, 36
Cluny, abbey, 12, 193, 218, 223; *see also* Mayeul, St
Cnut, k of England, 36, 37, 67, 68, 151, 241
coinage, 9, 12, 28–30, 36, 57, 162, 163, 164–5, 179, 239–40
Colchester, castle, 247
Cologne, 26
comes (count), title, 148–50
Compiègne, council (1023), 53, 66, 195
comtés, Norman, 57, 99, 114, 116, 150, 156, 195, 246
Conan I, ct of Brittany, 70
Conan II, ct of Brittany, 83
Conan, treasurer of Bayeux, 129, 130, 132

277

Conches, 101
  abbey, 101, 102, 115, 219
Conquereil, battle, 246
Conrad II, emperor, 55, 84, 242
Constance, queen of France, 68
consuetudines, ducal, 153, 157, 180
consuetudines, episcopal, 205, 211, 214, 216–17; *see also* jurisdiction, ecclesiastical
Consuetudines et Iusticie (1091), 29, 162–3
Conteville, 103
Corbeil, church, 216
Corbie, abbey, 32
Corbridge, 7
Cormeilles, abbey, 115, 169, 219
Cotentin, 16–17, 22, 103, 120, 153
  pagus, xii, 5, 7, 9, 10
  vicomtes and *vicomté*, 117, 157; *see also* Eudo; Nigel I; Nigel II
Coudres, 65
Couesnon, river, 10, 71
Coulombs, abbey, 62
Courville, 166
Coutances, 132
  bishops and bishopric, xii, 11, 12, 30, 98, 100, 105, 159, 207, 213, 261; *see also* Geoffrey; Hugh; Robert
  cathedral, 98, 214
  cathedral chapter, 217–18
  vicomté, 157
Crispin, family, 112, 117; *see also* Gilbert; Miles; William
Croix-Avranchin, La, 120
cross-border estates, 62–4
curia, 160, 161

Danelaw, 18, 19, 20, 23, 30
Davis, R. H. C., xv
Denmark, 36
Deux-Jumeaux, abbey, 31, 224
Dhondt, J., 136
Dieppe, 120, 130
Dijon, abbey of St-Bénigne, 32, 57, 193, 220, 221
Dinan, 83
diocesan synod, 212
Dives, river, 16, 116, 151
Dol, 10, 83, 249
Domesday Book, 258
Domfront, castle, 76, 79, 177, 255–6
Doué-la-Fontaine, palace, 246
Douglas, D. C., xiv–xv, 120–1, 134, 255–6
Dreux, 65

Dreux, ct of the Vexin, 66, 71
Drogo, *fidelis* of d Richard II, 124
Dublin, 7
Duby, G., 50, 105
Dudo of St-Quentin, xi, xii–xvi, xvii, 8, 10, 10–11, 13, 14, 21, 22, 25, 33, 34, 35, 56, 60, 73, 84, 129, 212
Dumas-Dubourg, F., 29
Dunstan, St, abp of Canterbury, 194
Durand, abt of Troarn, 203
Duvelina, 112
dux (duke), title, xiv, 148–50

Echauffour, 114, 213
Edgar, k of England, 29, 33, 239
Edward the Confessor, k of England, 37, 67, 68, 76, 84, 119
Efflanc, family, 103
Emma, first wife of ct Richard I, 14
Emma, queen of England, sister of d Richard II, 37, 68
Empire, the, 55; *see also* Germany, kingdom
England, kingdom, 49, 67, 76, 77, 83–5, 133
Enguerrand I, ct of Ponthieu, 72, 77, 101
Enguerrand II, ct of Ponthieu, 75
Epte, river, xii, 9, 56
Eric Bloodaxe, k of York, 7
Erneis Taisson, 110, 118–19
Eu, 10, 64
  college, 219
  comté and counts, 57, 99, 101, 116, 156; *see also* Godfrey; Robert; William
Eudo de Penthièvre, ct in Brittany, 83
Eudo, *vicomte* of the Cotentin, 109, 157
Eure
  département, 170
  river, xii, 26
Eustace, ct of Boulogne, 77
Evrecin, *pagus*, xii, 8, 26, 75
Evreux, 120, 132
  abbey of St-Sauveur, 115
  bishops and bishopric, xii, 176, 190, 210, 261; *see also* Baldwin; Gilbert; William
  comté and counts, 57, 99, 100, 115, 120, 156, 159, 166; *see also* Richard; Robert, abp of Rouen
exemption, monastic, 193–4, 197, 205, 214–15
Exmes, 57
Exupère, St, relics, 216

Index

Falaise, 74, 130, 131
Fécamp, 68, 117, 151, 152, 158, 211
   abbey, xvi, 30, 31, 33, 34, 62, 68, 70, 100, 104, 116, 121, 122, 125, 149, 150, 158, 167, 176, 189, 193–5, 196, 198, 206, 207, 208, 210, 219, 220, 221, 223
   abbots, *see* John; William de Rots; William of Volpiano coin hoard, xiii, 25, 26, 28–30, 37, 96, 239, 240
   domain, 104
   palace, 12, 13, 115, 247
   vicomté, 157
Ferté-en-Bray, La
   castle, 114
   college, 219
feudum, 122–3
fideles, ducal, 107, 170–1, 174
Flanders, counts and county, 5, 14, 27, 28, 47, 49, 50, 55, 57, 59, 61, 62, 66, 85, 105, 133, 134, 135, 179, 181, 195; *see also* Arnulf I; Arnulf III; Baldwin IV; Baldwin V; Robert I
Fleury, abbey; *see* St-Benoît-sur-Loire, abbey
Flodoard of Rheims, xiii, 6, 8, 9, 10, 11, 24
Fontenay
   abbey, 118, 207, 220, 221, 222, 224
   churches, 119
Fossier, R., xviii
Frutturia, abbey, 82, 223
Fulbert I, archd of Rouen, 260
Fulbert II, archd of Rouen, 260
Fulbert, bp of Chartres, 52, 59, 149, 194, 203, 209, 212, 216
Fulbert, tanner of Falaise, 151
Fulcoin, archd of Sées, 261
Fulk, archd of Rouen, 260
Fulk III Nerra, ct of Anjou, 25, 47, 48, 54, 67, 84, 246, 247, 250
Fulk IV Rechin, ct of Anjou, 52, 54, 81, 84, 249
Fulk de Guernanville, dean of Evreux, 216

Gaillefontaine, castle, 114
Garnier of Rouen, poet, xvii, 212
Gavray, *vicomté*, 157
genealogies, 34, 107–9, 112
Geoffrey, bp of Coutances, 98, 132, 197, 198, 201, 213, 214, 216, 217
Geoffrey II Martel, ct of Anjou, 47, 48, 49, 52–3, 54, 55, 61, 72, 74, 75, 76, 77, 78–80, 81, 82, 85, 177, 181, 246, 250, 255–6
Geoffrey III the Bearded, ct of Anjou, 52, 81, 82, 83, 150
Geoffrey I, ct of Brittany (Rennes), 66, 70, 83, 151
Geoffrey de Mayenne, 63, 78, 249
Geoffrey, son of Goscelin *Stantuin*, 124, 125
Gerald, ducal butler, 155
Gerald of Wales, 251
Gerard, abt of St-Wandrille, 220, 222
Gerard Flaitel, 210–11
Gerard, St, of Brogne, 32
Gerberoi, 249
Germany, 49, 99
   kingdom, 133; *see also* Empire, the
Gervase, bp of Le Mans, abp of Rheims, 76, 78
Ghent, abbey of St-Pierre-du-Mont-Blandin, 32
Giffard, family, 104, 105, 115; *see also* Walter I; Walter II
Gilbert, archd of Lisieux, bp of Evreux, 211, 261
Gilbert Maminot, bp of Lisieux, 211
Gilbert, ct of Brionne, 64, 72, 101, 125, 136, 159
Gilbert, *miles*, 126
Gilbert Crispin, 74, 112, 117, 122
Gilbert d'Auffay, 122
Giroie, 101, 118, 213
   family, 63, 64, 72, 73, 99, 118, 242, 243, 244; *see also* Arnold d'Echauffour; Robert fitz Giroie; Robert Giroie; William fitz Giroie
Giroie de Courville, 166
Gisla, daughter of k Charles III the Simple, 8
Gisors, 56, 77–8
Godfrey, ct of Brionne and Eu, 99
Godfrey, *vicomte* of Arques (or Le Talou), 104, 117, 159
Godgifu, sister of k Edward the Confessor, 66
Gonduin, *miles*, 126, 127
Gonduin, monk of Jumièges, 32
Gontard, ducal chaplain, abt of Jumièges, 225
Goscelin, archd of Bayeux, 260, 261
Goscelin, *vicomte* of Arques (or Le Talou), 96, 100, 102, 104, 117, 158, 159, 171

279

Gothenus (?Goscelin) archd of Rouen, 260
Gother, archd of Rouen, 260
Goz, family, 103, 107; *see also* Richard, *vicomte* of the Avranchin; Richard de Cruelly; Thurstan de Creully; Thurstan Goz
gravarium, 153, 161
Gravenchon, castle, 115, 120
Graville, castle, 115
Greenland, 3
Gregory VII, pope, 148, 192, 199, 200, 202, 228
Grestain, abbey, 103, 115, 206, 220
Grimboscq, castle, 115
Grimoald du Plessis-Grimoult, 167
Guerenfrid, castellan of Aumale, 72, 73
Guillot, O., xviii, 255–6
Guitmund of La Croix-St-Leuffroy, 204
Gunnor, second wife of ct Richard I, 108, 112, 118, 150, 213
Guy, abp of Rouen, 11
Guy, ct of Brionne, 73, 74, 75, 165–6, 167, 177, 256
Guy I, ct of Ponthieu, 75, 77
Guy-Geoffrey, d of Aquitaine, 82, 135, 149

Hague-Dike, Le, 19
Haimo, abp of Bourges, 53
Haimo *Dentatus*, 104, 135
Halphen, L., 255
Halton Moor, coin hoard, 239
hamfara, 22, 180
Harcourt, family, 103
Harold II, k of England, 60, 84, 202
Harold Hardrada, k of Norway, 7
Harold, Scandinavian chief of Bayeux, 13, 14, 34
Harthacnut, k of England, 68
Haskins, C. H., xiv, 125, 168–9, 258
Haspres, abbey, 32
Hastings, battle, 245–6
Hauville-en-Roumois, 122
Havise, sister of d Richard II, 66
Helgaud of Fleury, 60, 191
Héliot, P., 247
Henry, abt of St-Ouen, Rouen, 126
Henry II, emperor, 67, 241
Henry III, emperor, 55, 76
Henry I, k of England, d of Normandy, 62, 108, 129, 130, 148, 173, 251
Henry I, k of France, 46, 49, 59, 60, 61, 68, 70–1, 73, 74, 75, 76, 77, 81, 176, 255

Henry of Huntingdon, 61
Herbert, bp of Lisieux, 212, 214
Herbert I Wake-Dog, ct of Maine, 69
Herbert II, ct of Maine, 78, 80, 81
Herbert II, ct of Vermandois, 6, 10, 12, 29
Herleva, mother of d William II, 151
Herluin, abt of Le Bec, 125, 136, 224
Herluin de Conteville, 103, 109, 115, 119, 151
Herluin de Fierville, 243
Hermer, archd of Sées, 261
Hervey, abp of Rheims, 11
Hiésmois, *pagus*, xii, 69, 74
Hildebert I, abt of Mont-St-Michel, 70, 195
Hoel, ct of Cornouailles, 249
Holy Island, 2
homage, 127
Homme, Le, castle, 158, 165, 166, 175
Hougue, La, 152
household, 54, 179
    ducal, 116–17, 117–18, 155–6, 157, 159
    seigneurial, 102
Hubert, ducal *dapifer*, 155
Hugh, abp of Rouen, 28, 30–1, 35
Hugh, archd of Rouen, 213, 260
Hugh, bp of Avranches, 101, 158, 195, 211, 213
Hugh, bp of Bayeux, 100, 119, 159, 196, 210, 213
Hugh, bp of Coutances, 135, 210, 213
Hugh, bp of Lisieux, 107, 116, 170, 202, 210, 211
Hugh the clerk, son of Olivier du Mêle-sur-Sarthe, 243
Hugh IV, ct of Maine, 78, 82
Hugh, ducal butler, 155
Hugh the Great, d of the Franks, 14, 26, 27, 29, 31, 128, 240
Hugh Capet, k of France, 6, 25, 27, 29, 46
Hugh, a Breton, 83
Hugh Bunel, 243
Hugh 'the Dane', 28
Hugh de *Calvacamp*, 108
Hugh de Gournay, 75
Hugh de Grandmesnil, 77, 167, 170, 177
Hugh I de Montfort, 102, 117
Hugh II de Montfort, 117, 158
Hugh de Rocé, 81
Hugh of Flavigny, 100
Hugh Talbot, 107
Humphrey de Vieilles, 100, 101, 102,

Index

105, 112, 113, 118, 119, 153, 155, 159, 243
Humphrey, ducal chamberlain, 155

Iceland, 3
Ile de France, 51, 53, 62, 74, 105, 193, 220; *see also* Capetian principality
Inchkenneth, coin hoard, 239
inheritance, 118–20
Iona, coin hoard, 239
Ireland, 7, 36, 239
Isembard, abt of La Trinité-du-Mont, Rouen, 220, 227
Italy, 36, 193, 220
    kingdom, 55; *see also* southern Italy
Ivo, bp of Chartres, 108, 112
Ivo de Bellême, bp of Sées, 63, 70, 76, 78–81, 198, 212, 215, 217
Ivois, conference (1023), 67
Ivry
    castle, 166
    comté, 57, 99, 100, 156; *see also* Rodulf

Jersey, 120
Jerusalem, pilgrimage, 196, 246
John, abt of Fécamp, 196, 201, 202, 203, 208, 210, 211, 220, 221, 223, 227, 228
John, bp of Avranches, abp of Rouen, 136, 202, 205, 210, 214
John X, pope, 11
John XV, pope, 37, 198
John, son of Conan the treasurer, 132
Joscelina, Montgommery ancestor, 112
Judith, first wife of d Richard II, 66, 151, 153, 193
Jumièges
    abbey, 11, 12, 30, 31, 32, 33, 58, 100, 102, 120, 124, 149, 158, 193, 194, 198, 219, 221
    church of St-Pierre, 221
jurisdiction, ecclesiastical, 205–6, 214–15; *see also consuetudines*, episcopal
justice, ducal, 160–1
Juthael, bp of Dol, 83

Laigle, 114, 173
Lambert de Bellême, archd of Sées, 261
Lambert, son of Richard de Lillebonne, 118
Lanfranc, abp of Canterbury, 191, 199–201, 202, 204, 210, 216, 218, 222, 223

Langeais, castle, 246
laudes, 191
Le Maho, J., 135
Lemarignier, J. F., 55, 105
Leo of Ostia, 242, 246
Leo IX, pope, 198, 199, 201, 217, 227
Lessay, abbey, 224
Leutgarde, wife of ct William Longsword, 12
libraries, monastic, 32–3, 223
liege homage, 127
Liège, schools, 210, 216
Lieuvin, *pagus*, xii
Lille, 179
Lillebonne
    council (1080), 164, 180, 193, 199, 204, 205, 206, 215, 217, 228, 248
    domain, 104, 118
Lilletot, 102
Limoges
    council (1031), 198
    vicomtesse, 241
Lisieux, 221
    abbey of St-Désir, 116
    bishops and bishopric, xii, 159, 195, 202, 211, 213, 215, 261; *see also* Gilbert Maminot; Herbert; Hugh; Roger
    cathedral, 214
    cathedral canons, 116
    council (1054), 199
    council (1064), 162, 164, 199, 204
Loire, river, Scandinavian settlement on, 7
London, 131
    White Tower, 247
Longueville, 104
lordship, ducal, 168–72
Lorraine, 193
Lothaire, k of France, 14, 27
Louis I the Pious, emperor, 29
Louis IV, k of France, 6, 8, 10, 13–14, 128
Louis VI, k of France, 54, 62, 250
Lyre, abbey, 115, 169

Mabel de Bellême, 79, 80, 81, 104, 161, 243
Mâconnais, 50, 51, 52, 106
Maine, counts and county, 6, 9, 10, 33, 47, 48, 63, 69, 70, 73, 76, 78–9, 80, 81–2, 84, 242, 249, 256; *see also* Herbert I; Herbert II; Hugh IV
Maino de Fougères, 83

281

Malet, family, 102
Malger, abp of Rouen, 75, 154, 159, 167, 176, 197, 201, 202, 204, 209, 213, 227
Mans, Le, 249
   abbey of St-Vincent, 79
   bishops and bishopric, 48, 58, 82, 192; *see also* Avesgaud; Gervase; Wulgrin
   mint, 64
marchio (marquis), title, 26, 27
Margaret, sister of ct Herbert II of Maine, 82
Marmoutier, abbey, xvi, 56, 57, 58, 167, 225
Mathilda, sister of d Richard II, 65
Mathilda, wife of d William II, 76, 130, 151, 199, 250, 258
Maurilius, abp of Rouen, 77, 203, 210, 214, 217, 225
Mayeul, St, abt of Cluny, 33, 193
Melun, 25
Méresais, *pagus*, xii
Michael, bp of Avranches, 211
miles and *milites*, 51–2, 104, 109–10, 114, 122–7
Miles Crispin, 112, 200
Moncontour, battle, 49
monnéage, 154, 165
Montbazon, castle, 247
Monte Cassino, abbey, 246
Montfort
   family, 113, 175; *see also* Hugh I; Hugh II
   honour, 172
Montgommery, 74, 114
   family, 102, 104, 108, 112, 113, 175, 193, 221; *see also* Joscelina; Mabel de Bellême; Robert de Bellême; Roger I; Roger II; Sainfria; Wevia
Montivilliers, 102, 104, 115
   abbey, 148, 196
Montpensier, battle, 246
Montreuil, 213
Mont-St-Michel, abbey, 9, 12, 25, 27, 30, 31, 32–3, 33, 63, 64, 68, 70–1, 82, 100, 152, 170, 189, 193, 195, 196, 206, 214, 219, 220, 221, 222, 224, 258
Mortain, 98
   college of St-Evroult, 103
   comté and counts, 57, 82, 99, 103, 156, 159; *see also* Robert; Robert, brother of d Richard II; William Werlenc

Mortemer
   battle, 64, 75, 77–8
   castle, 166
Mouliherne, 76, 255–6
Moulins-la-Marche, 64, 114
Mount Sinai, 57
Muneville-sur-Mer, 103
murdrum, 22
Muriel, sister of bp Odo of Bayeux, 103
Musset, L., 10, 242

Namur, 106
Nantes, *pagus*, 4
Néhou, college, 219
Neufchâtel-en-Bray, 75
Neufmarché, castle, 57, 77, 177
Neustrian March, 5, 6
Nicea, 147
Nicholas II, pope, 199, 200–1, 202
Nigel I, *vicomte* of the Cotentin, 117, 158, 159, 171
Nigel II, *vicomte* of the Cotentin, 157, 158, 166, 167, 197
Nigel fitz Constantin, 243
nobiles, 51, 52, 106–7; *see also* primates; proceres
Norman Anonymous, 227–8
Norman, archd of Coutances, 261
Norman, archd of Sées, 261
Normannia, xvi, 56–7
Noron, priory, 243
Nouy, battle, 47, 74
Noyon, 9

Odo, archd of Sées, 261
Odo, bp of Bayeux, 119, 130, 131, 151, 154, 167, 168, 177, 190, 202, 205, 206, 209, 211, 214, 216, 250
Odo, brother of k Henry I of France, 75, 81
Odo I, ct of Blois-Chartres, 25, 246
Odo II, ct of Blois-Chartres, 47, 48, 55, 65–6, 68, 70, 71, 72, 74, 84, 240
Odo III, ct of Champagne, 77
Odo, ducal constable, 116
Odo, k of France, 5
Odo, *vicomte*, 117
Odo fitz Losfred, 107
Odo-William, ct of Mâcon, 55, 84
Odon, river, 96
Oissel, 17
Olaf Haraldsson, k of Norway, 21, 36, 37
Olaf Guthricsson k of York, 7
Olaf Sihtricsson, k of York, 13
Orbec, 64, 101

Index

Ordericus Vitalis, xiii-xiv, xv, 31, 34, 48, 63, 70, 74, 101, 108, 114, 116, 118, 148, 166, 172-3, 189, 190, 200, 201, 210, 211, 213, 222, 224, 236-7, 242, 243-4, 245, 249
Orkneys, 7
Orne, river, 96
Osbern, archd of Lisieux, 261
Osbern, bp of Exeter, 119
Osbern, dean of Rouen, 213
Osbern, ducal *dapifer*, 118, 151, 155, 158, 176
Osmund, archd of Rouen, 260
Osmund, 10th-century Norman noble, 34
Ouen, St, relics, 12, 33

pagus, xii, 156-7, 161, 180
    disintegration, 50, 51, 52, 53, 55
papacy, 198-202
papal banner, 189, 202
Papia, second wife of d Richard II, 151
parage, 127, 258
Pavia, 26
Peace of God, 53, 66, 163-4, 174, 176, 179, 195, 198; *see also* Truce of God
peasantry, 23, 94-5
Philip I, k of France, 46, 47, 60, 81, 149, 249, 250
Picardy, xviii, 10
Picquigny, island, 10
Pîtres, 20
    edict, 29, 163, 179
place-names, 7, 16-19
Plessis-Grimoult, Le
    castle 35, 114, 165
    honour, 168
Poitiers, abbey of St-Cyprien, 12
Poitou, 58
Poland, 36
Ponthieu, counts and county, 55, 63, 64, 77; *see also* Enguerrand I; Enguerrand II; Guy I
Pontlevoy, battle, 67
Pont-Audemer, 100, 105
Pont de l'Arche, 194
Préaux, 152
    abbey of St-Léger, 102
    abbey of St-Pierre, 102, 110, 115, 126, 220, 224
prepositi, 54, 179, 180
    ducal, 161
    seigneurial, 102, 161
primates, 106-7; *see also* nobiles; proceres

proceres, 51, 52, 55, 106-7; *see also* nobiles; primates
Provence, 51
Puy, Le, coin hoard, 26, 241

Quentovic, mint, 239

Radbod, bp of Sées, 69, 210
Rainald, ducal chaplain, later abt of Abingdon, 97
Rainulf of Aversa, 242
Ralph 'de Beaumont', abt of Mont-St-Michel, 82
Ralph, archd of Bayeux, 261
Ralph, archd of Coutances, 261
Ralph IV, ct of Amiens-Valois-Vexin, 48, 64, 75, 77-8, 166
Ralph de Gael, earl of Norfolk, 249
Ralph 'de Tancarville', ducal chamberlain, 104, 118, 154, 155
Ralph, early visitor to southern Italy; *see* Ralph I de Tosny
Ralph III, k of Burgundy, 84
Ralph, k of France, 6, 7, 8, 9, 10
Ralph, *miles*, 110
Ralph I de Tosny, 31, 35, 166, 241
Ralph II de Tosny, 122, 167
Ralph de Warenne, 112, 170
Ralph fitz Avenie, 243
Ralph I Taisson, 118
Ralph II Taisson, 118-19, 159
Ralph III Taisson, 207
Ralph *Torta*, 13, 34, 35
Ralph Tortaire, 130
Rannulf de Glanville, 251
Rannulf Flambard, 173
Rannulf, moneyer, 101, 132
reliefs, 127
Rennes, counts and county, 47-8, 70; *see also* Alan III; Conan I; Conan II; Geoffrey I; Brittany, counts and county
revenues, ducal, 152-4
Réville, burial, site, 20
Rheims, 210
    council (1049), 78, 198, 200, 201, 217, 227, 255
Richard de St-Vanne, abt of Verdun, 196, 198
Richard, archd of Bayeux, 261
Richard de Angerville, archd of Lisieux, 261
Richard, ct of Evreux, 115
Richard I, ct of Rouen, xiii, xiv, 13, 14, 15, 21, 34, 35, 37, 193, 198, 240
    Church, 30-3, 226

283

external relations, 25, 26–8, 245
government, 25–6, 28–30
Richard II, d of Normandy, xiv, 7, 21, 23, 24, 35, 37, 48, 57, 59, 62, 64, 69, 70, 71, 72, 84, 103, 118, 124, 134, 135, 147, 148–9, 150, 151, 163, 240, 241, 242
   Church, 191, 193–6, 205, 206, 208, 210–11
   external relations, 65–8, 73, 83, 245
   government, 99, 116–17, 152–62, 165–8, 170–2, 174, 180, 181
Richard III, d of Normandy, 57, 59, 69, 100, 109, 147, 150, 153
Richard, *vicomte* of the Avranchin, 115
Richard de Creully, 208
Richard de Lillebonne, 118, 157
Richard fitz Herluin, 62
Richer of Rheims, xvi, 25, 36, 240, 246
Rioul, 10th-century Norman noble, 13, 34
Risle, river, 156
Rivallon de Dol, 83
Robert, abp of Rouen, 30, 31, 37, 68, 70, 99, 100, 103, 118, 159, 195, 197, 209, 210, 212, 213, 214
Robert, archd of Evreux, 261
Robert, archd of Rouen, 260
Robert, bp of Coutances, 126
Robert, bp of Sées, 215
Robert, ct of Eu, 75
Robert I the Frisian, ct of Flanders, 249
Robert, ct of Meulan, 222
Robert, ct of Mortain, 82, 98, 103, 109, 119, 121, 151, 156, 177
Robert, ?ct of Mortain, brother of d Richard II, 99
Robert, ducal butler, 155
Robert I, d of Normandy, 37, 57, 82, 84, 99–101, 120, 147, 149, 150, 151, 163
   Church, 191, 195, 196–7
   external relations, 59–60, 63–4, 68–73, 83, 245
   government, 152–62, 165, 171, 175
Robert II Curthose, d of Normandy, 60, 82, 150, 173, 243, 249–50
Robert I, k of France, son of Robert the Strong, 4, 6, 65
Robert II the Pious, k of France, xvii, 46, 48, 59, 60, 62, 66–7, 69, 84, 181, 191, 195
Robert, *vicomte* (?of Caux), 117
Robert de Beaumont, 74, 101, 103, 107, 119, 126, 170
Robert de Bellême, 48, 102, 250

Robert I de Grandmesnil, 101, 118
Robert II de Grandmesnil, later prior and abt of St-Evroult, 170, 202, 207, 243
Robert fitz Giroie, 63, 80, 243
Robert fitz Humphrey de Vieilles; *see* Robert de Beaumont
Robert Giroie, 242–3
Robert of Torigny, 61, 107–9, 112, 135
Robert, son of Roger *Malpasnage*, 122
Robert, son of William de Bellême, 69
Robert the Strong, 5
Rodulf, ct of Ivry, 99, 113, 121, 156, 166, 210
Roger de Mortagne, archd of Sées, 261
Roger, bp of Lisieux, 212, 213
Roger, ducal butler, 117
Roger, *vicomte* (?of Caux), 117
Roger de Beaumont, 71, 101, 102–3, 109, 118, 119, 126, 166, 177, 205, 248
Roger de Clères, 101, 122
Roger de Fécamp, 114
Roger I de Montgommery, 100, 112, 117, 159
Roger II de Montgommery, xvi, 79–81, 82, 96, 102, 104, 107, 109, 112, 115, 116, 117, 124, 125, 136, 159, 167, 170, 177, 178, 207, 250
Roger de Mortemer, 64, 77, 166
Roger I de Tosny, 37, 101, 102, 109, 241
Roger, son of bp Hugh of Coutances, 210
Roger, tenant of Mont-St-Michel, 167
Rollo, ct of Rouen, xiii, xiv, xvi, 2, 4, 5, 7, 8, 9, 10, 11, 12, 13, 19, 22, 23, 30, 58, 84, 108
romanesque architecture, 220–1, 224
Rome, 55, 74
   council (1059), 199, 200–1, 203
Roscelin, canon of Rouen, 127
Roscelin, ducal chamberlain, 117
Rouen, xii, 2, 7, 9, 11, 12, 14, 20, 21, 33, 37, 70, 75, 83, 96, 98, 103, 128–9, 131, 132, 151, 152, 210, 240, 250
   abbey of La Trinité-du-Mont, 100, 102, 104, 110, 115, 122, 148, 169, 219, 220, 221
   abbey of St-Ouen, 11, 12, 30, 31, 33, 35, 58, 83, 110, 121, 122, 127, 154, 193, 194, 208, 219
   archbishops and archbishopric, xii, 11, 12, 30, 31, 35, 78, 100, 121, 190, 197, 202, 209–10, 212–13, 213, 215, 216, 220, 260; *see also* Guy; Hugh; John:

Index

Malger; Maurilius; Robert; William *Bona* Anima
cathedral, 80, 214
church of St-André-hors-Ville, 129
church of St-Eloi, 129
church of St-Laurent, 129
church of St-Lô, 30, 213
council (?1046), 197–8, 204, 213, 215, 227
council (1063), 199
council (1070), 199
council (1072), 199, 204, 228
council (1074), 199
ecclesiastical province, xii, 191, 199
mint, 12, 28–30, 129, 162, 240
slave-market, 23
vicomté, 118
Roumois (Rouen), *pagus*, xii, 8
Russia, 36
Ryes-en-Bessin, 211

Sainfria, Montgommery ancestor, 112
St-Aubin-sur-Scie, 75
St-Benoît-sur-Loire, abbey, 32, 57, 96
St Brice's Day massacre, 67
St-Céneri-le-Gérei, castle,
St-Christophe-du-Foc, 103, 153
St-Clair-sur-Epte, 'treaty', 2, 4, 8–9, 10, 11
St-Dennis, abbey, 12, 30, 32, 58, 169, 207
St-Evroult, abbey, 31, 63, 80, 98, 116, 136, 168, 169, 189, 202, 207, 208, 219, 221, 223, 224, 243
St-Fromond, college, later priory, 219, 224
St-Gabriel-sur-Seulles, priory, 208
St-Georges-Motel, 194
St-Germain-des-Prés, abbey, 9
St-James-de-Beuvron, 56, 57, 82
St-Lô, 98, 130, 131
St-Malo, 10
St-Marcouf, abbey, 224
St-Martin-du-Bosc, priory, 173, 206, 218
St-Pair, abbey, 31
St-Pierre-Azif, 120
St-Pierre-sur-Dives, abbey, 219, 221
St-Sauveur-le-Vicomte, college, later abbey, 219
St-Sever, abbey, 115, 219
St-Valéry-sur-Somme, 151
St-Wandrille, abbey, 11, 30, 31, 32, 58, 96, 106, 107, 109, 120, 121, 124, 148, 211, 215, 220, 221
Ste-Suzanne, castle, 249
Saintonge, 82

Samson, ducal chaplain, archd and treasurer of Bayeux, later bp of Worcester, 97, 130, 261
Saumur, abbey of St-Florent, xvi, 57, 151
Savigny-le-Vieux, 83
Sawyer, P. H., 19
Scandinavia and Scandinavians, 13, 14, 65
Norman connections with, 7, 23, 36–8, 239–41
Scandinavian archaeological finds in Normandy, 19–20
Scandinavian language, 15, 20–1
schools, episcopal, 216
Scotland, 36
Scottish Islands, 3
Sées, 70, 79, 80, 104, 130, 132, 177, 197
abbey of St-Martin, 79, 80, 81, 115, 116, 224
bishops and bishopric, xii, 11, 63, 69, 70, 159, 190, 208, 212, 213, 215, 250, 261; *see also* Ivo de Belléme; Radbod; Robert; Sigenfrid
cathedral, 98
Seine, river, xii, 3, 16, 17, 63
Seine-Maritime, *département*, 170
Senlis, 59
Séois, *pagus*, xii, 81
Sergius IV, ct of Naples, 242
Serlo, canon of Bayeux, 130
Sever, St, relics, 33
Sigenfrid, bp of Sées, 69
Sihtric Sihtricsson, 13
Sihtric, *vicomte*, 117
Simon, ct of Amiens-Valois-Vexin, 249
Sofria, Montgommery ancestor; *see* Sainfria
Soissons, abbey of St-Médard, 31
Soleure, coin hoard, 241
Southampton, coin hoard, 239
southern Italy, 98, 166, 214, 217, 241–5
Spain, 37, 241
Standard, battle, xv
Stephen I, ct of Troyes and Meaux, 74
Stigand de Mézidon, ducal *dapifer*, 155, 207
Suppo, abt of Mont-St-Michel, 82, 196, 220
Sven Forkbeard, k of Denmark, 7, 37, 67

Taisson, family, 99, 103, 104, 115, 127, 153, 222, 243, 244; *see also* Erneis; Ralph I; Ralph II; Ralph III

285

Talou
  pagus, xii, 8, 16, 194, 210
  vicomté, 104, 117
Tancarville, family, 155; *see also* Ralph, ducal chamberlain
Tancred de Hauteville, sons of, 242
Terslev, coin hoard, 239
Theobald I, ct of Blois-Chartres, 14, 246
Theobald III, ct of Blois-Chartres, 49, 74, 255
Thérouanne, 7
Thierry, abt of St-Evroult, 223
Thierry, abt of Jumièges and Mont-St-Michel, prior of Fécamp, 193, 195, 196
Thimert, castle, 81, 166
thing, 15
Thomas, abp of York, 216
Thurstan de Creully, 208
Thurstan Goz, 17, 117, 135, 159
Thurstan Haldup, 170
Tillières-sur-Avre, castle, 57, 65, 74, 81, 158
Tiree, coin hoard, 239
tolls, 97, 102, 153
toponymics, 113–14, 127
Torf, Beaumont ancestor, 112
Tosny, family, 99, 101, 103, 108, 113, 119, 153, 166, 241; *see also* Ralph I; Ralph II; Roger I
Touraine, 74, 246
Tours, council (1054), 203
Toutainville, 17, 18
Tréport, Le, abbey, 206, 219
Troarn, 100
  abbey, 115, 116, 167, 169, 207, 219, 220, 221
Troyes, county, 84
Truce of God, 168, 176, 204, 205, 210; *see also* Peace of God
Trun, 132
Truchetil, brother of Humphrey de Vieilles, 102, 112
Turmod, 10th-century Norman pagan, 13
Turold, Beaumont ancestor, 112
Turold, ducal constable, 155

ullac (ducal right to exile), 22, 163, 166–7, 180
Ursel, archd of Rouen, 260

Vaalse, coin hoard, 239
Val-és-Dunes, battle, 61, 73, 75, 101, 104, 167, 174, 176, 177

Valognes, 103, 130, 153
Varaville, battle, 75, 79, 80, 81
varech (wreck), 22
Vaudreuil, Le, 7, 194
Vernon, castle, 114
Vexin
  counts of, 72
  French, xii, 31, 62, 66, 70, 77, 108, 177, 249, 250
  Norman, 62, 117, 177
  pagus, xii, 8
vicomtés, 117–18, 156–8, 180
Vieilles, 100, 153
Villiers, church of St-Ouen, 79–80
Vita Lanfranci, 200–1

Waleran I, ct of Meulan, 66, 71, 74, 109
Waleran, son of Rannulf the moneyer, 132
Walter, ct of Mantes, 82
Walter I Giffard, 102, 119
Walter II Giffard, 75, 101
Walter, *vicomte*, 117
wardship, 127
Warenne, family, 112, 114, 135; *see also* Ralph; William I; William II
Wascelin, archd of Rouen, 260
Wedmore, treaty, 3, 4
Werner, K. F., 134
Wevia, Montgommery ancestor, 112
William of Volpiano, abt of Fécamp, 36, 174, 191, 193, 195, 196, 199, 203, 208, 218, 219, 220, 223, 225, 240
William *Bona Anima*, archd of Rouen, abt of St-Etienne, Caen, abp of Rouen, 225, 260
William de Rots, archd and dean of Bayeux, abt of Fécamp, 225, 260, 261
William, bp of Evreux, 211
William, ct of Arques, 75, 77, 101, 104, 107, 121, 158, 159, 176, 177, 197, 209, 256
William II, ct of Auvergne, 29
William, ct of Exmes and Eu, 99, 156, 202
William Werlenc, ct of Mortain, 82, 104, 156, 243–4
William I Longsword, ct of Rouen, xiii, xiv, 8, 9–10, 12, 13, 15, 19, 21, 27, 28, 30, 34, 164
William IV Iron-Arm, d of Aquitaine, 52, 135
William V, d of Aquitaine, 52, 55, 135, 149, 191

Index

William VI, d of Aquitaine, 49
William II, d of Normandy, xvi, 47, 48, 49, 57, 63, 71, 103, 106, 107, 122, 127, 130, 131, 135, 147–8, 149, 150, 189, 243
    Church, 191, 198–208, 211
    external relations, 59–62, 64, 73–85, 136, 249, 255–6
    government, 151–61, 162, 164–8, 170–2, 172–3, 176–9, 181, 248
    minority, 73–5, 101, 175–6, 197–8
William I the Conqueror, k of England; *see* William II, d of Normandy
William II Rufus, k of England, 54, 173
William Crispin, 177
William d'Arques, 104
William de Bellême, 63, 68, 69
William de Grandmesnil, 243
William de Montreuil, 236, 243
William de Moulins-la-Marche, 64, 110, 121, 170
William de Vernon, 177
William I de Warenne, 75, 101, 112, 166, 177
William II de Warenne, 108
William fitz Giroie, 63, 118
William fitz Osbern, 61, 109, 115, 118, 119, 155, 159, 166, 177, 178, 207
William Malet, 110
William of Apulia, xvi, 241, 242, 245, 246
William of Jumièges, xiii, xvii, 31, 35, 59, 61, 65, 66–71, 73, 74, 83, 100, 107, 114, 158, 163, 167, 196
William of Malmesbury, 61, 200, 249
William of Poitiers, xiii, xvii, 59–60, 62, 73, 78, 81, 83, 84, 150, 158, 166, 167, 176, 189, 202, 211, 216, 255–6, 261
William Paganel, 258
William Pantulf, 161, 243
William, son of Humphrey de Vieilles, 119
William Iron-Arm, son of Tancred de Hauteville, 242
William Talvas, 70, 79, 80
Wimund, *vicomte*, 117
Winchester, 173
    coin hoard, 239
Wulgrin, bp of Le Mans, 78

York, 20, 98
    kingdom, 3, 7, 14
Ypres, 179
Yver, J., 10, 22

287